THE JUST STATE

Richard Dien Winfield

THE JUST STATE

RETHINKING SELF-GOVERNMENT

HB
Humanity Books

an imprint of Prometheus Books
59 John Glenn Drive, Amherst, New York 14228–2197

Published 2005 by Humanity Books, an imprint of Prometheus Books

Inquiries should be addressed to
Humanity Books
59 John Glenn Drive
Amherst, New York 14228-2197
VOICE: 716-691-0133, ext. 207
FAX: 716-564-2711
WWW.PROMETHEUSBOOKS.COM

09 08 07 06 05 5 4 3 2 1

Library of Congress Cataloging-in-Publication Data

Winfield, Richard Dien, 1950-
The just state : rethinking self-government / Richard Dien Winfield.
p. cm.
Includes bibliographical references and index.
ISBN 1-59102-317-3 (hardcover)
1. State, The. 2. Justice (Philosophy) 3. Democracy. I. Title.

JC131.W63 2005
321.8—dc22

2004027186

For Citizens Kalindi, Manas and Rasik

CONTENTS

PREFACE

The Just State comprises the culminating installment in the reconstruction of ethics whose encompassing project I outlined in *Reason and Justice* (Albany: SUNY Press, 1988). Although the introduction and first chapter of *The Just State* trace the broad argument that must be covered before political justice can be addressed, I have provided more detailed treatment in the second parts of *Overcoming Foundations: Studies in Systematic Philosophy* (New York: Columbia University Press, 1989), *Freedom and Modernity* (Albany: SUNY Press, 1991), and *Autonomy and Normativity* (Aldershot, UK: Ashgate, 2001), which elaborate on property rights and moral autonomy; in *The Just Family* (Albany: SUNY Press, 1998), which systematically develops household freedom; and in *The Just Economy* (New York: Routledge, 1988) and *Law in Civil Society* (Lawrence: University Press of Kansas, 1995), which together systematically conceive civil society.

Reason and Justice appeared at a time when the Soviet Union and its satellite regimes were beginning to collapse, whereas *The Just State* was written during the prelude to and aftermath of the 9/11 Islamist terror attacks on New York City and Washington, DC. These convulsions and their continuing repercussions can no more prescribe what the state, society, and the family should be than can any other historical event. Nonetheless, they serve notice that one should never rest content with complacent labors of "deconstruction" and "reflective equilibrium," which resign reason to investigating the presuppositions and internal coherence of existing ideologies and practices. However settled a new world order and its pervasive consensus may appear, there is no excuse for abandoning the task of calling all givens into question and thinking without foundations. Only when that challenge is tackled can right be defended in theory, if not in practice, from its most resolute enemies.

INTRODUCTION

I POLITICAL PHILOSOPHY AND THE JUST STATE

What is the state? What should the state be? These would seem to be separate questions (one descriptive, one prescriptive), each requiring an independent answer. Political science, as a modern empirical discipline, has largely taken over the descriptive question by observing the acknowledged phenomena of political association and combing the data for any general patterns of political reality. No such empirical investigation can prescribe what the state ought to be, for any observations of political practice leave unanswered whether given political phenomena measure up to what politics should be. Far from providing any normative prescriptions, empirical science may at best observe what political norms have been advanced, how they have been followed, and what other phenomena have been connected to their appearance.

Yet even then it is questionable whether empirical political science can independently identify which norms and which institutions deserve being called "political." Modern political science may be happy to leave normative questions aside, but can its empirical investigations ever fulfill the descriptive task of determining what the state is? How can a positive political science establish what counts as political association in the first place without either baldly stipulating a definition of its own or following what some contingently given consensus has happened to label "politics"? If the answer be sought by simply generalizing about the phenomena that have been repeatedly identified as political, how can ensuing empirical investigation discover any "defining" features that may not turn out to be incidental commonalities absent from new or newly redescribed examples of whatever ends up being admitted into the political arena? Since all observations remain particular in time and place, none can ever certify what is universal and necessary in any putative "political" reality. Their descriptions may apply to those times and places under view, but never to all else, unless a leap of faith be made in assumption of the uniformity of the observed and unobserved. To arrive at any general conclusions, empirical political science cannot help but rely upon pragmatic assurances of family resemblances that are always subject to revision.

This situation may be inevitable, but it seems hardly benign if prescribing what the state should be were dependent upon an antecedent, merely descriptive determination of political reality. If the boundaries of political association are merely corrigible parameters of contingent conventions of description, leaving fluid the divide between the political and the nonpolitical, can any firm distinction be upheld between right and wrong politics?

Significantly, the celebrated pioneers of political *philosophy* have never even attempted to conceive what the state is prior to and apart from an investigation of what the state should be. Although they have distinguished between the just state and different forms of unjust body politics, the differentiation is invariably made in the course of conceiving the genesis or dissolution of normative political association.[1] Accordingly, the overarching identity of politics gets always established within the ethical investigation of normative conduct and institutions.

The absence of a descriptive philosophy of the state has its counterpart in the absence of a descriptive philosophy of the family, society, or any other convention. Because all such formations are institutions whose actual existence depends upon the arbitrary coordinated choices of rational agents, reason cannot independently dictate when, where, or whether they come into existence, nor the particular shapes that they will have. Since what conventions exist are contingent upon the concatenations of choice from which history arises, reason is incapable of providing a descriptive account and must hand over all describing to the corrigible labors of a historical, empirical understanding. Any attempt to specify what the state or any other institution *is* a priori is a futile exercise in nominalism that either surreptitiously apes empirical generalization or indulges in arbitrary speculation.

The possibilities of a prescriptive political philosophy are more sanguine. If ethics can overcome the challenge of nihilism and mandate that agents ought to participate in a form of association sufficiently resonant with common usage to bear the term "political," a normative conception of the state becomes possible that escapes the arbitrariness of nominalism while providing the standard by which deviating political formations can be distinguished. In that case, reason can conceive what the state should be and thereupon consider what might be entailed in its genesis and dissolution. Any resulting differentiation of political forms could then supply a rational typology for a historical understanding to employ in categorizing observed political phenomena. Although the latter descriptive undertaking will be in a position to apply political categories determined by reason, it will fall outside philosophical theory proper. Instead of engaging in the fruitless enterprise of conceiving political reality completely a priori, this subsidiary historical understanding will judge reflectively, interpreting empirical phenomena in light of rational concepts of what, if anything, is necessary in the rise and fall of valid political association.[2]

A philosophy of politics will therefore essentially be normative in character. Moreover, it will not be a separate discipline, developed independently from ethics. Political philosophy will instead be an integrated element in practical philosophy in general, receiving its constitutive boundaries from the conception of normative conduct within which it must be contained. Admittedly, the bare notion of normative conduct seems to leave open the possibility that the ethical and the political might completely converge, leaving politics the one and only valid practice and reducing ethics to political philosophy. So long, however, as nonpolitical conduct can have legitimacy, political association will be a particular sphere among others within a more general domain of right and wrong. This cannot fail to be true if the just state has normative preconditions, such as specific property, household, and social relations, without whose nonpolitical practices valid political association could not function. It can thus be no surprise that all the great attempts to conceive the just state have proceeded as part of more encompassing ethical systems, systems that have conceived why there should be political association in conjunction with determining what nonpolitical institutions ought to be and how the political domain should relate to them.

Before political philosophy can get underway, the principal obstacles blocking its path must be removed. These obstacles are twofold. First and foremost is the general challenge of nihilism, whose denial of reason's ability to prescribe conduct must be overturned if the possibility of ethics is to be secured, opening the field within which a normative politics might emerge. Even if nihilism can be countered, however, a second hurdle remains, lying in the particular difficulty that key features of politics pose to the normativity of political association. Unless these dual problems can be met, any normative mandate for a just politics will be in vain.

2 OVERCOMING NIHILISM

From the outset, the possibility of rationally justifying conduct seems trapped in a hopeless bind. Ethics cannot take any norms for granted without begging the question, but if ethics begins without any normative content it is caught dead in its tracks for the simple reason that what is devoid of normativity can hardly determine what distinguishes right from wrong. An investigation of ethics must begin without knowledge of any objective standards of conduct, yet obtaining such knowledge seems utterly impossible, for how can anything lacking in value, anything normatively neutral, anything that simply *is* provide any basis or direction for determining what *ought to be*?

One can readily identify a whole slew of enabling factors that must be at hand for conduct to take place: physical, chemical, biological, psychological, and linguistic conditions without which intelligent life and any interaction between agents would be precluded. Yet if these are preconditions of conduct, they suffice for all possible action without exception. Therefore, they can hardly serve to differentiate between the right and wrong conduct that they equally make possible.

Ethics seems paralyzed unless it jumps the gun and baldly stipulates something normative; yet if it does so, how can it ever uphold any divide between subjective preference and objective normativity? Is ethics to be left with an empty positivism, where all value is ultimately introduced by fiat, transforming the universal claim of any putative norm into a play for domination by its particular advocate, whose promotion of some ethics really expresses nothing but a will to power, imposing the perspectival aims of its author upon all other agents? And is politics nothing but the acme of this empty positivity, with rule exercising the ultimate license by which norms are handed down?

To escape paralysis, ethics seems to have but two possible avenues where what is normative might be discovered without taking it for granted. These complementary avenues are defined by the rudimentary structure of action in proper abstraction from any distinction of good and bad. Since all conduct involves behavior done on purpose, where an agent acts with an end in view, the value of conduct would seem to reside nowhere other than in the respective value of the ends willed by agents or of the form of willing by which those ends are pursued. The turn to each site faces the same basic challenge: of starting with neutral features of conduct and no normative commitments yet still arriving at the differentiation of right and wrong. Both avenues seem to be coevally given in the basic anatomy of willing as voluntary action, and each has spawned an imposing edifice of ethical theory, including complementary mandates for political justice. The proponents of both avenues and the advocates of nihilism are generally agreed on one point: that ethics has no other options but theirs. If indeed the resulting projects exhausted all opportunity for a rational determination of conduct, normative politics would be in jeopardy, for each of these fundamental strategies is plagued by dilemmas that call them into question. Nonetheless, the basic logic of their positions needs to be spelled out, for only by following them through can a third alternative be made intelligible, an alternative that escapes their limits and saves political philosophy from the impending triumph of nihilism.[3]

3 THE POLITICS OF PRIVILEGED ENDS

What one does or how one does it, the ends or the form of conduct, might seem to offer equally compelling starting points. It is, however, the end of conduct that logically comes first as a locus for developing ethics, as the historical primacy of teleological ethics at least illustrates. Several reasons give plausible priority to the recourse to ends as the key for evaluating conduct.

First, the end of conduct appears to cover both options insofar as an agent's aim can just as well be an action as a product of action. In acting to perform a type of action rather than to generate some product, the agent can regard what counts to be the form of the activity rather than the consequences that follow from the performance, all the while still doing so by attending to a governing aim of conduct. The end may consist in performing a type of conduct, but it remains an end all the same. A consideration of ends thus turns out to be the all-encompassing strategy for differentiating between right and wrong.

Second, a prime motive for making the form of activity the locus of normativity derives, as will become apparent, from a prior rejection of "material grounds" for conduct, that is, of allowing the value of an action to be determined by the content of its end. Indeed, it will only be by turning to the form of activity as a departure from any consideration of ends that this second alternative can hope to distinguish itself.

Finally, the turn to the ends of conduct seems inescapable the moment a justification for action is demanded. Since the mere being of conduct cannot serve to distinguish right from wrong, given how good and evil can both exist, conduct must find its measure in something separate from itself against which it ought no less correspond. Since the deciding measure cannot simply be arbitrarily chosen, it must not be a matter of convention, but must comprise a content given independently of choice, a content given by nature. Further, the privileged content must be immediate rather than mediated, for if it rests upon some ground, that ground must either be the real measure directly in virtue of its own content, or rest upon a further foundation in need of its own justification. Hence, to be valid, conduct must conform to some privileged, immediately given nature to have worth. Since conduct measures up to its standard through choice, rather than accident, the privileged content figures as the standard of validity in action by being the end that conduct aims to achieve. What else, then, but the end of action could serve to legitimate conduct?

Whether the end of conduct be action or its product, no distinction between right and wrong can possibly be established if every end is of value only as the means to some other goal. If all aims are merely instrumental, conduct can never have any genuinely definite justification. With every end the means for another, each act will have value only if the aim it or its product serves is of use to some further goal whose own value will then equally depend upon the instrumentality of what aim it furthers, with no achieved goal ever possessing a value in itself that could put an end to the ceaseless search for a reason to lend value to each and every undertaking. If the value of conduct is to lie in that of its end, all action will be in vain unless at least some end can be located that has value in itself. In that case, action in pursuit of that goal and the pursuit of any ends that contribute to its achievement will have a worth always eluding action unconnected to any intrinsic value.[4]

Moreover, if conduct can be distinguished according to whether it achieves an end in itself or realizes an end contributing to achieving what is for its own sake, then a hierarchy of value arises, with actions possessing worth in function of their position in the ascending subordination of actions that contribute toward the goal that is sought both for its own sake and as the overarching aim of all the activities instrumental to it. The very structure of the interconnected activities here engenders an impartial ordering of their worth without surreptitiously introducing any independently given values.[5]

This seeming solution to the aimlessness of conduct has one obvious problem, however. Although an end might be pursued for its own sake and as the governing rationale for subservient instrumental activities, its description has a self-defeating formality. Any end, be it an act or a product, could conceivably be sought for its own sake and then have its realization promoted by subordinate activities. Indeed, in the absence of any instrumental justification, whatever is sought for its own sake would have to be so pursued by a completely ungrounded volition, which might just as well make any other end its good. With an unlimited plurality of potential ends in themselves from which to choose, agents would have no grounds for favoring one line of conduct over another. In that case, being an end in itself would confer no more worth than being for the sake of something else and ethics would give way to a meaningless existence of indifferent behavior.

Only one measure can remove the dilemma presented by a plurality of ends in themselves and redeem the privileged role of ends in the justification of conduct: the plurality must be abolished by the discovery of a unique end that exclusively occupies the position of an end in itself. To do so, such an end in itself must no less be a master end, subordinating all other ends, be they products or actions, to the instrumental position of servants of its own realization. That master end will thereby comprise a highest good, constitutively defined as the one and only end for its own sake, an end that alone occupies that privileged height by equally subordinating all other pursuits to its own attainment. If such a highest good can be identified, ethics will be saved from the clutches of nihilism and conduct will be more than a will to power.[6]

But what could the highest good be and what place if any would political association enjoy under its banner? Since ends can be either actions or products of action, a first step in further determining the highest good lies in deciding whether it is an activity or a product. Although products are most commonly instrumental, ending up consumed in satisfaction of some need, they can also be valued for their own sake, as in the case of objects of fine art, protected from use and preserved to show themselves in their own right. Yet such objects are hardly one in number, nor do they subordinate any, let alone all other affairs to their self-manifestation. The highest good must therefore be not a product but an activity, an activity pursued for its own sake so as to no less subordinate all other pursuits to its own perpetuation. The master end is therefore a master activity, enjoying the sovereignty of being subordinate to no other end by lording over all other activities and their products so as to support its continued dominion.

If ethics can be no other than the philosophy of the highest good and the highest good must be a master activity, valid conduct will preeminently be a ruling activity that uniquely engages in a sovereign dominion over all other spheres of life. Such an activity will be the constitutive practice of a form of association to the degree that ruling cannot be a solitary endeavor but must involve either singly or jointly presiding over agents who submit to their dominion by acting in respect to the demands of the master agency. These subordinate agents may be different from their rulers and comprise a subject class or may conceivably be wholly or partly rulers of themselves, bifurcating their activities into self-government and action instrumental to rule.

The resulting association would seem to be no other than political, insofar as political association is not beholden to any higher authority and subordinates all other affairs to its own flourishing.[7] Of course, not all body politics satisfy this dual requirement, since many a government has historically been subservient to religious authority, kinship ties, or economic powers. Yet, these examples need not undermine the political character of a true master association, for they can compatibly amount to imperfect, partial embodiments of what politics proper can offer in radical distinction from all other forms of community.

If political association has the exclusive mastery demanded of the highest good then ethical conduct will preeminently be political activity and the good life will be fully realized in the life of the citizen who participates in rule. Not only will ethics mandate political association, but politics and ethics will converge to the extent that normatively valid conduct will consist in nothing but the activity of political association and whatever activities serve as governed prerequisites of politics.[8] Instead of deriving legitimacy by being an instrument for achieving nonpolitical ends, political association will here command authority as something uniquely for its own sake, realizing the highest good by actualizing the master activity that cannot coexist with any other pursuits either claiming value in themselves or serving some other competing end. The aim of politics will accordingly be exclusively universal with respect to the goals pursued within its domain. The end of the state will be the one over many, since all these other goals will be drawn into realizing political association's own all-encompassing end. Uniquely universal by being uniquely for its own sake, political association will be self-sufficient, for its own governance will involve insuring fulfillment of the functions furnishing the preconditions for its own perpetuation. Although individuals will act with instrumental value in pursuing these subordinate ends, they will behave fully ethically only when they will the universal end of politics, participating in the master activity of state rule.

This recipe for a politics that is an ethics of a highest good has cast a long shadow since its pioneering development by Plato and Aristotle. At first glance, it seems to meet the challenge of nihilism, for it promises a self-sustaining practice that has value without having to take for granted what is right. Every salient feature of the master activity of political association has followed from the normatively neutral structure of voluntary action and the basic theorem that ends can only endow conduct with value if an end can figure as a highest good. Moreover, the argument has provided the strongest of cases for political philosophy, making political association the ultimate substance of ethics, without which conduct becomes utterly pointless.

Nonetheless, the ethics of the highest good is haunted by a basic formality that threatens to rob it and its politics of all significance. The vexing problem is that any prevailing regime qualifies as the highest good because whatever power succeeds in dominating all other activities automatically qualifies as a master end, asserting itself for its own sake while subordinating every other end to its own. What composition the sovereign power has, how it governs and which activities it permits are all a matter of utter indifference so long as it reigns supreme. The indifference would be eliminated only if the attainment of rule were automatically connected to a specific form of government, with specific aims and specific subordinate institutions. Yet the incontrovertible possibility of different forms of rule dispels a unique exemplification, leaving each and every regime in the same precarious predicament. Insofar as being a master end leaves open everything about a regime but its supremacy, any insurgent force that successfully topples it while fending off all challengers wins equivalent legitimacy, but only in the pyrrhic sense of inviting the same contest of force against force to decide the issue. In effect, the political requirements of the highest good do little more than affirm that might makes right, an equation that eliminates any abiding distinction between is and ought, or convention and norm, leaving reason in full flight before the contingent contests of will. Political philosophy stands on the edge of collapse, for no distinction can possibly be drawn between political right and wrong or the validity of different regimes. All that is left to be done is offer Machiavellian counsels of prudence on how to conquer and retain power, counsels that can never emanate from reason alone, since the outcome of the struggle for power is always prey to empirical happenstance.

Can the ethics and politics of a highest good overcome this vitiating formality and provide further content sufficient to distinguish right from wrong and give meaning to political justice? Whatever remedial content is found must fulfill the same dual requirement of the highest good, of being both an end that is for its own sake and an end to which all others are subordinate, for if these features are lacking, the supplement's worth will depend upon some other factor whose own legitimacy is open to question. Yet how can one possibly determine what can so qualify as further filling for the master end, enabling differentiation between valid and invalid political association?

Nothing in the nature of what is will suffice, for what pertains to being will apply indifferently to all beings, be they good or bad. Nothing in the nature of the preconditions of political association will do any better since each and every body politic will share alike everything therein. Appeal to the nature of rational agency is of no use, either. If that nature is actual apart from convention, it has an immediate givenness that is always already at hand in any conduct.[9] If instead it is a natural potential whose realization depends upon choice, any injunction to realize that potential in practice only brings us right back to the problem of determining what it is that reason demands of conduct.[10]

If nothing that is can offer grounds for determining what ought to be pursued for its own sake as the master end, how can something normative be introduced without begging the question? The content of the highest good cannot be legitimated by any norm lying outside it, for if such an independent standard were introduced, it would be the ultimate principle of conduct, subverting the primacy of the erstwhile highest good while incurring the same dilemma of justification itself. But if no candidate for highest good can qualify in virtue of some separate ground, how can the content of one contender disqualify the competing content of any other? Each and every putative highest good must be fundamentally nonderivative and immediate. Yet, as the formality of might has exhibited, simply enjoying supreme mastery is something that leaves indeterminate the further content of the prevailing regime. In other words, no candidate can claim to be the only nonderivative and immediate possibility. Indeed, any content can occupy that role so long as all others are excluded from that privileged position.

Any attempt to show that a content is the bona fide highest good because all competitors actually depend upon it would require demonstrating two things: first, that all alternatives have been exhaustively explored and, second, that their dependence upon the bona fide master end is irretrievably necessary. Yet how can either proviso be established with any certainty, especially when the laurels of supremacy can be shared by any number of successive victors of contingent power struggles?

These dilemmas cannot be swept aside by the traditional device of distinguishing between legitimate and illegitimate regimes according to whether the rulers, be they one, few, or many, rule for the common good or for their particular interests.[11] As with the analogous recourse to some "rational potential," the appeal to a common good only relabels the highest good without adding new determination. If the common good be further identified as some rationally prescribed form of community or simply as the aggregate of the independently chosen aims of each agent, the favored description must count due to its immediate content or some separate foundation. Either alternative raises the same problems of justification that apply to the highest good—some privileged given must command exclusive normativity but nothing can be found to deprive other candidates from claiming the same honor in precisely the same way.

Relying upon a contrast between universal and particular ends only recasts the distinction between the master end and its subordinates, for how else can any putative universal end escape reduction to something particular unless it commands the exclusive position of being the only one over many? Nothing can count as a genuinely universal end other than the highest good, and the highest good can countenance no universal other than itself if the exclusivity of its ruling end is to be sustained.

If rule be right or wrong depending upon whether it serves the common good or particular interests, then governing loses intrinsic value and becomes an instrument for realizing the common good. But then, the common good would count as the only end that is for its own sake and that to which all other pursuits should be subordinated. Accordingly, the common good would be indistinguishable from the highest good and turn out to have the same formal features. If still the common good be given any separate identity, ethics faces an insoluble choice between competing universals, an impasse which is precisely what the turn to the highest good seeks to overcome.

The project of an ethics and politics of a highest good cannot escape these dilemmas any more than can any normative enterprise that seeks validity in some privileged given. Political philosophy need not, however, abandon the field to nihilism and the value-neutral descriptions of empirical political science. The collapse of teleological ethics directly suggests another possible strategy, the other option left open by the structure of voluntary action—namely, that the normativity of conduct be sought not in the ends willed but in the form of willing.

4 THE POLITICS OF THE FREEDOM OF DESIRE

The insolvable dilemmas of an ethics and politics of the highest good leave political philosophy with the challenge of distinguishing right from wrong despite reason's inability to prescribe ends whose content independently legitimates the practices that realize them. At the very least, the collapse of teleological ethics leaves the negative injunction that determining how conduct can have normativity and why and how political association should be are tasks to be fulfilled without relying upon the content of any ends.

This injunction might seem to cede victory to nihilism, for if no ends of conduct can be justified by reason and reliably employed to distinguish right from wrong, what ends agents choose and institutions promote seems to be a matter of indifference. And if that is so, how can any course of action claim superior worth over any other, or any regime claim authority on anything but its own might? In the absence of any a priori prescribable aims, would not politics always be opaque to reason, leaving political association prey to nothing but the contingencies of power, whose ends and arrangements are endlessly plastic and always relative?

Before the vertigo of a world without privileged ends, agents do enjoy one positive legacy: they are each equally liberated from all obligation to restrict their choice to any independently prescribed goal. The absence of a highest good sets all free of any rational tutelage that would mandate what individuals should desire and what mold of dispositions they should accustom themselves to acquire. Further, because the worth of actions can no longer be ranked according to what extent they promote the achievement of any privileged end, neither the conduct nor the motivations of individuals have any differentiated merit. With reason powerless to rank ends, each and every desire of each and every agent stands on a par. And since the ends favored by different patterns of disposition are equally indifferent, the corresponding character of individuals can have no differentiated value. With regard to obligation and with regard to merit, all individuals are free and equal.

The freedom and equality emerging from the demise of the highest good has, in the first instance, a purely negative character. It is a freedom from subordination to prescribed ends and a freedom from any privileged ranking of character. Of itself, this negative liberation hardly removes the specter of nihilism, for the absence of a highest good does not directly give freedom and equality primacy over oppression and inequality—each and every predicament is equally devoid of any rationally prescribable sanction as a privileged goal.

Yet, if the negative freedom accompanying the liberation from a highest good cannot count as an end in itself, might it still circumvent nihilism by endowing legitimacy not in virtue of being an end or serving any other, but by being that which allows conduct to have validity no matter what ends it pursues? This option brings to the fore the form of willing, that other element in the rudimentary structure of action that the pursuit of a highest good left out of account unless it were sought as an end in itself. To make the form of willing the locus of normativity is tantamount to treating how an agent wills as the deciding factor in whether conduct and institutions have legitimacy. This, of course, is precisely what is being done when the liberty of conduct is made the source of its legitimacy, for then what ought be asked is not which ends are pursued and achieved, but whether they have been willed freely. Instead of ranking conduct in respect to a highest good, distinguishing vice and virtue according to the ends willed, freedom and oppression, liberty and its violation, become the terms of ethical evaluation.

The turn to liberty may clearly involve a turn away from ends to a form of willing, but liberty hardly seems to be the only form of willing, let alone the one form that need be privileged. Just as the ends of action may be multifarious, so the forms of willing appear endlessly variable. If this is so, making the form of willing the focus of normativity seems to inject the same demand for hierarchy that led from the plurality of ends to a highest good. Otherwise something outside the form of willing must be introduced to adjudicate between the competing claims of different manners of volition, undermining the Archimedean role that the form should be appropriating from the matter of decision. Can the varieties of how agents will be ordered in any ranking as ends be subordinated to a master goal? What cannot be employed to differentiate modes of willing are the ends that are willed. But if what is willed is abstracted from, how multifarious can be the form that is left?

Whenever choice is made, the will is exercising a freedom of desire, acting in pursuit of whatever end it chooses to realize. Although here the agent allows the content of desire to figure as the ground of decision, insofar as something rather than something else is done on purpose, the absence of a highest good leaves the decision with no other basis than the preference of the agent, a preference free of any external prescription. Hence, while every such volition may have a different end, each act will share the same form of being an exercise of liberty, understood as doing as one pleases. If this ubiquitous form is privileged as the one and only source of value in conduct, ethics is left with an all too familiar strategy. Since all ends here have value only once they are chosen as objects of desire and all desires and characters are on a par, promoting the liberty of doing as one pleases is equivalent to promoting the satisfaction of chosen desires, with indifference to what and whose they are. Consequently, what results is not an injunction to do simply as one pleases. With all qualitative ranking out of the question, the freedom of desire asserts its hegemony by making the one and only ethical rule be that an action or institution is valid to the degree that it advances the *aggregate* satisfaction of desire, with the desires of *all* agents counting *equally* in the calculation. On this basis, if political philosophy is to retain any mandate, it must be demonstrated that political association increases the general happiness more than anarchy. By the same token, if any determinate conception of the valid state is to be drawn, it will depend upon establishing that the value of regimes can be assessed in terms of their impact upon aggregate desire satisfaction.

Can, however, any determinate counsels, let alone any universal prescriptions, be drawn by following the utilitarian calculus issuing from privileging the freedom of desire? If what desires individuals have is contingent, varying not only from person to person, but from moment to moment within each agent as well, the impact of any course of action upon happiness becomes inscrutable. Determining what effect any act or policy has is difficult enough once it enters the web of existence, with all its disseminating interconnections and reciprocal interactions. Yet even if consequences could be unambiguously ascertained, the contingency of desires subverts any estimation of resulting happiness. What desires might be held at one moment need not be had at any other, leaving agents with no reliable guide for choosing conduct that is appropriately useful. The value of any action or institutional policy remains indecipherable even after the fact, for not only can no certitude be had about the aggregate desire at any one moment, but all predictions about future desires are idle, leaving any current happiness subject to instantaneous vanishing.

If, on the contrary, desires had a discoverable common fixed character among and within individuals, a successful utilitarian calculation would still be impossible. Not only do the qualitative differences between desires resist any quantitative aggregation, but the freedom of desire still leaves indeterminate both which desires individuals happen to have chosen to fulfill and by which means. Appeal to the outcome of market transactions as a vehicle of commensurable calculation is of no avail, since the desire of individuals need not be limited to what has a price, nor be in any common relation to their buying power or commodity ownership. All these uncertainties make utterly unfathomable what circumstances will face other actions and institutional policies, both before, during, and after their execution.

Hence, even if it may be a truism that all agents aim at happiness insofar as they desire whatever they do on purpose and draw satisfaction from achieving their goal, the freedom of desire can generate no determinate rules for conduct nor any determinate institutional arrangements that will necessarily promote aggregate desire satisfactions. Just as the ethics and politics of a highest good cannot overcome the vitiating formality of the master end, so the ethics of the freedom of desire falls prey to the formality of its utilitarian principle. Once more, political association is left without direction: a utilitarian politics is either empty or fraudulent and a utilitarian political philosophy is a misnomer that clothes empirical speculation in the mantle of reason.

There cannot be any fit between reason and the freedom of desire simply because that freedom resists taking the form of a universal principle. Due to the contingent content of desire and the contingencies of its realization, the satisfaction of one desire need not promote nor be compatible with the satisfaction of any other. Not only may different desires interfere with each other's fulfillment, but the same desire may not be satisfiable when it is pursued by more than one agent. The absence of any preestablished harmony in the satisfaction of different desires and in the desire satisfactions of different agents prevents the form of willing of the freedom of desire from having the universality required of an ethical norm. There can never be any guarantee that one or more agents can actually do what they each please, not because of any impediments external to the pursuit of desire, but due to the lack of any inherent compatibility between desire satisfactions.[12] Because each exercise of the freedom of desire can interfere with its exercise by another agent, asserting its form of willing as a norm would present a universal ought that cannot be universally performed. Since no agent can be obliged to do what cannot be done, the freedom of desire cannot possibly be a norm commanding universal respect. Accordingly, no political philosophy can possible by erected on its basis.

If the form of willing is to supply the source of normativity for conduct, it must overcome the limitation that prevents the freedom of desire from disabling the challenge of nihilism. Somehow willing must obtain a form that can automatically be exercised without mutual interference. In other words, how an agent wills must be such that other agents *can* simultaneously will in the same manner. Or, negatively expressed, the way in which agents will must guarantee that what they thereby choose cannot prevent one another from exercising that common form of willing. If this requirement can be met, willing will have a form that at least fits the most minimal demand of ethical normativity: that what counts as valid be an ought that can be practiced, an ought that is not a privilege for the few who alone can fulfill it, but an ought that has universality for all who come under the sway of ethical obligation.

The predicament now facing ethics raises two questions: first, what can be this privileged form of willing, and second, can it suffice to distinguish right from wrong? Whatever content this privileged form may turn out to have may be a necessary constituent of ethical conduct, but this necessity will not itself guarantee that it be a sufficient condition as well. If the two questions of content and sufficiency can be positively answered, the fate of political philosophy will hang on whether the redeeming form of willing mandates any determinate type of political association. If, however, this privileged form is necessary, but not sufficient to render conduct valid, the normativity of politics will remain in abeyance until a further question can be answered, the question of how the lacking sufficient condition can be supplied.

5 THE ETHICS AND POLITICS OF PURE PROCEDURAL JUSTICE

The form of willing that insures that each agent's exercise of that form will be in harmony with that of every other agent is equivalent to the basic form of right. To exercise a right is to practice a freedom so constituted that it can be universally performed by all agents. The freedom in question is a *form* of volition in the sense that it does not bind the agent to any specific prescribed end. Instead, it leaves each agent an equal opportunity, that is, a certain range of discretion so limited that whatever action the agent chooses within that range can be performed without preventing other agents from enjoying the matching prerogative. By the same token, the form of volition of right is a form of *freedom* insofar as it leaves it to the discretion of each participant to decide precisely what action and end will be chosen in exercise of that form. Furthermore, because the exercise of right consists of individuals crafting their volitions so that they have a common mode that all can follow without contradiction, it involves a form a willing by which the participating agents will in a *lawful* manner. Accordingly, the freedom of right is a lawful autonomy that, unlike the freedom of desire, can figure as a principle of conduct, whose universality makes it specifiable by reason.

That the lawful character of right's form of willing allows it to figure as a norm is directly manifest in how each exercise of right involves observance of the duty to respect the same right of others. This conjunction of right and duty is always present the moment any right is enjoyed simply because the bearers of a right only exercise that entitlement by so circumscribing their discretion that the limit they impose upon themselves fits what is required to enable all other agents to exercise the same form of discretion. Since this mutual self-limitation both realizes an agent's own right and extends due respect to the corresponding right of every other bearer of the right in question, an agent determines itself as a bearer of right by willing in recognition of the rights of others.[13]

Once the lawfulness of right becomes the privileged form of willing from which conduct is to derive normativity, the differentiation of right and wrong seems to be an easy matter. No longer need ethics and politics struggle to distinguish vices and virtues in respect to an indefinable highest good nor tackle ever elusive calculations of which types of private action and public policy will promote the satisfaction of desires. Instead, the line between good and evil has a simple formula: whatever upholds right is normatively valid whereas whatever violates right is wrong. Once more freedom and oppression supplant virtue and vice, but now the freedom in question is not the license of desire, but the equal opportunities that the lawful form of willing entails.

The formal requirement of right is simple, but can it serve as a principle of conduct and valid institutions, determining what ought to be done? To function as a determining principle of valid practice, the form of right must have a character given antecedently to the practices on which it confers normativity. Otherwise, there is nothing to serve as a standard for evaluating the multiplicity of actions and institutions. It follows that the practices that get determined as normatively valid will have a content distinct from the antecedent principle of right by which they are sanctioned. Without that difference, they would merely reiterate that single form and lack not only the individuality by which any real deeds and institutions are distinguished, but the particular distinctions characterizing different types of conduct and association.

Moreover, if the lawful form of willing is to serve as the principle for legitimating conduct, whatever arises from its employment will have validity independently of any other factor. The privileged form will therefore serve as a pure procedural principle, for instead of sanctioning deeds and institutions by the contents they embody, it will justify whatever arises from its application. These qualifications, which attach themselves to the lawful form of willing the moment it functions as the principle of normativity, have fateful implications for its content and sufficiency.

To begin with, the bare notion of right, of a willing whose form harmonizes with all other volitions that embrace that form, has an empty formality unless it be given some further filling. If no heed can be paid to the quality of ends or consequent happiness, it is far from clear how one can determine which types of volition can or cannot be lawful. Any course of action that an agent can perform might pose as an exercise of right if all that counts is that everyone else may try the same sort of deed. Murder, theft, enslavement, sedition, betrayal, and every other seeming malfeasance could qualify, since each could be attempted on all sides, even if not all would achieve their aim. So long as any failure in so acting is not necessitated, the possibility remains that the type of volition could be undertaken by anyone.

If right is to have any determinate being, permitting some contrast between right and wrong, the principle of willing must have a lawfulness that includes some differentiating content. Given the inability of reason to establish a highest good and the inability of the freedom of desire to fit the form of right, the requisite content cannot be drawn from independently given ends or calculations of resultant happiness. On the other hand, because the form of right has been given the privileged role of generating the normativity of conduct and institutions, its content cannot already contain the identifying features of the conduct and institutions whose legitimacy derives from it. Accordingly, the right that has to serve as the principle of validity must be one that does not already involve an institutional reality. To figure as a pure procedural principle of normativity, the lawful form of willing must have a determinacy that remains ideal compared to the actual institutions to emanate from its Archimedean source.

The particular forms of right can be distinguished as different types of equal opportunity. This retains the lawfulness of the volitions involved, leaves room for different modes of freedom, and distinguishes different sets of rights and corresponding duties without binding the will to any given ends. Such binding would not only resurrect the dilemmas of teleological ethics but eliminate the freedom of discretion and the lawful form that such freedom possesses under conditions of right. Accordingly, what distinguishes particular equal opportunities are different mutually recognized prerogatives, involving types of ends and the types of coordinated agencies directed to them.

Of the determinate equal opportunities that distinguish particular forms of right, two have a distinctly noninstitutional character, enabling them to serve the aim of ethical construction: property right and moral right. Unlike family right, economic right, legal right, or political right, property and moral right can be exercised without direct participation in existing associations such as families, markets, legal systems, or states.

To enjoy the equal opportunity of ownership, individuals need simply embody their wills in external factors that they reciprocally honor as the exclusive domains of their respective volitions. How these respective factors relate to other considerations, such as interest and welfare, is a matter of indifference as far as simply having ownership is concerned. What makes the lawfulness of persons' volition have the specific determination of property is no more than that they each will an external embodiment as the recognized realization of their self-determination as owner. This particular type of right has an obvious primacy because no other equal opportunity can be enjoyed unless individuals have determined themselves as owners. Any further right is precluded because unless individuals have taken ownership of their own bodies, mutually recognizing that one another's body is the exclusive receptacle of each one's own will, they are prey to appropriation by others, whereupon anything an individual does counts as an exercise not of its own, but of some master's will.[14] Property right thus logically precedes all other forms of right as their common enabling condition and can be exercised without participation in any further institutions. For this very reason, property right has the greatest claim to figure as the Archimedean principle for procedurally generating the validity of practice.

Moral right might seem to be a plausible alternate or supplementary candidate for foundational employment since it can also be exercised without and, indeed, in express indifference to involvement in any institutions. In contrast to property right, the lawful willing of moral right consists in exercising equal opportunity to determine the scope of one's accountability in respect to one's self-selected purposes and intentions. As moral subjects, individuals enjoy the right to be held responsible only for that part of their action prefigured in their purpose and for those consequences of their action prefigured in their intention supplying the motive for their purpose. If moral right is to determine which purposes and motives are legitimate without illicitly appealing to a highest good or resulting happiness, it must acknowledge the right of each subject to determine individually what is good, that is, to acknowledge everyone's right of conscience. Conscience's determination of the moral good is a bona fide form of right insofar as when individuals acknowledge one another's opportunity to act on conscience, they exercise discretion in a lawful manner. Nevertheless, the subjective element in conscience's determination of right purpose and motive permits no definite commitments to any institutional arrangements. Not only may conscience dictate violating one's institutional duties, but what may be good for the conscience of one individual may be contrary to that of another, putting each in the quandary of being able to respect the conscience of another only at the expense of ignoring the competing claims of one's own. Moreover, although the unencumbered character of moral self-determination abstracts from all institutional involvements, it still presupposes property right since a person cannot recognize others as morally accountable if they count as embodiments of its will. Whatever one's chattel does is one's own responsibility. For these reasons, the determining process of moral reflection can hardly suffice as an unequivocal principle for ethical construction.

As a consequence, it can hardly be surprising that the effort to make the lawful form of willing the source of normativity has turned out to be a social contract theory, where an exercise of property right, i.e., contract, gives rise to institutions whose authority rests both on being the outcome of contractual agreement and on being the enforcer of the rights of ownership. To serve this foundational role, property right must function in two guises: first, as a generative ideal and second, as a regulative norm over derivative institutions that are not reducible to ownership, but draw their legitimacy by serving as a means to the realization of property right.

For property right to be the determining principle of valid institutions, it must perform its determining function in a condition where it lies at hand but valid institutions do not. Although the liberal tradition calls such a situation a "state of nature," it is not natural nor antecedent to society for it includes within its orbit not only the practice of property right but all other conventions that are not derivative of property right and that therefore do not yet enjoy normative validity. The state of nature often appears as just the plurality of individuals who enjoy their freedom of desire, having been liberated from the bogus obligations that an ethics of a highest good would impose upon their wills. That liberty of desire is recognized to be a threat to itself, and the search begins to find a universal form of willing that will give individuals the greatest mutually conducive opportunity. In order to be in a position to assign any rights to others, however, individuals must already be owners of themselves. Thus, property right must be at hand before any further obligations can be imposed. Under property right, no transfer of anything one owns can take place without the agreement of the owner, so any contractual agreement that enacts institutions has binding force only on the basis of preexisting property, which sets individuals in relation to one another as, at the very least, owners of their own bodies. Without recognition of that minimal ownership, no agent can qualify for participation in the privileged choice procedure by which social contract theory seeks to construct valid institutions, for unless one is recognized to own one's own body, no equal opportunity of any sort can be available. Far from being a natural given, such universal property right is a historical achievement, arising only when all impeding obstacles have been removed and individuals choose to interact in a correspondingly lawful manner.

If property right is to figure as an Archimedean principle, the question arises as to what, besides particular contractual transfers of the use and ownership of property, can issue from it. How can property right and, more generally, any procedural principle, give rise to something other than its own reiteration without succumbing to the influence of extraneous factors that have no legitimacy?

An obvious and oft-tried avenue consists in following out how the exercise of property right, albeit contingently possible, is subject to inherent difficulties that call for remedy, given the normativity of its own freedom. Indeed, since no other norms here have any legitimate standing, any move beyond property right must rely on nothing but what is required for property right to be realized. The mutual recognition process of property right constitutively contains the factor that inherently threatens its own maintenance: the capacity of choice that all owners must possess in order to select a factor in which to lay their will in relation to the domains of their counterparts. That capacity enables each person to disagree in good faith with the putative property claims of others, to opt for fraudulent misrepresentation to violate their property under the cloak of respect for right, or to trample on the ownership of others with open disregard for their entitlements, be it with direct criminal intent or negligence. The same capacity leaves the victims and onlookers alike with the options of returning wrong for wrong, disagreeing over the facts of the alleged violation, and feuding over what compensation and/or punishment is required to right the wrong. Even if all other parties agree on the allegations and the remedy, the perpetrator can always choose to resist their accusations and penalties, especially when no person enjoys any privileged authority to determine the actual property entitlements of each. The unconditioned normativity of property right requires that these obstacles to its realization be removed and their identity dictates the character of the remedy. Namely, a publicly recognized authority must be established to certify the property entitlements of each person, make known to all the authoritative formalities of property relations, provide an official public investigation and judgment of all violations of property right, and insure that whatever compensations or punishments it mandates are officially enforced. Further, since the public authority cannot fulfill its role unless it enjoys the recognition of all persons subject to its regulation, they must all be understood to have agreed to its governance, even if they may find themselves subject to its correction.

This familiar mandate for a public administration of justice, where justice is essentially focused upon the universal realization of property right, might seem to give political philosophy a lease on life by providing political association with its basic justification. The Archimedean principle of the lawful willing of ownership has succeeded in generating an institution over and above the private contractual relations of persons. In so doing, it has provided legitimation for a public authority whose promulgation of property law, a law of civil procedure, and a law of its own administration, whose judgment of cases coming under these laws, and whose enforcement of these laws upon the persons subject to its authority together constitute a rationally determined form of government that bears sufficient resemblance to common usage to warrant labeling as "the just state." Although the emergent body politic contains the realization of property right within its realm, its defining activity is instrumental in character. This instrumental, functional character is endemic to any institution that derives its legitimation from being the outcome of some privileged form of willing, for any such institution is an artifact, produced by that choice procedure. However the choice procedure be defined from whose exercise legitimate institutions are determined, those institutions enjoy validity insofar as they satisfy the antecedent demands of that privileged vehicle of ethical construction. A body politic that *is* for its own sake is incompatible with procedural ethics, for the founding procedure cannot be identified with what results from its process, which, as a derivative outcome, is constitutively a function of the working of that choice procedure.

This instrumentality might seem harmless, given how a vitiating emptiness plagued the self-sufficiency of the politics of the highest good. Yet several problems immediately arise from the instrumental character generic to the body politic issuing from property right or any other privileged choice procedure.

To begin with, because political association is here baptized as a means to realizing rights antecedent to its foundation and therefore independent of political practice, there is no inherent identity between politics and that for which it is an instrument. If the body politic were an association for its own sake, the mere fact of its existence would guarantee fulfillment of its legitimating aim. By being what it is, the state would automatically achieve what it is for—namely, political association itself. In that case, the state could do no wrong unless it undermined its own perpetuation. Of course, this leaves little opportunity to distinguish between political right and wrong or to evaluate different regimes, *unless* the state that is an end in itself has what teleological ethics could not supply: a concrete character involving more than lording over all other conventions, a concrete character eliminating the equation of might makes right. When, however, the state derives validity by realizing something different from political association, a discrepancy between political practice and its legitimating purpose is always possible. Better instruments might be provided not only by different regimes, but by institutions that are not at all political. And no matter what formation might be best able to perform the needed service, it could always deviate from its proper function since its being does not necessarily contain the attainment of its legitimating end.

Although this difficulty is the common bane of any instrumental relation, it has a special extremity when applied to politics. Whereas nonpolitical instruments can be compelled to perform their function by higher office, the supremacy of political association makes further external supervision of its operations problematic. For if the state is the highest public authority, how can its conformity with its validating aims be judged or enforced?[15] Social contract theorists perennially vacillate between asserting that the state can do no wrong and that persons have the right to rebel when they judge government to be in violation of its mandate. Their vacillation is understandable because neither option is supportable, and no other alternative lies at their disposal. To enforce property right, government must command recognition as authoritative, yet enjoying that recognition is formal insofar as public authority can still violate the antecedently determined strictures of property right even if no private individual has any authority to countermand it. On the other hand, if individuals enjoy the license to stand in judgment over government and repudiate its measures at will, public authority never commands the recognition on which the enforcement of right depends, leaving property right prey to the freedom of desire.

Any appeal to international intervention only transfers the dilemma to another level. If an international body wields authority over the affairs of states, their sovereignty is undercut and the international authority becomes a world encompassing state whose own rectitude becomes just as problematic as that of any state not subject to further subordination. If state sovereignty is preserved, as the very plurality of *international* relations requires, then any external intervention becomes an initiative of particular states whose authority is just as subject to question as that of the political association under their duress.

If this outcome casts into doubt whether political association can ever fulfill the function that procedural ethics requires of it, a more basic difficulty haunts the point of departure of any instrumental ethical construction. By serving as a determining principle by whose choice procedure valid institutions are to be derived, the lawful form of willing confers legitimacy upon something different from itself. Since the lawful form of willing plays this role as the exclusive source of normativity, the privileged procedure cannot itself derive legitimacy from anywhere else. This leaves the privileged procedure in a bind, for the only source of legitimation that it allows is a source from which it cannot itself derive validity. On its own procedural terms, validity is had solely by issuing from the privileged choice procedure. Yet because the choice procedure is a principle of ethical construction, endowing derivative institutions with normativity, it has a given character antecedent to what it endows with normativity. If the choice procedure had no given character, procedural ethics would have no determinate procedure to employ. Therefore the choice procedure cannot satisfy its own standard of normativity, for to do so, it must issue from its own process, something it cannot do without relinquishing the prior givenness on which its role as a determining principle depends.[16] To have normativity in conformity with its own requirements, the lawful form of willing would have to be determined by itself. Then, however, what endows legitimacy and what possesses legitimacy can no longer be separated. Instead of being a privileged procedure from which normative institutions derive, the structure of right would become the self-determined substance of normativity, forfeiting its ideal character as a noninstitutional principle of ethical construction and becoming the actuality of normative conduct.

Political philosophy appears to have reached an impasse. Procedural ethics cuts the ground out from under itself the moment it is called to account and required to meet its own standard of normativity. As soon as the privileged procedure is made to satisfy its own principle of justification, it cancels its own character as the antecedent determiner from which normative institutions are to issue. Yet if neither the end of willing nor any privileged choice procedure can provide normativity for conduct, can nihilism be evaded?

6 FOUNDATIONALISM AND THE LIMITS OF THE WILL TO POWER

With the successive collapse of teleological and procedural ethics, and the political prescriptions that derive from them, the conundrum of normativity has reasserted itself: value cannot rest upon antecedent value without begging the question, yet value can no more rest upon what has no value. Ought cannot be extracted from what is, but neither can it be extracted from any norm, for that only takes for granted what must be established in the first place. The dilemma is not simply ethical; it extends to all questions of normativity, epistemological and aesthetic as well. Plato's famous problem of the *Meno*[17] gave electric notice to its epistemological formulation: the truth cannot be known on the basis of what is not known to be true, but only upon knowledge of truth. But if acquiring truth depends on knowing what is true, truth cannot be acquired, but must always be had, seemingly precluding philosophy's search for truth.

In each and every domain, the problem has a common root: the presumption that normativity must rest upon a foundation. According to this presumption, ethical conduct must be legitimated by something apart from itself, just as knowledge claims are true by finding support in some separate reason, and aesthetic judgments are valid by resting on some other factor. Yet, no foundation can possibly supply the requisite legitimation because of the very structure of foundational justification. In the case of ethics, the legitimating ground can be something nonethical or something ethical, yet in either case, success is precluded. Conduct can never be endowed with normativity by what is not ethical, what is normatively neutral, for all this provides are implications of existence, which leave undetermined how to distinguish states of affairs that are right from those that are wrong. Alternately, to ground ethical value upon something of ethical value introduces a vicious circularity that takes for granted what must be established.

The general difficulty is starkly simple. If normativity be rooted in some foundation, what enjoys normativity is different from that which confers normativity. But then, the value-conferring foundation can never satisfy its own standard of validity. To be valid on foundational terms depends upon being derivative of the privileged foundation. The foundation can never meet that requirement because to do so it would have to rest upon itself, cease to be the privileged given upon which everything normative is predicated, and eliminate the difference between foundation and founded, between endower and recipient of normativity, on which foundational justification is based. Yet if the foundation from which validity is derived cannot have validity so long as it performs its foundational role, both its content and its alleged primacy are purely arbitrary, leaving normativity hostage to caprice.

If normative validity be restricted to foundational options, the impossibility of justifying foundations leaves little choice but to follow the grand narrative shared by Nietzsche, legal positivists, and postmodernists, and acknowledge that all norms ultimately issue from some groundless decision to impose principles which, because they claim universal validity, amount to a play for domination by the particular will that stipulates them. Unmasking the will to power underlying each and every ethics and politics might appear to be emancipatory, insofar as it undermines the universal claims of regimes that actually serve some dominating agency. The closet liberals among antifoundationalists would like to believe that such deconstruction paves the way for the institution of a multicultural democracy.[18] After all, if all privileged terms, be they ends or procedures, are arbitrary postulates, why not seek the fittest expression of the relativity of norms in granting each will an equal political voice, while insuring equal respect for the values of different cultural groups? But can the relativity of norms really give any succor to equal political rights and cultural toleration?[19] If *all* norms issue from foundations, the incoherence of foundational justification gives equal license to intolerant, undemocratic principles that cannot coexist with toleration of cultural diversity and universal suffrage. Hence, the appeal to multicultural democratic neutrality privileges a very particular set of values. If anything were to consistently follow from the unmasking of normativity as will to power, would it not instead be a politics of a new aristocracy that rules in explicit expression of its will to power, brazenly seeking to dominate others, without apology for the arbitrary particularity of its values?[20]

This invitation to fascism has theoretical force only if normative justification can be established to be endemically foundational. Admittedly, the variants of foundationalism in ethics do self-destruct in seeking to legitimate their own claims, which allows for their dismissal without need of any positive counterclaims. The self-destruction of foundational legitimation does not, however, validate the key claim that foundational argumentation exhausts justification. By itself, the collapse of foundationalism still leaves open the possibility of other avenues for normativity. Moreover, that possibility cannot be barred by antifoundationalists who identify justification with foundational justification because they can never coherently support that reduction. By undercutting the universal validity of argument, this defining move removes all authority from its own exhaustive extension of foundationalism. The grand narrative in which normativity is unveiled as will to power must itself be either an exercise of that groundless positing or a theorizing that escapes such deconstruction. If it is an expression of the will to power, it is just as ideological as any other power play and thereby forfeits any privilege over opposing views. If it is instead irreducible to the will to power, it refutes the absolutizing of ideology that follows from the identification of justification and foundationalism. Not only do these would-be antifoundationalists fail to uphold their claims, but by embracing the hegemony of contingent foundations over all normative argument, they advance privileged terms of their own—the rationally opaque historical conventions of value positing to which they subsume all discourse and conduct.

7 THE NORMATIVITY OF FREEDOM AND THE RECOVERY OF POLITICAL PHILOSOPHY

If the avatars of the will to power could focus upon the basic logic of foundationalism exhibited in each and every result of their deconstructions of value systems, it would become apparent that normativity cannot be inescapably bound to the appeal to foundations. Exclusive hegemony is simply impossible because when foundational justification seeks to be internally consistent, it not only eliminates itself, but gives way to a positive alternative that enables nihilism to be overcome.

The solution is radically simple and at one blow it removes the hold of foundationalism, demolishes the postmodern case for fascism, resolves the conundrum of ought and is, and makes manifest how conduct can have normativity even if neither the ends nor the form of willing can impart validity on their own.

All that is needed is to attend to what results when the foundations of normativity are called into account on their own terms. By distinguishing between what possesses validity and what confers validity, foundational justification stakes its own authority upon legitimating the privileged factor with which it endows derivative terms with validity. Whether the foundation be described as a privileged given, such as the highest good of teleological ethics, or as a privileged determiner, such as the choice procedure of social contract theory, it can satisfy its own standard of normativity only if it be founded upon itself. Yet, if the privileged foundation grounds itself, ground and grounded become identical, eliminating the distinction between source and recipient of validity, the very distinction by which foundational justification is defined. Instead of retaining the antecedently given character that a factor must have to figure as the foundation of derivative terms, the foundation that meets its own foundational criterion becomes something that is only what it has determined itself to be. The "source" of validity is no longer a prior standard at all and what has validity is no longer the derivative result of some antecedent ground. Rather than resting upon anything separate from itself, normativity is left residing in self-determination.

What determines itself is precisely what is not founded upon any antecedent foundation and what thus alone escapes the dilemmas of foundational justification. To ask *why* self-determination is the substance of normativity is therefore completely misguided if that question calls for some separate reason as justification. To demand some other criterion to certify the normativity of self-determination is doubly hopeless. On the one hand, self-determination cannot possibly be grounded on something else, for whatever is determined by a separate factor forfeits its self-determined character, which consists in being what it has determined itself to be. On the other hand, if one roots the validity of self-determination in something else, that other factor can only satisfy its own standard of validity if it relinquishes its foundational role and becomes something self-determined in its own right. In this way, any attempt to provide foundations for what is self-determined only ends up reconfirming the foundation-free, independent normativity of self-determination.[21]

There is simply no escape from acknowledging its unparalleled authority once the self-eliminating character of foundational justification is comprehended. If self-determination is not identified with normativity, normativity will reside in something determined externally by some validating factor. That ground of validity must, however, relinquish its distinction from what it validates if it is to meet its own standard of legitimation. But then, the only normative alternative to self-determination ceases to be an alternative, and the identity of freedom and normativity is left standing without any possible challenge.

Here lies exposed the key limitation of Enlightenment thinking, which rightly affirms the absolute value of autonomy in theory and practice, but which still conceives justification in the foundational mold and thus seeks to provide foundations for autonomous thought and action. This furnishing of foundations for autonomy makes Enlightenment thought easy prey to postmodern deconstruction, which exposes the unjustifiability of the Enlightenment's privileged grounds while presuming that theory and practice are still always conditioned by some, albeit contingent, grounding convention. That defining grounding has, however, a crucial result that both Enlightenment thought and its postmodern critique equally ignore: that autonomous thought and action, by being given foundations, get hopelessly misconceived. If autonomous reason and conduct be given grounds, such as transcendental conditions of knowledge or procedural legitimations of justice, they get reduced to derivative factors, determined by a two-tiered logic of ground and grounded.

Self-determination thereby gets conflated with the logic of positing, whose distinction between what posits and what is posited can never fit the identity of determiner and determined in the logic of genuine freedom. This identity between what does the determining and what gets determined is the essential unity that must be retained if freedom is to be in thought or reality.

One can readily anticipate that the same equation will hold all the more for conceiving or realizing political freedom, for unless ruler and ruled can be one and the same, self-government gives way to a division of political classes, where a ruling class imposes order upon a subject class and politics becomes an instrument of domination.

The removal of the difference between what confers and what possesses validity therefore not only overcomes foundations, but entails a rethinking of autonomy. This rethinking provides the resources for surmounting the paralysis that ethics faces once it is recognized that what ought to be cannot be derived from what is. That recognition leaves one option: that what is normative must derive only from what is itself normative. Yet this alternative seems hopelessly tautological: either ethics's search for valid conduct must presuppose normative standards or normative validity must be an empty slogan, out of which no content can arise that is not taken for granted. Ethical investigation here confronts the same sort of impasse at which Socrates left epistemology in the paradox of the *Meno*. In both cases an invidious assumption is made which the logic of self-determination eliminates: the assumption that determinacy is either given or determined by some other given determinacy. Only by assuming that right and truth have a given content or derive from some given foundation does normativity seem captive to insurmountable presuppositions. If, however, reason and conduct have validity in virtue of what they determine themselves to be, independently of any external, heteronomous conditions, the truth can be dictated by nothing but the truth and right can be measured by nothing but what is right, without either subject to predetermined standards. Instead of leaving normativity a slave to the arbitrary stipulation of an assumed determiner of content, a determiner whose identity is fixed prior to what it determines, the reflexivity of self-determination allows truth and right to obtain a content that emerges in the self-constitution of autonomous reason and autonomous action. Because what is self-determined is only what it has determined itself to be, ethics will redeem itself as a theory of free conduct by conceiving not some given principles from which derivative institutions are constructed, but rather the reality of freedom as its grounds itself, building a self-ordered system of those practices in which agents determine themselves in all the modes that self-determination can take.

The same identity of determiner and determined that allows normativity to acquire content without relying upon arbitrary givens equally enables conduct to escape the debilitating either/or of seeking validity in the end or in the form of action. Whereas teleological and procedural ethics privileged one of these elements to the exclusion of the other, the normativity of self-determination precludes setting them apart. Self-determination cannot simply be a matter of escaping the hold of antecedently prescribed ends by following the freedom of desire or willing in a lawful manner. The identity of free agency cannot be external to what is willed. Self-determination is not determination of something else by a determiner whose character is given prior to the act of determination. What gets determined is the self that does the determining. Only this reflexivity allows determination to be *self*-determination. Although choosing ends free of external dictate and exercising a mode of willing that others can equally pursue may well be necessary conditions of freedom, they are not sufficient. Genuine autonomy further requires determining the character of the agency that therein performs its lawful role. To be *self*-determining, agents must individuate themselves through their willing, choosing at one and the same time what to will and who it is who thereby acts. Only in so doing, can agents determine themselves as self-determining. If instead, agents are entirely individuated by factors external to their volition, who they are is determined from without, precluding any self-determined existence.

This does not mean that agents are devoid of any predetermined character, already individuating them before they exercise their freedom. Individuals cannot help but have unique spatiotemporal locations, individuated anatomies, and psychological and cultural histories individuated by factors beyond their control. All of these dimensions enable agents to be identified just like any other entity that is not self-determined. Nonetheless, if individuals are to engage in self-determination, they must add to their natural, biological, psychological, and culturally given personas a further artificial agency that they individuate through autonomous action. Because in so doing they exercise a form of agency that individuates itself, the end they thereby will is inseparable from that form. In freely determining oneself, one wills oneself as free. What gets willed is thus at one with the form of agency that does the willing. How one wills is accordingly identical with what one wills when volition is self-determined. Accordingly, if normativity resides in freedom, the end and form of willing are equal bearers of value.

This does not mean that what and how one wills have an independent parity. The form of autonomous willing is not indifferent to the content of its ends. To be willed autonomously, the ends must be such that they comprise an individuation of free agency, which signifies that they are fundamentally different from the ends at stake when the form of volition is not that of self-determination.

For this reason, consenting to natural hierarchies, where individuals are ordered by factors given by birth, cannot be an exercise of self-determination. Although individuals may submit to such an ordering voluntarily, in so doing what they will is not consonant with how they will. Only in choosing to relate to one another as autonomously individuated can individuals unite the form and content of their volition, freely willing themselves to be free.

This intrinsic connection of end and form in self-determined willing might appear perplexing, given how choice cannot be excluded from any volition. Choice, in and of itself, has a purely external relation to its ends since what one chooses, in virtue of choice, is arbitrary. The same faculty of choice is operative in opting for each and every end, for whatever one does, one employs one's capacity to select among given desires. This capacity is thereby natural, for in order to will into being any conventional form of agency and thereby determine an artificial form of willing, one must already possess the ability to choose. That ability cannot be a product of choice precisely because it is the underlying condition of every volition. Choice is thus given by nature, not convention, and comprises the natural form of volition presupposed by all artificial agencies that convention might spawn.

Nonetheless, the ubiquity of choice does not preclude the interconnection of end and form in self-determined conduct because freedom incorporates choice within a supervening structure enabling the determiner and the determined to coincide. The structure that allows choice to be a vehicle of self-determination is the convention of right, whose lawful universality and intersubjective practice entail a system of specific roles and ends giving the normativity of freedom its concrete character.

8 RIGHT AND SELF-DETERMINATION

Although each agent disposes of choice as a function of its single self, none can engage in self-determination alone. So long as an agent acts solely upon itself or upon another object, without reference to any other will, its volition takes the form of a technical activity, imposing some design upon a given material supplied by its own body or external factors. The agent may exercise the "second-order" choice of selecting among desires and rise beyond the immediate inclinations of instinct. Although this license affords the agent a liberty of desire, that liberty is doubly conditioned. Not only are the alternatives from which the agent may choose given independently of that volition, but no choice the agent makes can determine the character of the agency that executes that choice. The antecedent givenness of what is willed and that of who wills have the same source: the absence of unity between the determiner and the determined. This deficit is endemic to any unilateral volition because the form of such agency cannot be the product of its own willing, but must always remain the antecedent capacity of choice that selects among different objects of desire without ever determining its own agency.

The prime stumbling block to unraveling the enigma of self-determination lies in the failure to emancipate conduct from the parameters of the isolated will, which ethical atomism makes its principle. An agent who acts independently of any interaction with other agents can never surmount the dilemma of how to be agent and patient at once. To act by oneself, one must exercise a capacity of choice that is always the precondition, but never the product of one's volition. Each decision may have a different end, but each brings into play the same basic decision-making capability. Hence, although one may impose order upon one's own body, as well as upon other things, the activity of imposing form already possesses a form that is never the aim of its own imposition.

So long as an agent wills in respect to mere things or to agents treated as mere things, it can only individuate its volition in contrast to what do not count as instances of willing. This may allow the agent to be something other than that on which it imposes its aims, but it does not provide sufficient resources to distinguish one's act as a particular instance of willing, individuated from other instances in terms that derive from willing itself. Unless the will individuates itself in and through willing, it cannot obtain a character that is a product of willing and achieve the unity of patient and agent that is the basic element of self-determination.

The agent cannot surmount this limitation by willing in respect to its own volitions. To begin with, an agent's act of will cannot unilaterally will in relation to itself, since at the moment of willing, the agent's own willing is not yet at hand. Alternately, any attempt by the agent to individuate its will in respect to its own past or future volitions lacks that actuality of an independent volition to which to contrast itself. Any past volition has expended itself in already concluded activity, whereas any future volition has yet to transpire. Reference to either past or future willings amounts merely to including their representation within the aim that the agent entertains when acting. Instead of providing another individual volition standing over and against the current volition, these representations are merely absorbed within the aim of the one and only current act of will, which therefore still stands alone, devoid of the plurality it needs to be an individuated instance of self-determination. However the agent may orient its action in respect to its own past or future initiatives, its agency remains a capacity of choice whose form precedes its exercise.

The outcome is no different if an agent wills alongside other agents who each act without reference to one another. Admittedly, for an external observer, the mere plurality of agents offers multiple instances of willing that stand in the relation of particulars. So long, however, as the contrastive relationship between these examples of agency is not willed by the agents themselves, their distinguishing relation is imposed upon them, independently of their choice. Consequently, although they stand externally individuated as particular examples of volition, they are not self-individuated. Because they have not willed the relation between them that serves to individuate their volitions, the determination they possess as individual agents is not self-imposed. In virtue of their own agency, each individual possesses a capacity of choice that is identical to that of every other. What distinguishes them are the multitude of factors given independently of their choice that differentiate them spatiotemporally, anatomically, psychologically, and culturally. As far as their volitions are concerned, they remain a heap of atoms, whose aggregation in no way supplants the limits of unilateral agency with a conventionally determined form of willing.

If this situation were definitive of action, one would have to accept Plato's verdict that self-determination is as unthinkable as it is unrealizable and follow his conclusion that willing must be the act of one part of the soul upon another, just as political rule must be wielded by a ruling class upon a subject class, leaving agent and patient comprehensibly distinct.[22]

Choice, however, can surmount these limits of its unilateral exercise once one agent coordinates its choice with that of others. When agents pierce the confines of solitary action by willing with respect to each other's volition, they can exercise a form of agency that is the artificial product of the willing in which they engage, enabling each individual to interact as both patient and agent.

How this can occur is no great mystery. All it requires is a plurality of agents capable of recognizing one another's choices, making their choices known to one another, and acting in reference to one another's choices. The natural faculty of choice that each agent possesses as a function of the self need not undergo any inexplicable alteration—it merely need set itself in relation to that of others by means of its own capability.

If anything, the possibility of engendering an artificial agency that is both the product and the form of willing seems all too simple. In the abstract, every form of convention appears to unify agent and patient. Insofar as any association sustains itself through the coordinated activities of its participants, they all exercise determinate roles whose conventional character is given nowhere else but in the correlative practice that makes possible those enacted forms of agency. Master and slave possess their artificial roles by performing the activities animating the institution of slavery, just as members of a caste society are bound to their conventional personas through participating in the separated practices by which the world of caste reproduces itself. Indisputably, in each conventional community, participants perform specific roles whose differentiation is reproduced by those very performances. If this alone signified that every participant engages in acts of will that determine the agency they exercise, self-determination would become hopelessly formal. Each and every convention would be an embodiment of self-determination and the normativity of self-determination would collapse into an affirmation of might makes right.

What makes all the difference is whether the willing that defines an agent's role is mediated by the agent's own will. If one performs a conventional function whose design is dictated by others, independently of one's choice, then one's volition is molded by the dominating practice of others, to the exclusion of one's self-determination. By the same token, if their practice has as its object not the form of their own agency but the form imposed upon others, that practice is not self-determining, but a formation of a patient receiving its order from without. Similarly, any association that determines the roles of its participants in function of putatively natural differences, i.e., of factors given independently of the choice of individuals, such as gender, race, or hereditary rank, imposes forms of agency that preclude autonomy. Even though the privileging of natural difference is itself a form of convention, issuing from history's concatenations of choice, its practice constitutively prevents its participants from determining the character of the roles they therein perform. As in any institution where domination rules, the will that determines conventional roles is different from the will that executes those roles.

In order for convention to satisfy the reflexive requirements of self-determination, the artificial agencies that individuals perform must be emancipated from putatively natural differences and domination by privileged others. All participants must will with respect to one another such that their practical interrelation, as exhibited in their conventional roles, is determined by their will. In that case, the practice by which they are all individuated as agents will comprise a convention of self-individuation, where each agent participates in willing the relation to its counterparts by which its agency is differentiated.

This might appear a sheer impossibility, since if one agent wills its relation to another, that other has that relation imposed upon it, undercutting its autonomy. What eliminates this dilemma is a reciprocity of willing, where the relation one agent wills to another is at the very same time willed by that party. For this to be the case, agents must choose an end that sets them in relation to the volition of others so that the form of willing thereby exercised is the same as that of the volition to which their end relates them. In that case, when one agent wills itself in relation to an other, that other agent will have concurrently willed the same relation, for the end chosen by each party constitutively relates to a volition choosing an end of the same formal character. What each participant here wills is an end that can only be chosen when the agent to which it relates wills an end of the same sort in a volition that sets its agent in the same relation to its counterpart.

Such reciprocal willing is lawful in that each participant wills ends of the same general character in the same general manner. Such reciprocal willing involves a freedom from external prescription in that each party selects the particular end to be willed under the condition that it meets the formal requirement of fitting into a mutually willed interrelation. Such reciprocal willing thereby also involves an exercise of equal opportunity since all participants enjoy the same prerogative to select the specific aim that will allow the reciprocity of their relationship to be achieved.

Given these implications, it can be no surprise that the structure of willing by which agents individuate their agency and unite agent and patient is the practice of rights. In exercising any right, an individual wills an end that sets it in relation to the willing of ends by others who mutually tailor their choices so that they can enjoy the same prerogative without interfering with one another. In so doing, each participant enjoys an entitled agency that is determined by nothing but the coordinated volitions whereby what each party wills falls within the concordant boundaries effecting respect for the corresponding volitions of others that, for their part, concord with the like volitions of the rest. Consequently, in exercising a right, each party participates in determining the kind of agency it wields, as well as the content of its choice.

Because rights enable individuals to will in a manner that automatically harmonizes with all other volitions of the same sort, it is easy to focus upon the formal lawfulness that right possesses. The failure of an ethics of a highest good and the inability of the freedom of desire to function as a principle of conduct might suggest that this focus should be exclusive. Procedural ethics, of course, takes this route, privileging the lawful form of willing as the exclusive principle of ethical construction. This exclusivity only follows from the inability to derive normativity from the content of the end of conduct, taken separately from the form of willing, *if* one assumes that the end and form of willing cannot be united. The ethical atomism that takes the single will as the paradigm for conduct must accept that assumption, and it is thus no accident that social contract theory takes individual choice as its starting point.

Once the limits of ethical atomism are superceded by the intersubjective framework of right, uniting the character of agency with what is willed and making self-determination possible, the form of willing cannot have exclusive priority over the ends of conduct. Because rights are practices in which individuals determine themselves as individuated bearers of the universal entitlement they exercise, the ends willed in that exercise have a special character as well. Insofar as rights involve equal opportunities, what is willed in every exercise of right is an end whose individual content is free from prior prescription. The bearer of a right always self-selects what gets willed, but always does so under the formal requirement that the end in question relate harmoniously to the self-selection of similar ends on the part of all other bearers of right. For this reason, the content of the end has a conventional character that cannot be duplicated independently of the practice of right. The end may well have physical and psychological attributes shared by aims that figure within unilateral volitions in which the freedom of desire presides. Yet, because the only ends that can fit within the framework of right must stand in concordant relation to the rightful choices of all other bearers of the right in question, the permissible ends have that added conventional qualification. This conventional qualification includes the recognized meaning of comprising a determination of the agent as a self-determined bearer of right. In choosing an end that fits the frame of right, each participant no less chooses the factor by which its artificial persona as bearer of right gets individuated.

The most elementary self-determination, the exercise of property right, exhibits these connections of end and form in their barest configuration. To acquire property, one must lay one's will in some external factor, not as a mere object of desire of one's natural will, but as the embodiment of one's self-determination as owner. In taking property, one determines oneself as a proprietor, imposing upon oneself an artificial form of agency individuated by the factor in which one establishes one's ownership. What one wills in taking property is therefore not the satisfaction of a want, but the willing of an individuated domain of title, something that cannot be willed apart from the recognition of other individuals who have determined themselves as owners by simultaneously laying their wills in external factors that do not intrude upon the property of their counterparts. Accordingly, although what factor is chosen for appropriation is a matter of choice, the act of will by which property is acquired has an end that is conventional in character, defined by the self-determination of property right. In contrast to the dual formality of unilateral action, where the ends and form of agency are antecedently given, the interaction of owners enables both the content of what they will and the form of agency they exercise to be determined by the willing with which they each define their identity as owner and the domain of their property.[23] Each participant in the practice of ownership wills some property determination, a content that necessarily includes reference to the ownership of other persons insofar as the limits of each owner's property constitutively concord with those of every other owner. Each participant indeed has an antecedently individuated identity, thanks to the biological and psychological preconditions of agency. Yet each acquires a further self-determined identity as a unique owner individuated by the property in which the objectively recognized volition of ownership is exclusively embodied. Joint ownership is certainly possible, allowing for artificial corporate proprietors. Nevertheless, no property can be acquired, transferred, or conjoined unless individuals have succeeded in taking ownership of their own bodies, without which nothing they do can count as their own, rather than some slave master's, responsibility. Since no further self-determination is possible unless one retains title to one's body, this primary property has the unique character of being inalienable, although one can lend its use to others for a limited period of time without canceling one's recognized reality as owner and general bearer of right.

Although property right has an irremovable primacy owing to how no other mode of self-determination is possible unless one retains the recognized status of owner of at least one's own body, this does not make property right a privileged principle from which derivative institutions are constructed. As an exercise of self-determination, property relations merely individuate owners through some self-selected alteration of their domain of ownership without ever giving them some other institutional role. If the practice of property determined something other than the individuation of owners, it would cease to be a mode of self-determination and posit some separate product, which for its part, would not be self-determined, but a derivative outcome owing its design to that from which it emanates.

For this reason, neither property relations nor any other mode of self-determination can figure as the determining principle of other institutions, as procedural ethics would like to believe. Because normativity consists in self-determination and self-determination is self-grounding, the conventions of freedom can neither have nor figure themselves as juridical foundations. The practice of self-determination may depend for its existence upon any number of enabling physical, biological, psychological, and cultural conditions, but these conditions are the same that make conduct of any sort possible. For self-determination to be what it determines itself to be, all these enabling conditions of freedom must leave undecided whether the conduct they make possible will be right or wrong, autonomous or oppressed and oppressing. Instead of being or issuing from a privileged principle of ethical construction, the institutions of freedom are the actuality of normative conduct, existing for their own sake. Given the exclusive normativity of self-determination, no independent factor can legitimately preclude individuals from exercising any mode of freedom in which they can possibly participate, just as, given the foundation-free character of freedom, no situation in which conduct is feasible can preclude emancipation and render the struggle for rights a vain endeavor. Rights, understood as the reality of self-determination, should be realized without qualification. Ethics is, accordingly, nothing but the philosophy of right, charged with no other task than conceiving self-determination, that is, the practice of rights, in its totality. If justice is to retain its traditional meaning as what agents are due, justice can only comprise the complete realization of rights by which convention becomes a realm of freedom. Whatever scope an institution may have, be it a household, a society, or a body politic, if it is to be just, it must become a particular sphere of rights, of equal opportunity, of self-determination.

Yet if justice demands total emancipation and if ownership is not the only form of freedom, how are the possible modes of self-determination to be exhaustively determined and how are they to be realized in their totality without undermining one another? Although this question can be raised in the abstract without reference to politics, the fate of political philosophy hangs upon its resolution.

9 POLITICAL PHILOSOPHY AND THE SYSTEM OF RIGHT

With normativity at one with self-determination and self-determination an intersubjective practice of rights, political philosophy can have no other mandate than to be a theory of political self-determination that must not only conceive the necessary structure of political autonomy, but establish how political self-determination can sustain itself in harmony with the other modes of self-determination. The just state will accordingly be the realization of political freedom that upholds all nonpolitical rights as well. If, however, the different forms of freedom were to stand in any implacable opposition, an insoluble conflict of rights would ensue, leaving political justice and ethics in general at an impasse.

In this regard, the possibility of political philosophy rests upon two conditions. First, politics, whatever be its past history, must be determinable as an institution of freedom. Otherwise, political association can never have normativity and politics will cease to be a topic for philosophical conception. Second, political freedom must be compatible with whatever other forms of self-determination there be.

A complete answer to the second requirement ultimately depends upon an exhaustive determination of the different modes of self-determination.[24] Nonetheless, key elements of its fulfillment can be comprehended by considering the question of how a plurality of spheres of right must stand in relation to one another, no matter what specific content they have.

Three basic options are possible. First, the different structures of freedom may operate with no connection to one another besides their conjunction in individuals who exercise a plurality of rights either simultaneously or in succession. Second, the plurality of spheres of right may be united by an external agency, or last, one of the modes of self-determination may unite itself with the others in function of its own autonomy.

The first option of parallel indifference would apply only if each mode of self-determination could be realized independently of any of the others. Even then, of course, questions of coordination could arise if the claims of different rights intersected and required some adjudication to remedy incipient conflicts. It is already obvious, however, that a mere aggregation of spheres of right is out of the question. In one respect some systematic unity is required, for no mode of self-determination is possible unless the participants are already enjoying their rights as property owners. Because recognition as proprietor of at least one's own body is a normative precondition for participation in any further exercise of freedom, the integration of property rights with any further modes of self-determination is inescapable.

This does not mean that the unification with other spheres of rights will leave property right without any partial modifications. If the household be added as a sphere of rights, for example, the prerogatives of individual owners will become subject to supervening limitations in order to sustain conjugal and parental rights and obligations. Similarly, if a civil society be established, it too will require certain impositions upon private ownership in order to uphold equal social opportunity in the economy and before the law. And if political association supervenes as a sphere of rights, the imperatives of equal political opportunity and the expense of self-government will require their own modifications of unqualified ownership. By the same token, each of these further spheres will have to limit their modifications of property rights to particular restrictions, for if any were to cancel ownership in general or ownership of one's body in particular, they would destroy the minimal normative precondition of their own freedom. Ensuring both sides of the relationship, that property right be modified in conformity with the equal opportunities of further spheres of right and that those spheres still uphold property right in general, requires some concerted regulation. On occasion, participating individuals might conform to these requirements by accident. Yet, if the dual conformity is not automatically guaranteed by the separate functioning of each sphere, the unconditioned normativity of rights precludes leaving the required adjustments to chance. What should be without qualification should be guaranteed.

The second option, of allowing the spheres of right to be integrated from without, has correlative problems that prove to be of pregnant significance for political philosophy. If the modes of self-determination require integration by something outside them all, the reality of freedom is left hanging upon some agency that is not itself self-determined. That external aegis will, of course, involve activity of its own, but the supervening regulation will not be an exercise of right, in which the end and form of willing are determined by the agency itself. Instead, the integrating power will exercise a unilateral choice, selecting among independently given options with a given faculty of decision. This defining situation of any external integration places the whole edifice of right at the mercy of license. The putatively unconditioned normativity of self-determination is thereby rendered something dependent upon caprice. If the integrating power decides to fulfill its mission, the unifying order of the institutions of freedom is determined from without, undercutting the self-determined character of conduct. If, on the other hand, the integrating power chooses not to uphold all spheres of right in conformity with one another, no remedy is available to overcome its remiss. The possibility of nonfulfillment is endemic because the agency of the integrating power is a means to an end, separate from itself. Accordingly, the same contingency of compliance is at hand that plagues any instrumental action, a contingency that becomes a catastrophic problem when the highest ruling power is instrumental, as in procedural ethics. Because the means can be what it is without achieving its legitimating end, there never can be any guarantee that it will fulfill its sanctioned goal. When the instrumental agency has no higher authority supervising its operation, nothing can compel compliance, just as nothing can escape the caprice of this pinnacle of power. The entire fabric of right is left hanging in the balance, without any satisfactory resolution available.

Consequently, the normativity of self-determinations mandates that the integration of the spheres of right be achieved from within, as an exercise of one of the modes of self-determination. Only then can the self-sufficient, self-grounding normativity of freedom be maintained, for solely if an exercise of self-determination imposes the order integrating the spheres of right with one another, can freedom sustain itself, as it must to be what it has determined itself to be. So long as there be more than one sphere of right, an institution of freedom will be required to unite the different modes of self-determination together, integrating its own supervening regulation in conformity with upholding their concordant functioning. As a result, the reality of freedom will comprise a self-regulating system, presided over by a mode of self-determination characterized by willing the unification of the totality of right. Without this crowning autonomy, the entire realm of freedom forfeits the self-sustaining, self-grounding agency constitutive of self-determination.

It is this imperative that gives political philosophy its mandate. The system of right requires an institution of freedom that wills the integrated unity of the totality of self-determination. This institution must impose the order of the whole upon itself and do so as an exercise of right, by which all agents enjoy the equal opportunity to codetermine the system of freedom. The traditional governing role of politics here obtains its ethical, philosophically determined character. The identity of normativity and self-determination, taken together with the plurality of rights, mandates a self-rule that is conjoined with upholding all nonpolitical freedoms in conformity with equal political opportunity. Political philosophy therefore faces a dual challenge. Political association must be conceived as an institution of self-determination and, at the same time, political autonomy must be such as to uphold all nonpolitical freedoms in conformity with self-government.

At first glance, these complementary injunctions seem hopelessly at odds. How can political association be truly self-determining if its governance must be subject to the restriction of realizing the nonpolitical freedoms of the other spheres of right? Must not the sovereignty of political freedom be undermined if rule is required to protect independently given rights? And if political self-determination is distinct from these nonpolitical autonomies, how can the freedom of politics be sustained without abandoning nonpolitical rights to political caprice?

10 THE PROBLEM OF POLITICAL JUSTICE

These questions reflect two correlative features of political association that have persistently cast in suspicion the very possibility of political justice: first, the apparent absence of any end inherent in political association, and, second, the arbitrariness seemingly endemic to the sovereignty of state rule. The two features appear to be inextricably linked, for if politics is characterized by sovereign rule, nothing can constrain a state to embrace any particular end, whereas, if politics has no ends of its own, political association is set free to follow any course rulers may choose. On either account, political power seems to be an empty force, defined by little more than its supremacy over all other forms of association, a supremacy that is otherwise aimless and devoid of reason.

Not surprisingly, these dual dilemmas are tied to conceiving the pinnacle of political power as an exercise of choice, of the unilateral willing for which ends and agency are antecedently given and in which the reciprocity of right is absent. When, however, political association is conceived and actualized as a mode of self-determination, in which citizens exercise equal political opportunity as bearers of the right to participate in self-government, the ends of politics lose their arbitrary character. With normativity residing in self-determination, politics has a very determinate, indeed self-determined aim: realizing the political freedom of citizens as an end in itself. In each and every exercise of self-government, participating individuals will themselves as self-governing citizens, codetermining the form of the body politic to which they belong. To the degree that the exercise of equal political opportunity involves participating in the specific political institutions by which citizens engage in self-government, political freedom must always involve political decision making that reproduces the basic political framework enabling and comprising self-government. The reflexivity of self-determination thereby gives political freedom a very definite content for its ends, a content residing first and foremost in the constitutionality of politics. This constitutionality normatively consists in political arrangements necessary for the practice of political freedom. As such, it represents the constitution that the body politic must always retain in order for political rights to be realized, that is, for citizens to enjoy equal political opportunity and determine themselves politically.

Needless to say, determining the content of this constitutionality is one of the basic tasks that political philosophy must address. What complicates this undertaking is the already irrepressible implication that the constitution of political freedom is not just a political matter. At the very least, political right cannot be realized unless the property rights of citizens are upheld. Without all participants recognized as proprietor of at least their own body, equal political opportunity is impossible. Consequently, the problem of compelling the body politic to uphold nonpolitical rights collapses as a problem once political association becomes an institution of freedom. Then, at least in the case of property right, upholding this nonpolitical right is not a constraint upon political freedom, but something political association must continually do if the body politic is to sustain its own character as an institution of self-government. Therefore political association does not forfeit its sovereignty when it guarantees the property right of its participants. Rather, the body politic can only be an end in itself when it realizes political freedom, which can only be done in conjunction with sustaining the property rights that make possible equal political opportunity.

It is not hard to see that political self-determination will be jeopardized by oppression in any institutional sphere that impinges upon conduct outside it. If households remain ruled by domestic domination, where unequal family prerogatives limit the social and political opportunities of the underprivileged family members, self-government cannot function any more than it can when social privilege limits the political opportunities of the socially oppressed. To the degree that this is so, the emancipation of each institutional sphere is a precondition of political autonomy, which the ongoing practice of self-government must preserve in order to perpetuate itself.

Consequently, the upholding of nonpolitical rights is not a limitation upon sovereignty but rather a constitutive element in the realization and reproduction of political freedom. Self-government therefore hardly forfeits its autonomy by committing itself to respect nonpolitical rights in conformity with equal political opportunity. Instead, self-government is just that only so long as it integrates the nonpolitical freedoms with its own political practice.

This systematic unity of political and nonpolitical freedoms resolves the dilemma that plagues the instrumental predicament of procedural ethics and social contract politics. Whereas a body politic can never be compelled nor counted upon to realize ends that are separate from its own constitution, political self-determination cannot fail to uphold nonpolitical rights. Although nonpolitical freedoms may be enjoyed without political emancipation, self-government cannot exist unless citizens are liberated from the suppression of property, household, economic, and any other civil rights on whose maintenance equal political opportunity depends. Hence, if there be political self-determination, there cannot fail to be nonpolitical freedom as well.

The constitution of self-government therefore must include not only what is necessary to the organization of political self-determination, but also what is necessary for nonpolitical rights to be exercised in conformity with self-rule. For this reason, political philosophy must expand its scope to conceive the normative preconditions of political freedom and how their upholding by political association figures in the constitution of the body politic. Thereby, in both theory and practice, the end of politics will be an end in itself by drawing into its reach the totality of right.

NOTES

1. A classic example is Plato's account in bk. 8 of the *Republic* of the different forms of government as successively emerging from the dissolution of the ideal polis. See Plato, *The Collected Dialogues*, ed. Edith Hamilton and Huntington Cairns (Princeton, NJ: Princeton University Press, 1961), pp. 772–98. Although in bk. 5 (1316a) of the *Politics*, Aristotle duly questions Plato's claim that the sequence of forms of government is necessary, this does not undercut their connection to the normative concept of the just state. See *The Complete Works of Aristotle*, vol. 2, ed. Jonathan Barnes (Princeton, NJ: Princeton University Press, 1995), pp. 2089–90.

2. For an attempt to conceive the genesis of the just state and the other normative institutions it involves, see Richard Dien Winfield, *Reason and Justice* (Albany: SUNY Press, 1988), chap. 14, pp. 283–99, and Richard Dien Winfield, *Overcoming Foundations: Studies in Systematic Philosophy* (New York: Columbia University Press, 1989), chap. 12, pp. 271–93.

3. Because the logic of these options is conceptually determined, how closely historically given theories conform to them is contingent. Not only may historical theories be inconsistently developed, but they may combine elements from disparate strategies.

4. Aristotle provides the classic statement of this argument in chap. 2, bk. 1, 1094a20, of his *Nicomachean Ethics*. See *The Complete Works of Aristotle*, vol. 2, p. 1729.

5. Aristotle points this out in chap. 1, bk. 1, 1094a9–16, of his *Nicomachean Ethics*. See *The Complete Works of Aristotle*, vol. 2, p. 1729.

6. Aristotle works out this argument in chap. 2, bk. 1 of his *Nicomachean Ethics*. See *The Complete Works of Aristotle*, vol. 2, p. 1729.

7. Aristotle identifies the science of the highest good as the science of politics, implying these connections, in chap. 2, bk. 1 of his *Nicomachean Ethics*. See *The Complete Works of Aristotle*, vol. 2, p. 1729.

8. For these reasons, Aristotle's *Ethics* and *Politics* properly comprise one unitary science.

9. This problem applies whether the alleged nature is necessary or contingent.

10. These problems undermine Aristotle's appeal to human nature in chap. 7 of his *Nicomachean Ethics*. See *The Complete Works of Aristotle*, vol. 2, p. 1735. The appeal vitiates itself, since if the "human good turn out to be activity of soul in conformity with excellence" (1098a16–17), identifying that good merely directs us to ethics, instead of determining any further content of what it is to act in accord with reason.

11. Aristotle takes this tack in his *Politics*, chap. 7, bk. 3, 1279a–1279b (*The Complete Works of Aristotle*, vol. 2, p. 2030).

12. This is not the case with the desire for commodities that figures in economic freedom. Such desire is socially mediated by the interaction of the market, which makes its satisfaction by one commodity owner dependent upon its satisfaction by some other. Accordingly, conduct in pursuit of satisfaction of the need for commodities can, subject to certain public regulations, take the form of right. For a systematic account of how this is so, see Richard Dien Winfield, *The Just Economy* (New York: Routledge, 1988), pp. 103ff.

13. It needs to be emphasized that the recognition in question is always mutual. If recognized freedom is regarded instead as coming only from the sayings and doings of others, then a distinction can be drawn between recognized and actual freedom. In that case, as George Anastaplo points out, not everyone who is recognized to be free is actually free. For example, ex-slaves may be emancipated in the eyes of others, but they may need considerable purgation of previous dependent behavior and training in the independent exercise of rights before they can actively participate in the practices of freedom and become actually self-determining. See Anastaplo, *The Amendments to the Constitution: A Commentary* (Baltimore: Johns Hopkins University Press, 1995), p. 149.

14. For this reason, persons cannot take ownership of other factors unless their ownership of their own bodies is duly recognized.

15. For this reason, the connection of political power to any particular ends seems contrary to the sovereign character of the state. Hence, Max Weber can argue that the state cannot be defined in terms of the content of its activities, since hardly any end has not been pursued by some political association at some time or other. Rather, Weber concludes, the state can only be characterized, by its form, that of claiming the monopoly of legitimate violence within a territory. See Weber, *Political Writings*, ed. Peter Lassman and Ronald Speirs (Cambridge: Cambridge University Press, 1994), pp. 310–11. In *State and Revolution*, V. I. Lenin embraces this view, recognizing that it renders the state devoid of any inherent value, allowing it to be dispensed with entirely when the achievement of communism reduces man to his species being. See Lenin, *State and Revolution* (Moscow: Progress Publishers, 1965), pp. 18–19, 75, 90.

16. This problem has been acknowledged by many liberal theorists, but without abandoning procedural justice. Jürgen Habermas unperturbedly admits, for example, that the liberal project of realizing rights rests upon a dogmatic core: the idea of autonomy (Habermas, *Between Facts and Norms: Contributions to a Discourse Theory of Law and Democracy*, trans. William Rehg [Cambridge, MA: MIT Press, 1996], pp. 445–46). Robert Nozick also recognizes that any theory grounding norms in a privileged procedure begins with something not justified by being the outcome of that procedure but fails to see how this undermines his own Lockean liberal scruples (Nozick, *Anarchy, State and Utopia* [New York: Basic Books, 1974], pp. 207–208). And Ronald Dworkin points out that Rawls's choice procedure is predicated upon a deeper ethical view, requiring a justification entirely different from what contractarian, procedural ethics can supply

(Dworkin, *Taking Rights Seriously* [Cambridge, MA: Harvard University Press, 1978], pp. 169ff.). For a detailed analysis of how the foundational dilemmas endemic to social contract theory cannot be evaded by Rawls's appeal to historically given shared moral intuitions, which underlies his procedural ethics in both *A Theory of Justice* (Cambridge, MA: Harvard University Press, 1971) and *Political Liberalism* (New York: Columbia University Press, 1993), see Winfield, *Reason and Justice*, pp. 105–16.

17. Plato, *Meno* 80d, in *The Collected Dialogues*, p. 363.

18. Hilary Putnam, for example, claims that we need democracy because, as John Dewey argued, the absence of any final answers as to how we should live requires that we leave politics open to further discussion in which everyone has an equal say. See Putnam, *Renewing Philosophy* (Cambridge, MA: Harvard University Press, 1992), pp. 188–89. Richard Rorty makes analogous arguments in *Contingency, Irony, and Solidarity* (New York: Cambridge University Press, 1989), pp. 68–69. As Robert A. Dahl points out, however, if no ethical claim is superior to any other, one cannot justifiably maintain that it is better that everyone should participate equally in political life than that the stronger should rule. See Dahl, *Democracy and Its Critics* (New Haven, CT: Yale University Press, 1989), p. 180. Although Rorty dismisses the latter Nietzschean conclusion as madness (*Contingency, Irony, and Solidarity*, pp. 187–88, 190), it is too intelligible to ignore.

19. For a more detailed account of how the relativity of norms cannot give support to democracy, see Winfield, *Autonomy and Normativity: Investigations of Truth, Right and Beauty* (Aldershott, UK: Ashgate, 2001), pp. 152–60.

20. Friedrich Nietzsche, unlike his apologists, was not afraid to follow out these ramifications of diagnosing rationality as will to power. See "The 'Improvers' of Mankind" and "Expeditions of an Untimely Man" in *Twilight of the Idols* for classic examples of Nietzsche's affirmation of a consistent will to power (Nietzsche, *Twilight of the Idols/The Anti-Christ*, trans. R. J. Hollingdale [Harmondsworth, UK: Penguin Books, 1990], pp. 66–70, 78–115).

21. Hannah Arendt seeks a political solution to the problem of foundations by claiming that the legitimate act of founding be such that its act of beginning carry its own principle within itself, something she finds exemplified in the American Revolution insofar as the constituent assembly that drafted the constitution involved preestablished colonial governments that were then incorporated in the federal scheme of the new constitutional order. See Arendt, *On Revolution* (New York: Viking, 1965), pp. 165, 214.

Nevertheless, the founding activity of the constitutional convention is still different from the ongoing self-government of the constituted federal government. Hence, Arendt's "solution" still retains a distinction between legitimating and legitimated factors that is the common bane of foundational justification.

22. Plato *Republic* 4.430e–431a.

23. Hence, Michael Oakeshott can rightly observe, following Hegel, that "I and mine" is on any occasion the work of rules of recognition (Oakeshott, *On Human Conduct* [Oxford: Oxford University Press, 1975], p. 259). Oakeshott, however, mistakenly qualifies these rules as contingent products of a historically situated intelligence (Oakeshott, *On Human Conduct*, p. 259), as if the structure of self-determination could be grounded on something else.

24. For a systematic account of household freedom, see Richard Dien Winfield, *The Just Family* (Albany: SUNY Press, 1998). For a systematic account of social freedom, that is, of civil society, see Winfield, *The Just Economy* and Winfield, *Law in Civil Society* (Lawrence: University Press of Kansas, 1995). For further treatment of property right, see Winfield, *Autonomy and Normativity*, chap. 8–9, pp. 87–108. For further treatment of moral freedom, see Winfield, *Overcoming Foundations*, chap. 8, pp. 135–70, and Winfield, *Freedom and Modernity* (Albany: SUNY Press, 1991), chap. 6, pp. 61–75.

CHAPTER 1

THE PRECONDITIONS OF POLITICAL FREEDOM

1.1 METHODOLOGICAL PERPLEXITIES IN ADDRESSING THE PRECONDITIONS OF POLITICS

The normativity of self-determination mandates that political philosophy conceive a state realizing the equal political opportunity of self-government while upholding all nonpolitical freedoms. Accomplishing this task does not involve searching for privileged foundations upon which political justice is to be erected. Because normativity must be free of foundations and self-grounding, how the just state comes into being is a separate matter from what gives that state its legitimacy. If instead political justice were to derive validity from anything given prior to the establishment of self-government, politics would forfeit its character as a self-determined sphere of right that is an end in itself.

This normative independence does not signify that the genesis of the just state is completely unrelated to what political self-determination determines itself to be. Although what makes political freedom valid is its self-determined actuality and not the process by which it emerges, the internal constitution of self-government has implications for how it arises. Generally, if the just state is to come into being, whatever are the preconditions for political self-determination must be at hand. Of course, if any of these enabling conditions themselves rest upon factors that allow for their existence, then these too must have emerged.

Since the full series of these preconditions is predicated upon the content of the just state that they allow to come into existence, the account of the genesis of political freedom is theoretically posterior to the determination of valid politics. Only once self-government has been fully determined, is it possible to know what must of necessity transpire for political justice to emerge. The telos of that development, the actuality of the just state, must first be conceived in order for the proper generation to be constructed.

Moreover, the itinerary of that genesis can be determined after conceiving political self-determination without prejudice to the legitimacy of self-government. The identity of validity and self-determination signifies that even if the *existence* of the just state has specific prerequisites, the *normativity* of political freedom still in no way depends upon any prior process of foundation.

For this reason, the search for legitimating founding bodies of the just state is misbegotten. It may well be true, for example, that the American colonies had longstanding colonial legislatures that could delegate authority to confederation proceedings and then to a constituent assembly, permitting the constitution of a new republic to enjoy widespread recognition. Yet to claim, following Hannah Arendt, that this prefederal inauguration process is a unique solution to the legitimation problems of founding self-government is mistaken. The problem of legitimation is insoluble so long as normativity is sought in procedures antecedent to the functioning of self-government. If one locates the legitimacy of a constituent body in the character of some preexisting polity, the question arises as to how that prior polity enjoys legitimacy of its own, when it is not itself the just state that awaits enactment. If that antecedent polity has validity in virtue of its local embodiment of self-rule, that validity cannot rest upon a constituent body like the one it is supposed to legitimate. Then, however, the body conferring authority on a constituent assembly has a normativity independent of prior founding procedures, undercutting the need for such legitimation in the first place. Generally, if what is founded is the actuality of normative politics and political normativity is something for its own sake, no constituting body can have any comparable legitimacy of its own. Not only must the constituting body issue from a regime that is not yet fully politically emancipated, but the activity of founding cannot be identical with the activity of self-government to which it gives way in completing its founding service. At best, a constituting procedure can draw instrumental value for helping bring into being a body politic that is for its own sake, incarnating the normatively self-sufficient rule of freedom. This normative limitation of any political genesis only presents difficulties if one doggedly holds on to the foundationalist assumption that normativity must be conferred by something prior to what enjoys normativity. Once again, the only way to escape such foundational dilemmas is to acknowledge the normativity of self-determination and thus to locate the legitimacy of government in its realization of political freedom.

Whether political emancipation can only occur by means of constituent assemblies issuing from preexisting organs of local self-government is another matter. As the history of other establishments of representative democracies illustrates, the routes are manifold by which at least approximations of self-government can come into being. Although what gives legitimacy to the founded government is always the degree to which it realizes political self-determination, what in each case allows for it to operate is a certain level of compliant participation that various scenarios can secure. Foreign military conquest, such as that of the Allies over Nazi Germany and Imperial Japan, can be the vehicle for establishing forms of self-government that previously tyrannized populations quickly accept and invigorate. Political emancipation can be ushered in just as well by military coup d'états, internal reforms within one-party dictatorships, peaceful and not so peaceful decolonization processes, and any variety of other transmutations of political domination. In each case, what alone is required is enough popular recognition of and participation in the nascent body politic to allow it to function, together with nonpolitical institutions and cultural mores sufficiently compatible with genuine equal political opportunity.

Nonetheless, even if the route to political emancipation has a contingent variability and no role in the normativity of self-government, the conception of the just state cannot directly turn to political institutions without paying heed to their preconditions. These preconditions are normative and normatively neutral in kind, and each sort mandates a different consideration at the outset of political philosophy.

The normatively neutral preconditions of politics comprise the general enabling conditions of conduct, conditions that make possible all responsible action, good or bad, including all forms of political life. These are the astrophysical, climactic, biological, psychological, and cultural requirements that must be satisfied in order for conventions of any sort to be practiced. Without them, history is impossible, nor can any norms be laid down. Yet because these minimal conditions of agency and interaction are common to all conduct and all institutions, be they just or unjust, these conditions play no role in differentiating between right and wrong in general and just and unjust political regimes in particular. Still, because these conditions provide the minimal equipment with which conduct operates, political philosophy must presuppose what they are and accommodate their requirements if the political ought is to be realizable. Establishing their necessary conceptual character, however, is not the work of ethics, but the task of the philosophies of nature and mind, whose labors must thus precede the philosophy of right. Whenever nature, finite agents, or sheer possibilities of interpersonal relations are mentioned, these terms only have a noncontroversial significance on the basis of these prior achievements of reason. Since, however, these certified materials are general to conduct, their content does not otherwise enter into the determination of political or prepolitical rights.

The situation is very different with the normative preconditions of political freedom. Because self-determination has an exclusive and unconditional normativity, any normative preconditions of politics are themselves modes of freedom that, as such, ought to be upheld by the body politic. To be just, the state must accordingly tailor its activities to insure realizing these nonpolitical rights. Further, since these nonpolitical modes of self-determination comprise practices that allow for self-rule, the just state must preside over them both as antecedently conceivable and realizable spheres of right and as component elements of its own realm, necessarily integrated with the political self-determination that they facilitate.[1] To the degree that they make political freedom possible, these spheres of nonpolitical right must be prior in thought and reality, even if their antecedent existence may be enclosed within regimes that lack self-government or may be prey to violations that a just state can better remedy. In some way, these spheres of freedom must be capable of arising first so as to remove the prepolitical obstacles to self-rule that their absence entails. Yet, as normative institutions that just politics cannot do without, they must be incorporated within the state, subject to whatever partial modifications are necessary to enable political freedom to operate in conformity with their own.

This imperative presents an imposing challenge for the conception of the just state. If the state is to be determined in its regulation of nonpolitical spheres of right, the universal character of these spheres must be antecedently determined. Only then does politics have something necessarily determinate on which to intervene and only then can the summons of their political supervision be concretely defined.

This supervision has two broad tasks. On the one hand, political initiative must be taken to uphold prepolitical rights against the violations incipient in their own spheres and against the burdens that political participation puts upon individuals to the detriment of their exercise of prepolitical rights. To the extent that these subordinate spheres are enabling conditions of equal political opportunity, intervening on their behalf and modifying self-government to accommodate their practice are not external impositions, but internal imperatives for the realization of political freedom. Still, because the completely unimpeded practice of these freedoms can obstruct self-government, political initiative must be taken to prevent prepolitical rights from prejudicing the equal political opportunity of citizens. Not only must the just state make requisitions to finance its operations, provide for politically needed public works, and defend its realm, but it must partially restrict those exercises of prepolitical freedom that enhance the political advantage of some citizens at the expense of others.

All these imperatives inject a very determinate content into the ends of emancipated politics, a content that bears upon the constitution of self-government that the procedures of political participation must presuppose and reproduce. Political self-determination is therefore hardly an empty slate upon which a sovereign will draws any design it pleases. The universal structure of nonpolitical and political freedom entails very specific forms as well as ends for self-rule.

Political philosophy must therefore have at its disposal the conception of the different spheres of right with which to differentiate and define the freedom of the body politic in respect to its own normative preconditions. Furnishing the concepts of the other modes of self-determination is, of course, the defining occupation of the preceding remainder of ethics. Redeemed by the normativity of freedom as the philosophy of right, ethics must here proceed from the minimal autonomy of ownership through all the other freedoms leading to the threshold of self-government.

1.2 RAMIFICATIONS FOR POLITICAL PHILOSOPHY OF ANTECEDENT SPHERES OF RIGHT

Political philosophy must attend to four ramifications from the ensuing delineation of the antecedent spheres of right encompassed by politics.

First, owing to the normativity of self-determination, the basic rights of nonpolitical freedom must be politically guaranteed. Accordingly, the organization of self-government must accommodate the nonpolitical rights of citizens and noncitizens alike by insuring that equal political opportunity is maintained without prejudicing individuals' other rights and duties. Political philosophy misconceives the state if it determines political freedom in indifference to the institutional implications of this accommodation.

Second, because political self-determination is unconditionally valid, nonpolitical freedoms must be politically regulated so as to insure that their practice does not conflict with equal political opportunity. Once again, political philosophy will fail to grasp the actuality of political freedom if it ignores the institutional satisfaction of this requirement.

Third, to the degree that the exercise of nonpolitical rights is a precondition of political self-determination, self-government must uphold the nonpolitical freedoms so as to realize itself. A political philosophy that ignores this interconnection will once more fail to prescribe a regime of self-government that can sustain itself.

Finally, by guaranteeing, regulating, and realizing for its own sake the other spheres of right, political self-determination will equally distinguish its own autonomy from those it oversees. Because the prepolitical freedoms must be supervised in their totality, due to both their own normativity and their role as enabling conditions of self-government, political self-determination can only be fully distinguished if the spheres of right are determined in a necessary, exhaustive fashion. If political philosophy is to succeed in determining the specific character of political self-determination, it must thus do so in respect to the contrast between equal political opportunity and all the other antecedent forms of right.

1.3 THE RIGHTS OF NATIONS AND POLITICAL PHILOSOPHY

Before seriously embarking upon a differentiation of political freedom from the prepolitical forms of self-determination, political philosophy must contend with an alternate route for arriving at the minimal determination of politics. Instead of seeking to distinguish political association in reference to the prepolitical spheres of right, political thinkers have been tantalized by another strategy, especially attracting those who view the limits of political philosophy through the blinders of the foundational approaches of the past. This alternate route comes to political association from an entirely opposite direction. Rather than identifying politics by how self-rule operates in presiding over prepolitical relations, this approach locates the essence of the political in the opposition of the state to what lies beyond its borders.

The appeal to an international context as determinative of political association is not without plausibility. Certainly one of the most accepted distinguishing features of the body politic is that it expresses its sovereignty by wielding exclusive authority to determine how anyone and any institution within its domain may interact with what lies abroad. Although property relations, moral considerations, family ties, market activities, and social-interest groups may all extend themselves beyond national borders, political association characteristically retains the exclusive right to act in the name of the nation and draw the line between admissible and inadmissible foreign relations. Moreover, it falls preeminently to the body politic to protect and advance the national interest in an international context. Hence, states will have need of ministries devoted to national defense, the maintenance of foreign relations, and international commerce if they are to uphold themselves in face of one another.

To this end, it falls to the state to exact sacrifices at every level when necessary to sustain the body politic and all that it encompasses against foreign threat. Contrary to the instrumental thrust of social contract politics, where the state serves prepolitical ends, political association manifests its defining transcendence of civil concerns by requiring all other spheres to become instruments of national security. In this line, Carl Schmitt can argue that the concept of the political rests upon the opposition of friend and foe, where fellow citizens have a genuinely political bond only in putting everything else on the line in confronting the enemy of the state.[2]

Similarly, because each state finds its autonomy effectively limited by the geopolitical pressures, be they economic, cultural, or military, that foreign powers wield singly or jointly, it is tempting to follow H. L. A. Hart and determine political sovereignty by the international framework in which different body politics find their dominion differentially defined, be it by formal treaties or informal transnational arrangements.[3] Of course, one can add into the equation the impact of multinational corporate power and postcolonial legacies and conclude that any conception of politics that abstracts from the international conjuncture has left reality behind.

There can be little doubt that all of these international factors have an impact upon the internal organization of the body politic from the very moment one state confronts another. Nonetheless, the methodological question remains as to whether these internal ramifications mandate that the just state must be conceived from the start as one state in relation to others or whether the treatment of international relations itself requires the prior conception of self-government as it stands determined apart from foreign affairs. As with any institutional matter, philosophy will have a conceptually determinate convention to address only when normative relations come into play, either in fully realized or fragmentary form. For this reason, whatever order be mandated, the philosophical treatment of international relations must always involve reference to the spheres of right.

Of course, the one circumstance that could preclude any international element from entering into the structure of the body politic is the complete elimination of foreign interaction. This is conceivable in several ways. First, a state might be either the first or last political association in existence and simply have no foreign affairs. Second, a plurality of politically organized communities might exist but be separated by geophysical or intergalactic obstacles that leave each in an unperturbed isolation. Finally, the plurality of states could be supplanted by the consolidation of all nations into a single sovereign state, be it by agreement or conquest, transforming erstwhile international relations into provincial connections.

Each of these scenarios would be denied in principle by someone like Carl Schmitt, for whom the very identity of political association depends upon an opposition between the state and an external foe. If this were true, in the absence of a plurality of nations, political organization would either never arise or collapse into society, leaving kinship groups, markets, villages, and other prepolitical associations the exclusive forms of community.

The idea that an individual state cannot be in isolation might garner support from the very structure of rights. Just as an individual cannot be an owner, a moral subject, a family member, a market participant, a legal subject, or a citizen without standing in relation to other individuals who have determined themselves in accord with the same lawful form of artificial entitlement, it well seems that states cannot be what they are as national atoms, cut off from international relations. Certainly, if international relations involve rights of nations, no states can bear these rights without reference to the correlative entitlements of other states and the accompanying duty to respect them. Yet, the fact that international rights, like any other rights, consist in an interaction among right-bearers, neither guarantees that nations do have rights nor that a state could not exist in isolation, independent of any international entitlement. Just as an individual could be marooned without any opportunity to dispose of property, enjoy conjugal or parental rights, exercise market or legal autonomy, or act as a citizen, so the possibility of rights of nations does not preclude a state from realizing political and prepolitical rights without relating to other polities.

Indeed, the plural structure of rights suggests that political freedom need depend not upon relations between states but rather upon lawful relations among citizens of one and the same body politic. By exercising equal political opportunity within the frontiers of the body politic that their political participation continually renews, while exercising all of their prepolitical rights, citizens would seem to sustain a form of association distinctly different from any freedom not involving that political participation. Although Schmitt may be correct in castigating the instrumentalism of procedural justice for failing to generate distinctly political association, the limits of civil administration need not prevent political freedom from defining itself by means of its own domestic self-government. To the degree that citizens impose upon themselves the order of the whole totality of freedom while regulating the prepolitical spheres of right, their political activity reproduces an association distinctly different from the nonpolitical associations over which it presides. Although self-government must make the conventional ends of prepolitical rights part of its own, the political regulation and enforcement of prepolitical rights departs fundamentally from the prepolitical activity in pursuit of those ends. Whereas individuals will their self-determination as owner, moral subject, family member, and civilian in their nonpolitical practices, as citizens, these same individuals will the *state enforcement* of *every* person's prepolitical rights within the body politic, while further determining themselves as self-governing citizens, willing the form of the entire system of rights to which they belong. In so doing, citizens exercise a freedom that is supreme over all their other affairs. As such, their political engagement has a sovereign autonomy no other practice can rival. Moreover, precisely by imposing order upon itself without being subject to any external regulation, free political action exhibits an unequaled reflexivity. Finally, self-government possesses a defining universality of aim by willing the totality of right, a universality inseparable from the supremacy, sovereign autonomy, and reflexivity that simultaneously distinguish political self-determination.

Without such distinctly political practice already underway, at home or abroad, it is inconceivable how individuals could find themselves opposed to a *political* foe, against which they could act in a *political* manner. Prior to the formation of political association, individuals might well oppose others as tribal enemies, religious foes, caste pariahs, class antagonists, or social adversaries of any other form. Yet unless political association has arisen, individuals do not have a common sovereignty to protect from and advance against any adversary, a sovereignty whose domestically universal, all-encompassing self-determination alone empowers an agency for whom all particular ends are subordinate. Because political freedom gives itself its own ends in necessary conjunction with incorporating prepolitical spheres of right, the state does not need any external factor to sustain its identity.

Hence, contra Schmitt, foreign antagonism cannot be constitutive of politics. Rather, the opposition of states is predicated upon the domestic features defining self-government and the relation between politics and the other spheres of right. Although these features are the conceptually determinate elements that political philosophy prescribes for the just state, they equally apply to the relation between any other communities that warrant inclusion as political associations. Since only the normative concept of the just state can provide a universally valid determination of politics, all that can be said of necessity pertaining to political relationships, be they domestic or international, results from applying the categories of political justice to realities that stand in greater or lesser correspondence to them.

For this reason, it is fundamentally mistaken to follow Hart and deprive political autonomy of all intrinsic character by leaving it determined by whatever discretion contingent international conjunctures allow different states. Although states may well restrict the foreign and domestic options of other political associations, to do so, they must themselves possess the political structure both allowing for a plurality of states and empowering them to limit the sovereignty of one another. However goes the struggle between states, the opposition across national frontiers itself depends upon the prior emergence of political institutions over and above nonpolitical associations.

These considerations have key practical and theoretical implications. Practically speaking, they indicate that political association need not stand in relation to other politically organized communities. Theoretically, they mandate that political philosophy must first conceive political association as it is determined apart from international relations. Only once political association as such has been determined can political philosophy conceive the modifications incurred by the just state when and if it becomes a particular state interacting with others.

Whether that context of international relations involves rights of its own will therefore depend upon an antecedent determination of the domestic rights of citizenship and the prepolitical autonomies on which these rest. Furthermore, insofar as these domestic and civil rights are antecedently defined and enjoy an independent validity as modes of self-determination, they must be respected and upheld by any legitimate rights of nations, just as valid self-government must honor the nonpolitical rights of citizens. For all these reasons, the conception of international rights must follow the conception of the domestic rights of political and prepolitical freedom.

1.4 THE SYSTEM OF RIGHTS AND THE MINIMAL DETERMINATION OF POLITICAL FREEDOM

The minimal determination of political freedom is predicated upon the prepolitical spheres of right both because legitimate politics must uphold their freedoms and because self-government cannot operate unless its citizens have been emancipated from the oppressions that their emergence eliminates. Although this does not render these other modes of self-determination determining principles of political justice, political freedom's own defining autonomy cannot be conceived independently of their specification. Yet how are the spheres of right to be exhaustively identified? Two seemingly separate strategies beckon.

On the one hand, a complete taxonomy of the spheres of right can be developed by isolating the generic elements of self-determination and then conceiving all the possible particular forms that these elements can take. Of course, to be successful, this approach must locate some principle for guaranteeing the exhaustive character of the resulting differentiation.

On the other hand, the delineation of the spheres of right can be accomplished through a process of internal composition, following the structural requirements of political freedom. This entails starting with the most basic mode of self-determination presupposing no others, then advancing to a second type of right that incorporates no other but that elementary shape, continuing next to the further freedom that can operate on the basis of what the former provides, until finally the sphere of right is attained that brings political unity to the whole system of freedom. Here the order of conception follows the methodological proviso that nothing be addressed whose prerequisites have not already been determined. To the degree that these prerequisites are components incorporated within each successive shape of freedom, the order of conception is equally an order of constitution. In this case what guarantees completeness is the internal structure of the encompassing body politic. This is because whatever spheres of right constitutively enter into its formation are the only modes of freedom that can subsist with self-government. If there were any other nonconstitutive freedoms, they would be in the self-defeating situation of either standing at the perennial mercy of political license or depending upon the shackling of political freedom for their maintenance. Since political freedom can exist without upholding any sphere of right that is not an enabling condition of self-government, these nonconstitutive freedoms would conflict with state autonomy whenever citizens choose to ignore them, whereas guaranteeing their maintenance would require restricting political sovereignty by an external power. Either way, right would conflict with right, leaving ethics at an insoluble impasse. Consequently, only freedoms that are enabling conditions of self-government could belong to the coherent system of rights in which normative conduct must consist.

1.5 THE DIFFERENTIATING FACTORS OF SELF-DETERMINATION

Self-determination constitutively involves an intersubjective practice of rights where individuals exercise an artificial agency, whose generic character they will in choosing self-selected ends that meet the formal requirement of upholding some type of equal opportunity. In each case, autonomous agents will themselves as self-determined in some particular mode of right depending upon the type of ends they choose, the type of agency they thereby reproduce, and the corresponding type of equal opportunity that their particular type of lawful willing realizes.

By willing an appropriation, use, or alienation of property, individuals determine themselves as owners, in respect of other persons' rights of ownership. By determining the scope of their accountable deeds in respect to the conscientious purpose and motive with which they act toward others, individuals determine themselves as moral subjects in recognition of the moral accountability of others. By choosing to form a common home as codetermining spouses, consolidating individuals determine themselves as members of an emancipated household. By participating in the market and exchanging commodities, individuals determine themselves as bearers of economic rights, deserving of the equal economic opportunity to satisfy self-selected needs for the commodities of others in reciprocity with them. By joining into voluntary social-interest groups and partaking of a public administration of welfare, individuals secure their economic rights through further engagements of social freedom. By participating in the civil administration of justice, individuals interact as legal subjects enjoying rights of due process to have their civil rights upheld by law. And finally, by engaging in self-government, individuals determine themselves as free citizens.

Each of these modes of self-determination has become provisionally familiar through the theoretical achievements of the pioneers of the philosophy of right and the revolutionary practical transformations that have defined the rise of modernity. If, however, their examples are to serve as a heuristic guide for reconstructing the exhaustive system of right, the principle of their differentiation must be uncovered.

To begin with, property right presents self-determination in an immediate form. As in every mode of right, owners determine themselves as self-determined, but do so qua *owner* insofar as the reality of their self-determination consists in an externally given factor, immediately embodying their will to the exclusion of that of others. Anything that might underlie that embodiment as a mediating consideration plays no role in ownership. Preceding motives have as little relevance to property right as resulting impacts upon welfare. To determine myself as a proprietor, all that matters is that my will be recognized as inhabiting a particular external receptacle that, as such, does not intrude upon the correlative embodiments of other owners' wills. If self-determination is to exist without any further qualification, if the agent is to determine itself as having a recognized free determinate being and nothing more, property right supplies the minimal autonomy.

When, however, agents determine themselves through a mediated reality, a reality reflecting some determination provided by each agent's own will, moral accountability takes the stage. Individuals can always fashion their conduct in respect to independently given mediating factors, but their action is then defined by conditions dictating rather than dictated by choice, precluding their willing their own agency as self-determined. In order to determine the nature of one's own agency as something not just immediately embodied in some external factor, as in property, but as mediated by one's own volition, conduct must reflect contents both located in and determined by the agent's will. Given the structure of choice, this requirement is satisfied by making the self-selected purpose of conduct a mediating factor of self-determination, according to which individuals hold each other responsible only for what they do on purpose. In this fashion, agents determine themselves as agents whose actions are accountable in respect to that element (their "deed" proper) prefigured in the purpose with which they act. On this basis, they can then equally impute responsibility only to those consequences of each other's deeds that are anticipated in the intention supplying the motive for doing what they do on purpose. And finally, when agents take on responsibility for acting with the right purposes and intentions, and make this determination a mode of self-determination, they exercise the right of acting on conscience, sharing the prerogative to choose independently which aims and motives are valid while incurring the correlative duty to respect others' right to do the same. In each of these three dimensions of moral agency, individuals determine themselves as self-determined by defining the scope of their actions through self-specified internal features of their own volition.

The distinction between the basic structures of property and moral right provides a basis for specifying a third fundamental option for self-determination. Whereas property right provides free will with an immediate externalization, morality gives freedom a reality mediated by the internal choices of volition. In both cases, what is willed is an end that gives volition a particular content while individuating a particular type of agency, whose specific autonomy is exercised in recognition of and by other participants in the same mode of freedom. Agents individuate themselves as owners by laying their will in external factors that count as their property, whereas these same persons determine themselves as moral subjects by conscientiously choosing to act with purposes and intentions that are recognized to define what part of their action and its consequences are their responsibility. Although these exercises of right each realize a mode of self-determination, neither involves willing an end that contains the activity by which it is realized. Owners will an embodiment of their will, but property is different from the volition by which it is appropriated, used, or relinquished. Moral subjects act in respect to their independent determination of the right purpose and intention, but these contents of willing are aims that ought to be realized by the moral striving that seeks their fulfillment—not that striving itself. Although owners and moral subjects interact in recognition of the respective self-determinations exhibited in property and deed, they do not thereby will an end that contains their self-determined agency in an external embodiment. Property right gives freedom an external embodiment but one that is a mere receptacle of will, whereas morality makes action the focal point of self-determination but in respect to internal factors of volition that are yet to be externalized. For an end to combine both sides, the external reality of freedom and the internal determining of agency, what individuals will would have to reproduce the structure of interaction in which they participate. In that case, the end realized by their self-determination would already exist as the standing framework in which they exercise the right in question. In other words, the lawful interconnection of individuals, within which each exercises an equal opportunity reproducing their relationship, would be both the end and preexisting realization of their freedom. What they each will in exercising such a right would be an individuation of an artificial agency, whose role is made possible by the institutional convention within which and in reproduction of which it operates. Self-determination here takes the form of an ethical community of freedom, where individuals perform a normatively valid role predicated upon their membership in an association continually reproduced by the right, the equal opportunity, they therein exercise.

To the degree that self-determination wills either an external embodiment, an internal determining specification, or a reality both external and internal, rights fall unto three basic spheres: property, morality, and ethical community. In distinction from property and morality, ethical community comprises a mode of self-determination where agents exercise rights of membership, performing roles whose specific equal opportunities can only be enjoyed by belonging to a preexisting association whose own framework of right and duty sustains itself through nothing but the continuous exercise of that practice. Consequently, ethical community offers its members conventional satisfactions that can be had nowhere else, for the achievement of the ends generic to its roles reproduce its association. One cannot enjoy the happiness of fulfilling one's opportunities as a free and equal spouse unless one participates in an emancipated family, just as one cannot attain the satisfaction of earning a living through a self-selected occupation in reciprocity with others unless one enjoys equal economic opportunity as a member of a regulated market. And, of course, one cannot arrive at any of the political satisfactions of autonomous citizenship without participating in a self-governing body politic.

That ethical community situates its members in a preexisting association already realizing the rights to which their membership entitles them does not reduce property right and moral accountability to atomistic pursuits. To determine oneself as owner or moral subject, individuals must interact with other agents who do the same. Without this engagement with others, the reciprocity of right and duty evaporates and the will cannot rise beyond the technical assertions of unilateral choice. Yet the constitutive interaction of owners and moral subjects still does not involve membership in a standing association, involving the reproduction of institutional roles. Property owners are joined by nothing but the contractual relations they choose to enter or rescind, whereas conscience may call upon moral subjects to ignore their institutional duties. If the form of ethical community is itself differentiated in terms of the character of its ends and the scope of its association, it becomes evident that its institutional freedom can take three basic forms: that of a free household, a civil society, and a self-governing state.

When the ends of ethical community are particular and its association is particular in scope, individuals determine themselves as members of an institution whose shared good extends no further than the limits that separate its particular grouping from other comparable associations that pursue their own respective good in common. Within each such particular association, the members enjoy an equal opportunity to codetermine the life they lead in common, both in respect to themselves and as representatives of their association in interaction with outsiders. In this manner, individuals consolidate into a common home, therein acquiring their rights as spouses and potential parents to uphold the particular ends they jointly pursue in free domestic association.

When the ends are particular but the association is universal in scope, individuals pursue self-selected particular ends that can no longer derive their limit from that of their association, which is global, if not intergalactic in reach. Although the ends in question, as factors in a structure of right, necessarily relate their bearer to other individuals in their engagement in the same sort of self-determination, all participants are at liberty to define them as they may, subject to the proviso that their satisfaction is tied to the satisfaction by others of analogously self-selected ends. The ensuing network of commodity relations engenders a framework of equal economic opportunity, where individuals enjoy the right to pursue self-selected needs through self-selected activity in reciprocity with others, with nothing limiting the extent of their interaction than the possibilities of market expansion.

By contrast, when the ends are universal and the association is universal, individuals collectively determine the whole order of freedom in which they participate. Instead of limiting their concern to the particular shared interest of their household or to particular needs pursued in the limitless expanse of the market, individuals here determine themselves as members in an association where membership involves codetermining the order of the totality of right. Willing the universal realization of freedom and thereby willing an agency that defines itself by realizing every mode of self-determination, individuals comprise an emancipated political association. Because political freedom can be exercised by a body politic that stands in relation to no others, the universality of political ends can be reflected in the all-encompassing boundary of a one and only political community.

When, however, self-government is exercised by a community that stands in relation to other political associations, a field of international right opens in which the universal ends of political action are pursued within the borders of one state among others. In these circumstances, made possible, if not necessary, by political association in general, ethical community is universal in end but particular in scope, exhausting the alternatives for permutating end and scope under particular and universal.

If these differentiations delineate the basic anatomy of right, political philosophy can proceed to conceive the just state as an ethical community of freedom, universal in aim and universal in scope, upholding the freedoms of property, morality, family, and civil society in harmony with self-government.

What gives this enterprise added certainty and added precision is the order of constitution of the spheres of right, an ordering that reveals just how political freedom depends upon the other modes of self-determination. The coherence of the system of right requires that the encompassing freedom of politics preside over nothing but its own prerequisite nonpolitical autonomies and that there be no other nonpolitical rights than these. Otherwise, political freedom will stand in incipient conflict with other freedoms, undercutting them all. Consequently, the delineation of the spheres of right making self-government possible must exhaust the varieties of self-determination and, thereby, the normative preconditions of political justice.

1.6 THE ORDER OF CONSTITUTION IN THE SPHERES OF RIGHT

Property, moral, family, and civil rights stand in a relation of constitution both with regard to one another and with regard to political self-determination. This dual connection is manifest both positively and negatively. On the one hand, the spheres of right order themselves in a progressive inclusive complexity, with each successive practice structurally incorporating those that precede it. Each structurally prior sphere positively contributes to the composition of those that follow insofar as the agency of structurally posterior rights simultaneously engages in the agencies of the less inclusive freedoms. On the other hand, the absence of any of the structurally prior conventions of freedom entails obstacles to the exercise of the other rights in question. Consequently, property rights, moral accountability, household emancipation, and civil society can all come into being without self-government, whereas political freedom cannot operate without their emergence.[4]

1.7 PROPERTY RIGHT AND THE OTHER RIGHTS

The elemental primacy of property right is evident on both positive and negative grounds. Property right can be exercised without simultaneously enjoying moral, family, civil, or political rights insofar as individuals can determine themselves as owners simply by recognizably laying their will in some factor that does not conflict with the domains in which others have correlatively embodied their wills. Owners need not hold one another morally accountable, since title to property is itself indifferent to the purposes and intentions that may or may not conscientiously accompany its acquisition, use, or disposal. An Oedipus may stand guilty in the eyes of himself and others irrespective of his purpose and intention, yet still retain the status of owner that being a freeman minimally involves. Similarly, an individual may have property, yet be deprived of the right to freely marry and codetermine household affairs, since ownership in no way requires family membership of any sort. By the same token, persons may respect the property of one another without engaging in market relations and exercising any equal economic opportunity, supported by social-interest-group engagement and public-welfare guarantees. Nor does ownership require a regime of civil law, in which individuals enjoy rights of due process to have their civil rights legally enforced. Finally, owners need not enjoy rights of citizenship in order to enjoy property entitlements. Whether one is a noncitizen or a subject of an oppressive regime, one can retain ownership of one's own body and dispose over other items of property, for participation in self-government hardly plays a constitutive role in determining oneself as an owner.

By contrast, none of the other spheres of right can subsist without ascribing property rights to their participants. In each and every case, the reason is the same: unless individuals achieve recognition of having determined themselves as owners of at least their own bodies, nothing they do can count as an action of their own will rather than of some other master to whom they belong. Consequently, whenever individuals observe any further rights of one another,[5] their interaction must incorporate recognition of the personhood of each one, that is, of each party's established identity as a self-determined agent who cannot be legitimately subject to enslavement because each one's will already has an exclusive domain of its own. Whether this recognition take the form of a separate formality or simply be acknowledged as a constitutive part of every other exercise of right, it must be given its due if any further justice is to be realized. Without universal property right in operation, individuals are subject to various forms of bondage, be it outright slavery, serfdom, or domestic servitude, that not only interfere with their nonpolitical freedoms, but preclude the equal opportunity to political participation in which genuine self-government resides.

1.8 MORAL ACCOUNTABILITY AND ETHICAL FREEDOM

The right to moral accountability, to be held responsible only for that part of one's action and its consequences that are prefigured in one's conscientiously determined purpose and intention, plays a more ambiguous role than property in the constitution of right.

Moral right cannot fail to uphold property right, for if moral subjects lose recognition of their ownership of their own bodies, nothing they do can be ascribed to their volition. Their purposes and intentions may remain enclosed within the inviolable asylum of conscience, but everything external in their conduct gets referred to the will of their master, depriving them of any deeds that can reflect their conscientious purpose and intention. Consequently, to enjoy the right to moral accountability, individuals must simultaneously recognize one another as persons, inalienably owning at least their own body. This is why, in the order of constitution, property right precedes moral accountability and personhood—the agency of ownership structurally precedes moral subjectivity, the agency of conscience.

Although individuals must equally be owners in order to practice moral accountability, their moral interaction does not depend upon membership in ethical institutions of freedom. So long as individuals enjoy the status of persons, their responsibility can be imputed to conscience, even if they belong to households, societies, and states in which heteronomous traditions obstruct domestic, social, and political equal opportunity. Agents can still be praised and blamed only for what they do on purpose and only for those consequences of their deeds that they intended without automatically interfering with their participation in communities in which family, social, and political roles are defined independently of self-determination. Because conscience's determination of the right purpose and intention is subjective, its decisions may or may not conform to the demands of any existing association.

For this very reason, moral accountability might seem purely optional for an ethical community, which, properly speaking, realizes household, civil, and political rights. Indeed, since conscience might well collide with domestic, civil, and political rectitude, the institutions of freedom might appear better off if they could dispense with the gadfly of conscientious objection.

Admittedly, the family, civil society, and self-government cannot stand idly by when their members are driven by conscience to violate their institutional roles. Restraining conscientious decisions at odds with domestic, social, or political right is, however, very different from withdrawing all recognition of moral accountability. Just as property right must undergo partial limitation to comply with the obligations of conjugal joint ownership, parental duty, equal economic opportunity, due process, and equal political opportunity, so moral right must submit to partial constraint to integrate with the institutional prerogatives of ethical freedom.

What, however, of the remaining sphere, wherein moral self-determination does not intrude upon family, social, or political right? If ethical institutions were to restrict this exercise of moral right, a mode of self-determination would be restricted in the interest of something unrelated to freedom. Given that nothing pertaining to conduct can have unqualified validity apart from self-determination, any such imposition upon moral autonomy would be a wrong tainting the perpetrating associations. For this reason alone, any household, social, or political regimes restricting moral accountability beyond what their own rights require would be undercutting their own authority.

That moral accountability is not indifferently optional for ethical freedom is further evident by examining how wholly excising recognition of conscience impacts upon the internal functioning of household, social, and political community. What form will association take if individuals are unable to restrict their responsibility in function of their purposes and intentions, and the court of conscience counts as an illicit privileging of personal feelings with no further authority? To begin with, community obligations will never be mitigated by ignorance or unintended consequences, nor will association ever leave individuals free to consult conscience as an ultimate tribunal of conduct. Conscientious action will be not only unnecessary, but positively prohibited. Solely what is manifest in external behavior will count as essential. Although crime will still be distinguishable from nonmalicious wrongs, involving good faith contractual disputes or accidental harm to property, the element of intent will only figure negatively as a qualifier for punishment. The positive moral imperative to act with the right purposes and intentions will be absent, leaving individuals with only external incentives to uphold their community roles. After all, if individuals are not accountable for acting with valid motives, they will man their stations in each association as hollow conformists, liable to renege on their community obligations whenever expedient. This is not to say that moral agency must be recognized if ethical community is to function, nor that conscience will always corroborate ethical duty. Nonetheless, without respect for moral responsibility, any community spirit will be a fragile shell.

When, moreover, the moral stance is expressly excluded, that antagonism to freedom of conscience can hardly foster institutional autonomy in family, society, or state. The prohibition of moral right is demanded by any sacred or profane authority that imposes norms given independently of self-determination for the simple reason that these norms are imposed externally, without any regard for the personal knowing and willing of those subject to them. Needless to say, such a regime of traditional authority is equally an obstacle to the freedoms of every other sphere of right, to the degree that whatever order it imposes upon their arenas involves particular practices that deviate from property, family, social, or political autonomy.

1.9 HOUSEHOLD EMANCIPATION AS A PRECONDITION OF SOCIAL AND POLITICAL FREEDOM

Whereas property right and moral right are general preconditions of any form of ethical freedom, the emancipation of the household is a structural prerequisite of both civil society and self-government. The reconstruction of the family as an institution of right can precede the achievement of social and political justice because family community does not incorporate social freedom or political self-determination, whereas civil society and the free state both contain the families of their members. Nevertheless, the emancipation of the family involves an extrication of the household from both economic and political affairs that sets the stage for, if not coincides with, the demarcation of a civil society from a sovereign state presiding over newly separated spheres of family and society.

To take shape as an ethical institution of freedom particular in both aim and scope, the family must eliminate all vestige of the rule of natural difference by which tradition has left the household an arena of patrilineal-gendered hierarchy and heterosexual exclusivity. Individuals must reclaim the universal right to enter into mutually decided marriage, irrespective of race, hereditary rank, gender, or sexual orientation, and to comanage a joint conjugal property and welfare, subject to the proviso that in so determining their consolidated ownership and interest, they respect the rights of others without otherwise undermining their own.[6] To exercise their conjugal roles as a mode of ethical freedom, spouses must not only play an equal part in managing their household and representing its codetermined right and welfare outside the home but escape subjection to other kin relations that would undermine their mutual marital autonomy. Merging marriage with economic, political, or any other conventional power must equally be overcome when this interferes with the right to marry or prevents spouses from autonomously pursuing their own legitimate joint designs. When children enter the family, be it by birth or adoption, the same requirements apply to parents' right and duty to raise their progeny to autonomous maturity—no other kinship bonds or extrafamilial interests have any business to intrude so long as they are not required by other modes of right.

Accordingly, only through disengagement from the extended web of traditional kinship and the impositions of dynastic rule and caste nepotism can the family become an institution of freedom, where spouses and/or parents exercise a lawful willing reproducing a domestic association of conjugal codetermination and/or parental autonomy. Although this signifies that domestic emancipation depends upon the elimination of premodern social and political formations that merge kinship with rule and production, the positive freedoms of the emancipated household are structural prerequisites of social and political emancipation alike.

Family freedom is a direct precondition for each and every autonomy that individuals first win as members of a civil society. So long as spouses do not share equal responsibilities in families liberated from domination by wider kin groups or other traditional authorities, their hierarchical household roles block their equal opportunity to participate in the different activities of civil freedom. Any spouse who is subject to household domination is deprived of equal access to society, since inequality in domestic relations entails inequality in representing the family interest in the economy and before the law. Wherever family organization places a spouse under the authority of other kin, family membership becomes an obstacle to equal participation in the due process of civil law just as well as to equal economic opportunity, with its corollary participation in social-interest-group advocacy and social welfare benefits that secure economic autonomy. Unless family members have conjugal and parental autonomy, they cannot exercise their economic freedom of choosing how to satisfy their self-selected needs for commodities in reciprocity with others, nor secure the legal protection of their civil rights on an equal footing. Not only do unequal divisions of household chores shackle the career options of the more burdened, but any hierarchy in household management leaves the social ambitions of the subordinate family members hostage to the caprice of their household masters. Consequently, the household privilege of those who lord over other competent adult family members translates itself into the social privilege such as that which has allowed gendered hierarchy in the family to foster gendered disadvantage in markets, corporate bodies, and civil courts.

The ramifications for political freedom are obvious. Any deficit in household emancipation will interfere with the equal political opportunities of family members in precisely the same way in which unequal household duties obstruct equal social opportunity. Just as domination of one spouse by other kin obstructs equal economic opportunity, so it undermines equal access to participation in self-government. A family member who is compelled to take on an unequal share of conjugal and parental care can hardly have as easy access to social and political participation as the privileged household masters, especially if the latter dictate what activities outside the home are permissible. Moreover, to any degree that social disadvantage impedes the political opportunities of the socially underprivileged, family oppression that fosters social disadvantage doubly undercuts equal political opportunity. Not only does a lack of household emancipation directly impede the political participation of oppressed family members, but the social bondage it generates adds further insult to injury, subjecting the victims of family mastery to a social disadvantage that unfairly hobbles their political participation. Even if the state offers formal guarantees of universal suffrage and universal access to political office, vestigial household oppression will stamp the political arena with the political disadvantage that women continue to bear from gender-privileged family regimes.

Although household emancipation may free politics from the impediments to self-government that oppressive families represent, the retention of any domestic association might appear to be not only unnecessary but positively inimical to political self-determination.

Citizens may be unable to exercise equal political opportunity unless they recognize one another as owners of at least their own bodies, but individuals can just as well participate in civil society, earning a free livelihood in the market and enjoying due process in the courts, as join in self-government whether or not they be married or have any custodial duties over minors. Precisely because marriage is a particular ethical community whose rights and duties depend upon a membership that not all need share, there is no obligation to become a spouse any more than there is to become a parent. Moreover, life without kinship becomes generally practical once the family gets disengaged from rule and commerce and civil society insures the economic welfare of its members through public assistance.

Nevertheless, that some individuals can participate in civil society and self-government without family membership hardly challenges the political need for household emancipation. That unemancipated households restrict the political opportunities of some of their own members minimally entails that single individuals find themselves part of a body politic with second-class citizens, precluding genuine self-government. Of course, when traditional kinship infiltrates social and political relations with family attachments, the political options of nonfamily members are directly compromised by the absence of household emancipation. Hence, overcoming oppression in the family remains crucial for social and political freedom insofar as it removes the obstacles to autonomy that traditional kinship represents. Moreover, given the normativity of self-determination, any prohibition of family rights comprises an unconditioned wrong, even if individuals all choose to live alone or in informal relationships.

Nonetheless, that unemancipated families obstruct political freedom and that single citizens can practice self-government does not deflect the recurrent suspicion that even free families threaten the bases of self-determined politics. Latter-day liberals, such as John Rawls and James Fishkin, have suggested that the inherent differences in the quality of upbringing within particular families conflicts with the demands of equal opportunity of interest satisfaction.[7] Although their concern is with the prepolitical liberties to which liberalism subordinates political association, if social inequality subverts equal political opportunity, the unequal results of upbringing in families will threaten political justice. This would be the case if the unequal outcomes of differential parental care either cannot be remedied by public intervention both within and without the home, and present politically significant differences that even measures to shield political opportunity from social inequality cannot relieve. Yet the disparities in social opportunity produced by varying parental care are similar in kind to those resulting from factors extrinsic to family association. Hence the presence or absence of families is moot as far as political freedom is concerned. The alleged intractability of social inequality will present the same challenge to self-government whether or not families exist, not to mention whether upbringing occurs within or outside households.

The Platonic argument for the opposition between the good of the family and the good of the state fares no better. Because family membership generates a particular favoritism distinct from the common weal of political community, Plato concludes that at least the guardians must be brought up in common without knowledge of particular kin, so that they can have no interest divergent from that of the state.[8] The particular scope of family community may well give family members a special concern for their own household right and welfare, but does the partiality of family bonds necessarily subvert the universality of political ends? Is the state incapable of barring nepotism from the political arena and upholding equal political opportunity? And, more to the point, is household freedom incompatible with political autonomy? The jointly determined right and welfare of spouses is already subject to the proviso that it conform with the family rights of other households and not undermine the other rights of family members. Insofar as political freedom involves determining the totality of right, with the political realization of nonpolitical rights a constitutive element of self-government, justice in the state already contains family association in unity with political community. The diversity of the spheres of right would only challenge the universality of politics if that universality were an abstract one in many, collapsing all autonomy into the exclusive determination of collective decision making. In that case, politics would eliminate all nonpolitical autonomy, with self-government directly administering every affair that property right, moral accountability, conjugal sharing, parental autonomy, economic independence, and civil law make exercises of distinct freedoms. Then, no distinction could any longer be drawn between the public weal and any other. Instead, there would be left an immediate identity of "we" and "I," heralded by Plato in his *Republic* and embraced by modern totalitarian regimes,[9] who in their different ways all follow Rousseau in presuming inherent hostility between the general will of the state and individual interest, a hostility readily reducing virtue to selflessness.[10] Although such total politicization of practice may seem eminently conceivable, and conceivable as collective self-determination, the normativity of freedom to which it too lays claim prohibits the elimination of any other rights, provided, of course, that nonpolitical freedoms and self-government are compatible.[11] That very compatibility makes the universality of politics concrete, just as it enables prepolitical freedoms to operate without undermining political autonomy. Because the end of political freedom, the determination of citizens as self-determined in every mode of right, includes the end of the free family, the partiality of household community is an enabling element, rather than a countervailing subverter, of emancipated politics.

1.10 EQUAL ECONOMIC OPPORTUNITY IN CIVIL SOCIETY AS A PRECONDITION OF POLITICAL FREEDOM

Like the free family, civil society makes political freedom possible both by supplanting obstructing oppressions and by furnishing a constitutive component of a free political community. Civil society plays this dual enabling and constituent function in each of its arenas of social freedom: market economy, social-interest-group advocacy, public-welfare administration, and civil legality.[12]

Market economy reconstitutes commerce and production as a form of right, providing a social institution within which need as need for commodities becomes a self-selected particular interest for what others can provide under the condition of satisfying their own correlatively self-selected particular interest. Each participant in commodity relations cannot help but exercise an economic prerogative that is lawful in character, harmonizing with the economic opportunity of others to satisfy self-selected needs for commodities in reciprocity with others. Not only do market participants determine the content of their needs in accord with right, but they enjoy a freedom of earning by which they choose what activity to pursue to satisfy their commodity needs under the condition of meeting market demand and enabling others to earn a self-selected, but other-directed, livelihood in return. The ensuing nexus of exchange endows commodities with market determined use and exchange values, providing a framework within which exchange and production can be pursued for the sake of accumulating exchange value, engendering a competitive environment where independent enterprises must earn and reinvest a profit in order to remain solvent. Because commodity relations contain different types of earning activities, based upon the different forms that commodities can take, market participants cannot exercise their economic freedom without falling into classes defined by the mode of earning they practice. To earn in reciprocity with others, individuals must gain wealth through sale of their labor power, ownership of capital, or rent of commodities. Because ownership of capital can take various forms (including family, worker cooperative, share-holding, and public ownership), because the revenues from each form of earning can vary, and because individuals can have multiple class memberships (by simultaneously owning shares of corporations, renting property, and receiving wages), the self-selection of class need not be accompanied by any automatic economic advantage.[13]

Without commodity relations, individuals cannot choose how to earn to satisfy self-selected needs in reciprocity with others, that is, without markets, economic activity cannot take the form of right. Nevertheless, of themselves, markets do not secure the equal economic opportunity of which they are the necessary vehicles. Not only may individuals simply not succeed in finding market demand for what they have to offer, but the differences in wealth that continually result from commodity transactions can accentuate the barriers to market entry that hamper the economic opportunity of the relatively poor. This uncertainty in realizing economic freedom applies no matter how enterprises are owned; private firms, worker cooperatives, share-issuing corporations, and public enterprises are all susceptible to the same competitive pressures and market uncertainties that leave their own members with the familiar economic insecurity that haunts those consumers and producers with whom they must trade in the market.[14]

Individuals may combine in voluntary social-interest groups to promote their economic opportunity through joint negotiation in the market, fully abiding by the rights of commodity owners. Since, however, each such interest group can only fulfill its defining common interest by reciprocally satisfying the interest of other independent agents in the market, success is always contingent upon the decisions of others, who may or may not benefit from the collective achievements of their counterparts. Thus, although social-interest-group advocacy may sometimes enhance the economic opportunity of a particular sector of the market, it cannot alone guarantee equal economic opportunity, whose realization requires commodity relations, and therefore, capital accumulation.[15]

Because right has unconditioned validity, the economic insecurity left by markets and joint private-market intervention ought to be overcome. This imperative charges civil society to provide a public administration of welfare to guarantee equal economic opportunity. Accordingly, the realization of economic freedom has a threefold institutional organization: markets, social-interest-group advocacy, and a public policing of market activity, regulating free enterprise for the sake of every individual's economic freedom. The privately and publicly regulated markets of civil society provide a negative service on behalf of political freedom by superseding all forms of economic organization that leave production and distribution in the hands of traditional authority.

By making need a factor of self-determination, commodity relations supersede all economic formations where distribution and production are predicated upon "natural" needs, whose character is given independently of choice. As in all structures of right, the ends of economic freedom are conventional aims that cannot be willed apart from the autonomous practice in which they are embedded. The need for commodities is such as only to be satisfied by participating in market transactions where each party selects what commodity to seek from others and obtains satisfaction only on the condition of enabling some counterpart to do the same. Because the freedom of economic need is a matter of right, correlated with the same exercise of economic choice on the part of others, it has a lawful character that is absent when the needs that agents must satisfy are given by the contingencies of nature and external circumstance. This is why economic science has no other object than the market. All other economic formations are either devoid of lawfulness or follow a design that is the arbitrary posit of some central omnipotent economic authority. Contrary to Marx, it is only *without* commodity relations transforming need into a vehicle of self-determination that the economy remains a sphere of necessity, beyond which the realm of freedom begins.

With need dictated by external necessity, be it natural or conventional, the freedom of occupation is equally compromised. Since occupations proceed in function of the needs they seek to satisfy, when needs are imposed, so too is the character of the activities undertaken on their behalf. Moreover, since labor power can itself be the object of need and be offered as a factor of right in commodity exchange, the freedom of occupation is eliminated when markets fail to take hold of employment. If individuals are unable to decide how to earn a living in reciprocity with others, their livelihood gets determined either at the expense of the autonomy of others, as a unilateral exploitation of their activity, or by the external fiat of hereditary rank, ethnicity, race, gender, or some other heteronomous factor.

The decisive question is whether individuals can enjoy the equal political opportunity of self-government if they are submerged in nonmarket relations of production, whose needs and occupations are both determined independently of economic self-determination. To a large extent the answer already hinges upon the enabling condition that property rights provide for political freedom. Although commodity relations are not equivalent to property relations, because they insert ownership within the market's encompassing nexus of interrelated need and occupation, traditional economic formations will always entail removing the disposal of the factors of production from the domain of contractual agreement and subordinating them to other conventions. This applies most importantly to labor power itself, which, once taken out of the control of each person, leaves occupation subject to external determination precisely by restricting the "self-ownership" of each individual. To the degree that the breach of the freedom of occupation signifies a violation of basic property rights, it renders each person subject to a hierarchical domination that can readily extend to the political arena.

Of course, if individuals' role in production is decided independently of their will *and* economic position has any bearing upon political opportunity, the conditions for genuine self-government will be lacking. To the degree that economic subjugation inhibits the direct political participation of the economically oppressed as well as diminishes their ability to use economic resources to mobilize political influence, the persistence of traditional relations of production will jeopardize equal political opportunity.

Similar problems obtain when civil society's voluntary social-interest groups and public-welfare administration are absent, depriving markets of the private and public regulation required to guarantee equal economic opportunity. Traditional societies may supply other avenues to insure security to their members, but such measures will always guarantee livelihoods bounded by the hierarchies and "natural" restrictions that may leave individuals traditionally satisfied but politically hobbled.

A free-enterprise economy lacking sufficient social-interest-group advocacy and public-welfare policing may well underlie a political regime of universal suffrage and office open to all. Yet because free enterprise does not alone make a society civil, the abiding insecurity of economic freedom corrupts any supervening democracy into the "bourgeois democracy" that Marx and Lenin justly condemn for cloaking rule by the economically privileged behind the facade of self-government. Because economic inequality under conditions of free enterprise still subjects the underprivileged to an economic dependency limiting their resources for political action and leaving their political participation vulnerable to economic pressures, a regime of "laissez-faire" undermines political freedom.[16]

For their part, neither socialization through public ownership of all enterprise nor worker self-management can alone remove the economic domination that undercuts equal political opportunity. A centrally planned economy prohibiting private ownership of capital could certainly avoid the tyranny of vanguard party rule by following democratic collective control of economic management. Nevertheless, if such public ownership and management suspended all commodity exchange, individuals would lose the freedom of need and occupation that markets facilitate, without gaining any more political autonomy than state regulation of markets already provides. Moreover, as the history of "socialist" regimes bleakly testifies, nationalization of private enterprise leaves completely open what disparities in earning, consumption, and working conditions may prevail among different economic sectors, as well as within individual production units. Whereas the curtailing of market freedom prevents self-government from upholding the totality of right, equal political opportunity remains in jeopardy from the abiding threat of economic disadvantage that can affect political participation and influence.

The decentralized socialisms of "industrial democracy" and collectively self-managed communes fall prey to the same difficulties. Although industrial cooperative and commune members may have an equal say in their collective assignments of occupation and consumption, they still lose the economic autonomy to choose independently their needs and occupations by which equal economic opportunity is defined. Further, not only may economic inequality be imposed within cooperatives and communes, but the market interaction among them will continually generate the same disparities in fortune that afflict competing enterprises no matter how they are owned or managed. Hence, syndicalist socialism is no more a sufficient condition for political freedom than centrally planned socialism. Although both socialisms might be subject to a further public policing to guarantee economic equality, their common restrictions upon the forms of ownership and management of capital, together with the accompanying impositions upon the freedoms of occupation and need, make them obstacles to the self-imposition of the *totality* of right that politics should achieve. Public enterprise and worker self-management lose the latter liability only when they relinquish economic hegemony and take their due place as permissible forms among others that enterprise ownership and management can take. In that case, they figure as institutions of economic freedom in a market realizing the manifold shapes that capital can take, contrary to the narrow vision of the labor theory of value, which mistakenly conflates commodity production with privately owned, wage-labor-employing capital.[17] So long as they then undergo the private and public intervention that makes markets sufficiently civil, these alternate forms of enterprise shield politics from the oppressive economic formations that subvert self-government.[18]

1.11 CIVIL LEGALITY AS A PRECONDITION OF SELF-GOVERNMENT

The lawfulness inherent in right makes legalization an appropriate vehicle for guaranteeing the realization of every form of self-determination subject to external regulation. Because each entitled freedom of every agent is such as to coexist with the exercise of that same prerogative on the part of all others, each right is specifiable by a law capturing the common unity of volitions it represents. Although moral accountability is as lawful as any other right, the internal character of purpose, intention, and conscience precludes legal enforcement of conscientious conduct, other than respecting the negative injunction not to treat individuals as if they lacked moral responsibility. Property, family, and economic rights, by contrast, have external dimensions that make them obvious candidates for legal promulgation and enforcement, just as would be whatever political rights are ingredient in the public practice of self-government. Without legalization, each such freedom lacks an objectively recognized formulation with the appropriately universal content that can be supplied by legal enactment but not by uncodified tradition and custom.[19]

Because legality treats all legal subjects as not only equal before the law, but subjects of universal modes of conduct, any practices that lack that equality and universality are incompatible with legalization. For this reason, property right, household emancipation, and markets regulated on behalf of equal economic opportunity are prerequisites of civil law. In their absence, individuals are subject to personal bondage, family hierarchies, and economic ranks that stamp conduct with traditional differences to which particular decrees and commands but not common laws can apply.

Yet can civil law itself be a *prerequisite* of political freedom? Does not law emanate *from* political authority, first and foremost as enshrined in constitutionality, and then through the positive legislation by which self-government achieves rule by all over all? To the degree that political freedom involves rule by law, as well as under law, governing by enacting and enforcing statutes under constitutional guidelines, there can be little doubt that *some* law proceeds from political association. But can *all* law, let alone *any* law be political unless legality already prevails within civil society?

If all law were identifiable with the will of the sovereign, i.e., political in origin, common law and judicial precedent would be precluded.[20] The presence of such legal phenomena testifies to how law can be operative in civil society without state enactment. Although constitutionality may prove to be the ultimate seat of legal authority, law can stipulate the prepolitical rights of individuals in civil society so long as they generally recognize its legitimacy by predominantly interacting in respect of its mandates. Indeed, codification of civil law can occur without any parliamentary legislation simply by means of civil judges, lawyers, legal scholars, or other competent figures systematizing existing rules and customs into a publicized body of law that gains prevailing acceptance as authoritative. Although need might be felt for some foundational rule of recognition to identify what counts as law, such as that law is what is enacted by parliament and approved by the head of state, any such principle can only rest upon the fact of its own observance, for nothing else can confer authority upon it if it is the rule that makes rules valid laws. Consequently, a civil code can command authority simply in virtue of being generally recognized as that compendium of rules that is the positing of right.[21]

If this secures the possibility of law in civil society, prior to political association, what makes this possibility a prerequisite for self-government is the role that civil legality plays in upholding the freedoms that are themselves preconditions of equal political opportunity. Because civil legality gives prepolitical freedoms the objective and universal specification appropriate to right and then provides them with legal enforcement, it socially guarantees the modes of self-determination that individuals must enjoy in order to participate in self-government. Precisely insofar as property right, household emancipation, and equal economic opportunity are prerequisites of political freedom, the civil legality that insures the realization of these prepolitical rights is equally indispensable. Without legalization and legal enforcement, prepolitical rights lack a recognizably objective determination and an objectively secured actuality. Since a deficit on either score threatens individuals with oppressions that block their access to political activity, there must be law in civil society before there can be self-government by and under law.[22]

Moreover, if self-government turns out to require rule both

under and by law, self-legislating citizens must already stand in prepolitical relations that are congruent with lawful relationships. Otherwise, the nonpolitical associations of prospective self-governing citizens will conflict with their political autonomy. Since civil legality's enforcement of prepolitical rights achieves this congruence, it is indispensable to political emancipation.[23] Although civil legality does not itself comprise the rules of the game of self-government, it comprises the preliminary law without which that game cannot take place.[24]

1.12 PARTICULAR CULTURAL PRECONDITIONS OF POLITICAL EMANCIPATION

Because every exercise of right involves recognition of agents by one another, as expressed in the correlation of their respective volitions, the realization of self-determination cannot be indifferent to cultural practices that interfere with the recognition processes of autonomy. Although the intersubjective interaction of right may be accompanied by an indeterminate variety of psychological contents, cultural diversity always affects the relations between individuals that concern conduct.

Two features endemic to culture make it decisive for emancipation. First, unlike the inward vagaries of personal consciousness, culture is the common public endowment of a plurality of individuals, who give external expression to a distinctive shared self-understanding in the customs and productions that connect them under some cultural unity. Second, although culture may include expressly insignificant patterns of behavior, the cultural spheres of art, religion, and philosophy all lay claim to the highest values of humanity. In their respective modalities of beauty, faith, and reason, they each present some interpretation of what is held to be of universal importance. Since cultures will distinguish themselves by different estimations of how central self-determination is to normativity in conduct, they cannot all be equally amenable to the emancipation that political freedom brings to totality.[25] Whether this variance in cultural enthusiasm for freedom has implications for right is complicated by the different ways in which the three spheres of high culture (art, religion, and philosophy) provide their self-understandings of what is ultimately significant for humanity.

1.13 FINE ART AND SELF-GOVERNMENT

Although the creation, being, and reception of works of art have personal dimensions that might lead one to view each as a function of the self, they constitutively refer to others, and indeed, to rational agents in general, to whom art directs its imaginative union of meaning and configuration. Moreover, since art can be worthy of its universal address only by shaping matters of fundamental significance to rational agents, it must aesthetically transfigure ethical and religious themes, the two arenas of noninstrumental activity susceptible to sensible configuration.[26] Nonetheless, with the exception of performance art, where the artistic creation is itself a form of activity, the work of art does not directly enter the sphere of conduct. And even in such cases, artistic performance will be set off from prosaic life by the conventions of artistic transfiguration, preventing the fictions of theater from making all the world a stage. Of course, the creative process and the protocols of reception may well involve relationships impinging upon right, as when the production of art and the organization of its display utilize forms of oppression. Whether these violations of right are necessary to the creation and reception of any such works is another matter. If they are contingent to the art at issue, it is their engagement, rather than the art, that interferes with emancipation.

In order for any determinate form of art to play any necessarily facilitating role for political autonomy, some link must be established between the cultural existence of its beauty and the institutions of freedom. Artists may create and audiences may relish works that give expression to a self-understanding of humanity in which all striving of the self is an unessential epiphenomenon of an absolute absorbing all differentiation into a sublime unity, just as they may instead follow a classical bent and identify beauty with a vision of humanity in which everything essential is immediately joined to external appearance, ignoring the inner recesses of conscience and the pure abstraction by which personhood transcends all natural differences. Even if these artforms present truths incompatible with a complete realization of right, the fact of their contemporary production and appreciation need not preclude a degree of rectitude in conduct sufficient to sustain property relations, emancipated households, a civil society, or self-government. Because the creation and reception of art leave prosaic conduct largely untouched by their own workings, how aesthetic vision interplays with political commitment is essentially subject to external contingencies. After all, those whose artistic tastes reflect a different worldview may still act in "bad faith," participating in practices of right while pining with nostalgia for other ages. Admittedly, artistic allegiances may betray dispositions for other forms of community, but unless these dispositions manifest themselves in open rebellion to right, cultural dissidents may still man their stations in the regime of political freedom. When and if artistic leanings ever correlate with sufficient resistence to emancipation to block self-government is an empirical question for the ever corrigible interpretations of historical understanding.

For these reasons, political justice cannot depend with any necessity upon the removal or fostering of any particular forms of art. A culture giving highest place to rational autonomy may well find most compelling the artistic forms that give fitting expression to that self-understanding, forms that recognize the inability of exhausting autonomy in any sensible embodiment, substituting, for example, the open, self-propelled striving of the novel for the closed world of the epic.[27] Yet whether these forms must predominate before self-government can proceed is another matter. The indeterminacy of the relation is such that any politically enforced culture war to restrict artistic styles would be more of a bane than a blessing for emancipation or aesthetic achievement.

1.14 RELIGION AND POLITICAL FREEDOM

The case of religion is more ambiguous. The creation, display, and reception of a work of art can leave the prosaic world of conduct largely unscathed, even when subjecting it to the most withering unmasking. By contrast, religion can, if not must, draw the line between sacred and profane so as to intrude directly upon each and every sphere of conduct. Although religion might seem to turn more resolutely away from mundane affairs by seeking truth in not art's external union of meaning and configuration, but the inner recesses of faith, religion turns to the divine to discover how individuals should relate to it, and in so doing, to one another, to attain their own essence. Because how the divine is construed determines both how individuals view what is of ultimate importance for themselves and how they ought to come together in its pursuit, religion has the potential to conflict with any secular regime that invests validity in self-determination rather than holy authority.

The independent normativity of freedom is certainly incompatible with the privileging of any particular religious faith. Officially favoring one creed over another injects political inequality between believers in that faith and all others who do or might belong to the body politic.[28] Indeed, this poses problems for religion itself, with which civil society is bound to be concerned. Since politically privileging any particular religion leaves all others in a disadvantaged relation to the state, the independence of all these religions is jeopardized by giving one faith special political recognition. Moreover, privileging one religion may even compromise its own creed, if it recognizes the autonomy of individual belief and seeks only those who turn to faith without coercion.[29] Yet even if all citizens belong to the official faith, leaving none thereby disadvantaged, and that faith can consistently be a state religion, tying self-government to any particular religion lends autonomy a transcendent foundation at odds with the foundation-free validity of self-determination. Religious unanimity may enable all citizens to adhere voluntarily to the state religion, but in so doing, none enjoy the right to believe or not believe as they see fit, nor to govern themselves independently of any religious dogma.

Unrestricted toleration of religion, however, is equally incompatible with emancipation. Although some religions may be tolerable, others may not only be intolerant of one another, but demand the triumph of oppressive sacred law and practice over respect for rights. Insofar as religions are distinguished by how they represent the divine, and how this representation dictates different forms of worship and different prescriptions of what is of fundamental value in life, they cannot all be equally amenable to freedom. Only those religions that can let go of secular existence and allow individuals to enjoy self-determination in every sphere of conduct can ever harmoniously coexist with political freedom. Unless religions undergo the internal reformation that removes their own intolerance of rights, they remain an obstacle to emancipation.

If religion were merely a matter of inward belief, the problem would be little different from that posed by artistic refusals to accept the normativity of freedom. Art and religion could be equally tolerated, since neither would have any automatic bearing upon the prospects of emancipation. Yet, because religion involves not only faith, but religious community and religious regulation of behavior, the diversity of religion is not benignly contained within the pages of books or the walls of museums, theaters, or concert halls. The exclusive normativity of freedom mandates that states have no authority to restrict any religious practices so long as they do not intrude upon the observance of rights. When, however, religions trample upon the rights of their own coreligionists and/or individuals of different or no faith, the realization of freedom cannot be completed until these abuses are curtailed.

Political freedom therefore rests upon not unrestricted religious toleration, but the completed reformation of religion that brings religious practice into conformity with respect for right. How this occurs is a contingent affair of history, as contingent as the rise of self-government. Nevertheless, what that reformation must involve is mandated by the content of the different spheres of right.

Individuals cannot exercise their most rudimentary freedom as owners of property unless they have access to some external domain in which no other agency dwells. Nature must therefore be disenchanted if individuals are to be able to externalize their will in some factor that others can recognize to embody their self-determination as persons. If religion identifies the divine with nature, revering natural forces and investing the natural environment with spirit, humanity gets deprived of any space for self-determination. Accordingly, property rights, and all the other rights they make possible, become consistently attainable for believers only once they worship the divine as something distinct from nature.

Moral freedom's right of conscience can be respected only if religion grants its faithful two coordinate liberties—the entitlement to choose which creed if any one will adhere to and the entitlement to interpret independently one's religious doctrine. The moral autonomy to individually determine the good for which conscientious subjects hold themselves accountable is blocked by any religion that requires belief in its sacred doctrine and confers doctrinal interpretation exclusively to some clerical authority.

Religious belief and practice must further modify itself to conform to family right, which entitles individuals to marry without restriction to religious affiliation, race, sexual orientation, or anything else unconnected to the observance of conjugal and parental obligations. Family freedom will be violated so long as a religion rejects interfaith marriage, requires conversion of a nonobservant spouse, or mandates any other limitations upon marital autonomy and the equality of spouses.

The social freedoms of civil society mandate their own economic, legal, and cultural challenges to religious reform. To be compatible with equal economic opportunity and equal legal standing, religion must purge itself of all endorsement of social ranks defined by birth and other natural differences. Moreover, religion must acknowledge the authority of civil law and its legal enforcement of the rights of civil society. This requires the privatization of religion, whereby religious law relinquishes any hegemonic claims, leaving submission to its edict a voluntary private matter, subject to the limits that civil law imposes upon conduct in households and society. Only when religion accepts this privatization, ceasing to be an all-encompassing way of life, can faith conform to civil freedom and coexist in mutual toleration with other religions that similarly reform themselves.

On this basis, religion can be strictly separated from politics and the institutions of political freedom can operate without religious impediment. This separation entails that religious organizations be barred from fielding religiously defined political parties that vie for office, as well as that individuals relinquish any position of religious authority when they take public office. These measures are necessary to prevent subordinating political power to the particular interest of a religious faction, reducing self-government to a domination of one segment of the citizenry over everyone else. Because the capture of political power by a religious group jeopardizes not only equal political opportunity, but social and family freedom as well, the prohibition of religious organizations from entry into politics is as central a safeguard of civil society as it is a bulwark of self-government.

The reforms religion must undergo to be compatible with the institutions of freedom are not external impositions upon religion. While political self-determination and its enabling nonpolitical spheres of right need no foundation in religion or any other factor, the religious reformation required for political emancipation is equally dictated by wholly religious concerns. Because religion seeks in our relation to the divine what is of fundamental worth to humanity, the identification of freedom and value is of central theological significance. Any creed that religiously mandates oppression will be plagued by the dilemmas of foundational justification that can only be surmounted by acknowledging the exclusive normativity of self-determination. To fulfill religion's own vocation of finding the truth of humanity in our relation to the divine, religious faith must construe divinity so that our relation to it entails human emancipation. To present the divine's true injunctions to humanity, religious law must be a privatized law of freedom, entitling individuals to worship as they see fit and belong to their religious community voluntarily without obstructing anyone's rights as owners, moral subjects, free and equal spouses and parents, members of civil society, and self-governing citizens.

The ecumenical tolerance that results does not comprise a fatal capitulation to religious relativism. Far from undermining religion's constitutive claim to find our essential truth in humanity's relation to the divine, the privatization enabling religion to conform to right is what alone upholds religion's absolute truth. By privatizing its doctrine in accord with the institutions of freedom, a religion can tolerate other faiths while confirming the exclusive validity of religious doctrines whose divinity prescribes human emancipation.

No sacred text can present insurmountable obstacles to such reformation. Although fundamentalists would like to rigidify religious dogma by privileging a literal reading to the exclusion of all others, no text can interpret itself. Religious dogma is therefore always subject to reinterpretation. Given the dilemmas of foundational justification and the normativity of self-determination, theological debate will always face the challenge of reinterpreting sacred texts to enable them to satisfy the demands of right. Admittedly, some accepted understandings must be retained to allow reinterpretation to effect religious reform rather than to establish a new religion. Nonetheless, the experience of modern religious history testifies to how the most varied creeds are susceptible to reformation in an ecumenical spirit. For this reason, what warrants constraint are not religious texts but religious conduct in violation of right.[30]

1.15 PHILOSOPHY AND THE JUST STATE

The philosophy of right may conceive the normativity of self-determination and the universal determination of the realization of freedom. Nevertheless, conceiving what the philosophy of right seeks to know is not something that is a constitutive element of its object. Although no right can be exercised unless individuals preponderantly recognize their own entitlements and honor those of their counterparts, the recognition process of self-determination need not involve the philosophical conception of rights, which determines them in their systematic development. The practice of rights merely requires that participating agents have a working acquaintance with the due boundaries of their various prerogatives, an acquaintance that civil law first makes publicly available in authoritative form. When constitutionality sets within the state a separately articulated standard of its own normative operation, this must be sufficiently recognized by those who act in its light for the state to maintain its own identity. Yet the constitution is not the concept of political freedom any more than a working command of constitutional law is a philosophical wisdom that knows the concept of the just state in its truth. Even if the constitution duly conforms to the principles of political and nonpolitical freedom, it does not contain these principles in the fashion that secures for them their legitimacy. Whereas the constitution manifests itself at best in the form of right opinion, philosophical cognition must know its object together with the justification for that knowledge.

Accordingly, the realization of political freedom does not depend upon citizen-philosophers, who know why what they practice is beyond disrepute. Indeed, the institutions of freedom may function under the blessings of philosophical positions that neither escape the dilemmas of foundational justification nor realize their own inadequacy as legitimating ideologies for the practices they sanction. Whatever be the prevailing philosophical schools, they need not have any determinate impact upon political emancipation because they may be ignored or misinterpreted by the majority of citizens, because they may mistake the political implications of their own arguments, and because the recognition process of political and nonpolitical freedoms need not involve the philosophical conception of the rights in play. Hence, even if philosophy can alone ultimately determine what makes a state just, the existence of political justice does not depend upon philosophical cognition.

NOTES

1. For this reason, the "right to democratic process" is, as Robert A. Dahl argues, not "merely formal" because to exercise self-government all the resources and institutions necessary to it must exist. See Dahl, *Democracy and Its Critics* (New Haven, CT: Yale University Press, 1989), p. 175.

2. See Carl Schmitt, *The Concept of the Political*, trans. George Schwab (New Brunswick, NJ: Rutgers University Press, 1976), p. 26ff.

3. See H. L. A. Hart, *The Concept of Law* (Oxford: Oxford University Press, 1982), p. 218.

4. This connection is partly acknowledged by Jürgen Habermas when he observes that legality and the welfare state can exist without democracy. See Habermas, *Between Facts and Norms: Contributions to a Discourse Theory of Law and Democracy*, trans. William Rehg (Cambridge, MA: MIT Press, 1996), p. 504.

5. This includes the other rights of ownership, including the rights to acquire unowned external objects, to contract with others and exchange property, and to receive compensation for damages to one's property. All of these depend upon prior recognition of one's ownership of one's own body, without which no action can count as a disposal of property by the one who performs it.

6. For a detailed systematic treatment of this right, including examination of whether conjugal freedom can be compatible with the extended family and nonmonogamous marriage, see Richard Dien Winfield, *The Just Family* (Albany: SUNY Press, 1998), pp. 63–130.

7. See James S. Fishkin, *Justice, Equal Opportunity, and the Family* (New Haven, CT: Yale University Press, 1983), pp. 3–4, 35–36, 49, 71, 145, 156, and John Rawls, *A Theory of Justice* (Cambridge, MA: Harvard University Press, 1971), pp. 74, 301, 511.

8. See Plato, *Republic*, bk. 5, 457b–466d.

9. Hannah Arendt describes the identity of public and private interests as a central tenant of totalitarian regimes. See Arendt, *The Origins of Totalitarianism*, new ed. with added prefaces (New York: Harcourt Brace Jovanovich, 1973), p. 432.

10. These connections are drawn in Arendt's *On Revolution* (New York: Viking, 1965), p. 74.

11. Extending democratic decision making throughout society, as Norberto Bobbio proposes (see Bobbio, *The Future of Democracy*, ed. Richard Bellamy, trans. Roger Griffin [Minneapolis: University of Minnesota Press, 1987], p. 55), undercuts the specific structures of social freedom, without enhancing either political autonomy or social justice. Habermas questions similar proposals of Cohen for a democratic self-organization of society. See Habermas, *Between Facts and Norms*, p. 305. For a detailed investigation of the problems of "democratizing" civil society, see "Should the Economy be Democratized?" in Winfield, *Autonomy and Normativity: Investigations of Truth, Right and Beauty* (Aldershot, UK: Ashgate, 2001), pp. 141–51.

12. Habermas acknowledges that the civil freedom and welfare guarantees of civil society provide the social independence first making possible the actualization of political rights. He qualifies this relationship as, however, being merely empirical, rather than conceptually necessary (Habermas, *Between Facts and Norms,* p. 504). As we shall see, contra Habermas's qualification, any deficit in any area of civil freedom presents an obstacle to equal political opportunity. This is true, even if, as Habermas observes, how private and public prerogatives must be allocated in particular circumstances to uphold social and political rights is both contingent upon perceived historical conjunctures and a proper matter of political debate (Habermas, *Between Facts and Norms,* p. 314).

13. For a more detailed systematic treatment of these points, see Winfield, *The Just Economy* (New York: Routledge, 1988), pp. 102–49.

14. For further analysis of these problems, see Winfield, *The Just Economy,* pp. 157–68.

15. For a systematic investigation of the limits of private intervention in the market, see Winfield, *The Just Economy,* pp. 169–82.

16. The contradiction between unregulated markets and equal political opportunity makes it possible for markets and the pluralist democracy of "polyarchy" to be considered logically independent, as Charles E. Lindblom argues in *Politics and Markets: The World's Political-Economic Systems* (New York: Basic Books, 1977) p. 165, even while recognizing the indispensability of markets to the negative liberal freedom from government intervention (*Politics and Markets,* p. 164). Once, however, a fully civil society regulates markets to uphold equal economic opportunity, the resulting economic autonomy becomes a necessary condition of equal political opportunity.

17. For a more detailed examination of the limits and false implications of the labor theory of value, see Winfield, *The Just Economy,* pp. 111–33.

18. The manifold forms of enterprise that civil society can regulate in conformity with equal economic opportunity undermine the narrow vision of agrarian republicans like Thomas Jefferson, who, as Dahl observes, so identified the social independence necessary for democracy with family farming that they could not foresee how American democracy could persist after farmers became a tiny fraction of the citizenry (Dahl, *Democracy and Its Critics,* pp. 253–54). Such agrarian republicans tend toward Jean-Jacques Rousseau's presumption that only household autarchy can shield the citizenry from the play of private interests that market

activity fosters, a play implicitly assumed to be irreconcilable with the universal ends of politics.

19. For further discussion of the normative superiority of codified law over custom and precedent, see Winfield, *Law in Civil Society* (Lawrence: University Press of Kansas, 1995), pp. 91–94, 117–19.

20. Thus it is not surprising that, as George Anastaplo observes, the United States Constitution takes for granted the common law. See Anastaplo, *The Constitution of 1787: A Commentary* (Baltimore: Johns Hopkins University Press, 1989), p. 4.

21. For this reason, even prior to political legislation, civil law can acquire a legal codification that overcomes the indeterminacies plaguing common law's reliance upon custom and judicial precedent. Although common law *may* approximate the content that civil law should contain to uphold the rights of individuals in civil society, it cannot give them the properly objective and universal form that their due legalization requires.

22. To the degree that the modern democratic state realizes self-government to some significant degree, Max Weber can rightly claim that modern democracy and the modern lawyer belong absolutely together. See Weber, *Political Writings*, ed. Peter Lassman and Ronald Speirs (Cambridge: Cambridge University Press, 1994), p. 329.

23. Self-government's necessity for self-legislation, for which civil legality provides the medium, can first be systematically considered in conceiving constitutionality and the division of powers, something addressed in chap. 3 and 4.

24. Bobbio characterizes the relation in these terms, concluding that the "liberal state," whose juridical rule upholds civil legality and its civil freedoms, is the legal and not just the historical precondition of the democratic state. Nonetheless, as Bobbio duly notes, the democratic state no less upholds the social freedoms of civil legality, which must be maintained to sustain the democratic political process. See Bobbio, *The Future of Democracy*, p. 26.

25. For this reason, Habermas is only partly correct in claiming that the identity of political community depends primarily on the legal principles anchored in the *political culture* and not on an *ethical-cultural* form of life as a whole. See Habermas, *Between Facts and Norms*, p. 513. Because political freedom cannot be exercised without an emancipated household and a civil society, the "ethical-cultural" form of life remains crucial.

26. For a detailed treatment of why this is so, see Richard Dien Winfield, *Systematic Aesthetics* (Gainesville: University Press of Florida, 1995), pp. 106–61.

27. For an examination of how artistic style and worldview correlate, see Richard Dien Winfield, *Stylistics: Rethinking the Artforms After Hegel* (Albany: SUNY Press, 1996).

28. As Michael Walzer observes, when, as with the Puritan regime of Cromwell, religious sanctity is tied to rule, elections must give way to search committees of the religiously enlightened that seek other "saints" to run the government. See Walzer, *Spheres of Justice* (New York: Basic Books, 1983), p. 246.

29. Salvation, Walzer points out, is ordinarily regarded to be incompatible with coercive distribution. See Walzer, *Spheres of Justice*, p. 248.

30. For further discussion of these issues, with particular attention to modernization and Islam, see Richard Dien Winfield, "Modernity, Religion and the War on Terrorism," *International Readings in Theory, History and Philosophy of Culture* 18 (2004): 329–47.

CHAPTER 2

THE BASIC FEATURES OF POLITICAL SELF-DETERMINATION

2.1 WITH WHAT MUST POLITICAL PHILOSOPHY BEGIN?

The starting point of political philosophy is not a matter of convenience, contingent upon the interests or whims of any particular theorist or cultural community. Although the annals of political thought present a motley parade of beginnings, one start has exclusive authority. The mandate on which it rests is already apparent. The concept of the political can have theoretical necessity only as a normative conception of political justice, since otherwise it remains an empirical descriptive category devoid of strict universal application. .Given the exclusive validity of self-determination, the normative politics that political philosophy must address can be nothing other than the reality of political freedom. Therefore, political philosophy must begin with what comes first in the conception of political self-determination.

This injunction is not an empty mandate. What is primary in conceiving political freedom does not hang in midair, awaiting the eruption of some protean source of sovereignty. Political philosophy is not only a normative discipline, but the capstone of ethics that both consummates the system of right and presupposes the accounts of property, moral, family, and civil self-determination. Consequently, the starting point of the conception of political freedom already bears the imprint of the forms of right that precede it in thought and reality. From the outset, however, the determination of political right must be irreducible to the prepolitical practices that both make it possible and become incorporated under the domain of the sovereign state. Otherwise, the putatively political will fall back within civil society and never provide ends, activities, or agencies that escape the orbit of property, moral, household, or social concerns. To transcend civil society without appeal to factors extraneous to freedom, the minimal threshold of normative political association must nonetheless rely on nothing but what civil society furnishes. It must comprise a type of interaction that members of civil society can undertake without having to depend upon any further institutions that, being neither civil nor political in character, would have to be defined by heteronomous practices, determined by foundations of one sort or another.

Yet as much as the initial determination of valid politics transcends civil society and all that it contains independently of any external foundation, what comes first in political philosophy must be the most minimal specification of political justice, containing no further political relationship, but entering into every other dimension of normative politics. If instead any factors incorporating other political features were present at the start, political philosophy would beg its question, presupposing aspects of politics for which it must first give an account.

Because normative politics is political self-determination and political philosophy is the normative conception of political association, the starting point of the theory of political justice is the most elementary determinacy of political freedom, incorporated in all further aspects of self-government. Moreover, because political association has conceptual, as opposed to contingent empirical, determinacy only as normative political community, the minimal determinacy of political freedom, the starting point of the conception of political right, is the very concept of the political, a concept that possesses its proper theoretical independence and universality only by coinciding with the concept of political freedom.

As such, the identity of the legitimate beginning of political philosophy can be confirmed in two ways, one providing an indirect, negative certification, the other affording a progressive, positive vindication that becomes complete only when political freedom has its reality determined in its entirety. On the one hand, because the starting point of political philosophy must consist in the minimal determination of political freedom, it must contain no other independently given political element. Hence, the putative beginning must be conceived solely with what is provided by the antecedent conception of the prepolitical spheres of right, contained within the concept of civil society. No identifiably political factor can be permitted to play any foundational role, for free politics, like any other freedom, must be what it has determined itself to be. What is at issue is how individuals, enjoying all their civil rights, can will in respect to one another in a fashion constitutive of a distinctly political freedom, obtaining the supervening right of equal political opportunity. No *particular* political relationship nor any factor given independently of self-determination can possibly provide the required entry into normative politics.

On the other hand, in order to vindicate the putatively minimal determinacy of political freedom, all further aspects of just politics must be shown to incorporate it. If this proves to be the case, the ensuing determination of political justice will retrospectively validate the point of departure, demonstrating not that the start is the determining ground of all valid politics, but that it is the most elementary component shared by all facets of the just state. Because valid politics is political self-determination, the just state cannot have any foundation, political or otherwise. What comes first in the conception of the political is not a grounding principle of political justice, be it teleological or procedural but rather the minimal component ingredient in every other dimension of political association. What then is the minimal determination of valid politics?

Because political justice is a mode of self-determination, it must minimally contain what every structure of right involves: correlated volitions by which agents interact such that what each wills as well as what form of agency each exercises are determined by their concomitant actions independently of any externally given parameters. As a mode of self-determination, political action cannot help but comprise a lawful form of willing by which agents each exercise a range of discretion such that they all can practice that same type of prerogative without mutual interference. Accordingly, political association will combine right and duty such that the form of willing in which each participant engages will be both something to which each is entitled and something that can only be exercised by simultaneously respecting the right of others to enjoy the same freedom.

Further, insofar as political freedom can only be exercised within standing institutions of self-government, valid political association must exhibit the features common to every form of ethical community: that agents exercise a type of self-determined agency that can only be had by belonging to an existing association already realizing the freedom that its members enjoy in performing the roles in which their membership consists. Like any other ethical community, political association provides individuals with a right that they can only wield by belonging to an existing organization reproduced by the coordinated roles to which their participation entitles them. Consequently, the good at which they aim, a good lying in the realization of the self-determination in which their membership consists, is a good that can only be pursued by being already realized in the existing institution in which they participate.

Because these features of right in general and ethical community in particular do not individuate political freedom, political association must minimally involve further marks that uniquely differentiate political self-determination from nonpolitical conduct. As with every mode of self-determination, the individuating factors must reside in the constituent elements of freedom: the character of the ends, practice, and agency in play. Since self-determination indissolubly links end and agency together, such that the form of agency is what is willed, whatever is distinctive about political agency is interconnected with whatever distinguishes the ends of politics from those of every other activity.

2.2 THE FOUR CARDINAL FEATURES OF POLITICAL SELF-DETERMINATION: UNIVERSALITY, REFLEXIVITY, SUPREMACY, AND AUTONOMY

The end of valid politics stands distinguished from the ends of every other form of right in two respects: on the one hand, it incorporates all other rights within the political good, and on the other hand, it transcends them all by both willing their realization in common and willing the supervening activity by which political association realizes all forms of right in conjunction with its own presiding autonomy. By having this totalizing character, political association always involves a volition with an end that is universal in the specific sense of aiming at the realization of the totality of right, the totality of lawful, objective freedom, as a self-grounded whole. Whereas property right aims at a particular embodiment of the person's will in a particular external factor, whereas morality aims at realizing a subjectively determined good that is defined by the particular purpose and intention of the agent, whereas family freedom aims at upholding the particular good of a household, and whereas civil freedom aims at realizing the particular self-selected interests of economic agents under the protection of law, political action always aims at upholding the entire fabric of freedom in all its dimensions, seeking to impose the order of right upon the spheres of conduct it encompasses.[1] Whatever may be the ancillary purposes and interests that accompany political action, conduct is only political to the degree that it aims at governing, at imposing the form of the entire order of freedom upon the self-determined community to which it itself belongs.[2]

Due to the characteristic universality of the end of politics, political freedom is distinguished by a reflexivity that no other mode of self-determination can equal. Alone among the forms of right, political self-determination imposes the order to which it belongs upon itself and does so as the very object of its volition. Although illegitimate "states" may lack complete reflexivity by having a ruling class imposing an order upon a subject class excluded from governing, political freedom realizes an identity between ruler and ruled by achieving a self-government where political agents act upon their own activity, imposing the order of political freedom upon themselves.

For this reason, normative political association is neither natural nor artificial in character. Whereas inanimate natural things have a given determinacy determined in a nexus of external causality, the self-activity of political emancipation imposes its order upon itself. Since the reflexivity of political association is not blind, but operates through the conscious willing by political agents of a political good to which their own activity belongs, its realization depends upon the presence within itself of knowledge of its own form. Consequently, the structure of normative politics cannot be reducible to the organic unity of natural life. The living thing may sustain itself through the complementary interaction of its functionally differentiated organs, but none of these organs performs its function upon the basis of knowledge of the unity of the whole, nor with the self-determined purpose that allows. The concrete unity of the organism may be continually reproduced by the life process, but it remains something whose character is given independently of any knowing or willing internal to it. Although an artifact may exhibit the work of knowing and willing by incorporating a form imposed upon its matter by the conscious deed of some artificer, the artifact contains within itself neither its artificer, nor the knowing and willing by which it was produced. Normative political association, by contrast, contains the agents by and upon whose conscious deeds it is reproduced. This is what permits emancipated politics to be a structure of self-activity, exhibiting the reflexivity that neither merely natural nor artificial entities can possess.[3]

Whatever be the details of the institutional reality of self-government, each and every element in political self-determination involves this reflexivity by participating in the self-activity by which free politics renders right a self-determined totality. No other structure of right can possibly exhibit the same reflexivity for the simple reason that political activity aims at upholding their freedoms as well. Even though the configuration of the other spheres of right issues from the respective self-determinations of their participants, it is not directly self-imposed as the conscious end of their characteristic practices. Instead, the final form and interconnection of the other spheres of right rests upon the aegis of the encompassing freedom of self-government, whose supremacy allows free politics to have its unrivaled reflexivity.

This supremacy is the third cardinal feature of the minimal determinacy of political self-determination. It is indissolubly intertwined with the universality and reflexivity of political freedom. Precisely because the political good is a universal aim, encompassing all particular rights, it commands exclusive authority to determine the totality of right. Other freedoms may determine ends and agencies within their own particular sphere, but none determine the compatible shape and interconnection of each and every right, as political freedom alone does. Moreover, only political freedom determines the order of political association, even if the nonpolitical rights are preconditions of equal political opportunity. Precisely because upholding the other spheres of right is a necessary element in the self-maintenance of political freedom, the independent supremacy of political association is not limited by the prepolitical conditions of self-rule. By dictating and enforcing the final specification of the compatible realization of each and every right, political freedom determines is own preconditions and regulates their boundaries,[4] performing this service as an integral part of its own distinctively supreme agency. By contrast, all other rights ultimately depend upon political action for their legitimate actuality within the system of right.[5]

The exclusive supremacy of normative political association thus affords self-government an absolute autonomy distinguishing political freedom from all the other freedoms over which it presides. Whereas they must endure partial modification to achieve the integration within the self-ordered system of political community that secures their existence through freedom, political agents exercise an autonomy that is what it alone has determined itself to be.

The universality of aim, reflexivity, supremacy, and autonomy of the political all imply one another. By willing the totality of right, political freedom cannot help but act reflexively upon itself, reign supreme over all other spheres of right, and thereby enjoy an unrivaled autonomy. By willing reflexively, political agency cannot be particular in aim, for any merely particular ends would be contrasted to other independently given particulars, whose relationship would have to depend upon some other factor, leaving political agency part of an order it has not imposed upon itself.[6] Similarly, reflexivity cannot be achieved without supremacy and autonomy, for if politics were subordinate to any other agency, political association would not be what it has determined itself to be but receive its form from elsewhere. For its part, supremacy guarantees that political authority is subject only to itself and thereby reflexive, that its ends encompass all others and thereby enjoy universality, and that its rule is fully autonomous. The autonomy of the political equally entails reflexivity, universality, and supremacy, since dependence introduces an external determiner undermining the unity of ruler and ruled, makes the ends of politics' particulars contingent upon those of its master, and removes the supremacy of political association.

2.3 THE MINIMAL DETERMINACY OF CITIZEN

Because self-determination always determines not only the ends and practices with which its autonomy operates but also the type of agent in action, the minimal features of political freedom provide a basic determination of normative political agency. Like any other personification of right, this agency is given neither by nature nor in function of the self. Instead, it is a product of history, arising with the enactment of the intersubjective practice of self-government in which political rights have their actuality. Although the historical character of its genesis leaves contingent when, where, and if normative political agency ever arises, it has a timeless identity defined by the concept of right. The agency determining itself in and through political freedom when and wherever self-government emerges comprises the normative persona of the citizen, by reference to which all partial, illegitimate forms of citizenship can be identified and critiqued.

As the constitutive agent of political freedom, the citizen is minimally determined by the same cardinal features of universality, reflexivity, supremacy, and autonomy that distinguish political right. Agents determine themselves as citizens insofar as they will the universal aim of political association, an aim that simultaneously contains the concordant safeguarding of the nonpolitical rights making equal political opportunity possible and the perpetuation of the institutions of self-government within which individuals determine themselves as self-ruling citizens. The content of this aim gets further concretized through the specific modalities by which political freedom is exercised, but in every case it involves the constitutive good of political right, whose totalizing character affirms political and nonpolitical freedoms in unity. Individuals may always act in departure from this governing aim, but in so doing, they violate the entitled prerogatives of free citizenship and thereby obstruct the operation of self-rule. In order to partake of the reflexivity of political freedom, citizens must interact in terms of a realized equal political opportunity that has overcome any subordination to social, household, or any other nonpolitical institutions.

If any nonpolitical powers, be they secular or sacred, succeed in compelling government to serve their interests, no individuals can wield the bona fide political autonomy that imposes order upon the totality of conduct. If religious authority stamps its law upon secular affairs, free citizenship is just as much a hollow pretender as when dominant economic interests in an insufficiently civil society reduce self-government to a "bourgeois" democracy.[7] In either case, the subordination of political activity to nonpolitical powers prevents individuals from exercising an agency that reflexively imposes the system of freedom upon itself. Instead, the subject political life of individuals serves a good it receives from elsewhere, which may fit the foundational ways of tradition, but not the foundation-free practice of self-determination.

Similarly, if any individual or group enjoys political privilege, it lords over politically disadvantaged subjects, transforming its ruling activity into a unilateral domination, where an agent imposes form upon a passive patient. Even if the politically underprivileged retain some participation in governance, any abiding exclusion from other political functions renders those privileged functions nonreflexive, insofar as they are executed by some upon the whole, while transforming the common remain into a subject activity, that neither determines the totality of the body politic nor the limits of its own operation. For this reason, the reflexivity of free citizenship requires political equality as well as political autonomy.

The equal political opportunity endemic to the reflexivity of emancipated political agency does not preclude citizens from performing different roles, such as distinguish government officials from one another and nonoffice holders. So long as these roles are open to all citizens in a real, and not merely formal sense, with selections ultimately codetermined by the citizenry at large, citizens are never acted upon politically independently of their own political participation.

What free citizenship precludes are any distinctions among citizens that differentially restrict their respective political activity in a manner external to the capacity to exercise rights. Although Kant may be correct to connect economic and domestic subjection with different opportunities for political participation, his corresponding differentiation between active and passive citizens reflects not a legitimate recipe for political association but rather an admission of how an incomplete emancipation of the household and society hinders the realization of equal political opportunity on which self-government depends.[8] The same can be said of Mill's advocacy of weighted voting in function of the varying levels of education of individuals.[9] Although otherwise competent independent agents can hardly politic on a par with others if they lack the basic formation to comprehend and enter the debate over how to govern themselves, their political liability demands not a diminished franchise but remedial intervention to supply the cultural prerequisites for their equal political opportunity. Political justice demands that as long as individuals are capable of learning, they are entitled to an education sufficient to participate in self-government, an education whose specific political focus goes beyond the education to which all members of civil society are entitled so as to achieve equal economic and legal opportunity.[10] For this reason, educating citizens for democracy is not a precondition, but an integral part of the practice of self-government,[11] by which citizens secure their own equal political opportunity, rather than receive tutelage from experts in justice.

The historical exclusions of women, slaves, caste pariahs, servants, workers, and ethnic and religious groups from equal political participation present the same violation of the equality of political right without which political self-determination reverts to political domination and subjection. As with any form of right, all that individuals need to qualify for political emancipation is the basic capability of rational agency. Since self-determination has unconditioned and exclusive normativity, no factor can legitimate the exclusion of any competent rational agent from any of the spheres of right. For this reason, what joins individuals together as citizens of a free body politic is not any ethnic, religious, or otherwise apolitically defined unity. The identity of a citizenry is legitimately prescribed by nothing but their common membership in a political association respecting the equal political opportunity of its participants, independently of anything besides their competence as rational agents.

If to be a citizen should not be conditioned by any extraneous prepolitical differences, such distinctions should not intrude upon the relations between citizens within the practice of self-government. Since every right represents a form of equal opportunity, no sphere of right can accommodate differentiated roles that obstruct the self-determination to which all their participants are entitled. Although household and social bondage may hamper the political opportunities of individuals, the fact of these prepolitical oppressions cannot legitimate the political inequality to which they contribute. Rather, precisely because political emancipation is predicated upon the emancipations of family and society, the right to political freedom has revolutionary implications for household and social organization.

Any restriction of political office to natural-born citizens, such as mandated by the United States Constitution for presidential aspirants, therefore represents a violation of political right, even when citizenship is left open to immigrants, regardless of their country of origin. Permitting only natural-born citizens to hold certain political positions divides the citizenry into two classes, one with full access to all positions, another with restricted political opportunity. Far from safeguarding political autonomy from foreign domination, to which place of birth makes no necessary contribution, such measures undercut self-government. By privileging one sector of the citizenry with certain opportunities to rule over an underprivileged sector whose members are banned from occupying the same position, qualification by birthplace strikes a blow to political freedom. No matter how many other positions may be left open to all, the reflexivity of equal political opportunity is compromised in ways that can easily foster more pervasive political oppressions based upon privileging factors like birth that can be considered natural insofar as they are not chosen by the individuals to which they apply.

Citizenship does warrant certain residency requirements to cope with transients whose political membership lies elsewhere. They can hardly be granted rights of local political participation when they will not be around to be subject to the political policies they help impose. If they were given full political rights in whatever body politic they pass through, the permanent residents would find themselves subject to an absentee political agency that they cannot subject in turn. Accordingly, political freedom need not be violated by the presence of nonresident aliens whose civil rights are guaranteed but who are excluded from participation in the political institutions of their host nation. So long as these nonresident aliens retain active citizenship in some other self-governing state, their political rights remain respected, without detracting from the political freedom of their sometime hosts. As for their civil rights, these demand respect regardless of national frontiers since the freedoms of civil society are global in character, applying to individuals no matter what be their political identity.

The situation is more problematic when permanent resident

aliens are admitted into the state but still deprived of the political rights of local citizenship. Although such permanent resident aliens may retain citizenship in their country of origin, their enduring absence from their homeland deprives them of any effective participation in its political process. Hence, their permanent residency in a nation that still treats them as aliens amounts to a deprivation of political freedom.[12] Even if they retain the passport of their country of origin, they are stateless as far as the exercise of self-government is concerned. Since nothing can legitimate the deprivation of political right, host nations of permanent resident aliens have no valid grounds for not extending full citizenship to those otherwise competent agents who are allowed to live permanently within their borders.[13] Failing to grant this extension may all too often amount to a contemporary adoption of the ancient Greek anomaly of resting self-government upon the labor of a politically excluded subject class of guest workers.[14]

Not until all such limitations are overturned can individuals attain the most sovereign of agencies that self-determination can possess: the free citizenship that practices the lawful willing of the entire system of right, enjoying the self-governing agency that can only operate in and through the institutions of equal political opportunity.

2.4 THE MINIMAL REQUIREMENTS FOR CITIZENSHIP

Although the process necessary for the genesis of political freedom is systematically conceivable only after self-government has been fully determined, the requirements for citizenship enter into the minimal specification of emancipated politics since every dimension of free politics involves individuals who satisfy these demands. Primary among these requirements is the competent rational agency without which no right can be exercised. Accordingly, an obviously indispensable element in the qualifications for citizenship is the capacity of choice, given by nature insofar as everything conventional presupposes it. Possession of this natural endowment suffices to entitle individuals to engage in each and every freedom, since the exclusive normativity of self-determination precludes any justification for depriving competent agents of freedoms they can exercise. By contrast, individuals who lack the capacity of choice, either because of congenital deficiencies, illness, or accident, will be unable to fulfill the role of citizen in any meaningful way.[15]

Possession of rational agency is still not sufficient by itself for engaging in self-government. Because the exercise of prepolitical rights is a precondition for political freedom, autonomous citizenship further requires actual participation in these conventions. Since any deficit in these prepolitical rights undercuts the equal political opportunity of individuals, no one can engage in self-government unless their property, moral, household, and civil rights are duly respected. To the degree that all these rights are upheld in civil society through the administration of civil law and public welfare, citizenship requires that individuals enjoy equal civil opportunity in all its constitutive dimensions. To be a self-governing citizen, individuals must simultaneously enjoy property, moral, family, and civil rights, not just formally, but in accord with the standards of equal opportunity. So long as individuals have rational agency, meeting these requirements is not a burden upon the individual but rather an imperative of social justice that normative politics must fulfill.

Moreover, because political rights, like any others, can only be enjoyed by knowing what they are and how to exercise them in respect for the correlative entitlements of others, prospective citizens must receive training in the articles and modalities of political freedom adequate to engage in self-government on a par with their fellow citizens. This instruction must furnish not only knowledge of the general content of political and nonpolitical rights and the general anatomy of the practices they entail, but the linguistic competence and worldly orientation needed to make one's entitled aims known to one's fellow rights holders and to comprehend their actions in turn. Although part of such formation is contained in the education that should be already publicly guaranteed in civil society to secure equal household and social opportunity, it adds a distinctly political element of its own. To ensure equal political opportunity, the education in question must be made available to all prospective citizens with as equal quality as possible.[16] Making this education exclusively public is not necessarily a solution, since standards may vary among public schools, whereas private schools may do an equivalent job.[17] What counts is that relatively comparable quality education be offered in all schools and that everyone have compulsory access to comparable educational opportunities irrespective of differences in personal or family resources.[18] If instead, individuals are educated simply at the discretion of parents, future citizens may find themselves disadvantaged by parental neglect and poverty.[19]

In addition, since the exercise of self-government requires actual participation in the body politic, individuals can hardly act as citizens unless they reside first and foremost in the community within whose jurisdiction their political agency is to be wielded. To the extent that a history of past residence can testify to a standing presence within the political community, residency requirements can duly fall within the qualifications for citizenship.

Unless these conventional endowments of prepolitical rights, education, and residency are joined to the natural capacity for rational choice, individuals will be unable to function as self-governing citizens. Yet, precisely because these requirements are all that are necessitated by participation in an emancipated body politic, no other requirements ought to intrude upon the qualification for free citizenship.

For this reason, normative political association ought not deprive citizenship on the basis of ethnicity, national origin, religious affiliation, gender, race, sexual orientation, or any other factor unrelated to the capability for self-government. Although past discrimination may encourage a state to grant automatic citizenship to members of the historically oppressed group, as in the case of modern Israel and the emerging state of Palestine, this will reproduce the political discrimination it seeks to remedy if that state fails to extend equal citizenship to all competent permanent residents of its domain, irrespective of their group origin.

Minors who have the potential, but lack the actuality of independent rational agency, may be unable to participate in self-government until reaching recognized maturity. Nevertheless, so long as they reside permanently within a body politic, it can have no grounds for not giving them full rights of citizenship upon their becoming adults. In the interim of childhood, individuals remain under the authority of guardians precisely because they are recognized to lack the fully developed autonomy to exercise their manifold rights and respect those of others. Whereas this tutelage has as its legitimate end the bringing up of children to the point of being able to determine themselves in every sphere of right, the rights of minors have a prospective character anticipating their passage to full participation in the institutions of freedom. For this reason, the citizenship of minors does not give them rights and duties of political participation, for which they are yet unfit but rather guarantees them a seamless transition to active citizenship upon recognition of maturity.

2.5 THE BASIC TERRITORIALITY OF NORMATIVE POLITICAL ASSOCIATION

The minimal qualifications for citizenship already imply the basic territoriality of political association to the degree that residency has some connection to engagement in self-government. In order to exercise an agency that reigns supreme over every sphere of conduct, the citizen must participate in an association that has a determinate jurisdiction encompassing the activities over which as well as by which it rules.

Every form of freedom has a spatiotemporal reality since individuals actually determine themselves only by giving their wills recognizable objectifications predicated upon mutual recognition of the autonomous volitions of one another. Property relations provide the most basic and omnipresently recognized objectivity for willing insofar as one cannot determine oneself in any other fashion unless one's own body is recognized to be exclusively appropriated by one's own will. What distinguishes the objectivity of political freedom from the actuality of the other forms of right is the encompassing nature it must possess in order to reign free and supreme as the reflexive autonomy determining of the entire system of right. Because the conduct of every other form of right must be contained within the domain of political rule, political association must have a spatial boundary persisting over time. This boundary may be subject to alteration in shape, size, and general location, but it must retain some recognizably abiding limit marking the frontier of its political dominion from what lies beyond. Otherwise political jurisdiction ceases to be definite and the subordination of civil institutions to self-government becomes unmanageable. So long as some border gives unity to the dominion of self-government, political association may, nonetheless, just as well follow the wanderings of a nomadic community across a fixed territory as remain in place upon the drifting continents of some planet hurtling around its sun while spiraling within the tendrils of a fast-receding galaxy. Even fragmentation into noncontiguous territories, be they nomadic or relatively rooted, is possible, so long as the unity of a self-governing citizenry can be feasibly maintained.

No factor other than the practicalities of self-government has any legitimate role to play in dictating the territory of political association. Neither religious imperatives, customary cultural boundaries, nor geographical features have any independent right to prescribe the frontiers of a politically autonomous community. These factors may enter in when they affect the possibility of individuals uniting into a self-governing citizenry that can uphold its sovereignty against external and internal threats. Possession of a shared history and its resultant community of remembrance and cultural practice can provide sufficient national feeling to facilitate unification under one government,[20] but a common territorial heritage need not be necessary for shared political solidarity. Although the presence of different races, nationalities, and religions may impede formation of enough fellowship to engage in collective self-rule, national borders may include the most diverse populations, provided sufficient recognition of political unity can be fostered.[21] Widespread acceptance of the cultural pluralism of civil society is necessary for self-government to extend its frontier over a diverse population, but civil toleration will not be enough unless that motley group is sufficiently willing to unite as one self-governing citizenry, instead of seeking political identity in other unities.[22] When the historical and cultural backdrop of frontiers fail to bar political unity, state boundaries owe their legitimacy to their contribution to the realization of right. Since right has an unconditioned normativity extending beyond particular national borders, the legitimacy of a frontier depends upon its impact upon the right of not only the citizenry united under that territory but of other individuals whose own prospects for political self-determination may be jeopardized by how boundaries get drawn.[23] Precisely how this sorts itself out is a contingent matter, relative to historical conjunctures that themselves are subject to flux.[24] To the extent that this question concerns relations between states, its full systematic treatment must await the conception of international relations, which presupposes and thereby must follow the completed conception of domestic political sovereignty.

In any event, since each and every political activity stands in relation to the territory of the political domain to which it belongs, the territoriality of the body politic is as basic to the identity of citizens as it is to the practice of their self-government. Entry and exit from the territory is subject to control for no other legitimate purpose than upholding political freedom, together with the nonpolitical freedoms that it encompasses and presupposes. If citizens have a right to emigrate, it is not because their citizenship rests upon a prior consent, as social contract theory would imagine.[25] The ethical community of self-government instead allows its members the right to leave the boundaries of the state so long as doing so neither jeopardizes the ongoing activities of political freedom nor violates their household and social obligations.

2.6 THE MINIMAL DETERMINATION OF CONSTITUTIONALITY

Besides having a territorial jurisdiction, political freedom is necessarily constitutional. Constitutionality enters into the concept of the political, that is, into the minimal determinacy of political right, through the coalescence of three elements of political justice: the lawful nature of right, the situated character of the ethical community of political association, and the reflexivity and supremacy of self-government by which political self-determination upholds all non-political rights as part of its own operation. Needless to say, the constitutionality in question is normative. Approximations of body politics may operate without full-fledged constitutional government but only in function of their failure to realize political freedom.

Abstractly speaking, constitutionality comprises a body of law providing the internal standard for the self-regulation of political association. The lawfulness of right makes constitutionality possible in this basic respect insofar as what holds valid in each sphere of conduct is susceptible of determination by law. Because rights always involve prerogatives of freedom that are universal, guaranteeing that each party's exercise of right can proceed in harmony with those of every other, rights are properly specifiable as lawful entitlements. As such, their objective realization demands the conceptually determinate and universally available expression that can only be provided by public promulgation as a body of standing law.[26] Moreover, because the lawfulness of right has an unconditioned normativity that rules of externally, rather than self-determined, conduct can never share, the body of law that communicates rights in their totality has an irrevocable and incorrigible authority. Consequently, not only can political association's realization of right measure itself by an internal body of law, but that privileged legal standard of right can have a finality distinguishable from the corrigible positive legislation that a standing legislature implements to realize rights in face of the contingent circumstances confronting citizens at home and abroad.

This finality does not signify that constitutional law is devoid of any positive dimension, involving determinations that cannot be derived from reason. Although the universal principles of right are rationally determinable insofar as they are mandated by the concept of self-determination, every level of right involves specifications that are purely a matter of discretion. In property right, for example, the general grounds for punishment and compensation may follow from the concepts of malicious and nonmalicious wrong, but reason is powerless to determine precisely how long a confinement is required by a particular crime, nor exactly how much compensation is required for a particular tort. Nor, for that matter, can reason derive from the concept of contract what exactly should be the formalities by which contractual agreements are certified to be valid. Yet, because right demands some objective determination, a decision must be made, and if such a decision is to have binding force for all in an unambiguous way, it must take the form of legal specification. The same situation applies to the remedying of malicious and nonmalicious violations of every kind of right, just as it applies to determinations of what exactly comprises due household care by parents and spouses, due resources for enjoying equal economic opportunity and legal aid, and such political matters as terms of office and size of legislative, executive, and judicial bodies. In each case, the realization of right requires an objective determination beyond the scope of reason but requiring legalization. For these reasons, the constitutional specification of the principles of right cannot help but incorporate a positive dimension, even if the authority of the constitution stands over and above the positive legislating of parliamentary bodies.

Moreover, because the positive elements of constitutional law may require alteration in face of changing circumstances, at least these portions of the constitution are susceptible to amendment. More general principles of right, such as those that prescribe the basic equal opportunity of each sphere of freedom, demand protection from the unconstrained license of amending quorums. Otherwise, the constitution loses all necessary connection to the realization of freedom, permitting right to be obliterated with legal impunity.[27]

This threat should indicate why political freedom is not equivalent with the license of citizens to impose any institutional order whatsoever upon themselves. That unsituated and unmediated discretion is perniciously formal insofar as it leaves completely undetermined whether what a citizenry gives its consent to is a system of equal participation in self-government or a submission to tyranny.[28] Far from restricting the political liberty of citizens, normative constitutionality is what first constitutes individuals as agents institutionally associated so as to govern themselves. For this reason, the exercise of political freedom is fundamentally different from the constituting activity by which a constitutional order is produced. The latter constituent activity is not something for its own sake, since its end is a normative political order that comes into being when the founding constitutive activity extinguishes itself. By contrast, the constitutionally framed activity of self-governing citizens is an action for its own sake, reproducing the institutions of political freedom by and within which citizens determine themselves as politically autonomous.

Those who claim that political freedom only exists where citizens have a completely unconstrained ability to amend their constitution[29] fail to understand this distinction between the productive activity of constitution-making and the self-activity of constitutional political participation. On the one hand, they completely ignore how nonpolitical rights are prerequisites of political freedom that must be constitutionally guaranteed for self-government to be maintained. On the other hand, they equally ignore how emancipated political association is an ethical community, whose political good of self-government must already be embodied in standing institutions in order to be willed at all. Only through this dual omission could ideologues of right and left continue to harp upon the right of a "people" to be self-determined, as if political freedom could be wielded by a culturally defined group not yet organized as the self-governing citizenry of an existing constitutional state.[30]

To remove these misconceptions, the comprehension of how constitutionality is basic to political freedom must move beyond the lawfulness of right. Although this lawfulness makes constitutionality possible, that free political association is, and not merely can be, internally regulated by a body of constitutional law follows more directly from the structure of ethical community common to the emancipated family, civil society, and self-government. In each of these spheres, individuals exercise a type of autonomy that can only be had by belonging to an association already realizing the autonomy in question. The operation of political freedom exhibits this relationship most patently: individuals can only engage in self-government by being members of a state whose political institutions afford citizens equal political opportunity. Although these institutions are continually reproduced by nothing but the participation in self-government that they make possible, unless citizens are already situated within them, none can possibly exercise the rights and duties distinguishing political autonomy. Consequently, free citizenship exists only insofar as the body politic conforms to the institutional order of self-government. To the degree that self-government is itself inoperable unless it presides over a civil society containing emancipated families, recognizing the moral accountability of its members, and respecting the property entitlements of all persons, political freedom exists only when the principles of nonpolitical, as well as political, right actually regulate personal conduct and institutional practice.

Moreover, since each sphere of right is actual only insofar as participating individuals act in conscious respect of the correlative rights of others, the prevailing conformity to the principles of right is not blind. Self-determination does not just conform to the principles of right; agents can determine themselves only in conscious view of those principles. Hence, the effective regulation of conduct by the principles of right, which political freedom cannot fail to involve, presumes a prevailing common recognition of those principles. Whether published or not, those principles must be publicly available in some authoritative manner to sustain the prevailing recognition.

This structural prerequisite acquires necessity through the encompassing rule of normative political association. In order for self-government to realize its own constitutive equal political opportunity, the aim of political action must always be universal in the concrete sense of imposing order on the self-ordering totality of right. Citizenship must be such that citizens always will not only the perpetuation of their own self-government, but the upholding of the nonpolitical freedoms without which equal political opportunity is impossible. Citizenship can only be of this nature if it is the citizenship of politically self-determining agents, and they can only enjoy political autonomy if their political entitlements are so shaped that they always conform with the concordant realization of every sphere of right. This necessarily omnipresent prescription is the work of constitutionality, by which political association has its own bounds set so that political action is compelled to be free, that is, compelled to both perpetuate the practice of self-government and to uphold the consonant exercise of the nonpolitical rights that make equal political opportunity possible. Because this "compulsion" emanates from within the body politic, through the political promulgation of a constitution that is observed through political action, it does not reintroduce foundationalism. Because the constitution does not exist prior to or apart from the political order it internally regulates, constitutionality allows the body politic to ground itself. This is why the constitution is more than an empty writ only within the ongoing process of self-government of which it is a constitutive element. Before the engagement of that activity, the prospective constitution is merely a promise awaiting the fulfillment that only a correspondingly organized citizenry can achieve.

These minimal determinations of constitutionality cannot help but underlie every aspect of political freedom because without them, the preconditions of equal political opportunity are as much in forfeit as is the political rectitude sustaining self-government. Nevertheless, this initial concept of the constitution of valid political association leaves still undetermined *how* political institutions must be structured in order to operate in a self-regulating constitutional manner. Since the necessary anatomy of self-government is a nonnegotiable matter of political right, it ought itself to be constitutionally specified. Consequently, the ensuing conceptual development of the institutions of political freedom will carry with it a further concretization of the constitution, whose opening determinacy cannot help but be incomplete.

2.7 NORMATIVE PATRIOTISM

The territoriality and constitutionality of political freedom stamp the political allegiance of citizens with a twofold character. On the one hand, citizens are entitled as well as obliged to participate in upholding institutions of right that all rational agents should enjoy.

On the other hand, the territoriality of political right gives the right and duty of citizens a national focus that sets them apart from any other politically organized population. The full implications of this opposition can only be investigated in connection with international relations, which themselves presuppose the complete specification of the institutions of domestic politics. Nevertheless, the constitutional basis of citizenship already indicates that a legitimate national allegiance has nothing to do with kinship, class solidarity, ethnicity, religious community, or any other factor given independently of membership in a political association practicing self-government. If any of these nonpolitical factors are allowed to infect national feeling, the unity of the state gets bound to particular relationships external to equal political opportunity and the unrestrained exercise of political freedom. Even when the body politic is completely homogeneous with regard to the privileged factor, be it religious affiliation, ethnicity, or even kinship, and no citizens find themselves thereby excluded, the association of patriotism with nonpolitical concerns restricts the political prerogatives of citizens, both with regard to admitting new heterogenous citizens and to pursuing agendas unrelated to the heteronomous national character. Although these nonpolitical interests may warrant protection and promotion in civil society, even that is conditional on their compatibility with other independent civil interests, which any political hegemony would threaten. Only a patriotism for the sake of the national realization of right can escape these deformations. Such patriotism is indifferent to any cultural particulars apart from the general divide separating cultural practices that comply with rights from those that oppress. Nevertheless, normative patriotism rests upon feelings and symbolic representations of national political solidarity that a predominant portion of the citizenry share with one another, reflecting their recognition of membership in one state, rather than another.[31] Through this shared commitment to uphold collectively the freedoms of one body politic, with a history of its own, citizens can possess a patriotism in accord with justice that does not dissipate into a universal cosmopolitanism. Normative patriotism adheres instead to the concrete individuality of the territorially particular self-governing state, a totality whose concrete process now awaits determination.

NOTES

1. For this reason, the categories of contract are inappropriate for conceiving political relations. As Norberto Bobbio points out, following Hegel, whereas politics concerns the organization of the whole fabric of right, from which individuals are not at liberty to withdraw, the private law of contractual relations always involves resolution of particular conflicts between independent parties. Hence, when political relations are treated as private, as under feudalism, this represents a deformation of politics, subverting its universality, reflexivity, and supremacy. See Bobbio, *The Future of Democracy*, ed. Richard Bellamy, trans. Roger Griffin (Minneapolis: University of Minnesota Press, 1987), p. 121.

2. Michael Oakeshott attempts to lay hold of the universality of political association by characterizing it as concerned not with particular satisfactions and substantive outcomes but with determining the general conditions under which such satisfactions may be sought. See Oakeshott, *On Human Conduct* (Oxford: Oxford University Press, 1975), p. 174. This formal conception fails to recognize how politics has ends of its own, whose "satisfaction" always involves citizens determining themselves as self-governing and reproducing the institutions of political freedom, together with their prepolitical conditions.

3. Michael B. Foster discusses this point at length in *The Political Philosophies of Plato and Hegel* (Oxford: Oxford University Press, 1968).

4. In this respect, the state, to paraphrase Michael Walzer, defends the boundaries of all the other spheres of justice, regulating but not eliminating their own discrete arenas. See Walzer, *Spheres of Justice* (New York: Basic Books, 1983), pp. 15, 281.

5. For this reason, valid political association cannot be premised upon the consent of its members, as social contract theory would have us believe. Although a certain level of compliance is a condition for the existence of self-government, its authority cannot derive from any agency given independently of its own activity, such as the faculty of choice with which all individuals are endowed. If it did, politics would be subordinate to something else. The supremacy of political self-determination thus entails

that free political association is, as Oakeshott puts it, comprehensive, exclusive, and compulsory. See Oakeshott, *On Human Conduct,* p. 242.

6. This is reflected in how the equal voting right entailed by the reflexivity of political freedom means, as Max Weber observes, that individuals are treated not, as in every other sphere, in respect to their particular professional and family position, nor in relation to any other material or social differences, but simply as citizens, in expression of the unity of the body politic, rather than of the divisions of the various other spheres of life. See Weber, *Political Writings,* ed. Peter Lassman and Ronald Speirs (Cambridge: Cambridge University Press, 1994), p. 103.

7. The traditional Marxist notion of "bourgeois" democracy presumes that a market economy dominated by privately owned units of capital will automatically produce an economic class advantage for capitalists, equally automatically enabling them to disproportionally influence the democratic political process, transforming universal suffrage into an instrument of class domination. Although such domination is possible, it is hardly inevitable, given the different possible forms of private ownership of capital and their impact upon the distribution of wealth, the possible avenues of public regulation of the market, and the possibility of regulating the democratic political process to prevent private wealth from undermining equal political opportunity.

8. See Immanuel Kant, *The Metaphysics of Morals,* trans. Mary Gregor (New York: Cambridge University Press, 1991), § 46, p. 126.

9. John Stuart Mill, *Three Essays: On Liberty, Representative Government, The Subjection of Women* (Oxford: Oxford University Press, 1975), p. 286.

10. Although Mill correctly observes that universal education must precede universal suffrage (Mill, *Three Essays,* p. 278), the democratic state must insure that the precedence involves a tutelage in youth or in as brief a period as possible for those adults who miss a requisite education. To do otherwise is to condemn the body politic to a situation where political negligence politically privileges an educated elite. For this reason, as Michael Walzer notes, only the democratic state insists upon inclusive rather than exclusive schools to prepare future participants in political life (Walzer, *Spheres of Justice* [New York: Basic Books, 1983], p. 202). In doing so, it must insure that those schools maintain a relatively common standard, rather than replicating disadvantage through schools of widely varying quality.

11. Bobbio argues this point. See Bobbio, *The Future of Democracy,* p. 35.

12. This was implicitly recognized by Article 4 of the Revolutionary

Constitution of 1793, which, as Jürgen Habermas points out, defined the status of citizen such that active citizenship would be granted to every adult foreigner after one year of residence in France (Habermas, *Between Facts and Norms: Contributions to a Discourse Theory of Law and Democracy*, trans. William Rehg [Cambridge, MA: MIT Press, 1996], p. 509).

13. George Anastaplo suggests that resident aliens should be entitled to vote in local elections insofar as these elections are concerned with such civil affairs as property ownership and public schools, in which national loyalty need not arise. See Anastaplo, *The Amendments to the Constitution: A Commentary* (Baltimore: Johns Hopkins University Press, 1995), p. 222. Yet, if resident aliens have no real opportunity to exercise self-government in their land of origin, are there any legitimate grounds from depriving them of full citizenship in the one nation in which practical participation is possible?

14. Michael Walzer makes this point in *Spheres of Justice*. See Walzer, *Spheres of Justice*, pp. 54–59. He further notes to the extent that every immigrant and permanent resident can qualify for citizenship, territorial admission becomes all the more serious a concern. See Walzer, *Spheres of Justice*, p. 52.

15. For this reason, as Robert A. Dahl points out, a principle for inclusion into active participation as citizen that ignores judgment of competence is refuted by such examples as children and feeble-minded persons (Dahl, *Democracy and Its Critics* [New Haven, CT: Yale University Press, 1989], p. 128). Nonetheless, because such a judgment on competence requires weighing empirical evidence and considering incremental differences of capability, it is, as Dahl observes, inherently debatable (Dahl, *Democracy and Its Critics*, p. 128). Dahl accordingly offers the inclusion principle that the democratic polity should confer active citizenship upon all adults within its territory except transients and the certified mentally defective (Dahl, *Democracy and Its Critics*, p. 129).

16. Although illiteracy *may* prevent citizens from sufficiently informing themselves or from sufficiently expressing their political positions to participate equally in self-government, it cannot be a valid ground for disenfranchising voters when (1) measures can be taken to enable illiterates to become informed of party and candidate programs and participate as competent citizens, and (2) illiteracy reflects a failure of public authorities to provide equal educational opportunities to its citizens. Hence, the United States Congress was justified when, in 1970, it finally outlawed literacy tests designed to disenfranchise Southern blacks. See David P. Currie, *The Constitution of the United States: A Primer for the People* (Chicago: University of Chicago Press, 1988), p. 68.

17. As Walzer points out, private education can be tolerated so long as sufficient scholarships are available and private school pedigree does not provide privileged access to social and political positions. See Walzer, *Spheres of Justice*, p. 219.

18. Walzer argues that neighborhood schools are the ideal instrument of democratic education to the degree that they exhibit the same territorial principle as democratic political representation (Walzer, *Spheres of Justice*, p. 225). This presupposes that neighborhoods themselves are not distinguished by group identities, reflecting both historical dominations and traditional communities that subordinate the collective solidarity of the citizenry to either prepolitical particular interests or premodern hierarchies.

19. As Walzer notes, even if parents have equal resources, inequality in parental care can foster disadvantage among children. See Walzer, *Spheres of Justice*, p. 213.

20. Mill claims that although such national history may provide a prima facie case for uniting all members of the nationality under the same government, this is equivalent to letting the question of government be decided by the governed. See Mill, *Three Essays*, pp. 380–81. This equivalency would be true if one presupposes that neither any portion of nor the entire nationality is entangled with other groups in political solidarities that allow self-government within a state of different boundaries.

21. Although Mill rightly argues that representative government cannot operate without sufficient fellow-feeling and united public opinion among its citizens, this does not support his conclusion that free institutions are next to impossible in a country made up of different nationalities. See Mill, *Three Essays*, p. 382.

22. As Habermas points out, although democratic citizenship does require that every citizen be socialized into a common political culture, because self-government can accommodate a diversity of cultural forms of life, this does not extend to the whole of their socialization (Habermas, *Between Facts and Norms*, pp. 500, 514). Habermas's claim must be qualified, however, insofar as nonpolitical practices must be "socialized" if they obstruct equal political opportunity.

23. For this reason, Dahl is justified in arguing that a group's claim to autonomy is undermined to the degree that its achievement of political independence will imperil the freedoms of people within or without its own realm (Dahl, *Democracy and Its Critics*, p. 208).

24. As Dahl points out, the unit of democratic governance cannot be derived from the principle of majority rule—it depends upon other

assumptions that give that unit its legitimacy and jurisdiction (Dahl, *Democracy and Its Critics*, p. 204). Ultimately, what counts are that however units are demarcated, their boundaries should optimally conform with the actualization of self-government within each. In this respect, foisting political autonomy on a group that does not want independence can be, as Dahl notes, just as coercive as refusing independence to one that does (Dahl, *Democracy and Its Critics*, p. 208).

25. Habermas accepts the erroneous social contract view, arguing that the right to emigrate or to renounce one's citizenship implies that citizenship rests on at least tacit consent (Habermas, *Between Facts and Norms*, pp. 124–25, 497).

26. For a further analysis of why the realization of right requires legalization, see Richard Dien Winfield, *Law in Civil Society* (Norman: University of Kansas Press, 1994).

27. As Anastaplo observes, the amendability of a constitution suggests that there are separate enduring standards by which it, as well as positive laws, should be judged. See Anastaplo, *The Constitution of 1787: A Commentary* (Baltimore: Johns Hopkins University Press, 1989), pp. 188, 189, 228. Of course, the possibility of such standards, which ultimately comprise the principles of different modes of self-determination, equally indicates that any amendments should likewise be subject to judgment and that not every constitutional statute should be subject to repeal.

28. For this reason, the genuine sovereignty of self-government does not involve the freedom that Oakeshott attributes to the modern European state of having the authority and procedures to amend or repeal any law and thereby liberate itself from any fixture of its legal past. See Oakeshott, *On Human Conduct*, p. 229.

29. Michael B. Foster makes an argument of this sort. For a more detailed critique of this view, see "The Logic of the State" in Winfield, *Overcoming Foundations: Studies in Systematic Philosophy* (New York: Columbia University Press, 1989), pp. 249–69.

30. Hannah Arendt argues this point at length in *On Revolution*, detailing how the makers of the French Revolution tended to appeal to a politically unorganized people as the source of authority, in contrast to the American founders, who tended to acknowledge the politically organized character of the people qua citizenry. See Arendt, *On Revolution* (New York: Viking, 1965), pp. 70–71, 179, 181, 183.

31. As Habermas observes, the symbolic construction of a "people" produces the imaginary unity that allows the modern state to be a national

state. See Habermas, *Die postnationale Konstellation: Politische Essays* (Frankfurt am Main: Suhrkamp, 1998), pp. 99–100. This is in accord with right, provided the "people" in question is understood as a self-governing citizenry, whose shared commitment to join in self-rule transcends any subordination to cultural differences. Moreover, the "symbolic construction" cannot just transpire in language but must be realized in communal practices constitutive of collective self-government.

CHAPTER 3
THE PRIMARY INTERNAL ORGANIZATION OF POLITICAL FREEDOM

3.1 METHODOLOGICAL PERPLEXITIES IN CONCEIVING SELF-GOVERNMENT

The basic character common to every aspect of self-government may be provided by identifying normative political association as an ethical community whose end is concretely universal, whose activity is reflexive, supreme, and autonomous, and whose order is constitutional. Nevertheless, this identification does not determine how the particular features of political freedom are distinguished from one another. Until these differentiations are established, how self-government operates remains an open question. Where, then, must political philosophy turn to determine how the state should be organized to enable citizens to be politically autonomous while enjoying all their other rights?

As always, the order of consideration is mandated by the structure of the subject matter. Whatever determination of political organization follows upon the minimal specification of political freedom must itself be basic to any further aspects of self-government. If not, political relations will be inserted without any account of their own content or of the necessity of their introduction. Not only will their own structural prerequisites go unspecified, but any further specification will rest upon an incomplete edifice whose primary elements can no longer be coherently retrieved. Where then does the concept of the political find its first particular differentiation?

Although every exercise of political autonomy involves citizens willing the form of the totality of right to which their ruling agency belongs, the moment governing acquires any definition, political agency becomes distinguished into different necessary roles. Provided emancipated politics involves a determinate government with political offices of any sort, citizens play at least two distinct roles either simultaneously, in alternation, or simply separately: that of officeholder and that of nonofficeholder. Political association thereby acquires a manifold of relationships. Besides standing in common as members of the same constitutional state, citizens now relate politically to officeholders on the one hand and nonofficeholders on the other, whether they themselves act in one capacity or the other or in both at once.

In order for political officeholding to be compatible with the freedom of occupation of civil society, wherever government service is required, the filling of posts must be voluntary, at least so long as self-selection is sufficient to uphold self-government. This self-selection can operate both through candidacy for elective office and professional employment in government service for nonelected functionaries. These options can free government from conscripting citizens to perform particular services, which would place special burdens on some if not all were requisitioned, and unnecessary impositions on all, if voluntary employment could do what universal conscription aims to provide.[1] Such professional government service can be financed by equitable taxation, which allows citizens to contribute to the upkeep of the state without sacrificing their freedom to exercise the equal economic opportunity to which civil society is committed. By demanding monetary payment, duly graduated to secure equal economic and political opportunity, taxation allows each citizen to retain control over what goods they will buy and sell, as well as what occupation they will undertake.[2]

Given these arrangements, which allow officeholders and nonofficeholders to retain their social and political autonomy, citizens become further differentiated in terms of government organization. To the degree that government involves not just a distinction between office and nonofficeholding roles, but functionally differentiated offices, officeholders stand in a qualitatively complementary relation to other officeholders, as well as in a functionally distinguished relation to nonofficeholders. In other words, once there are particular government officials exercising different political roles, citizens must interact in regard to these distinct offices, whether in official capacities of their own or simply as self-governing civilians.

Moreover, if citizens cooperate politically through particular voluntary organizations (e.g., political parties) with their own functionally differentiated positions, and these organizations mediate between office- and nonofficeholders, self-government will involve the relation between citizens, their partisan political organizations, and government.

How any such government should be structured depends upon first whether political freedom requires organized government at all, and second, whether the organized government necessary to self-rule requires specific functions entailing particular branches of office. Whether democracy should be direct or representative hangs upon the answer to both issues, whereas the outcome of the latter question impacts upon how powers of government should be divided, as well as upon which possible configurations of legislative representation, of executive administration, and of authorizing powers are admissible.

Because these issues bear upon political organization at any level, they must be settled before addressing the respective merits of federal and centralized arrangements of self-government. Moreover, because how political organizations operate depends upon the structure of government, the basic questions of state organization must first be addressed before the legitimate principles of partisan political activity can be determined.

If all arbitrary assumptions are to be avoided, the answer to these questions can only be sought by relying exclusively upon the minimal determinacy of political freedom, which necessarily incorporates the nonpolitical rights making possible equal political opportunity, as well as the natural and psychological prerequisites of free agency that these already contain.

3.2 POLITICAL RIGHT AND RULE UNDER AND BY LAW

The internal differentiation of normative political association must give institutional realization to two features of political right whose abstract distillations have become accepted pillars of the modern constitutional state: rule by law and rule under law.[3] Although rule by law and rule under law have both been celebrated as keystones of political emancipation, this celebration too commonly reflects the deficient formalism of the lawful willing that procedural ethics elevates into the principle of normativity. What so often gets neglected here is how the lawfulness of right is tied to ends of a very specific content comprising the self-individuating determination of each respective mode of freedom. Without this further qualification by content, rule by law and rule under law have at best a formal value because, as is readily evident, neither automatically realizes right.[4]

Rule by law is regularly advocated as if the oppression facilitated by its absence suffices to make legislation just in itself. Rule exclusively by decree may be the fitting vehicle for the unlimited discretion of tyrants, who command specific individuals to perform particular deeds without ever imposing standing laws that could give their subjects any guaranteed prerogatives of their own. Yet even if government by law protects subjects from the unbridled arbitrariness of personal fiat, the settled common order it imposes until the next legislative repeal or revision may not be a bastion of right. Rule by law still leaves open what filling laws have, as well as whether their legislation is limited by any higher laws of constitutional authority. Admittedly, rule by law does effect an equal treatment since everyone falling under its jurisdiction is regulated by the same statutes. Nevertheless, equal treatment is not equivalent to respect for rights, since common laws may violate equal opportunity either by ignoring differences that affect autonomy or by imposing restrictions that trample upon everyone's freedoms. All citizens, for example, may be subject to the same flat tax rate, yet standing inequalities in wealth may make this particular formula of equal treatment a violation of equal economic opportunity. Alternately, legislation could forbid gay marriage, curtailing individuals' right to marry one another in function of nothing but the due requirements of conjugal self-determination.

Simply supplementing rule by law with rule under law can hardly remedy these difficulties. Admittedly, rule under law may be an obstacle to the unbridled choice of political masters. Further, unless those who legislate are subject to the law they make, legislators will impose law on a subject class excluded from self-legislation, precluding self-rule.[5] Nonetheless, the law that rules over government need not impose a system of self-determination. Ruler and ruled may equally be subject to the same highest laws, but these may mandate any variety of duties that diverge from the respect for rights. Constitutions need not, and perhaps, have yet to be, the internal political standard for the realization of the totality of freedom.

Given the exclusive normativity of self-determination, rule under and/or by law can command legitimacy only if the content of the law to which government is subject and the content of the law by which government governs consists in the realization of right. Any such content must be internal to self-determination, for if it were to originate from any other source, it would impose an order alien to freedom, an order owing its content not to itself, but to an antecedent foundation. Consequently, if rule under and/or by law were to have a content upholding the system of rights, this would be because self-government determines itself to be what it is by ruling under and/or by law. Then, both the form and content of rule under and/or by law would make it a necessary ingredient of political freedom.

Already, the constitutionality endemic to political freedom entails that self-government rules under law and that the law to which self-rule is subject is a law upholding the totality of rights. As we have seen, the normative necessity for constitutionality and its self-rule under law follows from three intersecting factors: the relation between political freedom and the nonpolitical freedoms that make equal political opportunity possible, the ethical community by which political self-determination must always be situated within existing institutions of self-government, and the general lawful character of right.

How rule under law takes shape in the internal organization of self-government coincides with the question of how self-government must be structured to realize its necessary constitutionality. Because of the exclusive validity of self-determination, the normative necessity of constitutionality, or of rule under law, is located in how political self-determination cannot operate without government under law, where the law in question has a content prescribing political and nonpolitical right. The institutional ramifications of this necessity only become determinate in conjunction with the coeval imperative of rule by law. What brings this imperative into play is the same general lawful character of right that contributes to the indispensability of constitutionality and its rule under law.

The general lawful character of right entails that the agency that determines itself by imposing the order of freedom upon the community to which it belongs does so in a lawful manner. In order for rule to take the form of right and be an exercise of equal political opportunity, participation in governing must always comprise a political prerogative connected by a common rule to that of every other citizen. Otherwise, what choice one citizen makes interferes with others choosing in the same manner, substituting political privilege for political right. This requirement is common to every exercise of right. What, however, gives political freedom not just lawfulness, but a necessary legislative character, is the reflexivity of political supremacy and autonomy. Because political activity always involves some sort of participation in the willing of the whole system of right, it centers around not just willing in a lawful manner but doing so while willing a content that is itself lawful. In other words, political freedom wills law, and more precisely, the law by which nonpolitical and political rights are objectively specified and enforced.

Constitutionality, encapsulating the situated character of political ethical community, might seem to eviscerate the legislative crux of self-government, especially when the constitutional law securing the universal principles of right contains elements mandated by the concept of self-determination that should not be susceptible to repeal by amendment. After all, if self-government requires the constitutional guarantee of all rights, which themselves comprise the fundamental laws of the system of freedom, what autonomous citizens constitutively will is the reproduction of a realm of self-determination whose law is already constitutionally promulgated. Why, then, need free political activity involve any further legislation? If self-government's self-realization consists in upholding the reality of right at each and every level within the state, why should this require more than an execution of constitutional law, for which additional lawmaking is superfluous? Self-government may be rule under law, due to the requirement of constitutionality, but why doesn't constitutional legality itself remove all rationale for rule by law?

Far from being precluded by constitutionality, rule by law is indispensable for constitutional self-government on two complementary grounds. To begin with, given the basic self-active structure of ethical community, where the preestablished order continually reproduces itself through the exercise of its members' rights, the constitution is a political reality, rather than an empty writ, only insofar as the form it articulates is predominantly willed into actuality in the activities comprising the political association for which it provides the inner standard. This does not mean that the normativity of political ethical community is a matter of conventional efficacy, where prevailing might makes right. It rather signifies that the structure of political freedom, which alone has normativity among body politics, exists only in virtue of a prevailing degree of rectitude. The question concerning legislation within the state is whether the self-realization of constitutional self-government requires positive lawmaking to make the constitution a living reality.

In the context of constitutionality, legislation is positive insofar as it is subordinate to the constitutional promulgation of rights, while possessing a further content of its own, which, otherwise undetermined by reason, must be decided by legislative discretion. Although such positive legislation may enjoy constitutional permissibility by not violating any constitutionally specified rights, it remains a superfluous option unless positive lawmaking is integral to the exercise of political freedom.

Abstractly speaking, the constitution is self-realizing insofar as it specifies the political institutions and their constitutive activities by which constitutional rule is upheld and reproduced. This distinguishes political association from the self-realizing unity of an organism, which sustains itself without necessarily containing an element knowing the form of the whole. In contrast to organic unity, constitutionality actualizes itself through a ruling agency that operates in function of its knowledge of the constitution, which must have an independent verbal expression in order to be an adequate object of conceptual comprehension. This is why constitutional self-government is not a merely natural entity, but a structure of spirit, exhibiting the specific self-activity of mind, which is determined by what it knows itself to be.[6]

Although the constitution has an antecedently fixed character, valid political practice must realize the constitutionally guaranteed principles of right in face of the changing conjunctures of domestic, international, and, for that matter, natural situations that bear upon the different spheres of freedom. Because these conjunctures have a contingent character that only corrigible observations can discover, how to respond to their exigencies cannot be derived directly from the concept of right.[7] Judgment must intervene to determine how the universal principles of justice are to apply to the particular perceived situation in families, society, foreign relations, and the environment at large. In no case could any individual or group of citizens claim any special expertise or aptitude privileging them to make the requisite judgment. Reason may determine the principles of right that define the nonpositive component of the just constitution. Nevertheless, rule by experts is precluded since all that is needed to perceive the given conjuncture and judge how the principles of right apply to it is the same basic rational agency with which individuals qualify for any ethical entitlement. Since each and every exercise of right involves agents respecting the correlative rights of others, recognition of the principles of right is already ingredient in their engagement in the institutions of freedom, as are the basic competencies of rational observation required for any recognition of the conduct of others. Although expertise may be needed to comprehend technical aspects of situations, including past activities of government, this information can be conveyed to generally competent individuals, without usurping their participation in deciding how to act thereupon.

If this saves popular participation from the specter of guardian rule, it does not of itself mandate that the judgment at issue is concerned with legislation. It could be a matter of executive discretion, where citizens en masse or as self-selected magistrates take particular measures decided by particular judgments in the way in which civil courts apply the law to contingent individual cases or how police enforce it on the beat. But can such action exhaust self-government without depending upon a prior attempt to legislate in face of these changing situations?

To realize equal political opportunity and comprise an exercise of self-government, whatever measures are taken must stand in a reflexive relation to the will of all citizens. That is, government must be of and by the citizenry, proceeding by an activity that addresses all citizens while emanating from all their wills, at least in some indirect fashion. Any alternate arrangement would transform self-rule into some unreciprocated relation of agent and patient.

On the one hand, if government acted only upon some citizens to the exclusion of others, rule would be an act of the state upon a part of itself, leaving the remainder unaffected. This imbalance would persist whether or not state action is undertaken with the codetermination of all or only a part of the citizenry. If all citizens participate in acting upon some of their compatriots, the unaffected citizens would exercise a nonreflexive domination, imposing order upon the others. These would be rendered a *relatively* subject political class, since whatever role they play in ordering themselves would be as subjects of a privileged political elite that remains above its own commands. If, by contrast, those citizens who are acted upon do not participate in determining the order imposed upon themselves, they become free citizens in name only, for they figure purely as passive patients of political action. Consequently, for governing to realize self-rule, it must address all citizens in common, which is to say that self-government must operate by wielding a political will that acts upon all citizens equally. Self-government must therefore command universally, which signifies that political self-determination is preeminently self-legislative. Of course, this necessity for rule by law is subject to the proviso that the content of legislation conform to the constitution of the system of rights, since any departure from this content will undermine equal political opportunity.

In so doing, legislation must uphold the universality of aim of political justice and not become corrupted into an instrument for satisfying particular interests. If the legislature becomes an arena in which representatives of competing patrons battle to fulfill the ends of some group at the expense of others, the universal jurisdiction of law does not prevent it from imposing rules subordinating some citizens to the satisfactions of others.[8]

For this reason, the connection between self-rule and rule by and under law is only half the story. If political action acts upon the whole citizenry, but is controlled by only some citizens, the lawful treatment of citizens as subjects of legislation does not apply to their political participation. Instead of exercising self-rule by law, citizens would all be legally regulated by a political power by which only those who participate in legislation would act upon themselves. Everyone else would be subject to a law they have not imposed upon themselves, eliminating equal political opportunity. Hence, not only does self-rule require that government exercise rule of and by the whole citizenry, but the rule by and under law that this entails can only conform to constitutional right if legislative activity is codetermined by all citizens. Only then can political legislation uphold and operate in function of equal political opportunity.

This line of reasoning, pioneered by Rousseau, retains validity only if freed from two assumptions on which its originator depended. One comprises the social contract foundation that conflates self-determination with the determining of a privileged determiner. The other consists in the assumption that the codetermination of legislation requires direct democracy, by which all citizens participate in person in legislative assemblies. When due account is taken of the foundation-free normativity of freedom and of how political freedom is inseparable from the upholding of the nonpolitical rights of property, morality, emancipated family membership, and civil society, the attraction of direct democracy quickly fades. Direct democracy proves to be incompatible with not only upholding the freedoms of civil society but the division of powers necessary for constitutional rule. Before this can be fully established, however, the relation between self-legislation, constitutionality, and the division of powers must be unveiled.

3.3 SELF-LEGISLATION, CONSTITUTIONALITY, AND THE DIVISION OF POWERS

With positive legislation established to be necessary for self-government, the dependence of political self-determination upon organized government becomes concretely defined in respect to how legislative activity must operate to be compatible with nonpolitical freedoms and the constitutionality that upholds them in their integration with political freedom. Because nonpolitical rights both have unconditioned normativity as modes of self-determination and are preconditions of political freedom, the self-legislation central to self-government ought, and indeed, cannot help but be constitutional in the normative sense of complying with an inner political standard prescribing the principles of the system of right in its entirety. Although putatively self-legislating regimes may enact laws violating rights, in doing so they undercut the equal opportunity of their own citizens on which the genuine reflexivity of self-government depends. Since the conformity of legislation to the realization of freedom is an unconditional imperative, it ought not be left to legislative discretion but should be politically guaranteed.

If those who legislate are themselves empowered to determine the constitutionality of their own legislation, all distinction between positive and constitutional law evaporates. Whatever the legislators will as law then immediately enjoys unchallengeable authority, emancipating the content of law from any necessary conformity with right and substituting the unconstrained arbitrariness of legislative will for the constitutionally situated volition of ethical freedom. Since no political will can set any limits to what such legislators legislate, the universality of rights collapses before the self-assertion of a single collective will that does whatever it pleases. Even if all citizens were to participate directly in such an unconstrained lawmaking, the formal reflexivity of their self-legislation cannot guarantee that the laws they enact uphold civil, let alone, political rights.[9]

If constitutionality is to be preserved, if politics is to actualize political freedom and the nonpolitical rights on which it rests, the agency that legislates cannot at the same time authorize the legislative proposals that it decides upon. A separate political power must independently determine whether the putative laws that legislators choose conform with right, as specified in the constitution. Only after this certification can legislative decisions count as binding laws of a self-governing body politic.

Needless to say, if the same citizens exercise both functions, the separation of legislative and authorizing powers becomes an empty formality, placing all rights at the mercy of a group with constitutional impunity. This peril remains equally in force if all citizens were somehow to exercise both functions, raising Rousseau's specter of a general will that can do no wrong, no matter how many other dimensions of nonpolitical and political rights it violates.

Although a *real* distinction between legislative and authorizing powers is necessary for constitutionality, the fact of separation will not suffice unless the authorizing power operates with an appropriate scope and finality. To uphold constitutionality and the very distinction between constitutional and positive law, a recognized authorizing power must certify the constitutionality of each and every measure that legislators decide upon *before* any take effect as law of the land. Otherwise, an interval of unbridled license is allowed legislators, a gap in the constitutional upholding of right, whose damage may be fatal to the body politic. After all, it is hardly unprecedented, let alone unimaginable, for a legislative body to legislate out of existence all countervailing authority and circumvent the certification that had erstwhile been required.

For this reason, judicial review of the constitutionality of legislation is a poor substitute for the authorizing power on which political freedom depends. Although a supreme court may lay claim to judging the constitutionality of laws applying to the cases brought before it, its judicial review is predicated both upon the prior operation of those laws and the particular initiative of individual plaintiffs bringing their cases to court. On either score, judicial review leaves the independent authorization of legislation a contingent matter, applying only to *some* laws and only to *some* portion of their effective career. Even when bringing a case to court leads to overturning a law, the prior reign of that statute has done its damage, which statutes of limitation as well as the mere passage of time may put beyond repair. These limitations are not removed by transferring all judicial review to a centralized constitutional court, as Hans Kelsen proposed and Austria first instituted in 1920,[10] unless dependence upon individual suits is removed and no legislative act becomes valid law until that court certifies its constitutionality.

Insuring that *all* legislation be publicly certified as constitutional by an independent authorizing power before counting as valid law is, however, only one requirement that must be fulfilled for political right to be guaranteed. The automatic universal jurisdiction of the authorizing power must be complemented by a finality of decision. No other political power can be permitted to override the constitutional certification of the authorizing power. This is particularly true of the legislators, for if they can overturn decisions striking down their legislative proposals, they recoup the unlimited legislative license that renders constitutionality an empty fiction. Such is the sorry state of presidential veto in the United States, whose overturning by a supermajority of Congress reduces the authorizing power of the president to an unreliable stopgap that judicial review can only partly remedy, given the contingent limits of court scrutiny.

These limitations underline how misguided it is to object to a separate authorizing power on the grounds that the finality of its constitutional certification undermines the political autonomy of citizens, as if unconstrained legislative supremacy unshackled self-government. Admittedly, if constitutional review were wielded by officials appointed without popular consultation and immune from popular recall, questions could be raised as to whether the authorizing power could give expression to the political codetermination of every citizen. These questions equally pertain, however, to legislators, for there is nothing in the function of these two powers that automatically confers on one or the other any greater connection to the political will of the citizenry. How legislators and authorizers are to be selected and how their terms are to be regulated are matters that can only be settled when these branches are specified in detail. What is already clear, however, is that unless legislative and authorizing powers are distinguished and properly empowered, selection procedures will be of no avail in preventing the erosion of constitutional rights.

Key to the due empowerment of the authorizing power is its strict limitation to certifying legal proposals that it neither formulates nor enforces. Only under that restriction can its unchallenged independence and finality realize constitutionality and uphold political ethical community. If the authorizing power played any role in determining the content of the legislation it supervises, it would usurp statutory power and wield a legislative will that can do whatever it pleases. Instead of submitting legislators to an independent constitutional certification, the authorizing power would illicitly combine legislative and authorizing prerogatives, eroding the protective distinction between constitutional and positive law. Consequently, the very sanctity of authorizing power depends upon its rigid abstention from any legislatively constructive intervention. If the authorizing power confirms the political validity of pending legislation, it must do so without adding any positive elements of its own. This does not mean that the constitutional authority must restrict its certification to an up or down acceptance or rejection of each legislative proposal in its entirety. Portions may be selectively excised provided doing so does not result in back door positive amendments.

Such restraint will allow the authorizing power to facilitate a legislated actualization of the constitution provided the certifying authority refrains from playing any role of its own in the subsequent execution of the legislation it confirms. If the authorizing power were to direct the implementation of law, either through public enforcement directed at all citizens or by presiding over the judicial application of the law to individual cases, the formal character of its certification would be circumvented. Even though the authorization of legislation leaves the latter's content unaltered, an authorizing power that usurps executive functions can then realize the law however it chooses. Such is the risk haunting presidential systems whose president is both authorizing head of state and executive head of government.[11]

Nonetheless, constitutionality is compromised if the authorizing power is completely indifferent to how the executive power enforces the laws that have been certified as valid. If the executive is left to do as it pleases, the constitutional constraints upon legislation are for nought. Although law is never equivalent to particular enforcements, if the execution of legislation is subject to no restrictions, the license of the executive will supplant rule by and under law with a tyranny of its own. Since the legislative power is restricted to making laws subject to the certification of the authorizing power, it is not in a position to supervise executive action. The authorizing power, however, is suited to the task, for in its constitutive role as the final determiner of constitutionality, it alone can certify whether executive enforcement of law remains true to the constitution. To avoid usurping executive power for itself, creating a combined authorizing and executive prerogative of effectively unlimited governance, the authorizing power must here exercise the same formality as it does in supervising legislation. Instead of instituting positive executive policies, the authorizing power must restrict itself to declaring invalid those executive measures that step beyond the pale of constitutionality. Since the executive power, as distinguished from legislative and authorizing powers, incorporates both administrative and judicial activities, the authorizing power is empowered to render void both administrations and court decisions that it deems unconstitutional.

Unlike scrutiny of pending legislation, validation of executive action cannot automatically intervene before each prospective executive initiative. Administrative and judicial measures are too manifold and dispersed to certify in advance. Indeed, in the case of specific government actions, they do not even have an "ideal" existence before the fact of their commission. Accordingly, constitutional authorization must here take the form of a *review* of individual court decisions and policy implementations, which may accordingly require organizational modifications within the authorizing power.

Of course, any punitive or compensatory remedies that follow from such authorizing judgments must be enforced by the executive power, which is to say that the executive must act upon itself to implement the certifications of the authorizer. If the executive fails to do so, it falls once more into illegitimate activity, forfeiting the recognition on which its own authority depends. Although executive officials may still persist in their unconstitutional deeds, they thereby act without any political validity and citizens have no obligation to submit to their administrations.

Needless to say, whatever protections the independent interventions of the authorizing power provide would be subverted if an executive power usurped legislative or authorizing powers on its own part, for either way, the combination of functions would jeopardize the constitutional integration of political activity.

These considerations underscore how without a separation of legislative, authorizing, and executive powers, rule by law and under law cannot be kept within the bounds that tie its exercise to the realization of political and nonpolitical rights. Constitutionality depends upon this separation, and constitutional self-government must minimally incorporate this division of powers into the workings of political self-determination.

3.4 THE LIMITS OF CONSTITUTIONALITY AND THE DIVISION OF POWERS

Constitutionality has validity so far as it comprises the order to which politics must conform to realize political and nonpolitical freedoms in their systematic unity. Clearly, if an authorizing power is not separated from legislative and executive powers, a particular branch of government can do whatever it pleases without ever violating the reigning constitutionality. Under this arrangement, constitutional conformity becomes an empty conceit, masking the domination of particular license. Nonetheless, the due separation of powers has very obvious limits. Intractable problems arise in several all too possible scenarios.

In the most benign case, where the authorizing power properly strikes down laws, administrations, and court decisions violating right, government may grind to a halt if the legislative power persists in producing oppressive statutes and/or the executive branch continually tramples on the rights of citizens and noncitizens alike. The integrity of the authorizing power cannot alone provide any escape from the impasse, since the formal certification it provides can never generate positive legislation or positive executive initiatives. What alone *may* remedy the situation is the selection of new legislators and executive magistrates. To this end, the authorizing power might be empowered to initiate whatever selection process is proper to self-government, something to be concretely determined in conjunction with the more detailed specification of the legislative and executive branches themselves. Whether the new bodies of legislators and executors will better satisfy the judgment of the authorizer, is, however, contingent.

The converse scenario presents wholly similar difficulties. If legislators and executors make laws, carry out administrative policies, and render court decisions in accord with right, but the authorizing power mistakenly or maliciously invalidates them, government paralysis occurs. Once more, the remedy *may* be found by replacing a body of officials, this time the authorizers, using whatever selection procedure accords with self-government. Of course, replacement offers no guarantee that the new authorizers will be any more amenable to right.

More injurious to right is the situation where the authorizing power is all too agreeable to rogue legislations and/or executive initiatives. In such cases where the authorizing, legislative, and executive powers collaborate in violating the rights of citizens and noncitizens alike, the injury is the same whether the oppression be effected in good faith or with open contempt for right. In the former case, appeal to the principles of self-determination in public debate *might* sway the collaborating powers to conform to genuine constitutional standards. In the latter case, any change of conduct would have to depend either on reversion to rectitude or other expediencies. When such remedies are lacking, citizens face a predicament where the due balance of powers fails to prevent injustice from being perpetrated under the banner of constitutional legitimacy.

Since pervasive injustice amounts to chronic disruption of self-determination in its various forms and impediments to nonpolitical freedoms obstruct equal political opportunity, the collaboration of errant authorizing, legislating, and executive powers does not cast in doubt the legitimacy of self-government. It would if it represented a bona fide exercise of political freedom that nevertheless stood at odds with right. A united rogue government, however, cannot help but disrupt political rights, minimally by upholding civil rights but violating equal political opportunity, and more egregiously by violating civil rights and thereby undercutting political freedom as well. Whatever the level of injustice, it signifies that self-government is not fully actual. In other words, so long as equal political opportunity is being realized, the division of powers cannot help but operate in conformity with right.

No greater guarantee of rectitude is possible, given the faculty of choice to which all political agents are party. Whenever sufficient numbers of legislative, authorizing, and executive officials choose to ignore the principles of right, and sufficient numbers of nonofficeholders submit to their governance, no division of powers can prevent self-government from degenerating into a charade of constitutional rule. The most that can be hoped for is that nothing less than massive collusion can render political legality at odds with right. The struggle to counter such an outcome is a continual occupation of free citizens.

3.5 THE EMANCIPATION OF THE DIVISION OF POWERS FROM CLASSICAL AND LIBERAL CONCEPTIONS

What valid constitutionality requires is far from congruent with the traditional division of powers into legislative, executive, and judicial branches of government that liberal theory made canonical. That division is oblivious to the requirement of an independent authorizing power. Instead, it allows legislative power to reign supreme, subjugating the enforcement activities of the executive and judicial branches to its antecedent statutory directives.

This privileging of legislative power does have the merit of expressly recognizing the essential role of rule by law in political freedom. By contrast, classical political philosophy never fully acknowledged legislative activity within the state, since the law to which teleological politics molds itself is something antecedently given, to be discovered by reason as a gift of external founders, rather than something to be made within the state as a constitutive activity of self-rule.

Although incorporating positive legislation within politics may be a necessary condition of self-government, it is no more sufficient than the distinction of executive and judicial powers that liberal theory appends to legislative supremacy. Although executive and judicial branches are here differentiated, they both fall within the broad function of implementing law that binds them as soon as it issues from legislative activity. Whether enforcing statutes upon the citizenry at large or applying law to individual cases brought to court, these two branches operate as subsidiary organs of legislative mandate. As a consequence, constitutionality has no institutional bulwark on which to rest, relegating liberal theory to choose between calls for slavish obedience to a legislator who cannot do any wrong or appeals to individual conscience to revolt against what each heart judges to be legislative license.

In theory, the remedy to this dilemma is first anticipated by Hegel's differentiation of a legislature from a head of state and an executive power, where the head of state exercises an authorizing function by dotting the line on legislation deemed constitutional. Although Hegel properly requires that all legislatively adopted bills be first approved by the head of state before counting as valid law, he fails to free his conception of feudal vestiges that obstruct the reflexivity and equal political opportunity of self-government. The authorizing power gets deformed both by being identified as a hereditary monarch, whose accession to power is expressly unmediated by the wills of the citizenry, and by exceeding the formal limitations of constitutional certification by providing a positive tutelage to the legislature. Whereas this latter intervention already undermines any possibility of citizens codetermining legislative activity, Hegel's legislature is further impaired as an organ of political freedom by being cast as an estate assembly, where noble birthright politically privileges a house of lords to counterbalance a bourgeois estate chamber.[12]

3.6 THE METHODOLOGY OF DETERMINING THE BRANCHES OF GOVERNMENT

These deformations highlight the need to carry through the division of powers in a manner consonant with the basic determinations of political freedom. This undertaking comes prior to the consideration of the alternatives of federal and centralized government, for constitutional self-rule at each and every level must incorporate the division of powers required for rule by and under law in conformity with right.

What does, however, get decided within the specific development of the branches of self-government are the controversies pitting direct versus representative democracy, presidential versus parliamentary systems, and the competing alternatives of legislative composition, pitting not only plurality/majority single-district representation versus the varieties of proportional representation, but corporate versus residential representation. Since each of these alternatives has ramifications for the organization of electoral systems and the electoral activity of political parties, these matters must also come into play in the specification of the branches of government. All of these issues are resolvable only by considering how the requisite division of powers must be structured to actualize political self-determination, upholding prepolitical rights in conjunction with the reflexivity, lawfulness, and ethical community of political freedom.

The basic differentiation of the three powers of government already delineates a framework to guide all further determination. To uphold the constitutionality on which self-government depends, the legislative, authorizing, and executive powers must be separated, so that the particular will of each cannot unilaterally substitute itself for the general will of the state. Instead, their activities must be so coordinated that the political self-determination of citizens can be actualized only when all three branches act in conjunction with one another, the legislature passing on legal formulations for approval by the authorizing power, which then hands certified statutes over to the executive for implementation. Although this complementary functioning depends upon the separation of powers, which stand as particular against one another, the activity of each must somehow be predicated upon the will of each citizen. If instead, any or all of the powers of government operate independently of the will of all or any citizens, those who play no mediating role will find themselves lorded over by an external force that forfeits the reflexive character of self-government.

The order for concretely specifying the branches of government is objectively determined by their structural integration. However, because each power relates to its counterparts in and through its own operation, finding an unequivocal starting point is far from easy. Further complicating matters is the connection between the composition of the three powers and the political process by which the citizenry at large relates to each branch. If, for example, legislators can actualize political self-determination only by winning their position in a preceding electoral process, the determination of the electoral system cannot fall from sight. Yet, because any election is predicated upon the nature of the position to be filled, specifying the legislative power seems just as paramount. The basic puzzle is inherent in the situated character of political ethical community: each political engagement in or out of office already presupposes the standing operation of the whole, without which none of these activities can be undertaken.

Be this as it may, the authorizing power does enjoy a certain primacy, insofar as it alone informs the particular activities of government with the imprimatur of constitutional legitimacy. Validating legislation and execution alike, with an authority no other political will can challenge, the authorizing power alone brings the political unity of self-government to actuality. In this respect, the authorizing power can merit Hegel's identification of it as the head of state, for until the authorizer certifies the work of the legislator, no statute can count as the will of the state, nor any executive act count as an implementation of constitutionally valid law. And only so long as executive action retains the approval of the authorizing power does it command legitimacy as a constitutional governance.

Nevertheless, the legislative power retains a functional primacy since until legislation is put forward, neither the authorizing power nor the executive have anything to do. Whatever guidelines constitutional statute mandates for the operation of the three powers themselves comprise nothing but a recipe for realizing the positive legislation by which self-government rules by and under law. Since, further, the executive cannot act until the authorizer has handed it certified laws to enforce, the authorizing power warrants treatment second, as a way station to a concluding consideration of the executive branch. Before turning to the successive determination of legislative, authorizing, and executive branches of government, two complications must be noted by way of anticipation.

First, because a multitude of specifications of the division of powers are mandated irrespective of whether government be federal or unitarily centralized, the branches of government are initially determined in abstraction from federalism. To the degree that federalism is at least a permissible option for self-government, the division of powers must be subsequently redetermined in regard to the modifications that a federal system entails.

Second, because unitary and federal government both have an internal domestic character, given independently of the relation between states, the basic determination of the branches of government under federal and centralized systems will abstract from international relations. Indeed, since political unity does not depend upon a plurality of states, the general concept of self-government would fail to possess the requisite universality if the differentiation of branches of government already reflected the contingent particular context of international affairs. Nevertheless, because the relation between states has structural ramifications for government as obvious as ministries of defense, diplomacy, and immigration, the division of powers must be reconsidered in light of how foreign affairs are to be handled by the branches of government. Insofar as each valid state will thereby acquire internal modifications on the basis of which international relations can proceed in conformity with political freedom, these organizational superventions must be conceived as a prelude to addressing the rights of nations.

3.7 POLITICAL PARTIES AND THE DIVISION OF POWERS

One last matter calls for inclusion in any systematic treatment of the division of powers—the role that political parties play in the workings of political freedom. This is a topic that has received relatively short shrift in normative political theory, as well as hardly any mention in constitutional statute, at least until recently.[13] It is tempting to attribute the pervasive neglect of parties in theories of the just state to the historical circumstance that the pioneers of teleological, liberal, and systematic political philosophy all theorized before mass parties had arisen and attained their predominance in modern politics. The grounds for neglect, however, lie not merely in historical contingencies. More crucial is a prevailing evaluation of political parties that has led much normative political theory to either ignore parties or expressly exclude them from the just state. This judgment rests on a common inclination to treat political parties as representatives of particular interests at odds with the universality of political action. Party partisanship allegedly subordinates the body politic to the parochial contest of factions, each vying to capture government for its own behalf.[14] Instead of embodying the general will of a self-governing citizenry, the party-ridden state becomes an instrument of partisan interest, which takes its final extreme in the transformation of government into a dispensary of party patronage. Then party machines render politics a means of private gain, subverting the sovereignty of the state over civil society.[15]

Underlying this repudiation of party politics and the corollary neglect of parties when conceiving the division of powers is a tendency to treat the reflexivity of politics as an abstract identity, where the general will gets conflated with the will of all, that is, with the aggregate of the individual wills of citizens as atomistically given in their personal preference. On this view, which pervades so much political thought from Rousseau through Carl Schmitt, the identity of ruler and ruled is only sustained when no intermediaries stand between popular opinion and state action and when popular opinion is itself undivided by factional disputes.[16] Self-rule appears to require both, for the exclusion of intermediaries allows popular opinion to have a direct expression in state action only if citizens are of one mind. Any disagreement involving shared political opinions would leave only the majority view present in the will of the state, leaving all other citizens alien to government policy. On the other hand, if citizens all had singularly different political positions, allowing for no grouping into factions, collective self-rule would be impossible. Political parties, however, comprise intervening bodies that relate citizens to government in terms of diverse political positions shared by different parts of the citizenry. The mediation and shared difference of party politics strikes doubly at the immediacy and unanimity of the identity conception and, from its point of view, doubly jeopardizes the unity of ruler and ruled constitutive of political self-determination.

Nonetheless, parties need not operate in function of the particular interests and particular prepolitical groups that give factions their bad name in traditional political theory. Although groups defined in these ways may invade the political arena and corrupt self-government, political parties can escape these deformations by comprising voluntary organizations advocating particular programs for determining the entire body politic and by allowing any citizens of a like political mind to join.[17] Because party organizations then rest upon differences of political opinion to which citizens can freely commit themselves irrespective of social and cultural distinctions, political parties retain the universality of end distinguishing political action and can thereby aspire to act for the political good of the entire citizenry. Further, since a valid constitution requires all political agents to always act in respect of the property, moral, family, social, and political rights of all citizens, political parties within a duly constitutional state will always be obliged to act for the sake of upholding these freedoms. Hence, instead of representing a particular interest, in the manner of a social corporate body, political parties will each duly advocate a specific view of how the state should govern so as to promote the rights of all citizens. Further, unlike mass movements that operate outside government institutions,[18] political parties will vie for office to put their political vision into practice. On this basis, the victory of one party or party coalition over others need not signify the capture of the state by some private interest and the reduction of government to patronage servicing.

These considerations dictate the basic parameters of citizens' right to establish and join political parties. All citizens are entitled to join in the party of their choosing provided the party in question is committed to respecting the nonpolitical and political rights of all and thereby to representing a particular vision of justice rather than a particular group from which others are excluded. Citizens do not have a right to form exclusionary parties limited to members of any particular classes, religious persuasions, races, ethnic or linguistic groups, genders, sexual orientations, geographical regions within the state, or other divisions extraneous to a difference in approach as to how to realize the political unity of self-government. Any such exclusionary parties would jeopardize the reflexivity and universality of politics by aiming to capture political power for a particular sector of the citizenry, to whom all others would be subordinate. It matters not whether the group claims to be the majority, as labor and or peasant parties have portrayed themselves in recapturing the state for the "people." So long as a party identifies itself with any particular part of the citizenry, the power it seeks can never be that of self-government, for it will always involve a rule over a subject class excluded from the reigning faction. That the faction promotes the interests of a historically oppressed group does not mitigate this injustice. Any political struggle defined by divisions between oppressed and oppressor only imposes a new bondage. To escape the divide of ruling and subject political classes, the parties vying for power must instead compete on behalf of different visions of how to uphold political justice and its prerequisite freedoms. Accordingly, the existence of more than one party is a requirement for democracy[19] not because it ensures a political voice to different interest groups, but because it leaves citizens free to advance different political positions in the pursuit of justice.

Accordingly, citizens cannot be entitled to form parties advocating the violation of rights. If they were, citizens would lay claim to a privilege to oppress others, contradicting the universality of rights and the exclusive normativity of self-determination. Citizens may retain a civil right to express views challenging the legitimacy of freedom, but moving from private speech to organized activity to seize state power on behalf of political wrong is a different matter.

Similarly, citizens do retain the right to enter groups advocating the interests of particular sections of civil society, but these social-interest groups do not have the right to enter the political arena and engage in the activities of self-government to which political parties properly direct themselves. Social-interest groups may lobby government officials and urge their members to influence party platforms, but if political rights are to be upheld, those who engage in self-rule must always act on behalf of the entire citizenry. If instead they ignore the universality of political aims and substitute the particular interest of a specific group, the reflexivity of political freedom gets subverted and the state becomes an instrument by which some sector dominates a subject group.[20] Then, the good of the nation becomes separated from all party activity in and out of office, setting the stage for distorted nationalist appeals supplanting the institutions of political freedom with movements standing above the state in the name of the people.[21]

These dangers make evident how the basic principles for legitimate party organization constitute a key element of political right. As such, these principles warrant a clear constitutional statutory statement enabling all citizens to have an objective and universal specification of their corollary rights and duties as party members. Upholding these constitutional strictures will, like all other principles of right, require positive laws and executive enforcement to certify parties and regulate their activities.[22] Hence, the political oversight of party organization must be addressed in determining the activities of the different powers of government.

Granted that political parties can and should act in congruence with the universality, reflexivity, and supremacy of political self-determination, and that this congruence needs to be enforced by government regulation, there remain two complementary challenges that parties seem to pose to the division of powers.

On the one hand, if the legislators comprising the bloc deciding legislation belong to a party or party coalition at odds with that of the head of state or of the chief executive and the cabinet, the conflicting party loyalties might deadlock self-government. Instead of refusing authorization only to bills of questionable constitutionality, a head of state could strike down any laws that oppose the party program to which the authorizer adheres. Similarly, the chief executive and the cabinet could seek to stymie the implementation of legislation passed by a hostile party bloc.

On the other hand, if the party bloc controlling the legislature is the same one to which the head of state or the chief executive and the cabinet adhere, party loyalty might seem to defeat the division of powers by subordinating the ostensibly separated branches of government to the actual unitary control of the ruling party bloc. In that case, the hegemonic party would seem to be in a position to do anything it pleases with state power.

These difficulties seem to loom large irrespective of how party candidates get selected. Whether caucuses of a party's elected officials, provincial or national party conventions, or provincial or national party primaries determine who runs for office on a party's banner, the complementary specters of "divided government" or unalloyed party rule will still haunt the division of powers.

If these problems are both insurmountable and sufficient to undermine constitutionality, political parties become a dilemma for self-government. If, instead, these problems can be mitigated without destroying the workings of political freedom, the division of powers must be so structured as to allow parties to be intermediary organs of equal political opportunity. Hence, the due determination of each power of government must address the role of political parties within its sphere.

3.8 METHODOLOGICAL PERPLEXITIES IN CONCEIVING PARTIES AND THE STRUCTURES OF SELF-GOVERNMENT

The place for parties in the workings of political freedom issues in the first instance from the basic parameters of political right. Citizens have a right to organize or join preexisting parties so far as doing so contributes to exercising their equal political opportunity. Given how political self-determination depends upon the perpetuation of nonpolitical freedoms, if political party membership is an organ of self-government, it will equally be consonant with the property, moral, household, and social rights of citizens and noncitizens alike. In this respect, citizens have the right to speak in public and assemble in public to advance their political agendas, either as independents or party members, so long as doing so does not undermine the political and nonpolitical rights of others. This does not give citizens complete license to speak and assemble in public, since certain forms of speech and assembly can constitute conspiracies to undermine the rights of others or acts of intimidation and aggression that violate civil and political freedoms. Although any political position can be discussed and analyzed, agitation actively working to impose oppression in politics, society, or the home is incompatible with the exercise of rights.

Yet, given the due limits of legitimate political speech and assembly, how can party activity make a contribution to political freedom that goes beyond what citizens can achieve in and out of office as independent, unaffiliated agents? Although political parties may operate in conformity with constitutional guidelines preventing them from impeding political and nonpolitical rights, the possibility of rectitude does not secure parties any essential, necessary place in self-rule. The question still remains open as to whether parties play any positive role, enabling them to be more than dispensable ornaments of citizenship. To find the answer, the basic options must be examined that political parties have under constitutional self-rule for mediating between citizens and government in accord with right.

First, parties can operate as voluntary organizations that seek to persuade as many other citizens as possible to act for a particular political program in whatever ways citizens participate in self-rule as individuals. In this capacity, political parties function as partisan molders of public opinion, like any public-interest group that seeks to influence the politics of citizens without itself vying for any government offices. Such party activity can readily respect the manifold rights of citizens so long as membership is open to all interested citizens and the proselytizing activity does not prevent individuals of opposing political positions from exercising their constitutional prerogatives.

Provided at least some citizens find among themselves enough political agreement to take joint action to persuade and mobilize others to take like-minded political action, political parties can emerge and offer their partisans a political clout outstripping the opportunity of political independents. Those who resist party affiliation find themselves in one of two situations of political disadvantage. They may find themselves holding political views without resonance among any other citizens, leaving them a voice in the wilderness, with nothing more than their personal resources to rely upon in trying to have any further impact upon political life. Alternately, citizens may encounter others who share their politics but with whom they take no joint partisan activity to influence the course of the state. In that case, their political efficacy remains a mere sum of individual efforts, lacking whatever additional powers of persuasion common organization can provide. Consequently, once citizens establish political parties and enjoy the benefits of common undertakings, party affiliation becomes a resource of which all citizens must avail themselves to escape political disadvantage.[23]

Admittedly, if party activity were limited to joint efforts at persuasion, with no specific role in governing, the political process would still function without any organized imprint of party divisions. Individuals in and out of office might well embody patterns of political behavior reflecting different party persuasions. Nonetheless, legislative, authorizing, and executive positions would all be filled by individuals whose party membership has no necessary consequences for their official duties. The divide between the citizenry at large and government officials would remain structurally unmediated by party organization.

This is true whether parties direct their political persuasion upon the citizenry at large or engage in lobbying of government officials. In either case, party activity is directed at influencing the political choices of individuals who, whether in or out of office, are left to their own designs when it comes to taking political action. Be they subject to general party propagandizing or to lobbying, citizens are left to act as individuals who may or may not be swayed by party views, rather than as party members who take political actions only possible in terms of their party affiliation. However persistent be such party advocacy, citizens can still take their political actions in complete indifference to the very existence of each and every party.

Insofar as these activities can proceed without violating any rights, they do still comprise a legitimate prerogative of citizens, just as permissible as the advocacy activities of social-interest groups. Nonetheless, this hardly exhausts the political options of parties. As several centuries of modern political history can testify, what distinguishes political parties from public-advocacy groups is precisely that parties do not limit their activities to nongovernmental activities of persuasion. Instead, political parties insert themselves directly into the political process to participate institutionally in the running of self-government. To the degree that this occurs, party involvement becomes all the more important for political opportunity.

Given the general framework of political freedom, parties can become more than instruments of political persuasion in two interconnected arenas. On the one hand, they can play an organized role in the selection of candidates for office. On the other hand, parties can enter government as such when officeholders act in their official capacities in function of their party membership.

To be legitimate, both of these interventions must not only operate in respect of the nonpolitical rights of citizens and noncitizens but equally uphold the equal political opportunity of all citizens. In other words, party involvement in the selection of officials and in the governing by officials will only be valid insofar as it serves as a vehicle of political self-determination.

Because political freedom entails constitutional self-government with rule by and under law, which requires a division of legislative, authorizing, and executive powers, the legitimate role of parties must be determined in view of these concrete aspects of the just state. Party involvement in the selection of officials cannot be determined in abstraction from the different roles of each power of government, nor from their interconnection. Similarly, how parties enter into the running of government can only be determined in respect to the specific functions of each power. For these reasons, the proper role of parties in self-government can only be duly conceived in conjunction with the determination of the different powers of government. Nevertheless, before determining each separate power of government, it is possible to anticipate general features of the role of parties in mediating citizens and government, no matter what power is at stake.

3.9 BASIC NORMATIVE ISSUES FOR PARTY INVOLVEMENT IN THE SELECTION OF GOVERNMENT OFFICIALS

Needless to say, in order for political parties to play any legitimate role in selecting government officials, self-government must allow for a distinction between officeholders and nonofficeholders that does not subvert self-rule. As we have seen, the division of powers entails such a distinction, since if all citizens engaged in legislation, authorization, and execution, the will of each power would be one and the same. Constitutionality would evaporate in face of a will of all that could do no wrong. The requirement for a distinction between officeholders and nonofficeholders applies irrespective of whether direct or indirect democracy applies to the legislative power, since even if all citizens were to legislate in person, they need not all participate in the authorizing and executive powers.

Of course, distinguishing officeholders from the citizenry at large does not guarantee that all officials warrant selection through direct, let alone indirect election. If party involvement in candidate selection is tied to electoral choice of officials, it will apply only to those officials and, indeed, only to those powers of government that should be filled by election. Determining the proper scope for electoral selection depends upon the functions of and relationships between powers of government. For example, posts in the executive branch that require special expertise may best require an examination system of recruitment, whereas officials in one branch of government may, at least under certain circumstances, best be selected by officials of another branch. Consequently, how officials should be chosen cannot be decided apart from the investigation of each power of government. Nevertheless, granted that some officials should be elected into office, parties may lay claim to a role in the nomination of candidates, as well as in the ensuing electoral process, provided party involvement sustains equal political opportunity and its prepolitical requirements. This proviso bears upon both the scope and manner of party participation in candidate selection.

If every citizen is to enjoy a right to run for those offices duly up for election, parties cannot have an automatic monopoly in candidate selection. Independent candidacies must be allowed, subject to those requirements that prevent the electoral process from being overwhelmed by legions of self-nominated office seekers. Otherwise, citizens' opportunity to participate in governing will be limited to the party faithful, leaving independents deprived of any equal right to rule.

Further, candidates should have the right to run as fusion candidates, that is, as the official nominee of more than one party. If fusion candidacy is prohibited, parties lose their right to nominate otherwise eligible candidates of their choosing, just as would-be candidates lose their right to seek the support of any citizen groups with whom they have political agreement. Such prohibitions are sometimes upheld as pillars of a two-party system designed to escape the instability of fragmented multiparty systems. Although a two-party political landscape is not illegitimate in principle, it violates political freedom if it results from anything but the unrestricted exercise of the rights to run for office and participate in political party activity. The fact that fusion candidacies make it easier for smaller parties to elect candidates is, if anything, an extension of equal political opportunity to their supporters.

In any event, when citizens join and/or support parties fielding candidates, the way parties select their own candidates, be they exclusive or coalition nominees, should facilitate rather than diminish the political choice of the electorate. Although party activity always involves consolidating individual political opinions into a joint program of a particular group of citizens, this move from the individual to the particular will only uphold equal political opportunity if citizens retain relative parity in determining the spectrum of political options.

In this regard, the distinction between party officials and party rank and file has important consequences. Although party officials need not be professionals, the emergence of mass parties provides both the financial basis and organizational responsibilities enabling as well as requiring parties to employ full-time functionaries, led by professional party politicians, who may rotate in and out of government office when the opportunity presents itself.[24] This provides a niche for individuals to earn a living from politics without holding paid government positions.[25] If professional party officials are not accountable to the party rank and file, but instead control party political activity, the equal political opportunity of the party rank and file is undercut, to the extent that it depends upon the mediation of political parties. This disparity of power among party members then gets ramified depending upon the role of parties in the political process.

Granted these considerations, whichever government officials in whichever power of government are electable by the citizenry, parties can mediate their choice provided some, if not all, candidates, run as members of a party or party coalition, which plays a role in their selection as a party candidate. Historically, this role has taken various forms, both within the same and among differing electoral systems.

A party elite can meet behind closed doors and decide upon both party platform and candidates, as well as negotiate campaign agreements with other parties.[26] Although this leaves the final selection of officials up to the electorate, if all candidates are nominated by party leaders without any input from the party membership, a narrow cabal usurps the power to decide the alternatives from which the general citizenry can choose.[27]

This concentration of nominating power can be mitigated by party caucuses that allow a wider spectrum of party activists to codetermine platform and candidates. Although attendance at such caucuses depends at least partly upon a self-selection by those party members willing to shoulder the major work of party organization, this still leaves party members at large, not to mention unaffiliated voters in general, without any role in determining party slates and program.[28] Opening party caucuses to the light of publicity may at least allow nonparticipants to observe the proceedings, but knowledge without choice is only one part of responsible involvement.

Provincial and national party conventions can extend participation to further sections of party membership, depending upon how delegates are selected. Schemes of corporate representation can assign delegates to different social-interest groups, defined by differences of occupation, race, ethnicity, language, religion, gender, sexual orientation, or any other prepolitical factor the party chooses to privilege. Delegates can be selected from local party caucuses or include a greater or lesser number of elected officials. If delegates act as corporate or regional representatives, intervening on behalf of some particular group of citizens rather than as advocates of a particular program for upholding the political and nonpolitical rights of all, party life risks turning into a contest for domination by one faction over the rest instead of a properly political contest between competing interpretations of the party's vision of political justice. Even if delegates adhere to duly universal aims, party members have at best an indirect connection to the proceedings, whose eventual outcome depends upon the will of the delegates.

A more inclusive participation in candidate nomination is provided by party primary elections, a course pioneered in the United States but largely ignored elsewhere.[29] Under a primary system, the choice of party candidate is left to voters who decide between whichever individuals have qualified to run for the party nomination. Primaries in the United States usually follow winner-take-all single-district representation models. Nonetheless, primary elections could be organized in ways which counter majoritarian imbalances with proportional representation schemes of one sort or another.[30] These, however, may so fracture primary voting as to end up leaving candidate selection to backroom parleys, as well as to so proliferate candidates as to hinder both their ability to make themselves known and voters' opportunity to inform themselves of the choices. Whether majoritarian or proportional selection is employed, primaries can further limit participation to party members or be opened to the general electorate. Whatever scheme be adopted, political opportunities will be limited by several basic conditions.

First, any inequalities in private resources that translate into campaign advantages will privilege some and disadvantage other candidates and their followers. This problem, however, is not specific to primaries, but extends to every election and must be addressed at all levels.

Second, although primaries place the choice of party nominees in the hands of primary voters, party platform is not thereby directly decided. At best, primaries can determine which programs are supported by the victorious nominees, but that determination hardly guarantees any unity across party slates. So long as primary candidates are at liberty to run for party nomination without having to adopt an independently determined agenda, any uniformity among primary victors will be a matter of chance. If there is to be a bona fide party platform, it will have to be developed and endorsed apart from primary elections, which is to say, outside the hands of the general party membership by whatever select party group takes charge of this undertaking.

Of course, the adoption of a party platform by the party hierarchy signifies little if the victorious primary candidates are at liberty both to campaign and to occupy elective office for the sake of a political program of their own individual choosing. One of the chief reasons why primaries have hardly been embraced outside the United States may well be that primary selection of party nominees reduces one of the principal means with which party organizations can discipline their elected members—namely, controlling their ability to run for reelection.[31] With smoke-filled rooms and party caucuses giving way to primary elections, even national party conventions get reduced to mechanical ratifications of prior primary results, unless no clear victor emerges. Under these conditions, much of the ability of parties to enforce partisan platforms falls by the wayside. Unless parties can somehow retain control of the resources for running subsequent campaigns, the primary victors can enter office free to act without concern for how party officials view their performance. If, however, campaign funding is left in the hands of party organizations, then the will of primary voters is liable to be frustrated.

Whatever the normative significance, primary elections' potential loosening of party unity is further accentuated when primaries are open to party members and nonmembers alike. Such open primaries do give every citizen a role in determining all the party nominees for office, which might be held to enhance equal political opportunity. Open primaries, however, thereby jeopardize the integrity of party differences by allowing the same majority of citizens to determine all opposing nominees. In effect, citizens forfeit their opportunity to choose among a full spectrum of political positions. Given consistent voter behavior and candidates in every party willing to curry popular favor, multiparty politics becomes a charade of tweedle dum and tweedle dee opponents, whose perennial political agreement leaves only personal "character" and "experience" as distinguishing marks.

Even when open primaries are prohibited, primary elections still circumvent party hierarchies by the direct appeal of competing candidates to voters who otherwise may have no other involvement in party activity than voter registration as a party member. By contrast, nomination by party caucus or party convention interjects the mediating activities of local party organizations, in which citizens can participate by self-selection, provided these organizations are duly open to all appropriately politically interested citizens. This does not guarantee that primaries leave voters mere spectators of party campaigns, with a withering away of grass roots party organization.[32] Primary campaigns may themselves be undertaken by grass roots campaign organizations, within which citizens have an opportunity to debate and influence candidate platforms. Moreover, grass roots initiative may be all the more encouraged when primaries prevent party insiders from monopolizing party affairs.

These various possibilities indicate that, in face of the Scylla and Charybdis of backroom nominations and open primaries, deciding which procedure for selecting party nominees best realizes political freedom is difficult enough in abstraction from the different functions and interconnections of the powers of government. Even apart from these concrete political considerations, however, the party nomination process can hardly be assessed without reference to how party organization should impact upon officeholders in their running of government.

3.10 BASIC NORMATIVE ISSUES FOR PARTY INVOLVEMENT IN GOVERNMENT

Modern political history has offered a slew of competing systems by which parties occupy government in fulfillment of some modicum of political freedom. Although their variety suggests a certain latitude in the form self-government can take, certain axes of difference point to perennial challenges that party involvement in government must resolve if political rights are to be upheld.

The prime contrast is provided by the polar roles of parties under parliamentary and presidential systems. Leaving aside one-party dictatorships that openly suppress the basic rights of political pluralism, parliamentary systems offer perhaps the greatest party integration in governing by empowering the party or party coalition controlling the legislature to appoint a prime minister and cabinet from its ranks, to wield some control in selecting authorizing officials, and to dismiss and replace officials who violate party discipline or lose its confidence. At the other extreme are presidential systems where the party formation dominating parliament does not directly appoint or dismiss executive or authorizing officials, nor does it have license to enforce strict party discipline in the legislature or in any other branch of government.

Under the parliamentary system, the predominant party or party coalition quite literally rules, with the prevailing party leadership disposing of the maximum levers for implementing the party platform at all stages of governing. The party in power is ensured not only of passing its legislative agenda, but of certifying its constitutionality and executing it in a spirit to its liking. If this hegemony is compounded by an electoral process where the party leadership determines campaign platforms, decides upon nominees, and controls campaign financing, the general party membership, not to mention the electorate at large, has the least opportunity to do more than ratify the policies of the party leadership. Yet even if caucuses, conventions, or primaries extend control of party affairs to a wider constituency, party control over legislative, authorizing, and executive powers still threatens the limits of constitutionality to the degree that the will of the party can thereby be a law unto itself.

By contrast, when party control of the legislature does not translate into party mastery over the executive or authorizing branches, the division of powers can retain its limiting functions, at least so long as "presidential" responsibilities do not illicitly conjoin prerogatives properly distributed among different executive and authorizing powers. What then optimally defines the role of party membership in the performance of office are the legitimate possibilities internal to each power of government. Although party membership warrants notice only insofar as it involves joint partisan action unavailable to independents, this ought not subvert the equal political opportunity of members of competing parties or of independents in or out of office.

How this should occur cannot be determined apart from an assessment of the specific function and organization that each power of government ought involve. Nonetheless, a few anticipations can at least clarify that party involvement in government has institutional ramifications.

This is perhaps most evident in the legislative branch. In legislatures, it has been common for party caucuses to choose committee chairs and chamber "speakers" and "whips," who perform leading functions in legislative procedures. When legislative elections alter which party or party coalition controls parliament, these positions change accordingly. All these party-mediated positions mark legislative activity with a party imprint to the extent that they facilitate the translation of party platforms into legislation. This typically occurs by the party leader of a legislative chamber guiding passage of the party legislative program, whose detailed elaborations and compromise adjustments get worked out by legislative committees, overseen by party chairs, before final adoption on the assembly floor. In this manner, party membership signifies more than a passive congruence between legislative positions. It instead involves an active coordination of the legislative process leaving independent legislators in an accessory position.

Although party discipline might seem to preclude real deliberation, as Carl Schmitt believed,[33] party involvement in the legislative process need not make legislative debate an empty formality. The elaboration of the party program into detailed legislation itself requires deliberation and debate. Moreover, party members still need to debate among themselves and with nonparty legislators to ensure that any legislative proposal actually be adopted, be it as originally formulated or as amended in compromise negotiation. These conditions apply even when a party can expel dissenters or prevent their future nomination on party tickets. No such measures can ever guarantee unanimity among party legislators when bills are put to a vote.

Similar conditions apply in the authorizing and executive branches. Wherever a controlling bloc of officials shares party loyalties, the presence of an underlying partisan agenda precludes neither deliberation nor initiative on their part. How this can legitimately proceed, however, is a question awaiting answer in the investigation of the three powers of constitutional self-government, whose determination now lies at hand.

NOTES

1. Universal military service can be avoided provided that (1) society is sufficiently civil to overcome the economic disadvantage that might make the poor disproportionate cannon fodder for a professional military, and (2) professional soldiers can be sufficiently trained and subordinated to civilian control to remove the threat of military rule.

2. In par. 299 of the *Elements of the Philosophy of Right*, G. W. F. Hegel argues this point, emphasizing how taxation allows the state to get the resources it needs from its citizens in conformity with their civil and political autonomy. See Hegel, *Elements of the Philosophy of Right*, ed. Allen W. Wood, trans. H. B. Nisbet (Cambridge: Cambridge University Press, 1991), pp. 337–38. Needless to say, taxation provides this service so long as it is tied to the election of salaried officials and to bureaucracy, that is, the professionalization of government service by nonelected functionaries.

3. As Norberto Bobbio observes, it is law, and not the private agreement of contract, which plays a constitutive role in political justice. Although contract may reenter in treaties between states, contract itself operates within the political sphere under the legal jurisdiction of the state. See Bobbio, *The Future of Democracy*, ed. Richard Bellamy, trans. Roger Griffin (Minneapolis: University of Minnesota Press, 1987), p. 120.

4. Jürgen Habermas seeks to overcome the formal connection by claiming that the rule of law and democracy are internally connected, both because the democratic process cannot operate without securing the private and public autonomy of legal subjects and because legal rights can neither be formulated nor implemented unless legal subjects democratically participate in their legal enactment (Habermas, *Between Facts and Norms: Contributions to a Discourse Theory of Law and Democracy*, trans. William Rehg [Cambridge, MA: MIT Press, 1996], pp. 449–50, 454). Admittedly, equal political opportunity cannot be achieved unless citizens enjoy the legal enforcement of civil rights, including equal household and economic opportunity.

Habermas, however, fails to recognize that civil legality can exist, and, indeed, has and does exist, without democracy. This reflects how civil society is a precondition of self-government and can therefore exist prior to political emancipation. For this reason, nations can be encouraged to erect civil society before being encouraged to complete democratization. Although the same revolution that overthrows feudal estate society and produces civil society simultaneously overthrows the feudal political order of estate assemblies, as Karl Marx observed in *On The Jewish Question* (Marx, *Early Writings*, trans. T. B. Bottomore [New York: McGraw Hill, 1964], pp. 29–30), the example of the French Revolution shows how the result may not be stable democracy but an autocratic dictatorship presiding over civil society.

5. Robert A. Dahl makes this point, acknowledging that rule under law is still insufficient to guarantee self-determination. See Dahl, *Democracy and Its Critics* (New Haven, CT: Yale University Press, 1989), p. 108.

6. For further exploration of this key character of political unity, see "The Logic of the State" in Richard Dien Winfield, *Overcoming Foundations: Studies in Systematic Philosophy* (New York: Columbia University Press, 1989), pp. 249–69.

7. As Michael Oakeshott observes, insofar as laws cannot be deduced from reason, legislative opinion cannot be demonstrably correct or incorrect. See Oakeshott, *On Human Conduct* (Oxford: Oxford University Press, 1975), p. 139.

8. Oakeshott bewails this deformation of parliament into a market where private interests clamor for awards from patron governments or bargain with one another for enjoyment of satisfactions. See Oakeshott, *On Human Conduct*, p. 312.

9. Consequently, Habermas is wrong in claiming that due judgment of the legitimacy of the law that citizens make is provided by the right to participate in the political processes that form legislators' opinion and will (Habermas, *Between Facts and Norms*, pp. 126–27). Not only do all these processes leave intact the autonomy of legislators, without which parliamentary debate and deliberation becomes eviscerated, but they contribute no separate authorizing power to check unconstitutional legislation.

10. See Arend Lijphart, *Patterns of Democracy: Government Forms and Performance in Thirty-Six Countries* (New Haven: Yale University Press, 1999), p. 225.

11. Lijphart observes that most contemporary presidential systems make the president simultaneously head of state and head of government. See Lijphart, *Patterns of Democracy*, p. 126.

12. As Bobbio points out, Hegel's estate legislature precludes political representation of parties by limiting itself to representation of corporate interests. See Bobbio, *Which Socialism?* ed. Richard Bellamy, trans. Roger Griffin (Cambridge, UK: Polity, 1988), p. 150.

13. As late as the twentieth century, Max Weber could still remark from his vantage in Weimar Germany that no constitution and no law acknowledges the existence of political parties, even though parties are the most important bearers of citizens' political will. See Weber, *Political Writings*, ed. Peter Lassman and Ronald Speirs (Cambridge: Cambridge University Press, 1994), p. 149.

14. On these grounds, Jean-Jacques Rousseau bans all factions, as if individuals could participate in self-legislation without coalescing into political groupings. Of course, he presumes that unanimity can reign, but that is begging the question.

15. As Weber observes, under such a spoils system, contending parties become utterly unprincipled instruments of position seekers, changing their electoral programs as needed to win the most votes. See Weber, *Political Writings*, p. 345.

16. When, for example, Hannah Arendt offers a council system as an alternative to the party system of parliamentary government, she assumes that citizens can participate in councils without forming political groups and reproducing the same mediations that the party system involves. (See Arendt, *On Revolution* [New York: Viking, 1965], pp. 267–69). This could only happen if citizens either act as unanimous clones or as unique surds lacking any political commonality allowing for party grouping. Whereas the former situation eliminates political plurality, the latter makes self-rule impossible. What the party system offers is a particularization that contains universality, enabling citizens to govern themselves in function of their plurality. Significantly, Arendt admits that the call to transcend the factional strife of the party system characterizes all imperialistic, totalitarian movements. See Arendt, *The Origins of Totalitarianism*, new ed. with added prefaces (New York: Harcourt Brace Jovanovich, 1973), p. 250.

17. Of course, as Weber observes, besides being organized dispensers of patronage or proponents of a political vision, political parties can also be a combination of these two types. See Weber, *Political Writings*, p. 152. The rise of a civil service bureaucracy curtails the opportunities for patronage dispensation.

18. Arendt distinguishes between parties and mass movements in respect to how the latter operate outside parliamentary institutions and

instead invade the household, cultural life, and the economy—the non-political spheres that Arendt tends to conceive as private arenas, following the ancient *oikos/polis* divide. See Arendt, *On Revolution*, p. 275.

19. Bobbio argues that a plurality of parties is the *conditio sine qua non* of democracy. See Bobbio, *The Future of Democracy*, p. 124.

20. This is what Arendt diagnoses happening in the "Continental party system," where parties are organized around different social groups, leading to domination by some groups over others, instead of proper self-government. Although she claims that this does not occur in two-party systems, it could if the two parties represent the interests of different sections of society, instead of different political visions. See Arendt, *The Origins of Totalitarianism*, pp. 112, 253–54.

21. Arendt discusses how this nationalist/totalitarian threat to self-government arises from the Continental party system, where social interest reigns supreme. See Arendt, *The Origins of Totalitarianism*, pp. 255, 260, 264–66.

22. What lies at issue are not hidden agendas, whose surreptitious intentions allegedly underlie party actions and programs but publicly expressed party platforms, membership policies, operational regulations, and activities both in and out of parliament. The latter are all eminently susceptible of external legal and administrative regulation, consonant with the workings of self-government.

23. Lani Guinier argues that groups are the appropriate units for political participation because the right to elect has no value at the level of the single individual, whose one vote is of itself of purely nominal significance. Unfortunately, Guinier does not have in mind political parties, but culturally defined interest groups, whose domination of political participation bodes ill for self-government. See Guinier, *The Tyranny of the Majority: Fundamental Fairness in Representative Democracy* (New York: Free Press, 1994), p. 93.

24. As Weber observes, the professional party politician inevitably results from the rationalization and specialization of party political work in the context of mass elections. See Weber, *Political Writings*, p. 216.

25. As Weber points out, if one seeks to live "from" politics, the likely options outside elective government office are journalism and professional party employment. See Weber, *Political Writings*, p. 352.

26. Bobbio claims that the relationship between political parties takes the form of contractual agreements, such as are covered by the civil code (Bobbio, *The Future of Democracy*, p. 124). This has some plausibility, since political organizations confront one another as independent parties to possible agreements. Yet, because what lies at stake in party negotiation is not

disposal over property, but joint political action, party agreements cannot have the strict binding force of contract, which always concerns what is and should be external to persons. Since, in contrast to property, the right to independent political action cannot be legitimately alienated, political parties are always free to pull out of party coalitions and other agreements with one another without facing any legal liabilities.

27. As Weber points out, when the party leader controls a party machine nominating candidates and keeping party legislators in check, government tends in the direction of plebiscitary rule, since the citizenry ends up affirming nothing but the control of that leader, who dominates parliament. See Weber, *Political Writings*, pp. 339, 343–44.

28. Hence Weber can observe that even mass parties with comparatively democratic forms of organization leave their ordinary membership, not to mention the mass of voters, participating in deciding on programs and candidates only in the formal sense that platforms and nominees are determined by the party leadership in view of winning their votes. See Weber, *Political Writings*, p. 150.

29. Arendt goes so far as to claim that parties, with the possible exception of those in the United States that employ primaries, usurp power from the citizenry, who only have the opportunity to ratify choices made by the party without their participation. This disempowerment allegedly compounds that effected by parliamentary representation, which Arendt, in line with the false identity conception of self-rule, views as a surrender of political participation by the citizenry, putting the monopoly of political action in the hands of elected officials. See Arendt, *On Revolution*, pp. 251, 273, 275, 277.

30. If, however, the entire legislature is selected with a proportional representation scheme using party slates, selection of individual candidates by primary election is largely precluded. See chap. 4 for further discussion of this issue as it bears upon the controversy between majoritarian and proportional election schemes.

31. James L. Sundquist raises this issue in connection with United States presidential primaries in *Constitutional Reform and Effective Government* (Washington, DC: Brookings Institution, 1992), pp. 251ff.

32. Michael Walzer suggests this outcome, ignoring how primaries leave open many opportunities for grass roots party organization to coalesce around primary election campaigns. See Walzer, *Spheres of Justice* (New York: Basic Books, 1983), pp. 307–308.

33. See Carl Schmitt, *The Crisis of Parliamentary Democracy*, trans. Ellen Kennedy (Cambridge, MA: MIT Press, 1985), pp. 6, 49–50.

CHAPTER 4

THE LEGISLATIVE BRANCH OF SELF-GOVERNMENT

4.1 LEGISLATION, DIRECT DEMOCRACY, AND POLITICAL FREEDOM

Self-government must involve rule by as well as under law because of the converging imperatives of legally enforcing rights, maintaining the reflexivity and universality of political self-determination, and upholding the entire constitutional system of freedom in the face of changing circumstances.

Each of these considerations appears to support and, indeed, require direct democracy in legislation, where each citizen personally participates in the activity of lawmaking. If all citizens join in the legislative process without any representative intermediaries, they would seem to participate in a lawful willing that enjoys the purest reflexivity. Whereas indirect participation through representative legislators differentiates official lawmakers from the citizenry at large, a participatory legislative assembly guarantees that those who impose law are identical to those who are subject to it. By the same token, whatever be the formula for determining the prevailing legislative consensus, direct participation insures that legislation issues from the most unmediated collective decision making of *all* citizens. Hence, the resulting law would seem to enjoy the most maximally universal origin, emanating as it does from the will of all citizens. Further, if interest be identified as the self-selected good of an agent, the direct participation of all citizens in lawmaking would stamp legislation as an expression of the most universal of interests, the general interest of the citizenry as directly codetermined in their legislative activity. Moreover, the task of realizing the constitution in face of contingent circumstances requires nothing more than the competencies of rational agency that each citizen must already possess to exercise any rights whatsoever. Consequently, there would seem to be no legitimate ground for excluding the citizenry at large from participating directly in legislation. Finally, given access to the virtually instantaneous communication of cybernetic connections or their future equivalents, the principal technical obstacles to direct mass participation would seem to have been overcome. Under these circumstances, failure to institute participatory legislation would seem inexcusably to restrict political autonomy to the periodic choice of representative legislators, who then monopolize lawmaking for themselves, impose their particular interests upon the citizenry at large, and thereby deprive politics of the universality and reflexivity on which genuine self-rule depends. But can direct democracy be applied to the legislative branch of government without enfeebling the legislative process itself and undermining the nonpolitical rights on which political autonomy rests?

The practicalities of participatory legislation have perennially been questioned on several fronts. To begin with, skeptics have commonly observed that an assembly of all citizens is only feasible if the body politic be no larger than a small city-state or Alpine canton. If this view were accepted, direct democracy might be redeemed simply by biting the bullet and conceiving the just state on the scale of an emancipated Monaco. Of course, Lilliputian states may be at risk of being devoured by leviathan neighbors, but this objection could be parried by putting hopes in alliances feeding off big power rivalry. That direct democracy could exist only under such geopolitical good fortune need not disqualify its legitimacy. This would simply mean that those who face less favorable conjunctures would have to aim for the imperfect alternative that provides the optimal political association under those circumstances.

Liabilities of political miniaturization could be circumvented, of course, by employing cybernetic interconnections to create a virtual direct assembly for an online citizenry of any size. Through such technology, all citizens could have access to each and every legislative proposal that anyone might introduce, as well as enjoy the opportunity to make amendments, counter proposals, or support arguments that every other citizen could instantaneously download. Finally, when the time came to decide on prospective laws, the votes of each citizen could be immediately registered and the results made universally known. Thereby the body politic can become transformed into a national chatroom, where each citizen has access to the same wealth of political information and equal opportunity to intervene in legislative debate and deliberation, where the entirety of the legislative process is transparent to each participating citizen, where the magnitude and complexity of a politically organized civil society would no longer seem beyond the grasp of direct self-legislation. No more would the limitations of representative legislation relegate direct participation to the subordinate pigeon holes of municipal ward assemblies or the nonpolitical self-management of social enterprises in pursuit of their particular interests. So, at least, beckons the reveries of the cybernetic empire of direct democracy. Yet, whether direct democracy be cybernetically elasticized or bound to the environs of a stadium, procedural problems cannot help but make participation in person a perniciously cumbersome undertaking.

If the engagement of citizens were limited to giving approval or disapproval to lists of legislative proposals, in the manner of referenda, a direct voice in legislation could be feasible, either in an Athenian assembly or a cybernetic virtual legislature. Whether participatory decisions would be blind or informed, however, would depend upon the size and complexity of individual bills and their aggregate number.[1] Unless each citizen were freed of other commitments and supplied with adequate staff and support to penetrate the mass of pending legislation, only the most paltry legislative calendar could be given more than perfunctory popular attention. Even then, however, the citizenry would have no direct involvement in determining the agenda of legislative decision making or the deliberative process honing final legislative proposals.[2] If proposed legislation were put to public vote by private initiative, in the manner of popular referenda, citizens would be hostage to whatever agenda the most active and influential social groups favor.[3] The most democratic input that could be hoped for would be an indirect say effected by selecting representatives to perform the decisive functions of legislative agenda setting and deliberation.[4] The resulting combination of representative deliberation and popular referenda would, of course, only be feasible when legislative production remains scant in volume and complexity.[5]

Any attempt to leave the entire legislative process to participatory democracy would face the immediate prospect of massive overload and paralysis, so long as citizens do not relinquish their plurality by acting and thinking as unanimous clones. Although each citizen-legislator would have a potential equal opportunity to propose laws, suggest amendments to prior proposals, debate contending interventions, and choose among competing proposals, none of these prerogatives can be exercised the moment any sizeable number of citizens attempts to join in the fray. No matter how cybernetically interconnected they be, citizens will have no time to peruse one another's respective proposals, amendments, or comments, nor even have the time to vote upon the myriad motions that must be made if direct participation is to be more than a formal possibility. If each citizen exercises the participatory prerogative of introducing a legislative proposal, every citizen would first have to become informed of all these proposals if they are then each to engage in debate about them, let alone to bring any to a vote. And if each citizen were to communicate an opinion about each proposal, they would all have to inform themselves of each such intervention before due responses could be made, which might then generate a further round of possible amendments, all of which would next have to be accessed by each participant, if they are to consider them and communicate their readiness to vote. That readiness would itself have to be registered by each and to each, leading to further exponential multiplications of advice and consent before any legislative outcome could be reached. In reality, any trace of real deliberation would disappear under an avalanche of unanswerable communications, which could only be circumvented by the self-abstention of the overwhelming mass of citizens.[6] Of course, in that case, the general lethargy of the citizenry would effectively render the few legislative activists representatives of their virtual assembly.

Compounding this impasse is the impossibility of maintaining any serious involvement in legislation without compromising the equal opportunities of oneself or others in the various spheres of right. The more citizens directly participate in legislation, the more cumbersome the legislative process becomes, imposing ever greater demands upon the time and activity of the citizen-legislators. To continue participating in legislation, active citizens must increasingly renege on availing themselves of full exercise of their nonpolitical rights. This may well put them at a disadvantage within the home or out in society, at least, if others are left free to take advantage of their family and social opportunities. Yet because political freedom cannot be exercised if individuals are not liberated from social or household domination, not to mention subservience to metabolism with nature, individuals can devote the lion's share of their activity to political legislation only if others attend to the family and social responsibilities that sustain engagement in law-making. If these ancillary individuals must be commandeered by the politically active citizens to fulfill the household and social activities from which direct legislators inevitably withdraw, a second-class citizenry gets created. No matter what other formal rights may be accorded them, the members of this subsidiary group cannot possibly enjoy equal political opportunity when they must limit their engagement in politics due to the family and social responsibilities from which their toils emancipate their overlords. This situation does not, however, subvert the reciprocity of right only in the political sphere. Because the directly legislating citizens must withdraw from active involvement in family and social affairs, they cannot help but violate the household and social freedoms of the others. Although the politically active citizens might seem to forego their own household and social rights by leaving these arenas to others, in doing so they subvert the nonpolitical opportunities of everyone else in two fundamentals ways. On the one hand, the political elite of direct democracy fails to perform the household and social functions that help others enjoy autonomy in the family and society. After all, if one group of individuals is left with a disproportionate share of household and social duties, that predicament is hardly an empowering "opportunity." Instead, it comprises a burden under which the household right to have one's joint welfare cared for by one's spouse is no more respected than is the economic right to exercise a self-selected livelihood in reciprocity with every other member of civil society. Moreover, the only way the politically active legislators can carry on is if furnishing the support necessary for them is required of the drones of the family and society. This requirement obviously subverts the latter's household and social autonomy, further compounding the political handicap under which they labor. For these reasons, the imposition of direct democracy in the legislative arena is incompatible as much with a free, family, and civil society, as with the reflexivity and universality of political self-determination. This is true whether citizen-legislators argue in person in a polis or commune assembly or interconnect in a virtual legislature inhabited by the privileged leisure class of cyberspace.

4.2 THE LEGITIMACY OF REPRESENTATIVE LEGISLATION AND THE BINDING MANDATE

The dilemmas of participatory legislation open the door for representation, but they do not themselves indicate how representative legislation satisfies the normative requirements of self-government. There is still need to overturn Rousseau's challenge that a citizenry allowing representatives to make its laws determines itself politically only when electing them, after which it relinquishes itself to rule by an external will.[7]

One route for parrying Rousseau's objection is to accept its basic assumptions and presume that a representative legislature is an organ of political freedom only when the will of each legislator is directly beholden to the will of its electors. What legislators enact will be an expression of the will of the citizenry only if a direct identity can be retained between the political aims expressed in the vote for the legislature and the laws passed by the elected legislators. For this identity to be sustained, legislators must be subject to a binding mandate, where what they vote in the legislature is required to conform to the legislative program on which they have been elected.

Although subjecting representative legislators to a binding mandate may be thought to preserve the political autonomy of citizens, it robs legislators of all independence of their own. To enforce a binding mandate in any literal manner requires that candidates for the representative legislature spell out their *entire* legislative program during the electoral campaign and that once elected, they restrict their activity in the legislature to introducing that legislative package, arguing on its behalf as it is originally advanced and voting for it in its original form. Of course, the supporting argument they provide is a pure formality, for if the binding mandate applies to all other representatives as well, no one is in the position to be swayed by the arguments of anyone else. Legislative deliberation is completely eliminated, for the binding mandate precludes representative legislators from engaging in any real efforts to persuade one another or to engage in any attempts to improve upon their original proposals or reach compromise agreements. Any of these initiatives would violate the antecedent identity of the binding mandate, which must fix the legislative acts of all legislators to their prior campaign promises. Indeed, if the binding mandate is to truly bind, the legislature cannot engage in any independent activity at all.[8] The vote for legislators should itself be a vote for legislation, since if the electorate's votes do not directly determine what legislation will be enacted, the legislature will have to engage in an independent lawmaking of its own that can no longer be anticipated in the electoral choices of the citizenry. The problem is that the only way in which the legislative vote of elected representatives can directly express the will of the electorate is if *every* victorious representative candidate campaigns on the same legislative platform. If any disunity reigns in the representative assembly, the only citizens whose wills can stand in identity with approved legislation are those who comprise a like-minded portion of the electorate, electing a majority of representatives, all bound to the same legislative program. Depending upon the electoral system, this prevailing electorate may or may not comprise a majority of all citizens. All other citizens will, of course, fail to have their choice expressed in resulting legislation. Accordingly, if political self-determination requires the direct identity that binding mandate seeks to redeem for representative legislation, the reflexivity and universality of self-government will never be realized unless political diversity never arises and citizens and their representatives are plural in name only. In the absence of that absolute unanimity, binding mandates will always leave some citizens unable to find an identity between their legislative preference and enacted laws.

In fact, *no* citizen will find legislation according with his or her choice if enough disagreement exists among electors and then among their elected legislators such that no group of like-minded representatives is sufficiently numerous to pass their favored legislation. In that case, either strict observance of binding mandates will make new legislation impossible or legislation will end up being adopted due to departures from the electoral pledges of representatives. In the latter case, the resulting legislation may diverge from the campaign programs of each and every candidate, leaving citizens with no legislation to their liking, at least as measured by the vote they cast in the previous legislative elections.

This impasse underscores how binding mandates only substitute for the direct identity of participatory democracy when legislative activity is completely eviscerated of any positive contribution of its own and the election of legislatures is tantamount to a referendum on legislative programs. Instead of making representative legislation a vehicle of political self-determination, binding mandates preclude real representation and reinstate rule by plebiscite with all the problems that direct democracy brings to the workings of political freedom and autonomy in family and civil society.[9] Once more, citizens confront a politically disempowering predicament. Either they relinquish all positive role in formulating the legislation to which their elected representatives are bound or citizens attempt to determine that legislative agenda, leading to a paralysis of participatory overload and a subversion of equal opportunity in the family, society, and the state.

The conundrums of binding mandate indicate how political freedom cannot consist in any immediate identity between the will of each individual, as expressed in the personal choice of legislation, and the will of the body politic, as provisionally given in approved legislation awaiting certification by the authorizing power. Although the reflexivity of self-government implies an identity between who rules and who is ruled over, the subject of political freedom is a constitutionally organized citizenry, exercising political and nonpolitical rights that all involve the interaction of a plurality of participants who differentiate themselves by acting in recognition of one another's distinct volitions. Any immediate identification of the will of each citizen with the will of the state abstracts from the contrastive determination that each bearer of right takes on in acting in function of the correlative acts of its counterparts. Even when some or all citizens agree on a candidate or a referendum proposal, this comprises an exercise of political right only insofar as it is predicated upon the recognition that that right remains effective when others opt for competing candidates or proposals. Otherwise, each citizen would will so as to preclude anyone else from enjoying an equal political opportunity to choose something different. In that case, the mutuality of political right would collapse into the unilateral assertion of a single will, unmediated by the political willing of any discernible others. For this reason, the principle of democracy cannot be identity without difference, as thinkers from Rousseau to Carl Schmitt have mistakenly assumed. Precisely because the reflexivity of politics characterizes the form of a political *community*, uniting a *plurality* of citizens within the activity of self-government, the identity of ruler and ruled is automatically bound with difference, and indeed, the self-imposed difference of political self-individuation. How this works itself out in the process of legislation transcends the bounds of direct democracy and binding mandate alike.

4.3 THE REPRESENTATION OF CORPORATE INTEREST VERSUS THE REPRESENTATION OF POLITICAL FREEDOM

The pitfalls of binding mandate representation extend not just to the immediate identity conception of political freedom underlying much nostalgia for direct democracy but equally to the representation of interest so often tied to binding mandates. In the abstract, interest can be conceived as the self-selected aim that any free agent pursues in exercising rights. Then, of course, the content of interest has no predetermined character, nor any universal filling beyond formal conformity with the lawfulness of right and the assertion of the mode of autonomy whose aims it involves. Interest, however, can also have an antecedently determined particular character, such as unites the economically determined interest of members of the same class. Since such particular interests are shared by a particular group and predetermined by their engagement in a certain type of self-selected economic activity, the issue can arise of tying representative legislation to the representation of such "corporate" interests. To the degree that members of civil society have a right to pursue their corporate interests, legislation should be concerned with promoting the achievement of that right in face of changing circumstances in global civil society. Moreover, because corporate interests are particular but shared, representatives can advance them on behalf of a plurality of affiliated citizens. If positive law should promote corporate interests, firm commitment to that task might seem to require corporate representation, whereby citizens with a common social interest would elect common representatives, who would then be committed to drafting legislation on behalf of their corporate constituents' particular shared interest. Since that interest is determined prior to legislation by the workings of civil society, binding mandate plausibly appears to be the fit instrument for insuring that corporate legislators do their duty. For if binding mandate ties the hands of legislators to an antecedently fixed legislative agenda, such an agenda seems most legitimately rooted in the class affiliations that the exercise of economic freedom ineluctably produces. Then, legislation is not beholden to contents given independently of self-determination. Instead, corporate legislation operating under binding mandate functions as a political organ of the particular interests ingredient in economic freedom.

So long as corporate legislators promote the shared interests of their social constituents, the legislative will they wield remains intimately connected to the type of economic activity their electorate has selected and expressed in their election. In this respect, the corporate electorate does not cease to be free after electing their corporate representatives. Because the latter remain bound to represent their constituencies' particular self-selected group interests, the social freedom of citizens continues to be politically effective in the postelection legislative activity of the corporate representatives.

This relationship applies to the social groups that are necessary to civil society, as well as those that depend upon contingent circumstances, both cultural and natural, to which civil societies may be subject. The corporations necessary to civil society are those corresponding to the different modes of earning that market relations make possible. These generate groups of wage-earners, owners of capital, and receivers of rent, which may, of course, overlap, given the possibility of individuals having multiple economic roles and multiple sources of income. Further, these same market relations equally engender tenant, consumer, and professional groups of various scope whose common interests can be pursued through the avenues of market activity and civil legality. On the other hand, the natural contingencies of bisexual reproduction may produce groups distinguished by gender and sexual orientation, just as historical contingencies of race, ethnicity, religious identity, and other cultural distinctions may produce particular bodies within civil society who share a common social interest sustainable in conformity with the rights of others. So long as these groups have a shared interest that is duly civil, that is, affirmable without depriving others of their household and social freedoms, civil corporatism can extend to noneconomic social factors to which corporate representation can give expression.

All of these cases might seem to defuse some of the conundrums of binding mandate. Since the corporate interest directly represented by corporate representatives is something common to all members of that social group, a social unanimity seems guaranteed, at least among that portion of the electorate to which each corporate legislative group is tied. Whereas citizens at large would have to be unanimous clones to avoid disenfranchisement under general binding mandate representation, corporate representation would seem to ensure that each social sector has its interest actually expressed in legislation, since all legislators within each corporate sector would be bound to legislate on behalf of a social interest belonging to each corporate member without exception. This identity, however, is problematic on two grounds.

On the one hand, possession of a common interest does not signify that each corporate member agrees on what legislative proposal best promotes that interest. Grounds for disagreement are unavoidable.[10] The legal advancement of a shared social interest must be drafted in the face of contingent circumstances, depending upon the choices of other members of civil society, as well as changing natural conditions and international conjunctures. Consequently, no one can claim with any absolute certainty what legal measure will most successfully uphold the welfare of any particular sector of society. Like any other positive legislation, laws promoting corporate interest are relative to both the current facts, which can never be known with absolute accuracy and completeness, and future developments that defy any necessary prognosis. Moreover, membership in a corporate group by no means ensures that one has a better idea of how to promote its interest than someone belonging to a different social sector. Given the abiding possibility of disagreement on corporate legislation, only the most fortuitous and fleeting unanimity among corporate members and their legislators can prevent divergences between the legislative preferences of some, if not all, corporate members and the legislation promoted by their representatives.[11] Moreover, if divergences due to independent contributions by representatives are to be precluded, the corporate electorate must already have given expression to every bit of legislation that its corporate representatives advocate. Once more, securing identity between elector and bound representative eviscerates legislation and reduces it to a wholly formal appendage to what are in effect corporate referenda.

On the other hand, even if unanimity were always to reign among corporate members and their legislators, the plurality of corporations guarantees that some, if not all, corporations will fail to have their desired legislation adopted intact by the combined legislature. Indeed, barring the fortuitous capitulation of other corporate representatives, the only corporation that will ever have its legislation adopted will be that whose representatives are sufficiently numerous to be able to vote through their legislative proposals. In that case, the citizens from other corporations will find their interest unrepresented in the resulting legislation. Alternately, if no corporation's representatives can unilaterally have their way in the legislature, compromise solutions will be the only avenue, precipitating the legislative initiative eliminating any direct identity between the choice expressed in the election of corporate representatives and adopted law.

Needless to say, what alone would remove this problem is the elimination of corporate plurality itself and the particularity of corporate interest. That would entail the emergence of a universal corporation with a universal interest, that is, of a "classless" society in which only one corporate interest remains—that of the social grouping that has achieved solitary hegemony. Any such solution, however, strikes at the roots of social freedom by canceling the right to pursue self-selected particular ends in reciprocity with others—the right constitutive of the basic structure of civil society. The diversity of corporations can only be preempted if this right to economic freedom is curtailed by limiting social activity to a single mode, such as would be accomplished through a universal proletarization sustained through total nationalization of all commerce.

Corporate representation therefore stands in a multifaceted opposition to political freedom. If corporate representation operates without eliminating the plurality of corporate interests, the resulting legislation cannot realize the reflexivity and universality constitutive of political self-determination. Corporate representation violates the reflexivity requirement insofar as legislation on behalf of a particular corporate interest comprises a law applying to the citizenry at large, as well as legal subjects in general (who include citizens and non-citizens alike), but emanating from a particular collective will representing a particular social body to which not all citizens or legal subjects belong. The discrepancy between author and subject of corporate legislation reflects, of course, the abiding particularity of corporate ends which simply cannot enjoy the universality of the bona fide political aim to impose the order of the whole body politic upon itself. If corporate representation seeks to avoid these limitations by suppressing the diversity of corporate interest and substituting one social interest for all, as in the proletarian dictatorship of so-called people's democracies, the negation of social diversity undercuts the freedoms of civil society on which equal political opportunity depends. Corporate representation thus ends up subverting political freedom either with or without a curtailment of civil rights.[12]

The root problem bedeviling corporate representation, that of squaring the particularity of corporate interest with the universality of rule by law, is a false problem on several counts. To begin with, the task of satisfying the interests of corporations in due conformity with equal economic opportunity is already addressed by the public administration of welfare that is a necessary ingredient in the workings of a free civil society. Its public regulation of the economy, which properly oversees corporate attempts to use the market to promote the welfare of each group's members, does have a legal dimension to the extent that every right deserves legalization as a means of obtaining an objective specification and an objective enforcement. This involves not only the provision of common goods that secure the economic opportunity of all, but supervision of the internal organization and market interventions of social-interest groups themselves. Corporate representation, however, is by no means required to legislate the proper regulation of the market so as to satisfy corporate interests in accord with economic right. Indeed, since the legislation in question aims to uphold the common conditions under which corporate interests can be justly pursued, it is not partial to any particular social group. Tying legislative power to groups defined by a specific social interest subverts the universality of the task at hand, which instead falls to legislators in their capacity as citizens, securing the order of rights in general, without special favor to any particular group. In this way, legislation on behalf of corporate rights retains the universality of end constitutive of political action. Instead of restricting its goal to the interest of a particular social class, which class representation might seem to ensure, legislation can promote the welfare of all social groups, which is the only context in which the particular ends of any become worthy of *political* implementation, in the normative sense of an exercise of political self-determination. Otherwise, legislation becomes a battleground of competing social interests, of class conflict, in which the victor lords over subject groups for whom rule by law can no longer count as an exercise of self-government.

Fascism's attempt to overcome the alleged conflict between society and state by injecting society into the political sphere[13] through corporate representation is therefore doubly erroneous. It ignores not only how class antagonisms can be resolved by the public administrations of civil society, but how self-government can protect equal political opportunity from being overwhelmed by social divisions precisely by freeing representation from corporate interest.

Corporate representation simply cannot achieve the proper integration of particular social interest and the universality of citizenship on any of the three dimensions of political self-determination. Because corporate representation makes laws emanating from a particular group on behalf of its own private ends, it forfeits the universality that action must possess to comprise a willing of the order of the whole body politic, that is, a willing of a political program. Although corporate representation may take hold of government and perform its own rule by law, the aim is always social in character and particular in scope.

Because corporate representation leaves legislation issuing from a particular will with a content just as limited, its lawmaking cannot exhibit the reflexivity of self-rule. The corporate laws instead impose themselves on the citizenry at large, leaving those from other social groups subject to a law of which they are not the author, while making the corporate legislators rulers of subject classes. On either side, the identity of ruled and ruler is lost.

Moreover, because corporate legislation predicates political activity upon particular social interests, the supremacy of political action is subverted. Instead of lording over civil society as an enabling condition of its own self-activity, rule by law suffers the feudal indignity of being subservient to social ends. However shared these corporate interests may be, they remain particular to a private group, which, as such, cannot possess the universality inherent in the aims of self-government. When legislation is organized on corporate lines, social position directly determines political opportunity, compromising the very distinction between civil society and the state. This is true whether the social groups given legislative privilege are defined by economic function, hereditary rank, race, gender, sexual preference, ethnic identity, religion, or any other factor given independently of political action. Nor does it matter how closely such groups are represented in proportion to the population of their members. Whatever their defining social difference and however they be apportioned, their representation by group replaces the independence of political freedom with subservience to prepolitical imperatives, each the prerogative of a specific group and each fixed apart from the distinctly political differences that distinguish opposing legislative programs on how to uphold the political and nonpolitical rights of all citizens in the face of current contingencies.

This is not to deny that underrepresentation of group members in legislative bodies can involve unequal political opportunity reflecting past and present oppression in society and state. Nevertheless, securing diversity in representation falls prey to the pitfalls of corporatism so long as representatives from disadvantaged groups participate solely as advocates of their group's particular interest. In that case, the identity of ruler and ruled is undermined as lawmaking becomes a battleground for competing groups to impose their particular will upon all. Self-rule can only be retained in conjunction with diversity when legislators of each and every group freely legislate for and in the name of the entire body politic. Then alone does equal access to legislative bodies extend political freedom, rather than political domination, to those who have historically been excluded from affairs of state.[14]

4.4 THE EMANCIPATION OF REPRESENTATION FROM BINDING MANDATE AND CORPORATISM

The dilemmas afflicting the direct identity of binding mandate and corporate representation set legislators free in two respects. On the one hand, legislative representatives are free to propose and vote constitutional laws as they see fit, independently of the antecedently expressed choices of their electorate.[15] On the other hand, legislators are emancipated from bondage to any given particular interests and are free to make law on behalf of the citizenry at large. On both counts, representative legislation ceases to be a formal appendage of electoral will.[16] Instead, legislators can engage in real debate with one another and do so for the sake of the genuinely political end of the civil and political freedom of the citizenry and the civil freedom of resident aliens.[17] In this capacity, representatives act as fiduciaries of the universal political aims of their constituents, rather than as delegates of and bound to particular interests.[18] For this very reason, legislators need not belong to any particular group in civil society, nor share any nonpolitical identity with their constituents.[19]

If legislators were to replace subservience to binding mandate and corporate interest by serving as agents of the particular welfare of a regionally defined electorate, these constitutive aspects of political freedom would once more be compromised. Although legislators may well be elected from geographically drawn districts, this break from corporate identity does not render them instruments of the special interest of that locality. If district election were to impose regional representation, legislators would be bound to a particular good, antecedently defined by geographic contingencies. The task of legislation would no longer be the pursuit of universal ends enabling rule to be reflexive and supreme but the imposition of a local agenda on the nation at large. Although it might appear that representatives would deprive their constituents of a voice in government if they did not favor local interests, the opposite is the case. Only if geographically defined district representatives advocate legislation on behalf of all citizens, directed at upholding rights without special deference to any particular group, can their lawmaking retain the reflexive character that allows members of the electorate to thereby participate in self-rule.[20] If regional interests instead trump the universal claims of political freedom, the electorate divides itself into prospective ruling and subject groups vying to dominate one another.[21]

The needed emancipation of representation from regional interests does not preclude federalism.[22] Federalism may, as much as any centralized system, fall prey to allowing particular local interests to intrude into the legislative arena by treating legislators as regional partisans. Federalism may also follow corporatist divisions, supplementing national corporate representation with provincial government organized on corporate lines, such as when different cultural groups can be accorded local autonomy. Although federalism may well be advocated as the best vehicle for insuring the representation of regional and/or cultural interests, it can equally be advanced as an instrument for allowing a decentralization of self-rule that remains consistent with the pursuit of universal ends at the national level. In that case, the national legislature operates as a representative body of the citizenry's self-legislation, realizing rights for the whole body politic, while provincial assemblies enable representatives of a particular region to make regional laws that address the general aims of that territory in accord with the civil and political rights of all members of the encompassing body politic. Even at the provincial or municipal level, representation will operate in accord with political freedom only by concerning itself with the universal political good of all individuals subject to its jurisdiction, without legislators privileging those who have elected them.

Nevertheless, to the degree that regional or municipal legislation applies to only a local sector of the citizenry, whose representatives impose it upon them with their indirect participation, it can only exhibit a reflexivity that is particular in scope, contiguous to that of other local bodies, all belonging to the same body politic. In this respect, self-legislation in local government is qualitatively distinct from national lawmaking.[23] Insofar as it bears the stamp of a particular subdivision of the citizenry, it could be said to fall within the public administrations of civil society, which operate below and subservient to the universal practices of political freedom.

Federalist schemes providing special representation to protect indigenous native cultures, minority linguistic groups, and other precarious communities are subject to the same limitations. Such schemes could only be legitimate if they protect practices compatible with the different spheres of right and if any special guarantees are legalized in the form of general statutes that apply to any civil group in similar straits. Further, any reservations of representatives for members of such groups could only abide by the requirements of reflexivity, universality, and the supremacy of political freedom if such representatives act on behalf of the entire citizenry, whose civil rights to enjoy legitimate cultural diversity are just as binding for representatives of any other section of the citizenry.

If, for example, aboriginal peoples or national groups are allotted federal privileges, giving them regional self-rule, dilemmas arise at both the local and federal level. If this regional self-rule is to accord locally with civil and political right, it will have to grant equal social and political rights to any permanent residents, whether or not they belong to the aboriginal or national group who lay claim to that region. If residents from other groups were prevented from entering, buying land or other real estate, using their own language, owning businesses, or voting or running for office, these federal regions would violate the property, social, and political freedoms of other citizens. If, however, they do not practice these injustices, the province will no longer be defined by aboriginal or national identity but will simply be one more geographically delimited locality that happens to be numerically dominated by a specific group.

Moreover, in the federal legislature, any representatives reserved for these regions would face the imperative of upholding the cultural rights of their region only in conjunction with promoting the rights of all citizens. This is hardly a limitation, for the citizenry's common rights to equal economic and political opportunity already require overcoming the disadvantages that historically have left aboriginal and national minorities in cultural jeopardy. If these universal entitlements are trumped instead by particular group agendas, parliament becomes a battlefield of different cultural factions, each vying for supremacy.

For these reasons, group representation for historically oppressed communities must transcend its own particular limits to accord with political self-determination. Other citizens may well be so indifferent to these cultural concerns and the affected groups may feel so politically alienated that political unity depends upon group representation to air these issues in the legislature. If legislators can transcend their cultural allegiances and be open to meaningful parliamentary debate, group reservations may facilitate the passage of fair statutory remedies. Of course, if conditions require such reservations for fair remedies to be debated, their passage may well be resisted by the other legislators.[24] After all, if cultural polarization rules the legislature, the group representation of minorities may have no effect upon what the prevailing majority passes.[25] Indeed, representation of regional cultural groups may only encourage cultural differences to harden into political divisions, imperiling collective self-government anew.[26] Whatever the outcome, such culturally defined group representation can at best comprise a historical compromise that should eventually be overcome.[27]

In every case, the emancipation of legislation from bondage to particular interests and binding mandate eliminates the reduction of legislative debate and deliberation to a formal exercise preempted by antecedent decisions. If the principle of democracy were the direct identity proposed by Rousseau, Schmitt, and advocates of participatory self-government, political freedom would be antithetical to real parliamentary autonomy. Yet, precisely because the universality, supremacy, and reflexivity of political conduct can only be retained when citizens participate in legislation indirectly through unbound representatives who are free to deliberate about how to make laws on behalf of the rights of all citizens, self-rule and the real independence of legislative representatives are actually intimately connected.[28]

Parliamentary party discipline might seem to undermine that independence and the identity of ruler and ruled. When representatives are elected as advocates of a party platform antecedently determined at party conventions, one party achieves enough parliamentary seats to pass legislation, and parliamentary representatives are required to vote their party program, legislative activity would seem to follow Schmitt's diagnosis of parliamentarism by degenerating into a formal rubber stamping of a legislative agenda decided at the time of their election. Representatives would play no independent role in formulating legislative proposals nor in attempting to persuade other representatives to change their positions. Speeches in parliament would amount to official party declarations, addressed to public opinion, rather than formulations of personal positions or attempts to win over opposing legislators.[29] Instead of comprising a deliberative process in which positions are developed and altered in a genuine give-and-take, parliamentary debate would be a pure charade, leaving completely intact the prior determination of legislation by the most recent legislative elections.[30] Of course, this could only be guaranteed if legislators are fully compliant with party discipline. Compliance could, of course, be secured by constitutional or positive statutes requiring strict adherence to party positions and forfeiture of legislative seat in case of violations. Alternately, compliance could be less rigorously achieved by regulating electoral politics such that candidates are as dependent as possible upon party organizations for election and reelection.[31] Both options would be stymied, however, whenever a single party lacks sufficient seats to pass its legislative program and parliamentary deliberations among representatives of different parties become necessary for the passage of any laws. Nevertheless, the tendencies of party discipline to stifle independent action in the legislature require attention in examining how representatives must act in order to realize political freedom.[32]

4.5 THE ELEMENTARY GUIDELINES OF LEGISLATIVE REPRESENTATION

Several guidelines are already evident independent of more concrete issues such as how political parties may or may not mediate the relation between legislative representatives and the electorate as well as the other branches of government, what electoral system should be followed, whether legislatures should be uni- or multicameral, and whether lawmaking should operate in a federal or unitary government. Although these matters of controversy all impact upon the activity of legislators, they themselves presuppose the following more basic considerations.

First, representatives should legislate on behalf of the freedoms of the citizenry at large rather than on behalf of any particular sector and its special interests. In other words, legislators properly have one task to fulfill, no matter what the particular focus of legislative formulation: to realize political justice in its constitutive sovereign universality with respect to the current conjuncture of domestic, not to mention, international affairs. Only then can lawmaking enjoy the universality of aim on which depends the reflexivity, supremacy, and autonomy of self-rule.[33]

Second, representatives should be free to formulate legislative proposals and independently participate in parliamentary debate, duly aiming to win sufficient agreement to pass the most emancipatory bills emerging from parliamentary deliberations.[34] Although this engagement requires freedom from binding mandates, it does not preclude representatives committing themselves to legislate the program on which they were elected. So long as a legislator regards that program as enduringly compelling, allegiance to electoral pledges need not stifle legislative autonomy.

Third, all such parliamentary debate must be made public to the citizenry. For this publicity to be real and not merely formal, it must include provision for sufficient means to make parliamentary debate and legislative proposals conveniently available as well as comprehensible to citizens. This involves not only accommodating linguistic differences among the populace but also making available records of legislative proceedings with aids to decipher technicalities that would otherwise cloak parliamentary activity from the real understanding of the public.[35] Such publicity is a key element in just representation since without full disclosure, citizens can neither know and evaluate the work of their legislature, nor recognize its lawmaking as an exercise of their self-government. If legislators are able to operate behind the backs of their fellow citizens, the legislature becomes a star chamber in which representatives who make the law monopolize knowledge of the legislative process, as if lawmaking were not of any concern for the rest, nor subject to anyone else's control.[36] Then the legislature relinquishes its representative character and becomes a law unto itself.[37]

Moreover, citizens must retain the right and have effective opportunity to give public expression to their own views in response to parliamentary debate. This opportunity can be exercised both as independents and through political party forums, and differences in social resources should not disadvantage citizens from having avenues for publicizing their positions. Whether undertaken by independents or party members, whether privately supported or publicly subsidized, public debate outside parliament cannot be allowed to have any binding effect upon the deliberations of representatives, since that would undermine parliamentary debate and the autonomy of legislators. Nevertheless, if citizens are deprived of equal access to this opportunity, their ability to hold their representatives accountable and influence the course of future legislation and legislative elections would be curtailed.[38] Only in these ways can citizens enjoy equal opportunity to determine the legislative agenda, to voice their views regarding different legislative proposals, and to register their satisfaction with the outcome of legislation in conformity with properly autonomous parliamentary deliberation.[39]

All the above considerations set limits, albeit approximate, upon the number of representatives that can feasibly comprise a working legislature of autonomous lawmakers. If representatives be too many, debate will become unwieldy and the publicity of parliamentary proceedings will be vitiated by the immensity and dispersion of deliberation.[40] Moreover, the political responsibility of individual legislators will become both diminished and obscured.[41] Breakdown into committees may evade some of the difficulties by allowing smaller groups to work out details of legislative drafts and subsequent amendments. Nevertheless, committees will still have to report their work to the entire body of legislators, whose ability to respond will be hampered by inordinate numbers. The same problems that afflict direct democracy will resurface on a lesser scale: with droves of representatives, only a withdrawal into passivity by most will enable an engaged few to keep proposals to a workable number, keep the pros and cons of debate at a digestible volume, and allow ensuing negotiation to come to a timely conclusion.

4.6 THE RIGHT AND DUTY OF ELECTING REPRESENTATIVE LEGISLATORS

Whereas self-government requires rule by law, with legislation formulated by representative legislators, free of binding mandates but obliged to legislate on behalf of the citizenry at large, the process by which representative legislators get selected becomes a key element in political self-determination. If the reflexivity and universality of political freedom is to be maintained, the procedures for selecting representatives must realize equal political opportunity both in respect to the participation of citizens in determining who shall be their representatives and in respect to taking office as a legislative representative. However these dual political rights be fulfilled, no citizen must be granted a privileged role in selecting legislators or privileged access to legislative office.

A lottery system for selecting legislators might seem to meet these requirements, insofar as determination by lot would give each citizen an equal chance to serve as a representative legislator. Indeed, such a system might be the one sure guarantor of political equality since social and natural inequalities would have no opportunity to influence the selection of legislators as such differences can when legislators are voted into office. Admittedly, selection by lottery can preclude unequal influence in the determination of legislators and give each citizen an equal chance to hold legislative office. Yet as much as equality may be a necessary element in each and every right, equality by itself does not provide for self-determination. What the equal chance of lottery selection does not offer is precisely any role for choice in either the selection of representatives or in the holding of legislative office. Under a lottery system, representatives are determined by an automatic procedure completely devoid of any exercise of will by citizens. Legislators are not chosen at all, properly speaking, nor do citizens choose to put themselves forward as candidates for legislative positions. Instead, the lottery mechanism preempts all such decisions, imposing equal passivity upon recipients of a wheel of fortune, instead of equal opportunity to exercise an entitled freedom.[42]

If legislation is to be an organ of self-rule, lottery must be replaced by legislative elections in which citizens enjoy dual rights: on the one hand, the equal political opportunity to codetermine who their representatives will be, and, on the other hand, the equal opportunity to choose to be electoral candidates for legislative office, provided their candidacy is consonant with the division of powers and the other elements constitutive of self-government. Whether the latter right excludes certain individuals from legislative candidacy because of their other political roles depends upon the further determination of the executive and authorizing branches of government, something that is itself predicated upon the initial constitution of the legislative branch. Whatever be such limitations, these dual rights hold irrespective of how legislatures are otherwise structured, as well as irrespective of what electoral system conforms to political freedom.

In each case, citizens incur political duties in conjunction with their political right. In order to have a right, rather than a privilege, to vote for representative legislators, each citizen is obliged to respect the correlative right of every other citizen to exercise the same franchise. Similarly, in enjoying the right to run for legislative office, each citizen is equally duty bound to honor the entitlement of all other citizens to do the same, subject to whatever qualifications right entails in conformity with the division of powers and other permissible elements of political freedom, such as term limits. In these cases, the duty concerns the rights of others. Is there, however, a duty to exercise one's rights to vote in legislative elections and to run for legislative office?

The very nature of representation precludes any literal application of a duty to put oneself forward as a legislative candidate. Although rights must be such as to be exercisable without violating the corollary rights of others, that does not mean that each right must be simultaneously executable. In the case of running for representative legislative office, a universal participation in candidacy would immobilize the electoral process, even if cybernetic facilities enabled every citizen to make their candidacy formally available to everyone else. Unless candidates gave their support to others, retracted their candidacy, and narrowed the field to a decidable set of choices, the election would be perennially tied, undermining the right to run for office and potentially paralyzing the legislative process.

Such difficulties do not afflict a duty to vote in legislative elections, as evidenced by the current enforcement of that obligation in various representative democracies.[43] Citizens can certainly be legally required to exercise their franchise and penalized for noncompliance just as they can be required to file tax returns and be punished for failure to do so.[44]

If, however, the feasibility of enforcing the duty to vote is undeniable, it is hardly true that the failure of all citizens to exercise their franchise necessarily jeopardizes the political freedom of themselves or their voting peers. Admittedly, the higher the turnout, the more citizens can be said to participate equally and in that respect, enjoy political equality.[45] Yet failure to participate need not signify any obstacle to equal political opportunity. Indeed, low turnout can itself be regarded as an expression of voter preference or lack thereof.[46] In particular, the abstention of a certain portion of voters determines what will comprise the minimal plurality or majority needed to win office.[47] Accordingly, abstentions, be they officially registered or not, comprise a specific form of political codetermination, rather than an impairment to electoral self-government.[48]

Admittedly, at some contingent level of voter apathy, a paucity of electoral participation can rob elections of a sufficiently legitimate mandate. Compulsory voting might ward off electoral decision making by a small minority, but it cannot remove the sources of apathy that make elections a tiresome tribulation for those who vote only under compulsion.[49]

4.7 THE FUNDAMENTAL REQUIREMENTS FOR THE JUST ELECTION OF REPRESENTATIVES

For the election of representative legislators to comprise an element in the exercise of political freedom, certain requirements must be observed that hold true irrespective of whether electoral systems be direct or indirect, majoritarian or proportional, centralized or federal. To begin with, conditions must be sustained so as to allow citizens to exercise their vote without being subject to illicit pressures, such as retaliations at home, at the workplace, or in other venues in which rights are at play. To this end, all such violations should be subject to the same remedies that apply to violations of right. If the retaliations against electoral freedom are exercised with malicious intent, they warrant treatment as crimes subject to punishment, irrespective of whether the retaliation passes from attempt to successful implementation. If there are victims, they are entitled to compensation from the perpetrators, be they malicious or nonmalicious agents of electoral compulsion. As with any matter of right, these remedies should be made legal, with adequate legal assistance publicly guaranteed for all participants in litigation, whether the case be civil and/or criminal.[50]

Further, elections should be immunized from such abuses by appropriately designing balloting procedures. The requisite measures bear upon the form of the ballot, the mechanism for registering votes, and the surrounding conditions of unimpeded access to polling. First, to insure that all citizens have access to the same voting device and a neutral environment, the ballot and election locale must be commonly provided by the state rather than separately furnished by particular private groups.[51] Although local geographic and cultural differences may require specific accommodations to enable all citizens to exercise their equal opportunity to vote, these accommodations must make available an equivalent voting facility. Second, any preliminary voter registration procedures must be as automatic as possible for individuals who qualify as citizens. If registration is instead left to private initiative, disparities in private resources that affect ease of registration will rob the disadvantaged of an equal opportunity to vote.[52] Further, the listing of candidates on the ballot must permit equal consideration by each and every voter. Linguistic differences as well as physical and psychological handicaps must be accommodated. Any ambiguous or preferential listing of voting choices must be avoided. Similarly, voting procedures must prevent any equivocal or partial registering of votes.[53] Moreover, the voting machinery must enable voters to freely opt for candidates without restriction. For example, the technical means for voting for "split tickets" must be made available when doing otherwise would curtail the political voice of citizens.[54] Finally, the voting system must allow voters to cast their vote with complete anonymity. This requires not just a nominally secret ballot, but a balloting procedure so fashioned that nothing perceivable in when or how voters enter and emerge from polling discloses their choice.[55]

Far from being an expression of liberal individualism at odds with democracy, as Carl Schmitt would have us believe,[56] election of representatives by effective secret ballot enables each citizen to codetermine who legislates for the citizenry without fear of reprisals. That each citizen registers his or her vote in secret does not signify that legislative elections become a private affair, summing up expressions of atomistic wills, supplanting the general will (*la volonté générale*) with the will of all (*la volonté de tous*).[57] Insofar as secret ballot facilitates, rather than impairs, the equal participation of every citizen in choosing who will legislate on behalf of the political and nonpolitical freedoms of the citizenry as a whole, citizens only affirm their political self-determination in voting anonymously. Instead of making a choice as an isolated individual, each citizen thereby chooses a legislative candidate, exercising a prerogative that cannot be enjoyed without belonging to a democratically organized body politic as a self-governing participant. In this respect, the will that each citizen wields in codetermining the universal political will of state legislation is not given independently of the encompassing political process of self-government, as it would be if the legislative will were a formal universal, related to independently given particulars.[58] Instead, the secret ballot of each citizen comprises an integral element of free political association, irretrievably situated within the ethical community to which each voter must already belong. The fact that citizens remain at liberty to divulge their electoral choice, whereas government officials may be legally compelled to honor confidentiality in certain official duties hardly confirms a depolitization in secret ballot.[59] Whether voters keep silent on how they vote has no bearing upon the political reality of their electoral participation. Of course, even when citizens refuse to disclose their vote, they remain just as able and entitled to participate in party activities in and out of office, as to intervene in public political debate as an independent.

Although secret ballot may shelter the electoral autonomy of citizens from illicit extortions, it is hardly sufficient to render legislative elections an exercise in equal political opportunity. Whatever be the mode of candidate nomination, the manner in which electoral campaigns are run and financially supported, the composition of legislatures, and the form of electoral system, the right to vote for legislators will be formal unless all citizens are guaranteed access to the activity of voting in both mind and body, without impairment of their nonpolitical freedoms. The time and place of legislative elections must be determined so that all citizens can make it to the polls in conformity with the exercise of their rights and duties at home and at work. When citizens' unprejudiced participation in voting requires it, the state must insure that care is provided for family members who cannot be left unattended, that paid leave from work be offered, and that conveyance to polling places be provided.[60] Physical access to voting must, of course, be complemented by making the voting procedure intelligible to all voters. Not only must voting materials be available in the language of every citizen, but the actual method of voting must be made as unambiguous and familiar as possible to all prospective voters. On both fronts, sufficient measures must be taken to overcome any obstacles presented by illiteracy and disabilities such as blindness, deafness, or dyslexia.

4.8 THE RIGHT TO LEGISLATIVE CANDIDACY

Guaranteeing these minimal conditions for the right to vote for legislators resolves only one side of the relation by which legislative elections realize political freedom. No less crucial is achieving equal political opportunity in the political processes by which individuals become candidates and then wage their electoral campaigns. Like the minimal conditions for exercising the right to vote, these minimal conditions for exercising the right to run for legislative office apply irrespective of the type of electoral system and the way in which legislative bodies are regulated. For this very reason, the general norms for legislative candidacy must be conceived before assessing such alternatives as majoritarian versus proportional representation, unicameral versus multicameral assemblies, and parliamentary versus presidential systems.

Needless to say, access to candidacy is as crucial to self-legislation as access to the ballot. If citizens have unequal opportunities to seek legislative office in a representative assembly, effective equal suffrage will not prevent certain individuals from exercising a legislative privilege that divides the citizenry into an active elite who makes the laws and a passive subject class who submits to the former's legislation. To avoid this destruction of self-legislation, citizens capable of political participation must enjoy the right to run for legislative office. Nothing extraneous to the basic qualifications for exercising political freedom must be allowed to deprive individuals of the opportunity to put their candidacy forward for representative legislator. Although citizenship may nominally extend to children and to permanently or temporarily mentally impaired adults who lack sufficient independent rational agency to engage in self-government, any permanent resident who can exercise political rights and recognize those of others is entitled to the full opportunities of political engagement. Even if permanent residents retain the ability to vote by absentee ballot in elections in the country of their official citizenship, permanent residency makes the nation in which they reside the real field of their effective political opportunity. Any restriction of that opportunity would violate right, which can only legitimately involve partial curtailments necessary to facilitate the realization of freedom.

Accordingly, any restrictions on legislative candidacy based on gender, sexual orientation, race, ethnicity, or religion are all inadmissable. By contrast, the right to run for legislative office could be duly restricted by, for example, term limits or prohibitions against dual officeholding provided that these are needed, respectively, to counteract the advantages of incumbency or to uphold the division of powers.

Less supportable are regulations that restrict legislative candidacy by any age qualifications different from those that certify the maturity recognized to be necessary, if not sufficient, for exercising rights in general. Although arguments have been made that legislative office demands greater experience than what eligibility to vote requires, any such claim implicitly appeals to standards of expertise that undercut selection by election rather than by examination. Leaving this incoherence aside, expertise cannot be a qualification for eligibility any more than teleological criteria of virtue, for, as we have seen, positive legislation must rely upon observation of current conditions and judgment to apply constitutional principles to the given situation. Every independent rational agent is capable of rising to the occasion of this task, given due assistance by experts in whatever technical matters lawmaking may address. Consequently, setting the age limit higher for legislative candidacy than for voting for legislative candidates creates different classes of political opportunity that impede, rather than facilitate self-government.

Equal political opportunity is further subverted if eligibility for candidacy is made hostage to residency requirements that go beyond the basic permanent residency status that entitles individuals to political rights in the body politic within which they reside. If legislative representation were a matter of legislating on behalf of the regional interest of the locality from which representatives are elected a case could be made for some period of local residency to insure some acquaintance with the particulars of that region. Since, however, legislation is properly for the sake of the universal end of realizing the constitutional rights of the entire citizenry in face of given circumstances, the parochial advantage of previous local residency loses its claim. Political carpetbaggers need not be shy so long as they advance the good of the nation. Removing all of these undue barriers to candidacy will strike a blow for equal political opportunity, but they will not suffice for achieving the full reflexivity of self-government if further nonpolitical and political factors render the formal right to run for legislator an empty promise.

4.9 THE CHALLENGE OF REMOVING NONPOLITICAL BARRIERS TO LEGISLATIVE CANDIDACY

Given how individuals cannot engage in self-rule unless they enjoy their nonpolitical freedoms of ownership, of moral accountability, of family membership, and of participation in civil society, it goes without saying that oppression in each of these spheres of right must be removed to enable citizens to exercise their right to candidacy. Yet even if these prepolitical emancipations have been achieved, room remains for elements of these legitimate domains to interfere with the right to candidacy. The task is to insure that nothing to which citizens are entitled as owners, moral subjects, family members, and participants in civil society undermines their equal opportunity to run for office.

In the sphere of personhood, wherein individuals enjoy the rights of ownership, the differences in property to which persons are entitled should not serve to prejudice access to elective office. In other words, particular property requirements ought not bar any citizen's candidacy. This applies to not only the market value of property but also its quality—e.g., candidates cannot be required to own a residence or other real estate in the district from which they are standing for election. Similarly, registration fees or escrow requirements for candidacy should not be imposed that would make political opportunities relative to differences in ownership.

Nor should persons' fulfillment of their duty to provide compensation for wrongs and to receive punishment for crime bar them from exercising their political right to run for legislative office.[61] Citizens' current incarceration or parole restrictions can disqualify them from legislative candidacy when they make participation in campaigning and subsequent exercise of office an impossibility. Imprisonment or parole are unlikely, however, to prevent a citizen from being able to vote for legislative candidates. Consequently, any disenfranchisement of prisoners or parolees constitutes a violation of their equal political opportunity. Analogously, prohibitions on the candidacy of convicted felons who have served their time are illegitimate subordinations of citizens who have no obligation to further curtail their otherwise constitutional activities. Any nation, such as the United States, that disenfranchises felons in and out of prison or disqualifies released felons from candidacy perpetrates political oppression.

Just as the righting of wrongs of ownership must not unduly obstruct political freedom, so the conflicts and controversies endemic to moral accountability cannot independently bar citizens from voting or running for office. Any moral litmus test for either political right not only falls prey to the inherent subjectivity of judgments of conscience but obstructs political freedom, which moral autonomy has no authority to trump.

Family rights and duties should analogously leave unobstructed every citizen's opportunity to become a legislator. Just as equal social opportunity requires that nepotism not be permitted to mandate a path to rags or riches, so family relationships must be barred from influencing access to candidacy. The political celebrity of family relations may inevitably pass its aura to other kin, but equitable access to publicity and other resources for campaigning can mitigate the political disadvantage of citizens of obscure lineage.

Conversely, family obligations must not be allowed to prejudice citizens' opportunity to run for office.[62] Although the imperatives of social justice already mandate public provisions for dependent care to enable individuals to pursue careers without disadvantage, participation in electoral politics adds another layer of activity to which family involvements must be accommodated, without the impairment of the household or political rights of the parties involved. Just as equal economic opportunity demands such allowances as paid maternity leave for parents of any gender or sexual orientation, so the office of legislator must make room for sufficient flexibility of scheduling and leave time to allow prospective and current parents to negotiate the demands of family and political right. Analogous accommodations apply to family emergencies, at least so far as they can be handled without undermining the legislative process.

Most challenging are the forces within civil society that threaten to subvert equal political opportunity as it applies to legislative candidacy. The institutions of economic freedom are notorious for generating inequalities of wealth and concentrations of economic power that threaten to transform the equal political opportunity of self-government into the privilege of oligarchy, where the economically powerful dominate the economically disadvantaged. This need not involve the feudal bonds where social position directly dictates one's relation to rule. Oligarchy can triumph even when civil society and state are demarcated provided political activity is left dependent on private means and significant inequality reigns in the economy of civil society. Under these conditions, self-government can readily degenerate into "bourgeois democracy," where universal suffrage and universal formal rights to run for legislative candidacy do not prevent the dominant economic group from using its economic leverage to control political life. Much of this violation to equal political opportunity can emanate from contingent social conditions reflecting the failure of civil institutions to enforce the equal economic opportunity to which members of civil society are entitled.

From a systematic point of view, what requires attention are not these contingent deformations of an insufficiently civil society, but the challenge to legislative rights posed by the workings of a fully just civil society, whose institutions of civil law and public welfare administration uphold equal economic opportunity as best as can be done. Although a just civil society should diminish economic inequality to the degree necessary for securing equal economic opportunity, this achievement does not prevent economic factors from threatening equal political opportunity.

To begin with, abiding differences in wealth and economic prospects can still influence the relative ease or difficulty of a citizen's election as a legislator. Equal economic opportunity does not entirely preclude certain individuals from enjoying independent means of livelihood that allow their undertaking substantial activity with little remuneration. For this reason, the office of legislator, not to mention every other full-time political office, must be paid a decent wage and benefits. Otherwise, only those who have additional sources of income will be able to survive election without suffering economic hardship.

Of course, if differences in wealth compatible with equal economic opportunity can affect the relative ease or difficulty of office-holding, the same will be all the more true of the opportunity to mount an effective electoral campaign. First of all, to engage in active campaigning without economic disadvantage requires that candidates be able to take leave from their normal occupation without prejudice to their career advancement and still maintain a reasonable standard of living for themselves and their dependents. Moreover, certain occupations, such as lawyering, may provide a flexibility and access to resources facilitating the opportunity to run for elective office.[63] If differences in personal wealth and occupation condition this opportunity, campaigning will only be possible for the more affluent and occupationally privileged sector of the citizenry, leaving the rest politically disadvantaged. Since what is at stake is a political right of concern to all citizens, the burden of guaranteeing living expense support for credible candidates and their dependents during a campaign should be borne by public subsidy, rather than by any particular employers or commercial partners.

Second, if the personal wealth of candidates and their supporters condition their ability to cover other campaign costs, such as media, travel, and organizational expenditures, political advantage will accrue to whichever candidates dispose of the greatest private contributions, especially if campaigning is allowed to extend over long periods of time. Compounding these inequalities in personal campaign resources of candidates and their individual supporters are the concentrations of economic power that can coexist with individual equal economic opportunity. Ownership of enterprises may be widely distributed by, for example, dispersed shareholding. Nonetheless, corporations and, for that matter, trade unions and other mass social-interest-group organizations can still mobilize sufficient wealth for their favored candidates to leave opponents at extreme disadvantage. Moreover, certain groups may be able to use their economic position to provide or withdraw key campaign resources, such as media or transportation facilities, in ways that decisively affect electoral opportunities. This political privilege may apply not just to wealthy proprietors of communications and transportation enterprises but to the most modestly remunerated employees whose jobs in key sectors enable them to decide which candidates can avail of politically crucial resources.

Further, some of these same organizations can mobilize large blocs of manpower under their control to give campaigns a crushing supremacy in human resources. Although the individuals involved certainly are entitled to give their time and energy to the campaign of the candidates of their choice, something different is involved when corporations and social-interest groups use their own economic and social leverage to pressure their employees and members to campaign.

If equal political opportunity is to be maintained in respect to legislative candidacy, public measures must be taken to counter these diverse economic bases of political advantage. On the one hand, the employment of private resources in legislative campaigns must be regulated to prevent private economic power from unfairly influencing electoral contests. On the other hand, public resources must be mobilized to guarantee competing candidates sufficient access to the voting public to enable the electorate to decide the race on political grounds rather than under the influence of unequal social power. Various options can be employed, such as publicly funded campaign subsidies for competing candidates, publicly enforced requirements that the media provide free publicity for every contender, and restrictions on the length and resources of campaigns.

Needless to say, some weeding of prospective candidates must be employed to prevent the number of competitors from overwhelming the capacities of public subsidy and the media, as well as the attention of the electorate. Petition requirements are one of the possible ways of limiting candidacies that can conform with equal political opportunity, provided, of course, that unequal private resources are not allowed to subvert the opportunity of would-be candidates to gather petition signatures. Although this raises an analogous specter of a plethora of petition gatherers, modest regulations could conceivably manage that problem. Finding effective remedies may not be easy, but political right mandates that measures be taken to insure that equal political opportunity is not subverted by ownership of nor employment in the media and other industries facilitating campaigning.

4.10 ELEMENTARY MEASURES TO OPTIMIZE THE DEMOCRATIC CHARACTER OF REPRESENTATIVE LEGISLATIVE ELECTIONS

To otherwise optimize the democratic character of representative legislative elections, five measures have been commonly advanced, irrespective of electoral systems, the number of legislative chambers, and the presence or absence of federal organization. These comprise extending direct election to all legislators, mandating the most frequently possible regular legislative elections, imposing term limits that reduce the advantages of incumbency, and furnishing easily executable procedures for the recall of individual elected representatives and for dissolving legislatures and initiating new general elections.[64]

4.11 DIRECT VERSUS INDIRECT ELECTION OF LEGISLATORS

Direct, rather than indirect, election of all lawmakers might seem to be an obvious ingredient in self-legislation, yet its significance quickly wanes in face of either the Rousseauian objection to representative legislation or the refutation of the identity conception of self-rule on which it rests. If political freedom required an immediate connection between the will of all and the general will of the legislature, indirect election would only reiterate the political usurpation committed by direct election of representative legislators. Whether selected by a prevailing group of voters or by a second tier of electors chosen directly by the voters, representatives will always legislate independently of the opinion of the citizenry, unless lawmaking becomes a formal appendage of a legislative referendum, where each election at every level selects candidates bound to a fully developed legislative program and no division reigns among the electorate. As we have seen, unless all legislative proposals are antecedently approved in legislative elections and all legislators and their constituents favor the same laws, the will of voters will diverge from the laws that their representatives finally adopt. Of course, even if binding mandate is enforced and unanimity rules, the determination of the legislative agenda will still be made behind the backs of the voting public by whoever formulates the positions put before the electorate.

In any event, once the link is severed between the preference of citizens and the lawmaking of their representatives, the further remove of indirect election diminishes nothing of significance to the identity conception of self-rule. As far as that position is concerned, there is either identity or difference, and degrees of difference are irrelevant to whether citizens rule themselves or stand subjugated to the body of legislators imposing laws upon them.

The distinction between direct and indirect election might seem to matter, however, once political freedom is duly recognized to require representation by legislators free to deliberate, debate, and independently formulate laws on behalf of the entire citizenry.

Then, the selection process of representatives appears to be central to the involvement of citizens in self-legislation, and indirect election puts one more barrier between citizen choice and legislation. After all, if representatives are selected indirectly, noncandidate voters relate to legislation only through a double mediation: first, through the will of the electors they select, and second, through the will of the legislators chosen by those electors. Admittedly, this double remove can remain congruent with equal political opportunity so long as all citizens' votes count equally in the selection of the electors, all citizens enjoy the right to run for both elector and legislator, and the conditions of fair campaigning are secured. Yet even then, do citizens not lose a degree of control over the selection of their legislators when indirect election puts a tier of electors between voters and the final choice?

The putative loss could be magnified by successive tiers of electors, each choosing a narrower circle of higher deciders, each diminishing the direct connection between the citizen's initial vote and the ultimate decision. Whatever the layering, do additional intermediaries undercut self-rule when political self-determination must be mediated by political diversity and legislative representation? As long as any indirect elections respect political equality, they do not subject citizens to a privileged cabal ruling over them. Rather, electors, like representatives, function as facilitators of self-legislation, enabling every citizen to have an equal say in choosing the delegates who will choose in turn their representative legislators. Citizens remain politically self-determining in indirect elections because they participate by exercising a political right all hold in common and the selection of representatives can still not proceed without their contributing decisions.

Significantly, when indirect election has been promoted, this is commonly done in express departure from equal political opportunity. The goal is instead to restrain the alleged arbitrariness or generality of popular rule and promote privileged groups of some sort. On these lines, electors would be chosen by voter groups privileging those allegedly possessing an enlightened political will wanting in the citizenry at large, or alternately, possessing a corporate interest that warrants legislative representation. This violation of political right at least has the virtue of consistency, for indirect election has nothing positive to offer self-rule that is not already contained in direct election of legislators.[65] Although indirect election may serve self-legislation without detracting from the identity of ruler and ruled, it does nothing for political freedom that cannot be gained by direct election of representatives. Whereas self-government necessitates legislative representation, legislative representation by no means requires indirect election. At best, it is a superfluous mediator that avoids doing damage to political opportunity. For that very reason, indirect election of legislators might as well be avoided simply for entailing an unnecessary layer of officialdom.

4.12 THE FREQUENCY OF LEGISLATIVE ELECTIONS AND POLITICAL FREEDOM

To determine how the frequency of legislative elections bears upon political freedom, due attention must be paid to the mediated character of legislative representation, whereby self-legislation operates not through a direct identity between voter preference and legislators' lawmaking, but through legislators' autonomy to debate and deliberate how to make laws to uphold the constitutional rights of all in the face of changing circumstances. The false identity conception of self-rule fosters the notion that legislative elections should be as frequent as possible to insure the greatest congruence between current public opinion and legislative practice. The shorter the term of representative office, the sooner voters can replace unpopular legislators and the greater the pressure on representatives to please their constituents or face a quick end to their legislative career. Increasing the frequency of legislative elections thus promises to approximate the same immediate union of voter and legislator sought by binding mandate and referenda. Not surprisingly, reductions of term length are prevented from realizing the holy grail of the immediate unity of ruler and ruled for the same reasons that defeat binding mandate and the whole gambit to render representation a direct expression of voter preference. Even if legislators faced immediate recall whenever their performance dissatisfies most of their constituents, each newly elected representative will still have the prerogative and need of taking legislative initiatives that cannot be completely anticipated by prior campaign pledges and prior preferences of the voters. Any diversity of political opinion will preclude complete congruence between voter choice and legislative action and any lucky unanimity will still presuppose the prior formulation of legislation without participation by all the electorate.

Similar limitations of the identity conception apply to those, such as Mill,[66] who argue against any staggering of legislative elections on the ground that this will prevent a shift in public opinion from changing the entire composition of parliament at one time. One can argue just as well that staggered scheduling of legislative elections can protect representation from momentary swings in public sentiment and preserve an element of legislative continuity that otherwise might be absent if all seats are up for election simultaneously. Consequently, the determination of election frequency, as well as the presence or absence of staggered scheduling, must be made on other grounds, grounds more truly reflecting the constitutive reflexivity, universality of aim, supremacy, and autonomy of political self-determination. This requires abandoning the pernicious quest for immediate identity and unanimity in legislation and addressing instead how electoral frequency enters into the mediated workings of self-rule.

Given that representatives should have autonomy but should equally be elected by the citizenry, the imperative to shorten term length loses much of its force. Since self-legislation is still at work so long as representatives have been selected by the electorate and exercise their prerogative to make laws on behalf of the rights of the entire citizenry, a greater or lesser frequency in legislative elections becomes largely a matter of indifference for political freedom.

Two polar extremes do pose problems that set boundaries to the term length. At a certain point increasing election frequency can impede the workings of legislation by compelling legislators to spend more time campaigning for election and reelection than in attending to lawmaking. This situation can easily overburden the electorate with overexposure to campaigning, diminish the significance of each election, and foster voter apathy. Moreover, the burdens of too frequent campaigning and too brief terms in office can interrupt the flow of legislative activity and prevent legislators from having the time to learn the ropes of parliamentary practice. For these reasons, it is hardly surprising that the United States is virtually alone in subjecting its legislators to a term as brief as the two-year stint that legislators in the House of Representatives must endure.[67] Exactly when the reduction of term length begins to impede self-government is a contingent matter, for which no exact a priori specification can be given.

The same can be said of the point at which extending legislative term lengths begins to undermine political freedom. The ultimate limit on length of elective office might seem definite enough—lifetime term for legislators. Yet the contingencies of lifespan, health, and retirement leave it an indeterminate appointment, of which little can be said for certain other than it frees representatives from contending with reelection or automatic removal from office. This may be thought to secure the independence of representatives, insulating them from the pressures that face those who covet reelection.

Such concern for independence from the vagaries of public opinion has often underscored the argument for lifetime appointment to an upper legislative chamber, structured to counter the vicissitudes of a lower chamber elected for relatively short terms of office. It also has figured prominently in arguments for lifetime appointment of constitutional judges and heads of state. Significantly, when lifetime appointments have been advocated for upper legislative chambers, this has often been tied to traditional substantive ends distinct from political self-determination and grounded in hereditary privilege. The result is an upper chamber modeled after a House of Lords, the preserve of a specific estate, reflecting a failure to emancipate both society and state from feudal divisions. Since the freedoms of civil society and self-government are incompatible with hereditary appointment and traditional social rank, the only redeeming virtue of lifetime legislative appointment could lie in securing the autonomy of legislative deliberation, which should apply throughout the legislature.

Legislative independence, however, hardly depends upon lifetime office. More limited terms need not jeopardize the proper autonomy of representatives. Not only may they have no desire for reelection, but guaranteed conditions of fair campaigning can encourage them to fearlessly fulfill their duties. Lifetime terms might well eliminate the advantages of incumbency in reelection campaigns, but once more other remedies to this problem are available, such as limits on the number of consecutive terms in office and public enforcement of equal campaign opportunities. Whereas lifetime office thus proves unnecessary for upholding legislative freedom or campaign equality, it has liabilities both specific to life tenure and shared with other extended term lengths.

First, the contingent length of lifetime legislative terms poses the practical problem of scheduling elections irregularly, which could be considered more than a technical issue if it were important that legislative elections be national in scope and be coordinated with elections for executive or authorizing officials. The significance of simultaneous nationwide legislative elections may depend upon the type of electoral system, with certain proportional representation schemes requiring voting for common party lists. Further, the coincidence of legislative elections with elections for executive or authorizing officials may crucially affect self-government if the relation of powers allows uncoordinated scheduling to facilitate "divided government." Under those conditions, the party winning the legislative election can differ from that voted into executive or authorizing positions and the ensuing opposition may foster political deadlock. Whether the perils of "divided government" are endemic to the division of powers under self-government remains to be seen in the treatment of the authorizing and executive powers.

What is not contingent upon this possibility or type of electoral system is a deepening challenge to self-legislation that lifetime legislative election may share with sufficiently extended term lengths. For some period, lengthy legislative terms may enable citizens to be subject to laws drafted by legislators that they have had a chance to elect. Presuming that the ranks of the citizenry continually absorb new adults, however, citizens who were not of age to participate in selecting the legislature will become more numerous, until a time is reached when a majority face a legislature that they did not elect. This problem of generational turnover haunted social contract adherents like Thomas Jefferson, who at one point suggested that the constitution expire once its ratifiers ceased to comprise the majority of citizens. At that junction, every nineteen years, according to Jefferson's actuarial tables, the new coterie of citizens would be empowered to ratify a renewed covenant that would enjoy the actual consent of the governed.[68] The foundational dilemmas of social contract construction render the issue of reratifying the constitution every generation a false problem. Nonetheless, self-legislation becomes suspect once those who are subject to law no longer predominantly comprise those who elected the lawmakers. Then the relation between representative and citizen loses one dimension of the reflexivity of ruler and ruled.

This predicament might seem most egregious for undercutting the answerability of legislators. When terms extend long enough to allow representatives to make law for citizens who mostly did not elect them, the day of electoral reckoning is all the more postponed for the new generation. However, increasing the frequency of elections need not be enlisted to ensure the accountability of legislators. Misconduct in office can be remedied both by self-regulation of the legislative chamber and by interventions of the executive under the guidance of the authorizing power. These interventions could involve reprimand and/or removal of specific legislators or dismissal of the entire legislature and the calling of new elections. Moreover, special avenues of recall could be employed without regular scheduling of more frequent elections.

When misconduct is not at issue and no occasion occurs for exceptional measures of recall or parliamentary dismissal by the executive or head of state, a remedy still lacks for tackling the separate issue of restoring the reflexivity of self-rule to legislation. So long as legislators conduct themselves constitutionally and enjoy sufficient recognition to avoid a breakdown in political association, citizens would have no recourse to reestablish their choice of representation until the next scheduled election.

Whether the same considerations apply to the authorizing power is a question that can best be determined in examining that branch of government in its own right. In regard to legislative representatives, the relation between lawmaking and the will of the citizenry certainly need not be mediated by lengthy terms to enhance any aspect of political freedom other than escaping the liabilities of terms so short that the demands of campaigning and of legislation collide. Accordingly, the reflexivity of self-legislation will be best upheld by scheduling legislative elections no less frequently than required to facilitate harmony between legislative continuity and electoral choice. The conditions determining that harmony are relative to all the geographical, biological, and cultural factors impacting upon the speed of elections and lawmaking. Since these factors are themselves contingent, reason can only indicate the outer limits within which an accommodation may be found.

4.13 LEGISLATIVE TERM LIMITS

The call for legislative term limits has the merit of not offering a surrogate for direct democracy, in the manner of binding mandate or the shortest possible legislative term. Prohibiting incumbent representatives from reelection could hardly fit the mold of identity politics, since constituents might well prefer the incumbent over any opponents. Instead, term limits are advocated to counteract the advantages of incumbency that can undercut the equal political opportunity of nonlegislators to run for legislative office. Incumbents can enjoy an electoral edge not only from their preestablished voter recognition but from using legislative office to garner further publicity, communicate the campaign message to constituents, raise campaign funds, and as a convenient sinecure whose responsibilities can easily be negotiated while engaging in active campaigning. By contrast, nonincumbents must contend with a paucity of voter recognition, reflecting an occupation that likely operates out of the limelight and offers little time for raising campaign funds and taking their political program to the electorate. Term limits can certainly remove at one blow the advantages of incumbency, but barring representatives from reelection equally limits the choice of the electorate. Voters may well prefer an incumbent, not only because of more appealing program and personal credentials but because of the further clout that seniority in legislative service may carry. Whether legislative seniority should be a basis for committee chairs and the like is certainly questionable, especially when historical dominance of a party in certain districts can disproportionately influence the legislative process through a seniority-driven stranglehold on parliamentary committees.[69] Yet even when seniority plays no such role in legislative committee assignments, the electorate may simply want to take advantage of the fruits of experience that seasoned incumbents can provide.[70] In any case, the restriction on voter choice is not ambiguous, for if the advantages of incumbency can be counteracted without term limits, this liability is sufficient to entitle incumbents to seek reelection.

Given the problem, remedies must be sought on two fronts: first, in restricting incumbents from using their position to their political advantage, and second, in providing nonincumbents with a fair share of campaign resources to remove whatever imbalance incumbency creates. On the one hand, incumbents must be prevented from using legislative office resources for campaigning. On the other hand, the general measures for equalizing campaign funding, media exposure, and general communication of candidate positions to the electorate must be tailored to neutralize incumbent advantage. In principle, there is no reason why such initiatives cannot restore sufficient equality of campaign opportunity to make restrictions on voter choice unnecessary.[71] Whether similar measures are adequate to remove all grounds for term limits on executive and authorizing officials will hinge upon a due determination of these powers.

4.14 RECALL OF INDIVIDUAL LEGISLATORS

Recall of individual legislators can serve different agendas of varying legitimacy. One use obeys the imperatives of the identity conception of self-rule, unseating legislators who fail to mirror current public opinion.[72] This employment misuses electoral choice by curtailing legislative autonomy, undermining the significance of parliamentary debate and deliberation, and transforming representation into a direct expression of the immediate preference of electors, rendering their plurality incompatible with the universality and reflexivity of self-government.[73]

Another use, seemingly more consistent with political freedom, recalls legislators to remedy misconduct. Whatever be the reality of the imputed infractions, recall has the disadvantage of substituting a positive or negative registering of popular opinion for any impartial investigation, indictment, and judicious weighing of evidence and application of the law. For this very reason, recall initiators can always allege misconduct to remove conscientious legislators who simply challenge public opinion.

Moreover, recalls, like referenda, are subject to manipulation by powerful groups well-positioned by concentrated wealth and other resources to organize whatever petitioning may be necessary to initiate recall and influence public opinion. The right to recall always leaves in question *who* will actually be able to mount an effective recall. So long as recall campaigns require significant means, it is always suspect whether equal political opportunity will be observed and whether the prior will of the electorate, as well as legislative freedom, will be subverted by social interests.[74]

Nonetheless, if legislator conduct could be policed by no other means, recall might be admissible by default. Yet, as already indicated, two powerful remedies are entirely feasible. First, the legislature can discipline its own members through duly impartial procedures open to public scrutiny. This option, can, of course, be corrupted by partisan conspiracies where legislators of the party controlling parliament expel their legislative opponents. These maneuvers can themselves be countered by the second alternative.

This relies upon the division of powers, which already charges the authorizing branch to suspend and remove officials who act unconstitutionally, while obliging the executive to enforce these measures. Although even here rampant collusion can poison political plurality, the eventuality of all powers of government violating their constitutional duties is tantamount to a breakdown of self-government, against which no constitution can automatically defend itself. Accordingly, self-legislation does not depend upon recall, nor is it a trustworthy enforcer of legislative rectitude.

4.15 ELECTIVE CALLS FOR NEW LEGISLATIVE ELECTIONS

Recall initiatives are originated by citizens acting as independents or as party partisans but not in exercise of any government office. By contrast, calls for new legislative elections characteristically fall within the prerogative of chief executives or heads of state, most often under parliamentary systems where new parliamentary elections follow votes of no-confidence requiring replacement of the prime minister by a decision of the new parliament. Such calls commonly legitimate themselves by serving to eliminate deadlocks between parliament and an unpopular prime minister, to enforce the accountability of an errant chief executive, and to bring into being a new legislative majority reflecting current public opinion. Using new legislative elections to remedy misconduct by a prime minister suffers from the same absence of judicial inquiry that plagues recall of individual legislators. Using new legislative elections to make parliament more closely mirror public opinion once more undermines legislative continuity and independence, none of which need be done when the true nature of representation is understood. Further, all of these rationales rest on the assumption that the call for new legislative elections properly falls to the discretion of either the executive or authorizing power. Whether this is compatible with the division of powers is a question better answered when the other powers are further determined. Then it becomes possible to systematically address whether parliamentary or presidential systems have any, let alone any privileged, legitimacy.

4.16 PARTIES AND LEGISLATIVE ELECTIONS

Legislative elections do not just relate individual citizens to the office of parliamentary representation. Legislative office may be predominantly filled by candidates who run as political independents, particularly at the birth of democratic government. As soon as common positions crystalize and political groupings emerge, citizens find themselves at a disadvantage unless they organize political parties and seek office under their respective banners.

Parties have a right to contest legislative elections and citizens have a right to run for legislative office on party tickets provided doing so is in accord with equal political opportunity. This mandates satisfaction of the general requirements that apply to party participation in elections for any branch of government. First, independents must retain their right to contest parliamentary elections and have access to a fair share of campaign resources. Second, parties should advocate different interpretations on how to realize political and nonpolitical rights in face of changing circumstances rather than the interests of particular groups vying for domination over others. Otherwise, party activity jeopardizes the universality, reflexivity, supremacy, and autonomy constitutive of political freedom. Third, parties should be open to all citizens of like political persuasion. Further, the selection of candidates by parties must reflect the will of the party membership. This requires navigating between the extremes of allowing a party elite to control the nomination process and opening candidate selection to nonparty voters. The former scenario leaves voter options hostage to a select few. By contrast, the latter scenario diminishes political choice by allowing one and the same majority to set the boundaries of the political spectrum, to the exclusion of political minorities. Either way, the rights of citizens to run for legislative office and to elect representatives are curtailed. Finally, candidates running under different party banners or as independents must have a fair opportunity to campaign. Equity of campaign funding must be sustained, both by limiting private contributions and by providing public subsidies. Such subsidies should be given to candidates themselves, rather than to parties, which could then use their control over campaign resources to enforce a strict party discipline at odds with the autonomy of representatives. When these measures prove insufficient to guarantee fair access to the media and other resources of campaigning, further initiatives must be taken, such as requiring equitable campaign coverage in the media. These aids should be made available to all candidates, subject to whatever impartial winnowing is necessary to prevent elections from being overwhelmed by a plethora of office seekers.

4.17 MAJORITARIAN VERSUS PROPORTIONAL REPRESENTATION

All these strictures pertain to party participation in elections for any government office. Nonetheless, their application is first systematically conceivable in regard to legislative positions because the authorizing and executive powers operate on the basis of the activity of the legislature. By contrast, the controversy pitting majoritarian versus proportional electoral systems ordinarily focuses not just first, but exclusively, upon the legislative power as mediated by political parties. The debate revolves around which alternative better secures equal political opportunity. This concern might allow the controversy to apply just as well to elections for the authorizing and executive powers. The debate over electoral systems, however, concentrates on legislative elections for several key reasons.

First, the legislature has no elected apex of command comparable to a head of state or chief executive. When one position is at stake, a winner-take-all solution seems inescapable. The plurality of legislators allows for proportional representation, although admittedly, proportional representation could be extended to the authorizing and executive powers not just at lower levels of command but even at the summit if collective leadership is permissible.

Second, the controversy between majoritarian and proportional electoral systems is often tied to the debate over presidential and parliamentary systems of government. Majoritarian elections usually get linked to presidential rule since the choice of president generally concerns a single chief executive and/or head of state, precluding proportional representation. Conversely, since parliamentary systems empower the legislature to select executive and, conceivably, some or all authorizing officials, proportional representation can reign supreme through application to legislative elections.

Further, the divide between majoritarian and proportional representation presupposes that candidates predominantly run on party tickets. Without party lists of candidates, proportionality can hardly be effected unless other shared differences be singled out to group candidates together. Some grouping is necessary since any vote short of unanimous triumph for one group slate will require seating only the fraction of a group's candidates proportional to that group's share of the vote. Of course, it is highly questionable whether any other shared differences besides party allegiances, such as race, gender, sexual orientation, ethnicity, religion, or occupation, can condition representation without subverting self-rule. Any attempt to tie proportionality to these extrapolitical factors will reinstate the liabilities of corporate representation and jeopardize the universality, reflexivity, supremacy, and autonomy constitutive of political freedom. Only proportionality in respect to the political grouping of party lists can retain the cardinal features of self-government.[75] For all these reasons, the debate over electoral systems falls first and foremost within the investigation of legislative elections and of the role parties play within them.

Proportional representation finds support on various grounds, some following corporatist agendas, some emanating from the identity conception of self-rule, and some more consistent with the bona fide character of self-legislation. In all cases, proportional representation is championed as a remedy to the disproportionate results of majoritarian, winner-take-all district elections. Under the majoritarian system, competing legislative candidates vie for territorially defined seats to be filled by the competitors receiving the most votes, either in a single round, or after sufficient run-off elections. Although majoritarian elections most commonly involve single-member districts,[76] where only one candidate gets seated, the majoritarian winner-take-all approach can be applied to multimember districts so long as representation goes exclusively to the highest vote-getters, without any reference to the aggregate vote of different party lists.[77]

Whether victory requires a plurality or an absolute majority in the first or second round or in ranked voting for more than one candidate,[78] the majoritarian procedure makes possible significant discrepancies between the relative vote totals received by parties and the relative number of legislators they seat. These discrepancies can readily foster two outcomes that seem most patently to thwart equal political opportunity. First, majoritarian elections easily allow a party winning a majority of seats each by the slimmest of pluralities to control the legislature with a minority of the total votes for legislative office. Since votes in the legislature are themselves winner-take-all in character, with a majority of a certain quorum[79] sufficing for passage of legislation, minority rule only gets further enhanced in subsequent legislative votes. Indeed, even when a majority elects the controlling party bloc in majoritarian elections, the bare majority of representatives needed to pass legislation may have been elected by a minority of voters.[80] Second, winner-take-all single-member district elections can easily shut out minority parties from any representation in the legislature if they fail to gain a sufficient plurality in any district.[81] Even when these extremes fail to materialize, only the most fortuitous distribution of votes among districts will ever allow legislative seats to reflect the actual relative vote totals of competing parties under majoritarian election.

Proportional representation seeks to minimize such discrepancies by allocating legislative seats in proportion to the vote totals of the respective parties. Of course, precisely how proportionality is to be achieved is subject to infinite variation, given how the number of legislative seats, the minimal threshold for party representation,[82] the magnitude of multimember districts,[83] the regional apportionment of seats,[84] the method for choosing victorious legislators from party lists, and the number of votes allocated to each voter[85] can all be modified.

Contemporary practice illustrates the range of options available for proportional representation, which may always involve multimember districts but otherwise offer tremendous variety in how winning candidates will be elected. The most common contemporary system is the list system, where parties nominate candidate rosters for multimember districts of varying scope, and citizens either vote for one list as a whole, with nominees taking seats in relation to their party's vote share and the order in which the party has listed them (the so-called closed list scheme), or citizens vote for individual candidates on a list, with nominees winning seats in proportion to their party roster's share of the vote in combination with the ranking of their vote total among nominees on their party's roster (the so-called open list system).[86] By contrast, Germany, New Zealand, and Venezuela follow a mixed system, with each voter casting one vote to elect a candidate by plurality in single-member districts and another vote for a proportional representation party list in a multimember district.[87] A further proportional vote option is provided by the so-called single transferable vote, where voters rank the list of candidates in multimember districts and candidates receiving sufficient first preference votes for election have their extra votes transferred to the second preference on the ballots in question, with this procedure repeated until all vacancies are filled.[88] A complementary approach is followed by the single nontransferable vote, where voters cast a single vote for one candidate in a multimember district, approaching a proportional result the greater the number of seats at stake.[89] Finally, under a cumulative voting system, voters are each allotted an equal quantity of multiple votes that they can distribute among candidates or candidate lists in concentrations of their choosing, enabling relatively small groups to elect candidates they strongly prefer.[90] Although these different schemes provide varying opportunities for voters to register their support of individual candidates, they all share the common features that give any formula of proportional representation a manifold appeal over and against majoritarian systems.

First, the proportional representation remedy can advantageously serve corporatist agendas[91] *if* (1) interest groups form subsidiary "parties" fielding candidates committed to that sector of the citizenry, and (2) citizens predominantly vote on correspondingly corporatist lines. These conditions cannot be guaranteed so long as all legislative seats are filled by general election, rather than reserved for representatives of certain groups in the feudal mold of an estate assembly. Unless citizens are subject to external restrictions, they always retain the capacity to run for office and to vote on purely political principles in indifference to the parochial claims of class, race, gender, religion, region, and any other extrapolitical interest. This very latitude is indicative of how proportional representation need not serve corporatist ends and the subversion of self-rule that interest-group politics entails. Given the exclusive normativity of self-determination, proportional representation can only command legitimacy if its independence from corporatism can be secured.

That independence is sustained when proportional representation is enlisted by the identity conception of self-government. A closer fit between voter preference and legislative representation well appears more likely by proportional than by majoritarian election. Except when total unanimity reigns, the majoritarian scheme always leaves losing voters without their preferred representatives and sometimes leaves most voters in that predicament. By contrast, proportional representation can allow all citizens to have representatives of their choice, at least so long as (1) all voters choose candidate lists from parties attaining the minimal threshold for representation, and (2) voters regard their votes as opting for a party representative, rather than an individual candidate. Under those two conditions, when legislative seats are filled from party lists in proportion to party vote totals, every voter elects a candidate matching his or her preference. Moreover, every victorious candidate is effectively elected by a unit of the electorate offering unanimous support, insofar as voters get grouped according to their common choice, rather than by territorial districting.[92]

Of course, the identity between voter preference and legislator still remains formal. No matter how proportionally allotted, the elected legislators cannot be held to the preference of voters in the manner of binding mandate without eviscerating legislative autonomy and parliamentary debate, paralyzing legislation in the case of sufficient parliamentary divisions and leaving the voters of the legislative minority "unrepresented" by the legislation passed by the majority. Indeed, when no party has outright majority support, proportional representation can foster situations where passage of legislation depends upon the assent of smaller and smaller party groups, with whom other party formations must ally in order to form a majority coalition. Under these conditions, the smallest fraction of legislators can block legislation or, alternately, secure passage of laws that no one else would otherwise support in exchange for letting other legislation through.

Although these outcomes defeat the abstract identity mistakenly conflated with the reflexivity of self-rule, that does not detract from the legitimacy of proportional representation. The abiding difference between legislative will and the will of all need not pose any challenge to political freedom once the autonomy of representation and parliamentary deliberation are given their proper due. Then, the evaluation of proportional representation hinges upon whether its operation is most compatible with equal political opportunity.

In this regard, proportional representation must be considered in light of all aspects of its impact upon the relation between citizens and the legislative process. At stake is not just how elected representatives correspond to voter choice, but how the procedures of proportional election affect the life of political parties and the political fortunes of independents, the range of political options facing voters, the breadth of parliamentary debate, and the ability of the legislature to effectively fulfill its constitutional tasks.

Even if political freedom does not rest upon any immediate identity between voter preference and legislative activity, whatever mediated connection prevails must satisfy the requirements of equal political opportunity. On the one hand, legislators cannot act without somehow operating on the basis of voter choice, and on the other hand, the choice of each voter must have as equal clout as possible.

From John Stuart Mill onward, advocates of proportional representation have suggested that both these requirements are better satisfied by proportional rather than majoritarian schemes. Although both electoral systems predicate legislator selection upon elections in which each voter casts the same number of votes, the proportional system, so say its adherents, prevents the votes for less popular candidates from being wasted. Majoritarian elections will have the identical outcome whether supporters of less popular candidates vote or not, since either way, seats are filled by the same victors. For this reason, majoritarian elections give whoever controls the gerrymandering of districts the power to determine whose votes will be wasted,[93] provided the voting patterns of constituencies remain relatively fixed[94] and the political options offered the electorate remain equally unchanged. Proportional elections permit most, if not every, vote to count, insofar as minority votes over a certain threshold determine which party or parties will occupy the seats left unfilled by the majority party or party coalition. Lacking this feature, majoritarian elections leave some voters with no effective role in legislator selection.

Indeed, proportional elections not only better guarantee that every voter's choice has some influence upon legislator selection but also better ensure that the elected legislature reflect voters' choices. Discrepancies between seat distribution and vote distribution among party supporters are certainly more likely minimized under proportional election. Nonetheless, this achievement comes at a certain price and may have a dubious effect upon ensuing legislation. In order for proportionality to be implemented, voting must in some degree involve party lists from which legislators get selected in relation to party vote totals. This poses several limitations upon voter choice.

First, it can restrict the opportunities of political independents, who must compete against regional or national party lists to obtain the minimum vote needed for seating in the legislature. Majoritarian elections may give independents a better chance, since winner-take-all single-candidate competition can enable unaffiliated individuals to triumph over party nominees within the more limited confines of a single legislative district.

Second, the use of party lists limits the ability of voters to choose the individual they wish to elect. To begin with, determining who will be the nominees on the party lists, as well as what order they will have when it comes to winnowing down the victors, presents a daunting challenge to general involvement by party members. In a majoritarian single-candidate district election, party members can manageably participate in primary elections for competing nominees who each have a chance to make their case to their constituents. Under proportional voting for party lists, party members face a much greater field of candidates, extending over a wider region or the nation at large. If primary elections were to be employed in nominee selection for party lists, party members would face the dilemma of choosing between an unwieldy number of candidates, who themselves would face the equally daunting challenge of informing potential voters of their credentials. Even if primary voters were given multiple votes to distribute among the candidates, and vote totals were used to select and rank party list nominees, the whole process would enfeeble primary selection by diminishing the chance for informed choice. For these very reasons, it is hardly an accident that primary selection of party nominees historically remains confined to majoritarian elections and only as a relatively recent innovation in United States politics.

As a consequence, proportional voting for party lists is haunted by the specter of party machine control of candidate rosters, as well as by the accompanying opportunities for influence peddling by special interest groups, who bargain to place their lackeys among the party lists. This undercuts not only voter choice, but the independent political leadership to be expected from genuine representatives.[95]

Of course, if voter determination of party list nominees is restricted and voting is done for party slates, citizens ultimately select not individual legislators so much as anonymous party representatives. This may be partly mitigated by open list voting or alternate proportional schemes in which voters cast multiple votes for individual candidates on party lists. Yet even here, the large number of candidates, the impracticalities of primary elections, and the aggregation of party totals still diminish the direct connection between a vote for an individual candidate and the outcome of proportional election.[96] This encourages the objection that proportional representation is of no significance in counteracting the exclusive say of the majority party coalition in legislation. Although proportional representation may allow minority parties to seat legislators, this has negligible effect if legislators operate as anonymous party functionaries, strictly bound by party discipline to follow the party program. Then, the autonomy of legislators is undermined, parliamentary debate becomes an empty charade from which independent deliberation and persuasion are removed, and the party groupings controlling the legislature pass exactly whatever laws are preordained in the party program. The votes that seated the parliamentary minority are as good as wasted, for the presence of that minority has no impact upon legislation.[97]

Although Carl Schmitt would maintain that parliamentary democracy arrives at similar results under majoritarian schemes in an age of mass political parties,[98] majoritarian election would seem less prone to this evisceration of the legislative process. Majoritarian electoral systems are amenable to primary elections that weaken the hold of party functionaries over candidacy, and single-candidate district election further enhances the political importance of the independent individuality of candidates. Consequently, majoritarian election commands a double advantage. By reducing parliament to a formal implementation of party program, proportional election undercuts its own redemption of minority party representation. And by subverting the autonomy of representation and parliamentary deliberation, proportional elections subordinate legislation to factional control, undermining the reflexivity, universality, supremacy, and autonomy of self-legislation.

If the difficulties facing independents and the limitations upon voter determination of party lists puts some tarnish on proportional representation, much of the majoritarian case is undermined by the limits to the facelessness of party legislative blocs. Even if party lists of nominees are determined by party elites, who wield this power to pressure legislators hoping for reelection, members of legislative blocs must still exercise individual initiative in formulating legislative proposals, forging new legislative compromises, and deliberating upon the continual surprises of parliamentary sessions. Although the still-lingering spectacle of "people's democracies" testifies to how draconian tyrannies can impose passive unanimity upon dummy legislatures, self-government requires the autonomy of legislators and real legislative deliberation and persuasion. Proportional representation can coexist with that autonomy and political pluralism makes it a virtual necessity. The members of parliamentary party blocs are hardly bound by Schmitt's diagnosis of parliamentary democracy. Instead, they can always take the chance of defying party leaderships and attempt to persuade their fellow cohorts and opposition legislators to support compromise amendments or entirely new bills of their own initiative.

Against this background, the presence of minority party blocs takes on a new significance. Given legislator autonomy and the correlative reality of parliamentary debate, it does make a difference whether a majority bloc faces an opposition and whether every significant political voice gets a hearing in legislative debate. Although the parliamentary majority may formally exercise total control, with no effective role for their opposition, that hegemony only operates if the majority acts as one agent, devoid of internal disagreement and impervious to the persuasive powers of opposing legislators. So long as members of parliament deliberate, debate, and vote with any independence, every legislator has an opportunity to influence the course of legislation. Then proportional representation prevents voters in the minority from wasting their votes by giving their preferred party representatives the opportunity to codetermine legislation.

For this reason, proportional representation diminishes the pressures for multiparty politics to coalesce into a two-party system, where the political options facing the electorate get narrowed to two relatively similar alternating parties, which alone remain viable because majoritarian elections permit representation only to broad-based victors, who must be close enough to the political center to win election. Under proportional representation, a plurality of small parties can retain a place in the legislature and escape the temptation to merge with others in order to ever give their supporters the promise of entry to parliament.[99] Accordingly, proportional parliamentary elections are likely to offer voters a greater choice of political positions, enable parliamentary debate to air a broader spectrum of political argument, and thereby allow more comprehensive coverage to the politics of the citizenry.

Securing this opportunity, of course, depends not just upon proportional representation. The workings of the legislature must equally be governed by procedures that prevent any legislative majority, or for that matter, any minority, from hijacking the legislative process and obstructing legislators' equal opportunity to prepare, introduce, and amend legislation, as well as to participate in ensuing parliamentary debate. To this end, excessive closure and openness must both be countered. Whereas parliamentary measures to curtail introduction of bills and amendments or to restrict debate can subvert legislator autonomy and parliamentary deliberation and persuasion, unrestricted filibustering can enable any persistent parties to paralyze lawmaking.

Yet even if parliamentary procedures are regulated in respect of legislative freedom, proportional representation may create a situation where no party has a parliamentary majority and the legislature is prey to two scenarios, each inimical to self-government. On the one hand, legislators may be seated from so many small parties that majority coalitions are continually at risk of fragmenting, leading to general legislative impasse and, in the case of parliamentary regimes, constant change of government. On the other hand, the same fragmentation may enable a small party to exercise disproportional influence over legislation when the survival of a majority coalition depends upon its participation. Either outcome frustrates self-legislation to the degree that citizens' equal opportunity to codetermine law is undercut.

Just these situations are typically used by majoritarian advocates to indict proportional representation. Of course, majoritarian elections can lead to similar results so long as no party wins a clear majority of seats on a winner-take-all basis. Nonetheless, it is commonly held that proportional representation more often leads to political fragmentation because majoritarian elections tend to overrepresent any majority party and shut out small minority parties, encouraging the formation of a two-party system. Majoritarian elections, however, can allow a party or party coalition with an aggregate majority vote to elect a minority of legislators, so long as its votes are unevenly distributed among districts. By contrast, proportional representation guarantees that the party or party coalition with a majority total vote will seat a corresponding section of the legislature. This may well result in a two-party outcome if the electorate so opts.[100] Of course, whether this diminishes fragmentation will depend upon how riven parties themselves are by competing factions. Hence, the liabilities of fragmentation in parliament are hardly a special curse of proportional elections.

Conversely, although proportional representation may allow the legislative process to be receptive to greater political diversity, this depends upon both how politically fragmented the electorate is and how politically monolithic parties are. Although majoritarian systems may allow for a political opportunism fostering two centrist parties offering little meaningful choice to the electorate,[101] political divisions may just as well produce an opposition of extremes. Moreover, the less fragmented the electorate, the less proportional representation will facilitate widened political debate, since fewer parties will likely gain a legislative foothold. Conversely, the easier compatibility of party primaries with majoritarian electoral systems may loosen the political bounds of each party and enable a two-party system to encompass as much or more political disagreement as does a relatively more focused and disciplined multiparty system under proportional representation.[102] Indeed, if party lists controlled by a party leadership tend to keep legislators in tighter step with party platforms, legislative debate may be more pro forma under proportional systems than under majoritarian systems fed by party primaries.

The final judgment on proportional representation rests on balancing the respective advantages of guaranteed legislative opportunities for minority parties and the respective disadvantages of limited voter control over party list nominees, diminished electoral chances for independents, and restricted opportunity to select individual candidates rather than party blocs. Because these are incommensurate considerations, without any clear qualitative ranking, and because their impact depends upon contingent conditions, what ultimately matters is that systems of majoritarian and proportional representation both be held to the other requirements for equal political opportunity. Only then can their respective liabilities be tolerated as inevitable borders of self-legislation.

4.18 SHOULD LEGISLATORS BE PROHIBITED FROM HOLDING EXECUTIVE OR AUTHORIZING OFFICE?

The early history of parliamentary self-government has offered contrasting views on whether legislators should be allowed to hold positions in other branches of government. Whereas the Constituent Assembly in revolutionary France barred members of the executive from sitting in the legislature and the United States Constitution prohibits legislators from holding any other public office,[103] England required cabinet ministers to be members of parliament. The historical opposition reflects a dispute over how the division of powers should be realized. On one view, any admission of executive, or for that matter, authorizing officials into the legislature subverts the division of powers, the bulwark of constitutionality. For the opposing position, the admission of members of government into the legislature facilitates political unity, reflecting how the different powers are mutually related organs, not independently given agencies whose wholly external restriction of one another would destroy genuine political unity.[104]

Dual officeholding can, of course, serve the supremacy of the legislative power in parliamentary systems of government, where parliament not only selects the chief executive and the cabinet but ordinarily does so from among its own members. Nonetheless, as the examples of parliamentary regimes in the Netherlands, Norway, and Luxembourg testify,[105] the legislature can appoint executive positions without dual officeholding, just as allowance of dual office can be enlisted to integrate the different powers without empowering parliament to select executive officials. Hence, dual officeholding is an issue independent of the controversy between presidential and parliamentary systems of government.

Under either system, the significance of dual officeholding upon the division of powers will depend upon the overlap of executive and legislative positions. The more those who control legislation are the same individuals who control the executive, the more the division of powers will be nominal. The more, however, leading executive positions are held by a relatively small minority of legislators, the more will collective determination by each power comprise divergent agencies. This will be most true when legislators in high executive office predominantly have party allegiances at odds with those prevailing in parliament. Yet, even when a chief executive and cabinet reflect the party composition of parliament, this need not signify that a single will pulls the strings in legislating and executing the law. The autonomy of representatives and the independent deliberation and persuasive powers of parliamentary debate preclude any automatic convergence.

Nevertheless, compelling grounds for requiring, let alone, allowing dual officeholding for representatives are lacking.[106] First, although executive as well as authorizing officials can certainly bring an expertise relevant to parliamentary deliberation, there is no reason why this cannot be brought to bear upon the legislative process by permitting officials to address the legislature, either in legislative committees or full session, whenever needed. Second, the demands of legislative service, like those of executive and authorizing office, are hardly fit for part-time occupation. All things being equal, full attention to the duties of lawmaking, limited by nothing but a legislator's other civil and household obligations, will better serve self-government than dividing effort between different government positions. Third, treating each office as an exclusive occupation will eliminate any of the possible compromises of the division of powers that can exist to some degree when legislative office is combined with executive or authorizing positions.

Although requiring government officials to forego family affairs would be a blow to household right, requiring government officials to relinquish other private employment need not be regarded as an infringement upon economic freedom. Government service can accommodate family responsibilities through the same adjustments that apply to any other occupation. Combining legislative with other civil employment, however, would jeopardize the effectiveness of legislative office while enabling legislators to subordinate their lawmaking to particular economic interests. So long as legislative service is remunerated sufficiently to uphold the economic opportunity of legislators, prohibition of simultaneous private employment does not undermine the economic rights of legislators and their dependents.[107]

For these reasons, it makes sense to place the personal economic resources of legislators and other government officials into "blind trusts" or the like to prevent officials from using their public employment for private gain. Admittedly, insulating the private fortunes of legislators from their public office has its limits, especially when legislators have spouses pursuing independent careers. Public scrutiny of household wealth and income can then be employed to monitor abuses of power.

4.19 THE PROPER SCOPE OF LEGISLATIVE ACTION

Although the legislature draws its mandate from the imperative for rule by law, legislatures have commonly wielded powers distinct from lawmaking. These nonlegislative activities generally fall into two categories—those verging on executive action, such as passing annual state budgets and approving treaties and declarations of war and peace, and those involving selection, supervision, and removal of either executive or authorizing officials.

All of these extensions of legislative action might appear to transgress the due limits of self-legislation and infringe upon the division of powers. Yet these parliamentary initiatives generally aim at upholding that division on whose basis they all operate. Whether they are appropriate vehicles for serving constitutionality is another matter.

The quasi-executive measures undertaken by parliaments themselves divide into domestic and international supervisions. Most prominent among the domestic initiatives are parliamentary fiscal decisions, whose specific character is often misconstrued.

Although yearly budgets, as well as specific ad hoc appropriations, commonly get approved as legislative bills, such measures lack the universality of standing laws. Instead of prohibiting or requiring types of action without limitation to time or place, budget appropriations operate as decrees, commanding specific government officials to make specific expenditures during a specific period.[108] The budget may dictate tax levies of a formula applying to all citizens and noncitizens alike, but even that mandate lacks the generality of a standing tax code, which remains indefinitely effective until repealed or amended.

For these reasons, neither annual budgets nor specific appropriations properly fit the job of the legislature as an organ of self-legislation. Legislation can remain true to this mandate at best by just making rules for taxation and for how executive ministries are to spend tax revenues, establishing general standing conditions for particular appropriations, be they annual or of any other limited duration.

Legislative approval of budgets and specific appropriations can, of course, serve another function, that of restraining the executive's license in levying the citizenry and spending public revenues.[109] Historically, this use of legislative approval to oversee executive action has taken two forms. On the one hand, it has been enshrined in constitutional requirements, such as those in the United States Constitution requiring congressional approval of government appropriation and spending.[110] On the other hand, the scope of legislative oversight has been expanded through positive law, as in that legislation whereby the United States Congress has wielded a so-called legislative veto, mandating congressional preauthorization of specific executive undertakings.[111] These extensions of legislative authority raise two questions: first, does enforcing the rectitude of executive action require intervention by the legislature, and second, does legislative intervention undermine the division of powers?[112] Although these questions can be properly answered only on the basis of determining the authorizing and executive powers in their own right, certain clarifications are not hard to anticipate.

First, the authorizing power has the resources to complement any self-regulation by executive bureaus through judicial cases filed by private as well as public plaintiffs. Moreover, the authorizing power can directly supervise executive action and suspend officials and halt activities that it deems unconstitutional. Both of these remedies do suffer from coming after the fact, which may be all too late to prevent serious violations of right.

Second, although the legislative veto has the advantage of forestalling suspect executive measures before they are undertaken, this might be thought to override the division of powers and enable the legislature to execute its laws as it pleases. The legislative veto, however, is subject to several limitations that reduce the threat of parliamentary hegemony. On the one hand, legislative preauthorization of executive action can only cancel plans; it cannot initiate positive implementations of its own design. Similarly, executive action is not usurped by efforts of the legislature to bring executive action under greater public scrutiny by holding hearings to investigate specific administrative activities.[113] Such hearings may shine the light of publicity over executive action, but they do not initiate any positive administrations of their own. Of course, a parliamentary system subverts much of this limitation to the degree that a legislature able to appoint and remove prime ministers and cabinets at will wields de facto positive control of executive action.[114] On the other hand, legislative veto still must contend with the supervision of the authorizing power, which can not only rescind such vetoes but counteract executive decisions that the legislature approves. Although much certification by the authorizing power comes after the fact, it is not unfeasible for authorizing officials to effect the same prior authorization that the legislature exercises under legislative veto.

These considerations leave the legislative veto admissible but dispensable. Because it need not subvert the division of powers, the legislative veto can be admitted, not as a due exercise of self-legislation, but as a check upon executive action. Nonetheless, given the availability of other avenues of keeping the executive within constitutional bounds, the legislative veto is dispensable.

Legislative approval of international treaties and declarations of war warrants a similar fate. To begin with, these legislative actions hardly comprise self-legislation proper. Both involve action with regard to other nations, rather than the reflexive self-activity of self-government. Declarations of war may inaugurate hostilities of indefinite duration, but they remain directed not at foreign nations in general but at specific enemies. Treaties, on the other hand, may establish standing rules governing the relations of participating nations, but they remain agreements between independent parties, rather than laws imposed by a representative legislature upon self-governing citizens. Multinational legislatures, such as the European Parliament, might seem to retain the reflexivity of self-government, yet so long as nations possess sovereignty, multinational legislation remains contingent upon treaty agreements, rather than upon a division of powers on which self-government depends. Not only may nations refuse to recognize the resulting law, but multinational legislation may impose limits that undercut the scope of domestic self-legislation.

Generally, none of these international measures originate in the legislature. Instead, the chief executive, head of state, or both combined as the empirical case may be,[115] introduce declarations of war or make treaties that then get submitted to parliament for final approval. The approval by the legislature then functions not as an act of self-legislation but as a check upon the chief executive or head of state. Given the international nature of the matters at hand and that parliament does not initiate the measures subject to its prior authorization, the legislature's role does not here jeopardize the division of powers. Instead, it prevents either the chief executive or head of state from taking foreign initiatives with unilateral license, a license parliament would itself wield if it had exclusive power to make treaties and declare war. Admittedly, other measures could be enlisted to make international conduct accountable. Executive action could be subject to review by authorizing powers, either by the head of state or through judicial review. Unless, however, treaties and declarations of wars require approval by the authorizing power prior to becoming official, any restraining veto will come too late to prevent errant executive actions from doing their international damage. Even more liable to pernicious delay would be any reliance upon citizen recall of executive officials, either through scheduled elections or elective recall initiatives. For these reasons, mandatory approval by the legislature of foreign treaties and declarations of war provides a satisfactory remedy, which could be dispensable only if the authorizing power fulfills the same task under the same restraints.

Of course, legislative certification of treaties and declarations can only do so much. If legislators collude with unjust leadership of chief executives and heads of state, parliamentary review of prospective treaties and war declarations can still allow the greatest infamies to be perpetrated. Conversely, when the legislature is controlled by parties opposing the party or parties of the chief executive or head of state, partisan differences can stymie any new international initiatives by the government. Needless to say, treaties and declarations of war that are in accord with right may be disapproved by parliament simply for political gain. Such situations of "divided government" can be minimized by parliamentary systems empowering parliament to appoint and remove chief executives, cabinet ministers, and certain authorizing officials. Although that prerogative ensures more party unity among the different powers of government, this very unity holds dangers of its own. If parliament can select chief executives and reject them at will, the predominant party coalition in the legislature exercises virtual, unchallengeable hegemony over treaty making and declaring war, at least so long as the authorizing power has no independent prerogative to veto these acts. As we have seen, if authorizing officials can only intervene after the fact, through judicial review or other subsequent scrutinies, the remedy may come too late to forestall international catastrophes.

4.20 PARTIES AND LEGISLATIVE ACTIVITY

Whatever the electoral system, the number of chambers of parliament, or the presence of federal or centralized government, the operations of the legislature bear the mark of the party organizations whose members win seats after running on party tickets. Although the enforcement of equal opportunity in running for office and the autonomy of representation set limits to party discipline, the same commonalities of political position that lead voters to identify with different parties permit representatives to act in parliament in function of their party membership, so long as doing so respects the legislative rights of all. Separate party caucuses, as well as party coalitions, may choose to elect a legislative leader, responsible for guiding their legislative strategy. This may encompass planning what bills should be introduced, how to organize parliamentary debate, what compromise agreements to forge with other groups of legislators, and persuading party legislators to act in concert. Similarly, whenever the legislature divides its labors between different committees focusing on different types of legislation and legislative concern, party blocs within each committee have a chance to elect committee chairs with some prerogatives to guide the work of the committee.

If party whips were to control unilaterally what legislation gets introduced and who can participate in parliamentary debate, the autonomy of legislators would be compromised. This is especially true if the predominant party or party coalition could block the introduction of bills and interventions by opposing legislators, or for that matter, if supermajority requirements for closing debate enable minority blocs to filibuster any proposal to death.[116] Legislative procedures should be tailored to prevent either from happening, for only then can party legislative leaderships lead in conformity with the autonomy of representatives, genuine parliamentary deliberation, and the equal political opportunity these make possible.[117]

Analogous provisos apply to legislative committees. If these follow procedures enabling committee chairs and their loyal cohorts to block bills in committee and throttle debate, parliamentary deliberation succumbs to the hegemony of the ruling party or party coalition, leaving legislative autonomy in peril.[118] Alternately, procedural rules facilitating filibustering in and out of committees can enable small coteries to bring self-legislation to a halt. Legislative committees have a legitimate role to play in conducting investigations and specialized debates to ensure statutory consistency and to help draft legislation in regard to complex problems. These technical undertakings do not, however, give license to restricting the spectrum of legislative proposals and of supporting debate and deliberation. Although committee scrutiny may give rise to new bills, it ought just as well follow the independent introduction of legislation to help that legislation take a final form adequate to its task. This does not preclude party groups from selecting committee leadership and voting in consort on committee resolutions, but it does set limits upon the prerogatives that committee chairs and committee majorities should wield.

These limits can counter the effects of winner-take-all elections of committee chairs, which can shut out minority parties from any committee control and disproportionally empower the majority party coalition. Of course, if proportional representation deserves any scope in the election of representatives, it should equally figure in determining committee chairs.

As for final votes on legislative bills, two complementary considerations must be addressed to secure equal political opportunity in a parliament of party members and independents alike: quorum and supermajority requirements. On the one hand, no parliamentary votes, nor any other parliamentary business can be allowed to count if there lacks a quorum of representatives sufficient to enable any actions taken to stand for those of the whole legislature, instead of for a particular faction of usurpers. To this end, it makes sense to set quorum requirements at that number of representatives whose vote would prevail if all seats were filled, that is, one more than half the total.[119]

On the other hand, parliamentary votes should not be left hostage to supermajority requirements that allow small factions to block any legislation they oppose. Although supermajority requirements have been advocated as bulwarks of minority rights against the tyranny of the majority,[120] positive legislation should always be constrained by constitutional guarantees that prevent any bills from violating the political and nonpolitical rights of legal subjects. Given due constitutional protections and the division of powers, supermajority requirements are not only unnecessary to uphold right but are also obstacles to the fulfillment of parliamentary deliberation and its realization of self-goverment.[121] Instead of allowing the equal political opportunity of constituents to gain expression in the majority decision of their representatives, supermajority requirements give minorities the power to stifle the general will of parliament. Instead of enabling political self-determination to be sustained rather than hindered by political plurality, supermajorities push toward their logical extreme in the Rousseauian demand for unanimity, at which point self-rule by a real diversity of citizens becomes impossible.[122] It should thus be no surprise that supermajority's minority veto is hardly a reliable protector of the interests of the disadvantaged. If anything, it is the perfect tool for upholding entrenched privilege by stalling reform legislation needed to remedy oppressions of minorities and majorities alike.[123]

4.21 SHOULD LEGISLATORS HAVE LEGAL IMMUNITY?

The accountability of legislators has two dimensions: accountability for transgressions of legislative duties and accountability for violations of other rights. Transgressions of legislative duties require rectification as much as any other wrongs. Although immunity has been enlisted to protect the freedom of legislators from sanctions,[124] so long as "politically" motivated suits and prosecutions can be duly screened and genuine transgressions can be rectified in ways that do not undermine due legislative autonomy, parliamentary immunity loses its justification as a bulwark of self-government. Given this proviso, suitable remedies vary according to the type of violation of office. These transgressions can involve unconstitutional lawmaking that authorizing powers can remedy by refusing to certify suspect legislation. Transgressions can also involve dereliction of duty, where legislators fail to appear and perform their duties as representatives, without, however, committing specific wrongs to other legislators. In these cases, the legislature can discipline its own members, through censure and removal from office, at least so long as the procedures be public and the accused have some recourse to appeal. Otherwise, party coalitions controlling the legislature could easily use these procedures to eliminate their opposition. By contrast, departures from legislative rectitude can also involve violations of the legislative rights of other representatives. Legislators may unduly prevent others from introducing legislation, participating in legislative debate, and casting their votes either by "peacefully" deviating from proper legislative procedures or employing force to intimidate and assault their peers. To the extent that such actions comprise malicious violations of the political rights of other legislators, they are crimes subject to punishment and compensation when damages ensue. Right requires that some impartial judicial process be employed to prosecute, try, and determine penalties and damages, when applicable.

If legislators were to enjoy immunity against such prosecution and trial, legislative right would itself stand in jeopardy. Legislators would have license to violate one another's parliamentary entitlements and undermine self-legislation. The situation appears otherwise, however, when legislators commit violations of right that do not involve official duties. In these cases, which may involve civil as well as criminal wrongs, prosecution and trial during the term of office of the accused could well interfere with participation in the legislative process. Some of this disruption can be averted through penalties for bringing nuisance suits and by winnowing dubious cases by judicial authorities. Nevertheless, when accused legislators warrant prosecution and trial for suspected nonmalicious and/or malicious wrongs, subjecting legislators to due process will likely interfere with their official duties.

Granting legislators immunity in such cases would allow the legislative process to operate without obstruction but at the expense of ignoring the rights of victims for compensation and the right of civil society to punish malefactors for their crimes. That liability could be ameliorated by either of two alternatives: (1) suspending prosecution of legislators for nonofficial wrongs until after their current term of office ends, or (2) appointing a replacement to handle legislative duties while the incumbent legislator is brought to trial.

Suspending prosecution until the end of term would not completely ignore the imperatives of compensation and punishment, but it would leave victims with no recompense for damages while incumbents complete their term and leave alleged perpetrators at liberty to strike anew. The problem of compensation would be parried, at least for the victim, if all victims had access to quick and automatic compensation, provided by a publicly funded universal personal damage insurance fund. Moreover, the perpetrator could still eventually be held liable for damages after leaving office and being brought to trial. The problem of delaying trial for serious crimes would be less tractable. Complicating either remedy is the possibility of accused legislators winning reelection, putting off trial even further. If this possibility were forestalled by prohibiting indicted legislators from running for reelection, their right to run for office would be sacrificed at the altar of unproven charges.

Replacing accused legislators would avoid some of these difficulties, but it would countermand the vote of the electorate for alleged perpetrators whose guilt has yet to be legally established. Electoral choice could be redeemed, however, either by snap elections to fill out the remainder of the accused's term or by using indirect election, perhaps by provincial assemblies, by a caucus of legislators of the same party or by vote of the entire legislature. These avenues would then make immunity for legislators unnecessary for upholding the integrity of self-legislation.

4.22 SHOULD THE LEGISLATURE BE UNICAMERAL OR MULTICAMERAL?

All of the preceding considerations apply to the legislative power whether it be uni- or multicameral. Whatever enables the selection of representatives and parliamentary procedure to serve self-government in a single-chambered legislature applies just as well to the members and activities of any plurality of chambers. For just this reason, some other factors must be sought to legitimate any preeminence, let alone any exclusive mandate, for multi- as opposed to unicameral legislatures.

Historically, the emergence of multicameral legislatures has reflected varied agendas, most prominently aiming at representing traditional hierarchies, social and cultural groups compatible with civil society, or provincial regions under schemes of federalism, or merely to curb legislative license by balancing chambers against one another.

To begin with, multicameral parliaments have given legislative expression to the divisions of premodern estate assemblies, where hereditary rank has entitled lords to an upper house of their own to counteract the lawmaking of a house of commons. Such arrangements depend upon residual feudal privileges that conflict both with the universal freedom of ownership, the marital freedom of an emancipated household, the equal social opportunity of a civil society, and the equal political opportunity of self-government, which presupposes the emancipation of household and society from traditional relationships that distribute family, social, and political roles according to distinctions independent of self-determination. Accordingly, any such organization of multicameral legislatures is opposed to right and illegitimate.

Second, multicameral parliaments have been advanced as vehicles of corporate representation, where different legislative chambers are exclusively assigned to particular social-interest groups. Given that legislation will only be adopted through the cooperation of the different chambers, their corporate division will ideally insure (1) that none of the groups having a chamber of its own will have its interests sacrificed in legislation, and (2) that no group interests will gain expression in law unless they harmonize with the group interests of every other legislative chamber. On this basis, a multicameral corporate parliament will serve an agenda seemingly compatible with political and social freedom: it will integrate civil society and state by insuring that law serves corporate interests and that corporate interests determine themselves politically in a way that secures the mutual respect and harmonization of the different sectors of society.

Of course, the moment the legislature is divided into separate corporate chambers, the universality of political representation becomes suspect. To begin with, if multicameral corporate legislatures are to provide any semblance of equal political opportunity and the reflexivity and universality of aim that goes along with self-rule, two conditions must be met. First, whatever set of groups gain chambers of their own must together include the entire citizenry. If any citizens are excluded from these groups, the multicameral corporate assembly will leave these nonmembers with no role in legislation. Lawmaking will then cease to be self-legislation and instead comprise the rule of a privileged set of groups over the entire citizenry. Second, even if all citizens belong to the groups allotted chambers of their own, equal political opportunity will be absent if any citizens belong to more than one group and have the opportunity to vote or run for legislative office in multiple chambers.

Needless to say, neither all groups nor all assortments of groups compatible with a civil society satisfy these dual requirements. Among those that can are groups necessary to civil society and groups contingent upon given divisions of race, ethnicity, religion, sex, and any of the other natural or cultural factors that may or may not sort members of a free society. The ground of necessary social-interest groups lies in the commodity relations of a civil society, which automatically group market agents into classes distinguished by types of commodity ownership, corresponding types of earning, and corresponding types of revenue. These economic classes are generic to social freedom and have interests whose fulfillment is predicated upon the satisfaction of the complementary interests of their counterparts.[125] Moreover, civil freedom entitles members of civil society to advance their joint class interests through corporate groups so long as these groups do so through market activity and civil litigation respecting the civil rights of others. Admittedly, individuals in civil society may engage in multiple economic activities, making them simultaneous members of more than one class and, if they so choose, members of more than one corporate advocacy group.[126] Nevertheless, a system of class legislative chambers could escape the political inequality of multiple representation by restricting individuals to voting for candidates and running as a candidate in only one chamber.

The need for political representation by class presupposes that shared, but particular, economic interests cannot be satisfied unless political privileges be assigned by class, e.g., that voting for representatives to a certain chamber and running for office in that chamber be restricted to those belonging to or exclusively aligning with those classes. This assumption might apply if civil society were a laissez-faire society, in which equal economic opportunity is left at the mercies of markets and social-interest-group activity. Since, however, neither markets themselves nor social-interest-group activity can protect equal economic opportunity from monopoly power, unequal development, business cycles, and recurring disparities in wealth, health care, shelter, education, commercially relevant infrastructure, and other prerequisites of economic welfare, society is not genuinely civil unless it involves a public administration of welfare that intervenes upon the market to guarantee every member's social freedom.[127] This civil intervention is a neverending occupation, given the contingencies of market conjunctures and extramarket conditions that affect economic welfare. Nevertheless, through its ongoing efforts, the integration of all classes into civil society is upheld to the degree that the economic interests of all members are publicly secured, without leaving any over- or underprivileged. Admittedly, this undertaking is a task that few contemporary societies have sufficiently fulfilled, but that failure does not diminish its standing as a fundamental civil duty. Indeed, because equal political opportunity is imperiled if equal economic opportunity is not maintained, self-government must occupy itself with insuring that this public intervention is upheld. Because rights are at stake that deserve legal enforcement, the legislature has an obligation to enact legislation sufficient to maintain the public administration of welfare within civil society in face of changing conditions. Nevertheless, the need for legal public enforcement of equal economic opportunity does not at all mandate that the requisite law be made by a legislature divided into corporate chambers. The aim of these interventions is not the satisfaction of any particular social interest to the exclusion of others, but maintaining the general conditions for equal economic opportunity, and, by extension, for equal political opportunity. The task at hand therefore has the universality of aim proper to political action, where individuals determine themselves not as members of a distinct social group, but as citizens, acting as equal partners in the collective governance of the whole body politic and the society it incorporates. Consequently, a division of chambers by class is superfluous for upholding and harmonizing social interests.

Further, the end of self-legislation is by no means limited to legally realizing particular social interests in reciprocity with one another. All the other dimensions of right, including above all the political end of self-rule are constant concerns of positive legislation, concerns that transcend the horizon of class allegiance. If the legislature is divided into different chambers in function of social interests, lawmaking as a whole becomes subsumed under social concerns, substituting a balancing of particular group agendas for the reflexivity, universality, supremacy, and autonomy of political self-determination. Although corporate chambers may guarantee that no group has its interest overridden, it risks leaving politics captive to group rather than national aims.

Analogous limitations apply to any scheme of dividing parliament into chambers reserved for groups differentiated by religion, language, ethnicity, tribe, race, gender, or any other contingent cultural sorting compatible with civil society. Once more, the rights of individuals belonging to each of these groups are already obligatory concerns of any legislative chamber, no matter how it be configured. Any intentional discriminations entailing restrictions of family, social, or political opportunities on the basis of these cultural differences constitute crimes warranting punishment specified by law. Of course, if damages are incurred, the victims also deserve compensation from the perpetrators. Further, any deficits in equal opportunity that result from historical discrimination require legally enforced remedies that counter these barriers to the exercise of right. All of these initiatives serve nonpolitical and political freedoms to which all citizens are entitled, rather than particular interests that apply to part of the citizenry. Consequently, the task of guaranteeing the rights of members of different cultural groups provides no justification for dividing the legislature into separate chambers, differentiated by cultural factors. Once more, any such legislative division would, at best, be purely redundant. In each and every chamber, legislators would have the same obligation to uphold the rights of all citizens, as well as the nonpolitical rights of all noncitizens. If legislators instead showed partiality to their defining group they would violate the universal aims of political justice and subvert the reflexivity of self-rule and the supremacy of political over particular cultural ends.

Distinct group rights could only be deserving of political guarantee if they accord with family, civil, and political freedoms, which preclude exclusionary privileges in household, civil, or political relations. Granting a group exclusive control of a legislative chamber for the sake of its own welfare would challenge this accord, even if all citizens could be assigned membership in a group with its own chamber. To entitle particular groups to distinct legislative chambers would allow citizens to engage in legislation only in function of some group identity, given independently of specifically political differences, a requirement underpinning the separate but equal rationale invoked by apartheid and "Jim Crow" regimes. Even if group identities are drawn so that all citizens fall into one such group, and each chamber has equal veto rights over legislation, the division contributes nothing of positive value to self-government. If legislators take their group identity as decisive for their legislation, lawmaking gets subordinated to group agendas alien to the universal aims of political justice. If instead, legislators in each group chamber transcend their group horizons and exercise their political right and duty to pursue different political programs for upholding the rights of all citizens, the division of chambers becomes a redundant duplication. Even then, however, if the chambers represent different numbers of citizens, the veto power of each chamber would compromise equal political opportunity by giving disproportionate voice to the citizens whose chambers represent comparatively fewer people.

These liabilities might seem largely mitigated when multicameral assemblies serve federalism, where representatives are drawn from different provinces, which exercise some degree of regional autonomy. Instead of providing social groups a separate chamber, federalist schemes structure at least one chamber on regional terms by guaranteeing each province a certain number of representatives without regard for the relative number of voters in these districts.

The provincial regions may owe their identity to preexisting states with or without a unitary ethnic, linguistic, and/or religious identity. Alternately, they may be arbitrarily drawn geographic areas, whose provincial government serves simply to decentralize government power and enhance the opportunities for local involvement in self-rule. What makes these federalist chambers part of a multicameral system is that they get balanced against at least one other chamber organized on other lines.

Of course, a federalist scheme could suffice with a unicameral legislature, leaving the legislative power exclusively wielded by representatives whose numbers reflect some measure of equal representation of different regions.[128] That federal representative democracies have opted instead for multicameral legislatures reflects the obvious limitation of a unicameral federalist parliament. Since regions would have some modicum of parity in the assembly, any significant difference in regional citizen populations would grant citizens in the least populous regions a disproportionate representation, while underprivileging the legislative influence of citizens from the most populous regions. This breach of equal political opportunity has been partly counteracted by complementing a federal chamber of representatives with another chamber in which representatives are elected by relatively numerically equal sections of the electorate. If the assent of both chambers is necessary for any legislation to be enacted, the legislators in the nonfederal chamber can at least foil statutes reflecting the disproportionate legislative power of less populous provinces in the federal chamber. For its part, however, the federal chamber can foil statutes adopted in the other chamber in expression of the legislative privilege wielded by these less populous provinces.[129] For this reason, any retention of a federal chamber impinges upon equal political opportunity, at least so long as provinces differ in population.[130]

Such compromise may have historical justifications when conditions make it impossible to realize political freedom in any fuller approximation. On these lines it has been argued that the constitutional compromise engendering a United States Senate guaranteeing each state two seats was necessary to secure any durable national independence and preclude colonies from separately expanding the slave trade and extending slavery to the new territories that they each might annex.[131] Even if this is true, the theory of the just state must still abstract from such particular limitations and consider what the state ought to be, given sufficient conditions for self-government. Then, bicameral legislatures with a federal chamber offer questionable restrictions upon equal political opportunity.

This liability is compounded by the implicit rationale underlying equal representation for provincial communities—that representatives in a federal assembly are elected by province to represent their separate regional interests. If representatives were to act on this basis, legislation could never achieve the reflexivity of self-legislation. Instead of coalescing into a general will that makes law for the sake of upholding the rights of the entire citizenry, lawmaking would become a contest of competing particular aims, guaranteeing that any adopted law would serve a certain set of regional interests to the exclusion of others. Lacking the universality, reflexivity, and supremacy of genuine political self-determination, such region-bound legislating would secure the domination of one part of the citizenry over another. Just as representation cannot legitimately revolve around corporate concerns, so any structuring of parliament in terms of regional interest corrupts the political autonomy of representatives and the political freedom of their constituents.

This leaves one last rationale for multicameral legislatures, a rationale that has been invoked to redeem the federal organization of the American Congress[132]—that dividing parliament into different chambers of distinct composition will curtail the license of any prevailing block of legislators and make for superior deliberation and law. If a multicameral legislature had legislatures structured identically, with representatives being selected on the same basis for identical terms, the plurality of chambers would be a superfluous redundancy, offering neither mutual moderation nor any deeper consideration.[133] If chambers are merely cloned, whatever transpires in one will likely transpire in the rest. The question, then, is what differences in composition could possibly secure political justice to a greater degree than in a unicameral legislature.

If equal political opportunity is to be strictly observed, every chamber must insure that representatives are each selected by approximately equal numbers of the electorate, without unfair duplication. Otherwise, the inequality haunting corporate and federal representation gets perpetuated under the same or different guise. Further, representatives must not be exclusively tied to particular sectors of the citizenry. Even if legislators are elected from specific districts, rather than in at-large elections, they must be free to serve the good of all citizens, without partiality to any subcommunity.[134] Given these provisos, chambers can permissibly diverge in respect to numbers of legislators and populations of constituencies, lengths of term, and scope of legislative responsibility.

Chambers with different numbers of legislators might generally enhance the prominence of legislators in the smaller chamber, while casting a relative obscurity over representatives in the larger chamber. Of itself, this disparity offers little advantage to self-government. Although prevailing coalitions in each chamber might differ somewhat, the mere numerical difference in representatives provides no reason for any substantial disparity in relative party strength. Any political difference between larger and smaller chambers would be purely contingent, as would any benefit from retaining such differences instead of relying on the political divisions at play in a single chamber.

Similar results follow from diversifying chambers by term length. Whichever chamber has longer term lengths enhances the independent role of its representatives, at least insofar as they have more time to legislate before facing the demands of reelection or retreating into private life. Yet the contribution of this enhancement to self-legislation is just as indeterminate as that produced by any manageable variation in numbers of representatives. Moreover, if longer term length offers any independence from the vicissitudes of public opinion, there is little reason to apply it differentially in different chambers instead of having a unicameral parliament with extended terms.[135] The disparity in election dates will allow the chamber with shorter terms to reflect shifting political fortunes before the other chamber faces its next election. This may enhance political divisions between chambers, facilitating a legislative impasse when chambers become controlled by opposing party coalitions who fail to reach legislative compromise agreements. Such an outcome could also increase the likelihood of "divided government," where elected authorizing and executive officials stand opposed to ruling coalitions in the legislature. This likelihood could be diminished by coordinating the term lengths of different chambers with one another and with term lengths for elected authorizing and executive officials. Yet any difference in term length between legislative chambers will promote the chances of deadlocks between chambers. In the absence of any advantage for political freedom, this liability is enough to disqualify chambers differentiated by term length.

If neither number of representatives nor length of term can be privileged factors for distinguishing legislative chambers, can differences in legislative jurisdiction contribute to self-government? Significantly, the arguments underpinning the allotment of different legislative functions to the United States Senate and House of Representatives depend upon the admission of provincial representation into lawmaking. If provinces should not be granted equal say on any legislation when that conflicts with equal political opportunity, some other basis must be sought for giving one chamber exclusive privilege, for example, to ratify treaties and declarations of war, approve the appointment of high authorizing or executive officials, or to originate fiscal appropriations. Yet if chambers are not differentiated with respect to corporate or provincial agendas and variations in number and term length of representatives have no positive impact upon self-government, little resources remain for privileging one chamber over another on any specific areas of legislation. In that case, what one chamber may collectively decide about some particular matter will have no intrinsic priority over what any counterpart would decide if given the same legislative opportunity. Since the division here gives exclusive jurisdiction to one chamber, the plurality of chambers cannot contribute to any check upon legislative license, except perhaps where their jurisdictions overlap.

In the latter case, any check would be independent of diversification by jurisdiction, composition, or term length. If, however, chambers basically duplicate one another in respect to how their members are elected and on what and how they legislate, any mutual limitations become nominal or completely contingent at best. The mere redundancy of legislative consideration guarantees neither any enhancement in the general lawful realization of right nor any enhancement in any exercise of political freedom.[136]

Moreover, the very need for restricting the will of a legislative chamber by another legislative element is questionable. Although a legislative chamber may always pass bills of suspect constitutionality, the division of powers should give the authorizing power sufficient means to counter any legislative violations of rights. Of course, general collusion between the different powers can always defeat the limits of constitutionality. Still, no multiplication of legislative chambers could protect against that breakdown of self-government. Chambers may concur on illicit legislation. Alternately, even if one chamber refuses to endorse the violations of any others, a colluding authorizing power and executive can make that refusal negligible. For these reasons, a division of chambers wins no support from the imperative of keeping lawmaking within the bounds of right.[137]

NOTES

1. Max Weber points out that budgets have never been put up for approval by referendum precisely because referenda only allow a yes or no decision, precluding the debate and compromise which any budgetary decisions or any other significant legislative matters ultimately require. See Weber, *Political Writings*, ed. Peter Lassman and Ronald Speirs (Cambridge: Cambridge University Press, 1994), pp. 128, 225.

2. As Weber observes, when any technically complicated laws are left to adoption by referendum, the formulation of the proposal is prone to be left in the hands of hidden vested interests. See Weber, *Political Writings*, p. 227.

3. Moreover, as George Anastaplo observes, increased reliance on referenda initiatives tends in the direction of a plebiscitary democracy where the power of the executive gets enhanced over and against the legislature. See Anastaplo, *The Amendments to the Constitution: A Commentary* (Baltimore: Johns Hopkins University Press, 1995), pp. 226–27.

4. As Robert A. Dahl observes, any large meeting is inherently a "representative" system since a few speakers end up having to represent the voices of all those who are unable to speak. See Dahl, *Democracy and its Critics* (New Haven, CT: Yale University Press, 1989), p. 228.

5. Arend Lijphart notes that referenda, usually held to be the most extreme instruments of majoritarian democracy, can actually serve an anti-majoritarian role by allowing small, but active minorities to challenge prevailing majority-approved legislation and campaign for their proposals (Lijphart, *Patterns of Democracy: Government Forms and Performance in Thirty-six Countries* [New Haven, CT: Yale University Press, 1999], pp. 230–31). This possibility only confirms the liabilities of referenda as surrogates for direct democracy identity politics.

6. This dilemma is not contingent upon any assumptions concerning human abilities to multitask, for no matter how elastic capabilities may be, every increase only multiplies the explosion of point and counterpoint.

7. See Jean-Jacques Rousseau, *The Social Contract and Discourse on the Origin of Inequality*, edited with an introduction by Lester G. Crocker (New York: Washington Square Press, 1967), bk. 3, chap. 15, p. 99.

8. With binding mandate, to paraphrase Hannah Arendt, the work of the legislature has degenerated into mere administration and the public realm of parliamentary debate has vanished. See Arendt, *On Revolution* (New York: Viking, 1965), p. 240.

9. For these reasons, Arendt is justified in describing rule by plebiscite as an unbridled rule of public opinion that eliminates citizens' right to vote, select, and control their government. See Arendt, *On Revolution*, p. 231.

10. As Michael Oakeshott notes, an "interest" never specifies a particular performance (Oakeshott, *On Human Conduct* [Oxford: Oxford University Press, 1975], p. 42).

11. For this reason, advocates of group representation must do to groups what Rousseau does to the citizenry as a whole: secure its homogenous unanimity at the expense of any internal plurality. So, for example, Lani Guinier observes that group representation presupposes that legislators represent unanimous, rather than divided constituencies (Guinier, *The Tyranny of the Majority: Fundamental Fairness in Representative Democracy* (New York: Free Press, 1994), p. 140).

12. The inherent particularity of corporate interests insures that this subversion occurs whether or not the parliamentary representation of corporation exactly matches the relative proportions of their membership among the citizenry or whether or not citizens belong to multiple corpo-

rate groups. Dahl raises the former issue in questioning the democratic credentials of corporate representation. See Dahl, *Democracy and its Critics*, p. 297. Weber raises the latter issue in pointing out that multiple corporate membership by individuals means that any system of corporate representation will fail to meet the equal political opportunity standard of a "popular assembly." See Weber, *Political Writings*, p. 91.

13. Arendt formulates Mussolini's interpretation of the corporate state in these terms. See Arendt, *The Origins of Totalitarianism*, new ed. with added prefaces (New York: Harcourt Brace Jovanovich, 1973), p. 258.

14. Arendt fails to recognize these features of genuine representation and therefore still considers representative democracy to violate the reflexivity of self-rule. Her remedy of a pyramid of assemblies, rising from the ward level, does not escape any of the mediations of representation that she mistakenly seeks to overcome. See Arendt, *On Revolution*, pp. 241–42.

15. This freedom from binding mandate is recognized in how, as Norberto Bobbio notes, the French Constituent Assembly, which produced the Constitution of 1791, came to view the parliamentary deputy, once elected, as a representative of the nation, rather than of the electorate. See Bobbio, *The Future of Democracy*, ed. Richard Bellamy, trans. Roger Griffin (Minneapolis: University of Minnesota Press, 1987), p. 29.

16. As Weber points out, the intellectual quality of parliamentary debate depends on whether legislators not only address the great problems of the nation, but conclusively decide them (Weber, *Political Writings*, p. 145). Only with freedom from binding mandate, can parliament exercise both options.

17. As Jürgen Habermas observes, when representatives are elected as participants in freely conducted parliamentary discourses, voting power has not just been delegated (Habermas, *Between Facts and Norms: Contributions to a Discourse Theory of Law and Democracy*, trans. William Rehg [Cambridge, MA: MIT Press, 1996], p. 181), as under binding mandate.

18. Bobbio draws this instructive contrast between representatives regarded as fiduciaries of their constituency's universal aims and as delegates of a constituency's particular interest. See Bobbio, *The Future of Democracy*, p. 48. As he points out, such delegates engage in mandation, transmitting demands made by those they "represent," rather than in the genuine legislative initiative of representation (Bobbio, *The Future of Democracy*, p. 126).

19. As Bobbio points out, how "what" is represented gets defined has implications for "who" can be the representative. If the representative duly

represents the universal ends of political freedom, then it is no longer essential that the representative be, for example, of the same professional category as the person represented. See Bobbio, *The Future of Democracy*, p. 47.

20. Significantly, Guinier presumes that territorial constituencies involve representation of geographically drawn interests. She objects to this as a violation of individual autonomy insofar as residents may neither have freely chosen their place of residence, nor share interests simply because of their geographic location. What she fails to recognize is that the indifference of territorial constituencies to any self-selected interests is precisely what makes them a fitting unit for the universal ends that allow representation to conform to self-rule. See Guinier, *The Tyranny of the Majority*, pp. 81, 129, 136–37.

21. As Bobbio points out, sectional representation may be suitable in certain nonpolitical contexts, such as university or industrial affairs, where decisions must be made within a technically circumscribed orbit. When, however, the governance of citizens is at stake, citizens must be represented by individuals distinguished not by the sectional interests they represent, but by the political visions they support. See Bobbio, *The Future of Democracy*, p. 51.

22. Anastaplo points out how salient features of the federal system of the United States Constitution reflect this autonomy of representatives. To begin with, members of the new congress are called representatives and senators, not delegates, as under the Articles of Confederation. Second, each state is allotted two senators, who vote separately, which would not be required if they were bound by the interest of the state they represent. Third, senators are not subject to recall before the expiration of their term of office. See Anastaplo, *The Constitution of 1787: A Commentary* (Baltimore: Johns Hopkins University Press, 1989), p. 37.

23. Carl Schmitt draws this distinction in proper respect for the universality of political representation. See Schmitt, *Verfassungslehre—Achte Auflage* (Berlin: Duncker & Humblot, 1989), p. 240. What he fails to recognize is that democratic representation realizes the universality of political aims precisely by allowing voters and nonvoters to codetermine the selection of legislators who legislate on behalf of all, irrespective of their political disagreements. For this reason, the reflexivity of self-rule can be maintained without the homogeneous identity that Schmitt wrongly ascribes to democracy, following the lead of Rousseau. Political diversity does not prevent universal franchise from enabling all citizens to affect electoral outcomes equally, whether they vote or not, so long as differences in social

and household organization are not permitted to undermine equal political opportunity. As Schmitt himself observes, the electoral decision of every citizen enters into determining the victor, since even abstentions decide what will comprise a sufficient majority or plurality to carry the day. (See Schmitt, *Verfassungslehre*, p. 240.)

24. Hence, although Guinier may claim that group representation fosters, at least in the United States context, coalition building among racial and political factions (Guinier, *The Tyranny of the Majority*, p. 140), this may just as well further marginalize disadvantaged minorities, as the Republican "Southern strategy" proved when it supported racial gerrymandering to create a solid conservative majority in predominantly non–Afro-American congressional districts.

25. As Guinier observes, if voting remains racially polarized, representatives elected by a racial majority can completely ignore minority voters without risk of any electoral consequences. See Guinier, *The Tyranny of the Majority*, p. 89.

26. As Guinier observes, prejudice among group representatives may merely shift the "gerrymandering" problem from the electorate to the legislature, leaving minorities with just as little influence on legislation. See Guinier, *The Tyranny of the Majority*, p. 65.

27. As Will Kymlicka notes, these forms of "political 'affirmative action'" are "most plausibly seen as a temporary measure on the way to a society where the need for special representation no longer exists." (See Kymlicka, "Three Forms of Group-Differentiated Citizenship in Canada," in *Democracy and Difference: Contesting the Boundaries of the Political*, ed. Seyla Benhabib [Princeton, NJ: Princeton University Press, 1996], p. 158.) As such, they fall into the prehistory of the just state.

28. This connection between self-legislation and the autonomy of legislative representatives is ignored by those who seek to legitimate representation by holding what Habermas calls the "rationalist assumption" that only a representative legislature's framework for feasible deliberation allows the common good to be properly determined. See Habermas, *Between Facts and Norms*, p. 185.

29. Weber aptly describes parliament under the reign of party discipline in these terms. See Weber, *Political Writings*, p. 170.

30. For this reason, Bobbio describes party discipline as an open violation of the veto on restricted mandates that are so central to representative democracy. See Bobbio, *The Future of Democracy*, p. 30.

31. Such measures could include selecting party nominees by party

officials, be it in smoke-filled rooms, caucuses, or open conventions, instead of through primary elections, and channeling campaign funding, be it private or public, through party officials, rather than passing it directly to candidates. James L. Sundquist discusses how these measures can be employed to maintain party discipline. See Sundquist, *Constitutional Reform and Effective Government*, rev. ed. (Washington, DC: Brookings Institution, 1992), pp. 264–70.

32. Another likely consequence of party discipline on parliament is, as Weber observes, that legislative office will tend to be sought only by party hacks and representatives of vested interests, since independent personalities and advocates of any stature will not seek positions from which the responsibility of leadership has been eliminated. See Weber, *Political Writings*, p. 191.

33. Guinier points out that this view was prevalent in the British Parliament, whose members were regarded not as delegates of individual constituencies but as equal members of Parliament who represented all of Britain. See Guinier, *The Tyranny of the Majority*, p. 128. Edmund Burke, for example, argued that "Parliament is not a *congress* of ambassadors from different and hostile interests . . . but parliament is a *deliberate* assembly of *one* nation, with *one* interest, that of the whole" (cited by Guinier, p. 270). By contrast, Guinier herself ties representation to the representation of self-selected interests, claiming that voters have representation only when they choose who represents their interests. Not surprisingly, she tends in the direction of the identity conception by demanding that every citizen's vote count for some representative's election. See Guinier, p. 150.

34. As Mill points out, this unfettered discretion of representatives meets some of the alleged deficiencies of majoritarian electoral systems by giving a chance for opinions other than those of electoral majorities to be heard in parliament. See John Stuart Mill, *Three Essays: On Liberty, Representative Government, The Subjection of Women* (Oxford: Oxford University Press, 1975), p. 334.

35. Of course, adopted legislation must equally be made intelligibly available to all legal subjects, since, to paraphrase Oakeshott, law prescribes conditions of conduct that can be freely followed only in being understood (Oakeshott, *On Human Conduct*, p. 261).

36. As Bobbio points out, the publicity of all acts of government is crucial not only because it enables citizens to know what those in power do but because public scrutiny itself operates as a form of control, inhibiting outrages that might easily occur in secret. See Bobbio, *The Future of Democracy*, p. 34.

37. As Bobbio observes, Carl Schmitt in his *Verfassungslehre,* duly connects representation and publicity of power, going so far as to argue that secret sessions can never be representative (See Bobbio, *The Future of Democracy,* p. 82). Yet, as we have seen, even though Schmitt may recognize that representation can only proceed in the public sphere, he fails to see how representation can realize the reflexivity of self-rule.

38. Habermas analogously argues that parliamentary debate can provide for equal political participation only if it remains open and receptive to information, arguments, and suggestions from a pluralistic public sphere, relatively undistorted by the effects of power. See Habermas, *Between Facts and Norms,* p. 182.

39. These are the criteria of effective democratic participation listed by Dahl. See Dahl, *Democracy and Its Critics,* p. 109. Any other implementation would be incompatible with the legislative autonomy necessary for sustaining the reflexivity of self-government.

40. Mill notes these problems but offers the extreme solution of a non-elected Committee of Codification that would have exclusive power to draft bills to which the legislature could make no changes but only vote yes or no or remit to the committee for further reformulation. See Mill, *Three Essays,* p. 224. Mill's Committee of Codification resuscitates Rousseau's notion of a Legislator who can guide the general will to do no wrong by leading it to ends given independently of self-government. Neither Mill nor Rousseau provide sufficient argument to preclude a moderately sized legislature from ably effecting self-legislation.

41. In this respect, Weber claims that the United States Senate draws its superiority over the House of Representatives from its smaller membership, for the fewer the deliberators, the more unambiguously are political responsibilities manifest both to each participant and to those they lead. See Weber, *Political Writings,* p. 230.

42. Selection by lottery would, as Anastoplo puts it, undermine the belief that the citizenry are in fact governing themselves. See Anastaplo, *The Constitution of 1787,* p. 94.

43. Lijphart reports that whereas the Netherlands abolished compulsory voting in 1970, voting remains compulsory (as of 1996) in Australia, Belgium, Costa Rica, Greece, Italy, Luxembourg, and Venezuela. See Lijphart, *Patterns of Democracy,* p. 285.

44. Habermas suggests that compulsory voting is totalitarian in spirit, even though it could be implemented without otherwise compromising any features of the democratic process. The fact that, as Habermas main-

tains, the legally constituted status of citizen depends upon a significant level of voluntary compliance with democratic practice does not mean that citizens cannot predominantly voluntarily comply with a duty to vote. See Habermas, *Between Facts and Norms*, p. 499.

45. Lijphart makes this point. See Lijphart, *Patterns of Democracy*, p. 284.

46. Accordingly, when Mill argues that suffrage is strictly a matter of duty, where each citizen is under an absolute obligation to serve the public interest (Mill, *Three Essays*, pp. 302, 304), he fails to take into account situations where abstention from voting may provide just that service.

47. Carl Schmitt makes this point. See Schmitt, *Verfassungslehre*, p. 239.

48. Arendt describes the right to exclude oneself from political participation as a negative liberty, "freedom from politics," unknown to Rome or Athens, which renders political participation an act of self-selection, demonstrating that one cares for more than private interest (Arendt, *On Revolution*, p. 284). This ignores how political freedom is bound up with ethical community, something equally ignored by any social contract doctrine that derives political obligation from individual choice. "Freedom from politics" is relinquishment of the status of citizen and exclusion from self-government, rather than an exercise of self-determination.

49. Moreover, as Anastaplo argues, compulsory voting hardly encourages voters to become properly informed about the electoral issues and vote with thoughtfulness. See Anastaplo, *The Amendments to the Constitution*, p. 226.

50. For a systematic account of these basic features of malicious and nonmalicious wrong, their remedies, and how righting wrong must be made legal, see Richard Dien Winfield, *Law in Civil Society* (Lawrence: University Press of Kansas, 1995), pp. 45–52, 85–96, 151–55.

51. As James L. Sundquist points out, only with the reforms of the Progressive Era did United States election ballots cease to be printed by party organizations and instead become a "single publicly printed ballot, marked in secret," following the originally Australian innovation (Sundquist, *Constitutional Reform*, p. 112).

52. As Guinier points out, the United States has the dubious distinction of being one of the few democracies to leave voter registration to private initiative instead of having the government register voters in a virtually automatic procedure. This policy compromises equal access to electoral participation in function of the social inequalities of citizens that affect the ease of their participation in voter registration. See Guinier, *The Tyranny of the Majority*, p. 32.

53. The morass of the Florida presidential elections of 2000 presented glaring examples of both shortcomings: varied voting machinery that led to higher rates of ballot disqualifications among heavily Democratic voters and a punched ballot system whose hanging, pregnant, and dimpled chads left the voting opportunity of thousands jeopardized by a cloud of uncertainty.

54. In this respect, proposals to require voting for presidential and congressional candidates of the same party would limit voter freedom in ways in which voting for a single presidential/vice-presidential ticket might not. See Sundquist, *Constitutional Reform*, p. 128.

55. For example, as Sundquist points out, voting machines with the familiar single ticket lever device enabled observers to distinguish split ticket from single ticket voters by the longer time they spent in the voting booth. See Sunquist, *Constitutional Reform*, p. 113.

56. Schmitt, *Verfassungslehre*, p. 245.

57. Ibid., p. 246.

58. G. W. F. Hegel appropriately contrasts the formal universality of Rousseau's *volonté de tous* with the concrete universality of the *volonté générale* in the first addition to ¶163 of his *Encyclopedia Logic*. See Hegel, *Logic*, trans. William Wallace (Oxford: Oxford University Press, 1975), p. 228. Only the latter concrete universality is congruent with the ethical community of self-government.

59. Schmitt makes this bogus claim. See Schmitt, *Verfassungslehre*, p. 246.

60. Initiatives of this sort must remedy such situations as that Guinier describes afflicting poor black rural communities, whose access to polling is compromised by relative scarcity of cars, lack of public transportation, and unaffordable taxi rates. See Guinier, *The Tyranny of the Majority*, p. 11.

61. The traditional social contract view that criminals forfeit all their rights, fall back into a state of nature and stand at war with civil government suffers from the fateful mistake of all procedural theories of justice—that of grounding valid political association in a privileged prepolitical exercise of will. For further critique of the liberal misconception of crime and punishment, see Winfield, *Law in Civil Society*, p. 171.

62. For a systematic account of the due scope of family rights and duties, see Winfield, *The Just Family* (Albany: SUNY Press, 1998).

63. Max Weber points out how the high incidence of lawyers among parliamentary representatives and elected officials in general can be tied to the specific advantages that occupation offers to individuals seeking a springboard for a political career. As Weber observes, lawyers not only have

training in the law and in fighting with words, but they have an office infrastructure that can be utilized in campaigning, they do not have large fixed capital or labor forces requiring their continuous supervision, they commonly share group practices whose partners or associates can temporarily fill in for them, and they can ordinarily return to their practice without sacrificing their position. By contrast, entrepreneurs are comparatively indispensable to their businesses and are more likely caught up in its daily management. See Weber, *Political Writings*, pp. 110–11.

64. Schmitt lists all but the last as measures for realizing the identity principle of democracy, adding as well, initiatives to insure the greatest majority of voters (so as to approach the ideal of homogeneous unanimity), and the greatest possible extension of referenda to decide policy issues (Schmitt, *Verfassungslehre*, p. 252). If any of these measures are to retain validity as instruments of political freedom, it will be not as aids to an immediate identity of ruler and ruled but as vehicles of equal political opportunity, enabling each citizen to codetermine equally the choice of unbound representatives, legislating on behalf of the citizenry at large.

65. As Mill observes, "every benefit of indirect election . . . is attainable under direct." See Mill, *Three Essays*, p. 299.

66. Mill, *Three Essays*, pp. 321–22.

67. Sundquist points this out. See Sundquist, *Constitutional Reform*, p. 154.

68. Thomas Jefferson describes this option in his letter to John Adams of September 6, 1789, cited in *Social and Political Philosophy*, ed. J. Somerville and R. E. Santini (New York: Doubleday, 1963), pp. 261–66.

69. Such was the case in the United States Congress, during the period in which the Democratic Party exercised a virtual one-party rule in the South.

70. As Anastaplo points out, legislative term limits subvert the institutional memory of congress, permanently excluding our more experienced elders, something no other major enterprise or government elsewhere would think of doing. See Anastaplo, *The Amendments to the Constitution*, pp. 209–10.

71. Guinier suggests that cumulative voting can promote the political turnover sought by term-limit advocates, at least to the degree that minority voters can consolidate their votes behind minority candidates and evade the stranglehold on office of entrenched majorities (see Guinier, *The Tyranny of the Majority*, p. 16). It is far from clear, however, that cumulative voting will not suffer from identical, if not more pronounced problems of

incumbency advantage, especially if group allegiances harden into fixed political polarizations.

72. The 2003 California gubernatorial recall election thus reflects the same erroneous identity conception of democracy that underlies California's frequent recourse to referenda.

73. As Bobbio observes, such recall was instituted by the Paris Commune, duly appreciated by Karl Marx, and then prescribed by V. I. Lenin in *State and Revolution* and inscribed in various Soviet and people's democracy constitutions. See Bobbio, *The Future of Democracy*, p. 49. It should not be a surprise that none of these regimes were examplars of political plurality and constitutional self-government.

74. As Bobbio points out, Lenin's statement that "all party officials are without exception revocable at any time" does not indicate who is the mandator of revocable mandate. If the mandator is a small group, sectional interests may trump the will of the citizenry, whereas if the mandator is a large group, it will require an organization to effect, giving it potentially undue influence. See Bobbio, *Which Socialism?* ed. Richard Bellamy, trans. Roger Griffin (Cambridge, UK: Polity, 1988), pp. 81–82.

75. Guinier characterizes the unit of proportional representation as political rather than regional, which is apt, given her understanding of territorial representation as a bogus form of interest representation. See Guinier, *The Tyranny of the Majority*, pp. 81, 122. When, however, territorial constituencies elect representatives exercising due legislative autonomy, the district is just as politically defined as the whole body politic. Significantly, Guinier still identifies the political character of the unit of proportional representation as a voluntary interest constituency (Guinier, *The Tyranny of the Majority*, p. 92) indicative of her inability to distinguish civil interest from political ends.

76. This is still very much the less-followed path among contemporary democracies. According to Guinier, single-member-district, winner-take-all systems are found in only five Western democracies, including the United Kingdom and the United States. See Guinier, *The Tyranny of the Majority*, p. 18.

77. As Lijphart points out, whereas majoritarian election schemes can be applied to single- or multimember districts, proportional representation requires multimember districts. See Lijphart, *Patterns of Democracy*, p. 150.

78. Australia employs an alternative preferential majoritarian voting system where voters register their rankings of candidates and the winner emerges by amassing an absolute majority of first preferences either directly or as a result of successively redistributing highest preferences for the

weakest candidates to their supporters' second preference. See Lijphart, *Patterns of Democracy*, p. 147.

79. As Anastaplo points out, the bare majority of total seats in a legislative chamber ordinarily qualifies as a minimum quorum, since that number can prevail even if all legislators are in attendance. See Anastaplo, *The Constitution of 1787*, p. 28.

80. Mill makes this point. See Mill, *Three Essays*, p. 249.

81. Mill somewhat overstates this point, claiming that winner-take-all voting inevitably leads to the complete disenfranchisement of minorities. See Mill, *Three Essays*, p. 248. Guinier similarly overstates the situation that results when a majority bloc continues to be voted into power election after election. She claims that a majority whose control is fixed and permanent has total power, since it need not worry about defectors and faces no checks to its domination (Guinier, *The Tyranny of the Majority*, p. 4). This "tyranny of the majority" could only result if the majority bloc was totally monolithic and constitutionality and the division of powers on which it rests were entirely overthrown. Guinier herself later somewhat retracts her claim, acknowledging that the majoritarian paradigm, following the United States example, constrains majority tyranny through checks and balances, federalism, and judicial review. See Guinier, *The Tyranny of the Majority*, p. 80.

82. As Lijphart observes, the minimal electoral threshhold does explicitly what district magnitude does implicitly—namely determine the lower limit of possible party representation. See Lijphart, *Patterns of Democracy*, p. 153.

83. As Lijphart points out, the greater the district magnitude, i.e., the number of members in a multimember district, the more elected representatives will reflect the proportional vote totals of the different parties. Small parties will have greater difficulty winning any seats in small districts, whereas a district extending the entire breadth of the state will offer them the best chance of representation. See Lijphart, *Patterns of Democracy*, pp. 150, 152.

84. The most proportional results will be achieved when a single nationwide multimember district precludes malapportioned regional districts, as in Israel and the Netherlands. See Lijphart, *Patterns of Democracy*, p. 156.

85. Guinier, for example, advocates a cumulative voting system, where each voter has a plurality of votes to cast, which can be concentrated among candidates as the voter sees fit. This will allegedly allow racial minorities to seat legislators in a racially polarized body politic. See Guinier, *The Tyranny of the Majority*, pp. 15, 93, 152.

86. For more detailed descriptions, see Lijphart, *Patterns of Democracy*, pp. 147–48.

87. Ibid., p. 148.

88. Ibid.

89. Ibid., p. 149.

90. Guinier advocates such a system in *The Tyranny of the Majority*.

91. Mill, for example, enlists proportional representation to ensure that every class achieves parliamentary representation. See Mill, *Three Essays*, pp. 270–71.

92. Mill makes this point. See Mill, *Three Essays*, p. 257.

93. Guinier discusses this issue, presuming the constancy of voting behavior and voter options. See Guinier, *The Tyranny of the Majority*, pp. 121, 135.

94. Guinier observes that when racial prejudice pervades an electoral majority, that majority tends to be fixed (Guinier, *The Tyranny of the Majority*, p. 103). The same could be said of any ingrained group attachments that prevent citizens from acting in pursuit of the political and non-political rights of all.

95. Weber tellingly analyzes this problem. See Weber, *Political Writings*, pp. 217, 351.

96. These attenuations between voter choice and individual candidates under party-list systems counteract Mill's argument that proportional representation allows for more eminent and better qualified representatives since candidates need not depend upon local influence for their election, as in majoritarian territorial district election systems but can win by means of national reputation. See Mill, *Three Essays*, p. 258.

97. This situation holds true even if cumulative voting were extended to the legislature, as Guinier suggests (Guinier, *The Tyranny of the Majority*, p. 118). Although that might sometimes allow certain minority blocs of legislators to consolidate all their votes behind an intensely favored measure, this could always be stymied if majority blocs are sufficiently committed to bar its passage.

98. See Carl Schmitt, *The Crisis of Parliamentary Democracy*, trans. Ellen Kennedy (Cambridge, MA: MIT Press, 1985), pp. 6, 19–20, 49–50.

99. Arend Lijphart discusses this connection between majoritarian and two-party systems on the one hand, and between proportional and multi-party sytems on the other. See Lijphart, *Patterns of Democracy*, pp. 64–65, 71, 87. Guinier also discusses the connection between majoritarian district elections and two-party systems. See Guinier, *The Tyranny of the Majority*, pp. 85–86.

100. For these reasons Dahl can rightly maintain that the connection between two-party systems and winner-take-all single-member district elections is a historical peculiarity, rather than a strict necessity. See Dahl, *Democracy and Its Critics*, p. 157.

101. As Lijphart observes, those who endorse two-party systems for moderating the cleavage between major parties ignore how this may leave voters no meaningful political alternatives. See Lijphart, *Patterns of Democracy*, p. 63.

102. In this connection, Lijphart notes that the American primary system allows party dissidents a greater chance to win nomination than in proportional systems with less application for primaries. As a result, those dissidents have less reason to form minority parties. Accordingly, the lack of small parties in a majoritarian system need not signify a restriction on political diversity. See Lijphart, *Patterns of Democracy*, p. 164.

103. See Art. 1, § 6 of the Constitution of the United States.

104. Hegel maintains that prohibitions on dual officeholding reflect this pernicious misconception of the division of powers. See the addition to ¶300 in Hegel, *Elements of the Philosophy of Right*, ed. Allen W. Wood, trans. H. B. Nisbet (Cambridge: Cambridge University Press, 1991), p. 339.

105. Lijphart, *Patterns of Democracy*, p. 124.

106. Weber observes that countries with parliamentary government consider it absolutely indispensable for leading statesmen to be members of parliament, insofar as there is no apparent reason why a parliamentary deputy suited to a leading position should be required to uproot himself politically before he may take up such an office. Under that requirement, Weber argues, parties are "beheaded" while the government gains officials in specialized areas who lack both expert knowledge and the influence of a member of parliament. See Weber, *Political Writings*, pp. 168–69. What this argument ignores is how top executive officials can continue to be leaders of their party and bring all the experience and prestige of past legislative tenure to their executive office.

107. Although these concerns, which apply to any secular occupation, also support the prohibition of dual holding of clerical and political office, the need to separate religion and politics provides an independent justification for requiring clerics to resign their positions of religious authority before taking political office.

108. Hegel points out this difference between legislation proper and budget appropriations in the remark to ¶544 of the *Philosophy of Mind*. See Hegel, *Philosophy of Mind*, trans. William Wallace and A. V. Miller (Oxford: Oxford University Press, 1971), pp. 274–75.

109. This nonlegislative role is reflected in how, as Mill observes, parliament is not expected to originate taxation or expenditure but is only asked for its consent, retaining as its sole power that of refusal. See Mill, *Three Essays*, p. 215.

110. See Art. 1, §§ 7–8 of the Constitution of the United States.

111. Sundquist discusses the history and ramifications of this "legislative veto" in *Constitutional Reform*, pp. 294–303.

112. Mill, for one, considers the legislature the proper power to watch and control the executive, following the liberal predilection to privilege the legislature at the expense of the other powers of government. See Mill, *Three Essays*, p. 226.

113. Weber duly considers the power to hold such hearings a key element in preventing democracy from degenerating into authoritarian rule. See Weber, *Political Writings*, p. 224.

114. Weber observes that so long as the parliament's only means to influence the executive is to deny it finances or refuse assent to its legislative proposals, parliament can engage only in "negative politics," whereas if, as in a parliamentary system, the legislature appoints the prime minister and cabinet from its own ranks, the situation is radically different. Weber considers the former situation of parliamentary "negative politics" to entail an authoritarian state, whereas he views the parliamentary system to offer a popular democracy. What he neglects is the situation where parliament makes laws of its own, subject to validation by the authorizing power, without parliamentary appointment and dismissal of the executive. See Weber, *Political Writings*, p. 166.

115. The United States presidency combines the chief executive and head of state, although the authorizing powers of the president lack finality and suffer from limited scope, given how presidential veto can be overridden by Congress and supplemented by Supreme Court judicial review.

116. Anastaplo properly indites both interest-driven state referenda and "supermajority" rules (including filibusters) in legislative bodies as measures that undermine the deliberations of the citizenry's elected representatives. See Anastaplo, *The Amendments to the Constitution*, p. 194.

117. James L. Sundquist recounts how the attempts of congressional party caucuses to enforce strict party discipline through threats of party expulsion, forfeiture of committee positions, and related penalties were duly abandoned by the 1930s in the United States Congress. See Sundquist, *Constitutional Reform*, pp. 258–59.

118. Efforts to contain the autocratic power of committee chairs in the

United States Congress are described by Sundquist in *Constitutional Reform*, pp. 259–61.

119. Anastaplo, *The Constitution of 1787*, p. 28.

120. Guinier makes this argument. See Guinier, *The Tyranny of the Majority*, pp. 16–17. Dahl points out that only unanimity, such as Rousseau upholds, can prevent a majority from harming a minority, since when citizens are politically homogenous, they cannot harm others without harming themselves (Dahl, *Democracy and Its Critics*, p. 161). Although this eliminates "minorities," it still does not preclude self-submission to violations of right.

121. Anastaplo, *The Amendments to the Constitution*, p. 105.

122. As Dahl points out, when the supermajority requirement reaches its limit in the demand for unanimity, self-government by a plurality becomes impossible. See Dahl, *Democracy and Its Critics*, p. 153.

123. Dahl, *Democracy and Its Critics*, pp. 153, 156.

124. So, for example, legislative immunity has been advanced in the United States to insure that representatives are free to debate without fear of sanctions elsewhere. See Anastaplo, *The Constitution of 1787*, p. 39.

125. For a systematic account of the classes of civil society, see Richard Dien Winfield, *The Just Economy* (New York: Routledge, 1988), pp. 142–56.

126. This possibility of multiple class memberships has important ramifications for economic justice. See Winfield, *The Just Economy*, pp. 146–47.

127. For a further account of why markets cannot independently guarantee equal economic opportunity, see Winfield, *The Just Economy*, pp. 157–68. For a systematic account of why private social-interest-group intervention cannot secure economic welfare either, see Winfield, *The Just Economy*, pp. 169–82. For a systematic account of the normative principles of public civil intervention in the market, see Winfield, *The Just Economy*, pp. 183–232.

128. This option was followed by the Articles of Confederation, whose loose federation of states could make due with a single-chamber legislature as a consistent expression of its privileging of states' rights at the expense of equal political opportunity for all citizens at the national level. See Anastaplo, *The Amendments to the Constitution*, p. 7.

129. As Dahl points out, those who claim that equal representation for states in the United States Senate serves to protect minorities are refuted by the historical record, which rarely if ever shows senators from relatively unpopulated states using their disproportionate power to serve political

and social rights rather than maintain minority oppression. See Dahl, *Democracy and Its Critics*, p. 186.

130. The United States Senate represents an extreme example of this violation of equal political opportunity. Arend Lijphart points out that the one-tenth of the United States that lives in the least populous states control 40 percent of the Senate, whereas one-fifth of Americans control a comfortable 55 percent of the Senate. See Lijphart, *Patterns of Democracy*, p. 209.

131. See Anastaplo, *The Constitution of 1787*, p. 193; and Anastaplo, *The Amendments to the Constitution*, pp. 133–34, 148.

132. See Anastaplo, *The Constitution of 1787*, p. 195.

133. For this reason, as Dahl points out, the Scandinavian countries eliminated their second chambers, which had ceased to represent the undemocratic privilege of traditional upper houses. See Dahl, *Democracy and Its Critics*, p. 157.

134. For this reason, it would make little sense to institute a second chamber for the purpose of making room for opinions, free of dependency upon group interests, a purpose for which Arendt claims the United States Senate was designed. Given the due autonomy of representation on which self-rule depends, any legitimate chamber would be concerned with debating political opinion. The House of Representatives would therefore not be a chamber for the representation of interests, as Arendt depicts it, any more than the Senate if legislators attend to the universality and supremacy of political ends. See Arendt, *On Revolution*, pp. 229–30.

135. Arendt maintains that the Senate was originally designed to guard against rule by public opinion (Arendt, *On Revolution*, p. 228), but it is dubious whether this imperative legitimately requires two houses of Congress, appointment of senators by state legislatures, or equal Senate representation for each state.

136. Anastaplo maintains that the differentiation of House and Senate has produced two chambers sufficiently different in composition and experience to make it more likely that legislative proposals will receive thorough consideration (see Anastaplo, *The Constitution of 1787*, p. 195). If the difference rests on longer term length and statewide election for senators, the alleged likelihood is all too indeterminate.

137. Mill concurs with the general thrust of these arguments, observing that a democracy otherwise unchecked can be little restrained by any second chamber. See Mill, *Three Essays*, p. 335.

CHAPTER 5

THE AUTHORIZING BRANCH OF SELF-GOVERNMENT

Constitutional self-government requires that laws passed by the legislature obtain validity only through subsequent authorization by a separate power, a power playing no role in formulating the legislation to which it grants or refuses constitutional certification. If this validating power lacks either comprehensive or final authority, constitutional right remains jeopardized by legislative license. Any restricted scope of authorization allows some laws to evade constitutional scrutiny, whereas any limits on finality allow the authorizer's decisions to be overridden by some threshold of legislative defiance. Conversely, if the authorizing power extends beyond certifying the constitutionality of legislative or executive initiatives, it usurps unlimited power for itself.

These guidelines do not, of course, guarantee that judgments by the authorizing power will always accord with right. Laws may well be struck down that conform to constitutional principle, just as legislation violating right may well be certified.[1] Nonetheless, these possibilities do not diminish the greater danger that unrestrained legislative power represents. The rejection of otherwise constitutional laws does not threaten any positive wrong, whereas collusive authorization of oppressive legislation only allows what an unchecked legislature could do on its own.

5.1 INADEQUACIES OF TRADITIONAL ALLOCATIONS OF AUTHORIZING POWER

The parliamentary system of government sanctioned by social contract theory[2] exhibits the dangers incipient in failing to endow an authorizing power with sufficient scope and finality. Investing sovereignty in the legislative power, the classical liberal model establishes a head of state whose will is law. In this guise, parliament not only drafts legislation but immediately invests its bills with validity. Since the legislature thereby reigns supreme, no political authority can call into question the "constitutionality" of legislation. The legislative general will can do no wrong.

The American model takes dual steps to counter this predicament and remove sovereignty from the legislature: on the one hand, the chief executive wields a veto power over congressional legislation, while on the other hand, the Supreme Court judges the constitutionality of laws applying to cases brought before it. Although these measures point in the right direction, they lack the comprehensive scope and finality required for proper authorization, while mixing the authorizing power with legislative and executive functions.

Admittedly, the veto power given the chief executive does possess comprehensive scope insofar as all congressional legislation comes before the president to be signed into valid law or rejected. The presidential veto, however, lacks finality in two respects. First, Congress may override any veto with a two-thirds majority, leaving the president powerless to block the most flagrantly oppressive legislation. Second, the Constitution has a virtually unrestricted amendment procedure by which any vetoed bill can be adopted as constitutional law with the sole exception of measures altering the representation of states in the Senate.[3]

Compounding these problems is the attachment of authorizing prerogatives to a chief executive who not only presides over the implementation of law but can originate legislation as the effective party leader of a major block of legislators. To the degree that the president initiates legislation through subordinate legislators and then wields the power to authorize it as effective law of the land, the constitutional limits on congressional license stand at risk before the manipulations of an executive in chief who rules as chief legislator.[4] Analogously, insofar as the president commands how law is enforced, presidential control over legislative authorization may tend to widen executive license provided the power to curtail unconstitutional administration gets retained by the authorizing organ. In this respect, the American model anticipates the errant conflation of head of state and head of government in the president of contemporary presidential systems of government as well as of certain parliamentary regimes, such as those of Botswana and the Union of South Africa.[5]

The judicial review appropriated by the Supreme Court overcomes some of the above limitations upon finality insofar as legislation overriding presidential vetoes can still be declared unconstitutional by the highest court.[6] Nonetheless, the relatively unrestricted amendment process still allows any judicial review to be circumvented by the adoption of new amendments. Furthermore, the Supreme Court exercises judicial review only over laws figuring in individual cases brought before it. This means that judicial review operates only upon legislation that already has counted as valid and that not all laws are subject to Supreme Court authorization. Rights may be legislatively violated both because relevant cases never get brought to court, and because those that do come, come too tardy to prevent violations that could conceivably corrupt or completely dismantle remedial judicial procedures. Even if judicial review were to count retroactively,[7] providing remedies to past victims of unconstitutional law could require formidable future litigation, too late for some and burdensome for others. These predicaments testify to how judicial review lacks the comprehensive scope requisite for protecting constitutionality from legislative usurpation.

The situation is analogous regarding judicial intervention to restrain the executive branch from transgressing its proper prerogatives. Although the Supreme Court can address the constitutionality of executive actions, their review must always come after the fact, through reactive litigation.[8] That may be all too late to remedy the worst potentials of combining executive and legislative prerogatives.

These difficulties are directly addressed by the institution of a centralized constitutional review procedure, such as suggested by Hans Kelsen[9] and adopted in differing degrees by various European regimes, many of whom follow parliamentary as opposed to presidential government. On this scheme, adapted to meet the requirements of finality and comprehensive scope, a central constitutional court passes final judgment on all legislation before any bills are allowed to count as law. No longer does judicial review depend upon individual litigation that leaves some laws without any scrutiny and gives all laws some initial period of unchallenged legal validity. On the other hand, by retaining a judicial form for the authorizing power, the central constitutional court scheme leaves the door open for future review of previously authorized legislation whose constitutionality may become questionable in face of hindsight and altered conjunctures. By providing opportunity for individual cases to be brought to court, the constitutional judiciary reserves its own corrective for its automatic review of pending legislation.

Of course, the finality of authorization of such a constitutional high court depends upon two factors: the inability of the legislature to override its judgments and the restriction of constitutional amendment powers. If the legislature can overturn authorizing decisions, even if only by supermajority votes, constitutionality is at the mercy of whatever coalition of legislators commands sufficient numbers. Similarly, if the constitution is entirely amendable and the amendment procedure is successfully navigable by some part of the citizenry, constitutional review presents no firm barrier to the subversion of right. These threats have more than a domestic dimension. Even if the national parliament cannot bypass constitutional court decisions and the national constitution cannot be amended to invalidate each and every judicial review, the empowerment of transnational legislatures and courts can make domestic barriers irrelevant. The finality and comprehensive scope of any national authorizing power gets undermined if international bodies are permitted to trump domestic jurisdictions.[10]

5.2 THE PRINCIPLES OF CONSTITUTIONAL CERTIFICATION

However constitutional review be administered, the concept of constitutional self-government entails common principles of constitutional interpretation. As a structure of ethical community, constitutional self-government exists only insofar as an authorizing power operates in an institutional context where the constitution already specifies the principles of political and nonpolitical rights and where these strictures already predominate in the practices of property relations, moral interaction, households, civil society, and politics.

In order for the constitution to achieve a commonly available objective determination of right, it must be written, that is, have an authoritative discursive articulation, rather than being left in the indefinite form of an unwritten body of custom. Custom, be it parliamentary or judicial, is always subject to incremental change and never unequivocally present in single examples or particular aggregates of behavior. Consequently, the absence of a written constitution leaves constitutional review problematic, since no higher law is unambiguously present with which to certify the constitutionality of pending legislation.[11]

Having a definite, written constitution is not, however, sufficient for an authorizing power to engage in its proper activity. Where there is a definite, written constitution, but it significantly diverges from the principles of right and/or where the prepolitical institutions of right are absent or largely deformed, any recognized authorizing power finds itself under revolutionary obligations. Instead of exercising an ethical freedom, which reproduces existing institutions of right, the authorizing power must exercise moral conduct and aim at bringing into being an order of justice that ought to be but whose establishment depends upon some personal initiative. This initiative is properly guided by the concept of the institutions of nonpolitical and political freedom and by pragmatic concerns of how best to establish those institutions in the face of existing domestic and international circumstances.

The authorizing power of the just state is predicated upon the overcoming of this moral, revolutionary situation. Instead of certifying legislation by a standard not yet embodied in constitutional law and existing institutions, the authorizing power faces the task of finding the rational standard that lies both within constitutional statute and in the institutions that predominantly accord with constitutionality. The very existence of self-government depends upon a prevailing recognition of the principles of right, a recognition expressed both in predominant interpretations of law and predominant practices. This recognition includes acknowledgment of the authorizing power itself, since otherwise nothing the authorizer does could command actual respect as an official undertaking. Consequently, the authorizing power constitutively exercises its interpretive prerogative within an already existing consensus that regards this prerogative as legitimate and binding.

Of course, this recognition of the authority of the authorizing power has limits conditioned both by shared understandings of constitutional law and by contingent shifts of public opinion. If the authorizing power interprets constitutionality in ways widely viewed to deviate radically from the constitution as it is embodied in existing practice, the authorizing power may become regarded as a rump usurper, whose judgments lose authority. Alternately, if enough citizens come to repudiate the constitutional principles of self-government, the most just constitutional certifications will be predominantly ignored by a citizenry already largely deviating from rectitude. Either situation ushers in a constitutional crisis, threatening a total breakdown of self-government.[12] Between these extremes the authorizing power has an interpretative prerogative that can always elicit disagreement under the broad framework of shared understandings of constitutional self-government. Two levels of interpretation are always at stake.

First, the authorizing power must interpret the constitution itself. Although self-government inherently contains a constitution predominantly conforming to the concept of political freedom, the meaning of constitutional statute cannot be reducible to a philosophical determination of self-government. The constitution should well contain statutory guarantees of the fundamental rights of ownership, moral autonomy, and family, social, and political self-determination. Nonetheless, constitutional statutes contain an irreducibly positive element, underivable from the concept of right, specifying the particulars of the organization of government and its relations to prepolitical spheres of freedom. These constitutional features are positive in that they cannot be derived from the concept of right but must be chosen and agreed upon if self-government is to have a sufficiently determinate framework within which to operate. Consequently, constitutional interpretation always addresses conceptual and positive elements, both of which must be understood before legislation can be authorized. The interpretation of either of these elements can always be questioned, but any legitimate interpretive debate must center upon locating in constitutional statute meanings conforming to the principles of right. To uphold the constitutionality of self-government, the authorizing power cannot engage in a free-wielding constitutional construction that offers principles in accord with right that have no plausible basis in any existing constitutional statute. Nor can the authorizer legitimately find meanings in constitutional statute that have no plausible connection with self-rule and its prepolitical conditions. The integrity of constitutional interpretation always rests upon retrieving the unity of existing constitutional language and the principles of self-determination. Although this labor cannot be performed outside of a preexisting ethical community, this contextuality is not the historicized, formal foundation of a judicial Hercules who upholds the consistency of our "moral intuitions," whatever these may be.[13] Ethical community is genuinely ethical only insofar as it exists in essential conformity to right, whose due conception is as free of juridical foundations as the institutions of self-determination that only an autonomous reason can legitimate.

The above considerations get incorporated in the second level of interpretation, where the authorizing power must apply its understanding of the constitution to particular legislative proposals, which must themselves first be interpreted to have their constitutionality evaluated. Since passed bills are collectively determined by the legislature, antecedent parliamentary debate can shed light on what legislators likely intended their work to signify. Of course, any such indicators are themselves in need of interpretation. This brings to the fore the need for some shared bearings beyond interpretation to defuse the specter of an unbreakable hermeneutic circle, or, to be more precise, spiral, where every interpretation is itself subject to further interpretation. This need for an accepted basis of fixed shared meanings cannot fail to be met at several levels. To begin with, unambiguous shared meanings are automatically at hand in natural languages whose intersubjective intelligibility is the precondition of any deliberation, debate, and communication of legislation. Second, shared understandings cannot fail to be at hand in the prevailing recognition of the constitutional framework that is a necessary ingredient of the ethical community of self-government. These transparencies allow for both the intelligibility of constitutional evaluation of positive legislation and for the possibility of debating among rival judgments. Only when the meaning of the constitution and of pending legislation are each held communicably determinate can constitutional certification operate. That does not preclude questioning aspects of the respective interpretations of constitutional and positive law, but it does presume large underlying agreement. Even when, however, consensus reigns on the particular meaning of relevant constitutional statutes and pending legislation, room for disagreement still remains since positive legislation can never be strictly deduced from constitutional statute. Evaluation of the conformity of legislation to constitutional principle always requires an act of judgment that remains inherently debatable.

Nonetheless, the debate must always be cast in terms of constitutional validity. If any lower standard is either openly or tacitly followed, the authorizing power misuses its office. In that case, the authorizer risks forfeiting its authority in the court of public opinion, as well as incurring whatever official remedial measures are constitutionally mandated for holding the authorizing power accountable.

A prime example of such corruption of authorizing power is partisan rejection of bills that, though constitutional, advocate a legitimate legislative policy opposed by the authorizer, either individually or as a loyal member of a party opposing the party bloc controlling the legislature. Presidential veto has often operated in this way in the United States, forestalling legislation passed by congress when it runs counter to the party of the president but not to the constitution. Through this use of the limited authorizing power of the presidency, the president acts as virtual legislator in chief, rather than as constitutional guardian.

5.3 ITEM VETO AND THE CERTIFICATION OF LAW

When the authorizing power misuses constitutional certification to favor one legitimate legislative proposal over another, the ability to employ an item veto power can have wide-ranging partisan consequences. By enabling the authorizing power to strike down portions of legislation selectively instead of disqualifying entire bills containing any illicit element, item veto reduces pressures to accept unwanted provisions that would otherwise be bound to other acceptable parts of the same legislation. Whether this promotes right depends, of course, on the content of the various provisions and on the general importance of untying the hands of the authorizer.

If the authorizing power fulfills its due mandate and accepts or rejects legislation solely on its constitutionality, item veto seems to present few drawbacks and substantial advantage for the cause of political justice. First, if only one section of legislation is unconstitutional and the rest can separately keep its integrity, item veto serves the cause of guarding constitutionality while facilitating legislative freedom. Striking down an entire piece of legislation because of one detachable item unnecessarily defeats the will of the legislature, at least so long as the remainder of the law could discretely retain legislative approval. Of course, if any doubt were raised on this score, the surviving portion could be sent back for formal legislative approval. If this reconsideration were automatic, item veto might seem to be eviscerated, for whatever legislation finally passes would do so without any veto attached. Nevertheless, item veto does not thereby become superfluous, for it specifies what part of legislation is unconstitutional and thereby focuses legislative reconsideration.

Admittedly, exercising item veto for appropriate constitutional ends will have some ramifications for the balance of power between parliamentary factions. Minority party blocs will have less room to pressure other legislators in those cases where no legislative faction alone has sufficient numbers or cohesion to get its bills enacted. No longer will legislative provisions be tied together in an all or nothing package as far as constitutional certification is concerned. Of course, legislative groups holding the balance of power in divided legislatures will still be able to insert their favored provisions as a price for allowing bills to be passed, but the prospect of entire laws being vetoed on account of one provision will cease to apply. Diminishing that opportunity might seem to serve equal political opportunity by undercutting the disproportionate power of swing legislative blocs. So long, however, as parliament has more than two parties, the uneven compulsions of coalition building are unavoidable.

5.4 SHOULD THE AUTHORIZING POWER HAVE THE PREROGATIVE TO DISMISS THE LEGISLATURE AND CALL FOR NEW LEGISLATIVE ELECTIONS?

If the legislature is to be kept within the bounds of constitutional lawmaking, it is not enough for its legislation to be certified by an independent authorizing power enjoying finality. Legislators must also be made to respect due parliamentary and legislative election procedures allowing representatives to exercise their legislative rights. Insofar as these procedures should be made legal, their implementation falls to the executive branch in exercise of its authority to enforce the statutes that guarantee legislative autonomy and electoral fairness. This enforcement conforms to the separation of powers to the degree that such executive interventions play no role in formulating legislation or in securing passage of any particular laws. Can there be further circumstances, however, where the authorizing power is itself obliged to intervene to uphold legislative rectitude?

A common point of intervention in the annals of parliamentary government is when the head of state dismisses parliament and calls for new elections. This initiative is most frequently precipitated by votes of no-confidence, where parliament rescinds support for the prime minister whom it had earlier selected from among its members. If parliamentary government retained exclusive validity, this situation could be generic to self-government. If parliamentary government is instead but one admissible form of political freedom, if not a discreditable mutant, some broader need must be located for empowering the authorizing power to terminate the legislature before the expiration of its elected term and to order new elections. Although deciding among these options requires settling the controversy between parliamentary and presidential systems of government, the power to dismiss parliament and call new elections has endemic features worth considering apart from this divide.

Whatever its occasion, the power to dismiss parliament and call new elections has the virtue of conferring no more than a negative role to the authorizing branch of government. Since the selection of the new legislature remains under the independent control of the electorate, the authorizing power cannot usurp any command over the positive content of legislation. The right to dismiss parliament may give the authorizer power to momentarily suspend whatever legislative agenda is underway, but that interruption suspends itself with the election of the next parliament, which enters office free to go its own way subject to constitutional certification. Although the authorizing power can always threaten to call new elections unless parliament makes laws to its liking, this threat can still not compel any specific laws so long as representatives fulfill their obligation to legislate with autonomy on behalf of the rights of all.

Furthermore, any threat to dismiss parliament will undermine the authority of the head of state if it manifestly diverges from the legitimate grounds for calling for new elections. Using the threat of parliamentary dismissal to control the content of legislation clearly deviates from the aim of resolving crises of confidence pitting prime ministers against parliamentary majorities. More essentially, threatening new elections to compel particular legislation violates the division of powers by enabling the authorizing power to lay hold of lawmaking and turn constitutional certification into an instrument of absolute domination.

Given these limits, the question arises as to what positive contribution to self-government could be provided by any power to dismiss parliament and call new elections. Intervention by the head of state is hardly required by a parliamentary system since a vote of no-confidence by parliament could be resolved by allowing the same legislators to select a new prime minister. This would remove any chance of the head of state using parliamentary dismissal to breach the division of powers and influence the content of legislation. If parliament is united in dismissing the prime minister but too divided to agree on a successor, the ensuing impasse could be resolved in several ways without giving the head of state any authority to dismiss parliament and call new legislative elections. First, votes of no-confidence can be structured so that a prime minister cannot be dismissed until after parliament comes to an agreement on who the successor will be. If this requirement proves too stringent to allow for any removal of unpopular prime ministers under conditions of parliamentary splintering, votes of no-confidence without agreement on a successor can be automatically followed by new parliamentary elections, which, of course, might or might not resolve the impasse. Both of these scenarios, like any in parliamentary systems, presuppose that opposition between the prime minister and parliamentary majorities is a sufficient ground for removing the chief executive before term end and that parliament should select the successor. Each of these presuppositions is very much open to question, as shall be seen in the concrete determination of the executive power in its relation to the legislature.

If, then, the head of state need not dismiss parliament and call new parliamentary elections to resolve opposition between the prime minister and the legislature, is there any legitimate ground for the authorizing power to retain those options? With the executive empowered to enforce laws regulating parliamentary conduct and the authorizing power already able to strike down unconstitutional legislation, parliament can do nothing in violation of its duties that is not already subject to these remedies. The only other rationale that might support intervention by the head of state would be appeal to shifting public opinion that produces a new divide between the legislature and its electorate. Even if such a divide were sufficient for curtailing the legislative term of representatives, it is questionable whether the head of state should have the prerogative to declare when new elections are necessary. Voter initiatives for recall might be more trustworthy, provided procedures existed to prevent vested interests from dominating those intitiatives at the expense of equal political opportunity. In any case, given the incoherence of the identity conception of representation that underlies any attempt to match legislative representatives with immediate registrations of voter opinion, the whole appeal to shifts in popularity is devoid of legitimacy. The only circumstance that would make such shifts significant for self-government would be when upheavals in public opinion are accompanied by pervasive disobedience to constitutional governance, a condition verging on political breakdown. Then calls for new elections come too late.

Under any conditions, two exercises of political freedom would be compromised by empowering the head of state to dismiss parliament and call new elections before term end. First, the vote of the electorate in the preceding legislative elections would be nullified. Second, the right of representatives to occupy their office till term end provided they act with legislative rectitude would be violated. Given that these infringements are not entailed by any positive contributions to self-government, they are inadmissible.

5.5 THE FINALITY OF AUTHORIZING VALIDATION AND THE ACCOUNTABILITY OF THE AUTHORIZING POWER

Preventing domestic or transnational legislatures or constitutional amendment procedures from overriding constitutional court decisions may fix legislative power within the limits of right. Yet the very finality enabling authorizing decisions to secure constitutionality raises the problem of how the authorizing power will be kept accountable for its own operations.[14]

A basic precondition for accountability common to every power of government is transparent publicity for all official activities. Unless what authorizing officials do in performing their duties can be known to every citizen, the possibility of holding them to account becomes either beyond reach of all, or else a prerogative for a privileged coterie, destroying the unity of ruler and ruled. For this reason, all investigations and judgments on the part of the head of state and other authorizing officials must be made public in a form allowing intelligible access to all citizens. If expertise is needed to decipher the technicalities of authorizing decisions, this must be made available as well. Nonetheless, insuring openness does not itself prevent official misconduct.

Limiting the authorizing power to approving or disapproving pending legislation to whose formulation it cannot contribute and doing so with full public disclosure still seems to leave two opposite possibilities for violation of right. On the one hand, the authorizing power may collaborate with the iniquities of the legislature by validating oppressive, properly unconstitutional legislation. By that means, a cabal of legislators and authorizers can wield unlimited control of government, at least so long as the executive power follows its formal duty to enforce validated statutes and a sufficient number of citizens obey. Conversely, the authorizing power may refuse to validate proper legislation, immobilizing the legislature and leaving government reliant upon past statutes to tackle not always congruent circumstances.

Both of these options may follow the party allegiances of legislators and authorizers alike, at least if both powers are filled in a partisan manner. When both branches are in the hands of the same party, their collusion lets that party reign supreme. This may occur in good faith, when authorizers judge the laws passed by their party members in parliament to be genuinely constitutional. It may also occur maliciously, when authorizers follow party loyalty and validate laws they know to be unconstitutional. When authorizers belong to a party opposing that controlling the legislature, party loyalty can translate into legislative deadlock, with no passed bills receiving validation. Once more, this can occur in good or bad faith. In the latter more likely case, made all too familiar in the United States by partisan presidential vetoes,[15] authorizers reject laws they recognize to be constitutional but oppose as party partisans.

Of course, authorizers may also fall prey to rank corruption, selling their decisions to the highest bidders, or simply shirk their responsibilities and leave passed bills in limbo. All of these possibilities must be addressed in determining the organization, appointment, and accountability of authorizing officials.

5.6 BASIC STRUCTURAL IMPERATIVES OF THE AUTHORIZING POWER

To determine how the authorizing power should be organized, the primary concerns of comprehensive scope and finality must be satisfied in ways suggested by the scheme of a centralized constitutional court, supported by limitations on constitutional amendment and transnational governance, as well as by some way of remedying abuses by authorizing officials. Whether such a scheme suffices, however, depends upon more than achieving success in limiting legislative license. Although keeping legislative activity within the boundaries of constitutional rights is the task immediately given to the authorizing power, two other relationships play equally constitutive roles in its operation. One involves the relation between the authorizing power and its executive counterpart. The other concerns the relation between the authorizing power and the political self-determination of the citizenry, as mediated through political parties. These concerns are interrelated. Unless the authorizing power can pass validated law on to the executive branch and insure that execution conforms to constitutional guidelines, self-government stands at risk of executive tyranny. Alternately, unless the authorizing power operates as a vehicle of self-rule, the safeguarding of constitutionality becomes foreign to political freedom. These issues bear upon the institutional organization of authorizing authority, the selection of its officials, the safeguarding of their independence, and the enforcement of their own answerability.

5.7 THE AUTHORIZING POWER IN RELATION TO THE EXECUTIVE BRANCH OF GOVERNMENT

Precisely because the authorizing power functions as the facilitating link between the legislature and executive, conceiving its relation to the executive branch poses difficulties that do not apply to determining how authorization relates to legislation. Since the authorizing power first operates in relation to the prior activity of the legislature, once the legislative branch has been conceived, everything is at hand for determining how authorization functions in reference to statutory enactment. With the executive branch, the situation is reversed. Although the concrete relationship between the authorizing power and the executive depends upon how the executive is structured, the organization of the executive is itself predicated upon the antecedent functions of legislation and authorization. Nevertheless, the organic unity of powers constitutive of constitutionality already mandates some connections, albeit by way of anticipation.

To begin with, however executive agencies be structured and however chief executives, cabinet officials, and their subalterns be appointed and administratively regulated, the authorizing power has a twofold relationship to government, understood broadly as the executive branch of state. First, the authorizing power gives the executive its legal charge, since by validating legislation, the authorizing power at the same time obliges the government to administer what now counts as law of the state. For this very reason, the executive is answerable to the authorizing power, which has the ultimate responsibility of certifying that government has fulfilled its charge of enforcing legislation. Since this enforcement is tantamount to realizing the constitution in face of contingent circumstances, both domestic and foreign, the authorizing power is responsible for monitoring the constitutionality of executive action in general.

The first of these mandates is the least problematic. To give the executive its legal charge, the authorizing power must insure that whatever legislation is judged valid gets communicated to all relevant government agencies. Furthermore, so far as the authorizing power not only judges all pending legislation but has appellate procedures for reviewing the constitutionality of previously authorized legislation, all such judgments must be equally transmitted to the administration for enforcement. Of course, in every case, what gets certified as valid law is a public as well as administrative matter. Unless each judgment of the authorizing power is also effectively publicized, citizens and noncitizens alike will be unable to know the law to which they are subject and for whose enforcement government is accountable. Accordingly, the authorizing power must insure the communication of its validations to not just government officials but the inhabitants of the state at large. For these purposes of publicity, the authorizing power must dispose of adjunct facilities going beyond the judicial operations of a centralized constitutional court. Given the limited task of this communication, a bureaucracy within the authorizing power can suffice.

Much more demanding is the second principal occupation of the authorizing power: overseeing the constitutionality of government activity. Whatever its field of scrutiny, this oversight involves three dimensions: surveying what the executive branch does, judging the constitutionality of surveyed executive activity, and remedying violations of constitutional rights. How these three dimensions are effected varies according to the type of executive activity at play. Broadly speaking, the enforcement of legislation takes two forms: the public administrations of state agencies on citizens at large and the judicial application of law to individual cases.

Supervision of the judiciary by the authorizing power is an

undertaking distinct from the appellate function by which the constitutionality of laws is reviewed. Whereas the latter review concerns the constitutionality of statutes, judicial supervision here concerns the constitutionality of court action itself. Policing the judiciary can occur through the avenue of individual litigation, suing derelict judges for civil damage, as well as by bringing criminal prosecution when rights have been maliciously violated. Individual litigation, however, cannot be counted on to deal effectively with all judicial abuses for the simple reason that it leaves scrutiny of judicial action contingent upon the initiative of private individuals, who may or may not go to court. Accordingly, the route of litigation must be supplemented by a supervision of civil and state courts by an appropriately empowered office of the authorizing power.

Nonjudicial executive action calls for its own authorizing watchdog agency, equipped to investigate, evaluate, and determine remedies for constitutional violations. Needless to say, here as much as in regulation of the judiciary, implementation of any remedial judgments will require executive acts of its own, be it negative measures dismissing officials and canceling programs or positive measures replacing officials and reorienting policy administrations. Although this reliance upon executive action to remedy executive action might seem to be hopelessly circular, it reflects the basic interdependence of the powers of the state, none of which can function if any other has completely thrown off its integration into political unity. Such political cancers can occur, but the fact that they may spell the death of the body politic does not reduce authorizing restraints to empty gestures. As with any element of constitutionality, the actuality of political authority depends upon a prevailing recognition of right, exhibited in rectitude by office- and nonofficeholders alike sufficient to sustain self-government.

5.8 THE AUTHORIZING POWER AS HEAD OF STATE

In its dual capacity as authorizer of legislation and constitutional watchdog of executive action, the authorizing power determines itself as the genuine head of state. Although the legislature and executive are equally indispensable for self-government, neither wields the authority to supervise the activities of its counterparts. Each may aim at realizing the constitution in face of changing circumstances at home and abroad, but only the authorizing power engages in subordinating the other powers to the constitution.

This subordinating function can be organized in various ways. It can be centralized under a head of state whose office handles all authorizing duties. Alternately, it can be distributed between an authorizing figure who validates all legislation by certifying its constitutionality and checks unconstitutional executive action and a central constitutional court that handles appellate considerations of preexisting statutes and individual prosecutions of executive conduct. Either way, the authorizing power presides over legislation and administration as guardian of constitutionality.

This very primacy casts in relief the question of how the authorizing power is to be held accountable without undermining its authority over legislature and executive. To no small extent, this issue bears upon how the head of state is appointed, what the term of office shall be, and under what conditions, if any, a reigning head of state can be removed from office and/or be judged and punished for transgressions of duty.

5.9 THE SELECTION AND REMOVAL OF THE HEAD OF STATE

If parliament is given the power to appoint the head of state, the autonomy of the authorizing power is immediately compromised, at least to the extent that the head of state owes its office to the approval of the legislature. Admittedly, the continued force of this approval can be countered by lengthening the term of office up to the ultimate limit of lifetime tenure and by granting the legislature no power to impeach and remove the head of state, nor to alter salary and benefits.[16] Then, no matter what the expectations of the legislature, the appointed head of state can uphold constitutional right against legislative license without fear of reprisal. Still, permitting the legislature to appoint the validator of its legislation raises a conflict of interest that should be avoided unless no alternative is available.

Of course, if the legislature not only enjoys the power to appoint the head of state but further retains the power to judge, remove, and punish its authorizer, the independence of the head of state evaporates, unless every whim of parliament is in preestablished harmony with the judgment of the protector of the constitution. Under these conditions of legislative supremacy, the head of state is perennially hostage to votes of no-confidence, votes that may merely serve the partisan interests of a parliamentary majority that will tolerate no obstacle to its legislative agenda.

Analogous problems apply if the chief executive, the cabinet, or any other executive officials wield the power to appoint, impeach, remove, and punish an allegedly errant head of state. The head of state's power to curtail unconstitutional executive acts is compromised the moment the term of office of the head of state is made dependent upon the will of any executive official.

The problem is the same one that allows any combination of executive and authorizing functions, or for that matter, of legislative and authorizing functions, to jeopardize the independent safeguarding of the constitution that the head of state should otherwise effect. Just as legislators and executives should wield no power to appoint or terminate the head of state, neither should a head of state retain any position in the legislature or executive. These strictures apply equally to members of any constitutional court, who should be immunized from legislative or executive reprisals and equally barred from performing legislative or executive functions. Dual, or for that matter, triple officeholding for authorizing officials serves only to undermine the division of powers, without affording any advantage that cannot be obtained through communications between officials from the different organs of state.

The resulting predicament might seem to call for the solution provided by constitutional monarchy, where, following Hegel's proposal, the head of state enjoys a lifetime term of office based on hereditary succession. Although a duly limited constitutional monarch could exercise authorizing powers without being subject to any pressure from the legislature or the executive branch, that very independence leaves once more unresolved the problem of how to maintain the accountability of the head of state and how to enable the head of state to relate to the citizenry as an agency of their political self-determination.[17]

Both of these questions can be jointly answered by placing the selection of the head of state in popular election and setting limits to the length of each term of office, as well as to the number of terms a head of state can hold, *if* incumbency advantages cannot be countered.

If all citizens exercise the right to elect the head of state, or for that matter, judges on a constitutional court, the authorizing power stands as closely related to their self-rule as the legislators they vote into office. This congruence, of course, defeats any argument that parliament should be the ultimate guardian of the constitution because leaving constitutional review to separate authorizing officials places constitutional safekeeping in the hands of unelected appointees unaccountable to the citizenry.[18] Instead, the same imperatives apply to each power. Just as legislators can represent the political autonomy of citizens only insofar as they act independently for the sake of the whole body politic, so an elected head of state can realize self-rule only insofar as the authorizing power is wielded freely on behalf of all citizens for the universal ends of constitutionality.[19]

By contrast, indirect election would always diminish the democratic stature of the authorizing power by making it beholden to a plurality or majority of whatever group appoints the head of state, a plurality or majority patently distinct from that of the citizenry itself. Whether those appointing the chief of state are elected officials of the national legislature or executive, or provincial governments, indirect election leaves the authorizing power dependent upon some particular center, rather than an independent expression of the citizenry's self-rule. For this reason, Max Weber is on the mark in calling direct election of the head of state the "palladium" of genuine self-government.[20]

Direct election of the head of state may be necessary to effect self-government, but it will only be sufficient if the elected authorizers escape the confines of binding mandate and corporate representation. Any scheme to distribute the office of the head of state among representatives of different interest groups, be they defined by race, language, religion, gender, or any other prepolitical factor, would undercut the universal claims of the authorizing authority. Instead of upholding constitutionality in relation to legislation and execution, a corporate head of state would subordinate the regulation of the legislature and government to a competition among sectarian concerns. Whoever prevails would do so at the expense of political freedom, for the victorious guardian of "constitutionality" would impose the will of some groups upon the subject will of others.

This limitation would apply to any scheme for dividing the head of state into a council of representatives of different political regions, at least so long as the authorizing officials elected by region fulfill their office as representatives of regional interests rather than of the political unity expressed in the constitution. If election by region produced instead an authorizing power devoted to the universal end of self-rule, it would surmount sectarian deficiencies in the same way in which legislators elected from geographically defined districts do by upholding the rights of all.

Similarly, the political deformations of binding mandate would be perpetuated by any arrangement subjecting the head of state to immediate recall whenever public opinion diverged from authorizing decisions. Once again, genuine political plurality would be sacrificed to the unilateral domination of identity politics. Reduced to a direct expression of popular will as it is immediately given, the head of state could never be the agent of every citizen's political self-determination unless the plurality of citizenship was obliterated. The same dilemma would recur that afflicts any application of an identity conception to legislative elections—so long as the electorate has any divisions, the only individuals whose wills would be politically recognized would be those in the prevailing majority, who themselves would exercise not self-rule but domination over a subject class.

These difficulties need not be encountered by term limits, either with regard to term length or the number of terms that a head of state is permitted to serve. The same considerations that apply to legislative elections pertain here. As long as the elected head of state has a fixed term, the authorizing power can retain autonomy over and against the vagaries of public opinion. How long the term should be entails the same practicalities that apply to legislative terms. If term length be too short, officials will face replacement or the demands of reelection before having an opportunity to settle into their position, learn the ropes, and effectively perform. Conversely, the further term length is extended, the less opportunity the electorate has to use new elections to hold accountable the officials it earlier chose.

Although judges on constitutional courts are often appointed for life terms to guarantee their independence from public opinion, this supposed remedy eventually compromises the link of the authorizing power to political self-determination. Once most citizens confront a highest tribunal that they have not chosen, the authorizing power is at pains to exhibit the reflexivity of self-government. Giving members of a central constitutional court more limited terms need not undermine their autonomy any more than limited terms undercut the independence of legislators. So long as terms are fixed, recall initiatives are precluded, and electoral campaigning is regulated on behalf of equal political opportunity, constitutional judges face no undue pressures to betray their official autonomy.

Similar considerations apply to limits on reelection. Once more, what applies to legislative elections carries over to elections of the authorizing power. Although prohibitions of reelection restrict the freedom of the citizenry to choose whomever they prefer as head of state or constitutional court officials, limits on number of terms counter the advantages of incumbency that may otherwise damage equal political opportunity. If campaign finances, access to publicity, and the length of campaigning are all publicly controlled to counter incumbency advantage and insure equal political opportunity to all credible candidates, term limits become unnecessary restrictions upon voter choice and the freedom to run for office.

Worries that an absence of term limits will allow popular heads of state to amass dangerous power have little foundation if the authorizing power is held within its constitutional limits and election campaigning is regulated to counter incumbent advantages. The mere fact that a head of state holds office for term after term does not itself alter the negative character of constitutional certification of legislation and constitutional supervision of the executive. So long as the head of state can only strike down legislation and executive actions and not independently initiate positive laws or implementations, longevity in office need not involve any threat to self-government.

The term limits on United States presidents respond to a different, all too imperfect situation where elections remain captive to incumbent advantages and the president combines authorizing functions with executive powers while presiding as virtual chief legislator when congress is controlled by the president's party. Although these conditions may give term limits some justification, the problems addressed are not thereby resolved and call for different remedies.[21]

5.10 IMMUNITY AND THE POWER OF PARDON

Although the head of state does not stand above the law under conditions of constitutional self-government, the preeminent role of the authorizing power might seem to endow it with two complementary suspensions of legal subordination: the power of pardon and immunity from criminal prosecution and civil liability. Unlike certification of legal validity, the power of pardon does not exercise judgment over the law. Instead it recognizes the validity of the application of law to a particular case but suspends that application by precluding any further punishment. To have legitimacy, the suspension of pardon must serve the cause of right. Yet how can the overriding of unimpeachable punishment be in the interest of self-determination? Since valid punishment is always a response to malicious violations of self-determination, pardon would only serve right if the further execution of the due penalty threatened a disturbance of the fabric of self-government, including those civil institutions on which political freedom rests. Such conditions are not unthinkable and the supreme validating authority of the head of state gives it an unrivaled credibility to judge when suspension of an individual verdict is necessary to prevent fissures in the institutions of right.

Nonetheless, if the head of state, or for that matter, any other official, commands final power of pardon, nothing can prevent abuses where pardon is used to nullify the righting of wrong without any securing of an otherwise imperiled system of freedom. The remedies for removing a derelict head of state could be employed but only after the fact, leaving preceding pardons in place. This limitation could only be surmounted if removal of a miscreant head of state could retroactively void pardon decisions made during the period in office determined to be suspect.

Although such removal would apply to official misconduct, immunity from prosecution for nonofficial wrongs might seem more desirable for the head of state and constitutional court judges than proved to be the case for legislators. Indicted individual legislators could readily be replaced on an interim or permanent basis without impugning the legislative process. Owing to the concentration of authorizing power in the head of state and the comparatively small membership of a constitutional court, holding top authorizing officials legally accountable while in office would put a greater strain on authorizing operations. Still, granting immunity from criminal prosecution and civil suits would trump the righting of wrong only if official authorizing duties could not be handled by replacements on an interim or permanent basis. The most acute dangers would concern the head of state, whose continuous work of validation would require immediate relief by a successor or successors chosen without damage to the division of powers. Replacement could be secured by standing rules of succession, specifying some other authorizing official to replace the indicted head of state or constitutional court judge until the next election for head of state. If instead, the legislature were empowered to choose a successor some threat of legislative domination could arise. This would be especially true if prosecutions could be politically engineered, enabling parliament to undermine an impartial head of state and appoint a compliant accessory to its own bid for hegemony. A less perilous course would consist of allowing the chief executive to step into the breach and appoint an interim successor. Although this could weaken the authorizing power's supervision of executive action, it would at least not subvert the constitutional certification of legislation. In any event, because viable options do exist for righting wrongs by authorizing officials without undermining the upholding of constitutionality, legal immunity is not warranted.

5.11 MUST THE HEAD OF STATE BE ONE INDIVIDUAL?

All the above considerations apply to the election of the head of state, whether its office be commanded by one individual or jointly by several. Given the extent of authorizing functions with regard to pending legislation, judicial review, and executive action, a single individual can hardly be expected to fulfill all duties of the head of state. Nevertheless, the question can be asked as to whether the office of head of state should have at its apex a single individual or a sovereign council.

Historically, the functions of head of state have been allotted in different ways, according to which dimension of authorization is at stake. Judicial review has ordinarily been exercised by a supreme court involving a council of highest judges, where the presence of a chief justice has not prevented authorizing judgments from being jointly decided by all the judges. On the other hand, where heads of states have presided over the government, dismissing prime ministers, or calling new legislative elections, they have tended to reign as single individuals.

Although the finality and comprehensive scope of authorization calls for a united and exclusive will, it is far from self-evident that this requires the head of state to be a single individual, as Hegel has argued.[22] Although the demands of timely action set some limits on how massively plural the head agency can be, a single leader may be no more decisive than the joint resolve of a small group. So long as publicly established procedures specify what actions by a highest authorizing council count as sovereign decisions, the united individuality of the authorizing power is sustained.

Similarly, the accountability of the head of state need not be diminished by extending headship to a council. Whether through subsequent election or other means, citizens can hold responsible one individual just as well as a group. Nonetheless, a collective headship opens the door to tensions that a single head of state can forestall. Instituting collective leadership can open a Pandora's box, where all parties, subcultures, or other corporate bodies demand representation, challenging the unity and universal aim of the authorizing power.[23]

5.12 THE AUTHORIZING POWER IN RELATION TO CITIZENS AND THEIR POLITICAL PARTIES

The authorizing power comprises a multiplicity of officials, one or more presiding as head of state at the apex of authority, supplemented by a central constitutional court and subsidiary individuals to assist in the technical tasks that facilitate constitutional certification of laws and executive action.

Constitutional self-government depends not just on all these authorizing officials performing their duties as guardians of the constitution. They must also undertake these tasks as functions of political freedom, exhibiting the reflexivity as well as the universality and supremacy of aim constitutive of political self-determination. For this to be achieved, the leading officials of the authorizing power must act on the basis of the will of the citizenry. Although the leadership of the authorizing power must act with an initiative of its own, like autonomous representatives, whatever action it takes must be predicated upon a preceding choice in which all adult, competent citizens are entitled to participate. In other words, the chief authorizing officials must be elected into office, for only then will their official activity be mediated by the will of the citizenry and comprise an exercise of self-rule.[24] Once more, the identity of ruler and ruled cannot involve any direct correlation between voter choice and authorizing decisions. If it did, self-rule would require the elimination of electoral plurality and the elimination of any autonomy of action on the part of authorizing officials. Any political diversity among the citizenry would prevent decisions by the authorizing power from having any immediate fit with the will of all, just as any initiative on the part of authorizing officials would transcend the immediate expression of voter choice. For all citizens in their plurality to relate to the independent action of the authorizing power as an element of self-government, two parallel conditions must instead be satisfied: On the one hand, every voter must have an equal opportunity to determine the outcome of the election as well as to run for authorizing office. On the other hand, the elected authorizing officials must act on behalf of the constitutional rights of all citizens rather than in advocacy of some particular interests.

These dual requirements by no means entail that all officials of the authorizing power be selected by general election. Functionaries who provide technical assistance in preparing and carrying out authorizing decisions instead require certain expertise that should be tested as a condition for appointment. Since such functionaries are concerned with providing the means for enabling authorizing decisions to be effected, rather than with determining those decisions themselves, their selection by qualification rather than by election does not undercut the mediating role of the electorate. So long as the leadership of the authorizing power is elected into office, every act of their underling bureaucracy is predicated upon the election of their superiors.

For this very reason, candidates for head of state and constitutional courts need not have any special expertise beyond the general political competency that qualifies citizens to vote and run for any elective office.[25] Although a central court of constitutional review might seem to require trained jurists, a lay court could suffice, provided it has at its disposal whatever legal expertise is required to comprehend the meanings and coherence of both constitutional and positive law. If instead appointment to the central court depended upon expert qualifications, elections would be an inferior instrument for choosing among candidates, as would be selection by other elected officials.[26] Conditioning eligibility upon such credentials as a law degree might be thought to suffice as a preselection before allowing the electorate to choose among qualified candidates. If, however, expertise was essential, appointment should fall entirely within the hands of other experts, qualified to evaluate their peers.

These relationships all become further concretized through the operation of political parties as vehicles of political freedom. Although individuals have a right to run for authorizing office as independents, the sorting of political opinion makes party membership a key element in the exercise of political opportunity. Individuals will have good reason to run as party candidates in order to garner campaign and electoral support, as well as to be effective in office. As voters, citizens will need to consider the oppositions of parties in deciding how their vote can best determine government action.

Consequently, whenever leading officials of the authorizing power are elected as party members, the question arises as to whether party allegiance will undermine the upholding of constitutionality. Two polar situations circumscribe the range of alternatives: On the one hand, the chief authorizing officials may be members of the same party that wins control of the legislature and/or the leading executive positions. On the other hand, party membership may be divided, so that authorizing officials face a parliament and/or an executive controlled by opposing parties. Party hegemony over two or more branches of government raises the specter of absolute rule by the dominant party, whereas divided party allegiance poses the threat of an impasse paralyzing self-government.

As we have seen,[27] party control of the authorizing power and one or more other powers of government does not itself threaten constitutionality. To begin with, common party membership does not signify automatic unity on issues of constitutional certification. What legislation gets passed by the dominant party coalition may not seem constitutional to authorizing officials even if they share the general political positions of that coalition. Moreover, party leaderships cannot impose strict discipline on authorizing officials, not to mention legislators, particularly if equal opportunity is properly upheld in political campaigning. Officials can always stand by the prerogatives of their position in the face of party pressures even if this compromises renomination. Furthermore, party domination of the opportunity to run for office is duly countered by freeing the funding of campaigning from party control. In addition, partisan unity need not threaten constitutionality so long as party differences fall within the range of legitimate political diversity. As long as this remains the case, authorizing certification will remain within the bounds of right. Constitutionality stands at risk only when unconstitutional collusion between powers of government has reached such proportions as to comprise a breakdown of free political association. Then, the problem transcends party membership and requires solutions falling beyond the internal workings of self-government.

The problems posed by party oppositions are equally limited. To begin with, the mere fact that the dominant party coalition in parliament opposes that of the authorizing power hardly entails that constitutional certification will be refused for all its legislation. So long as party differences remain within the spectrum of political right, the authorizing power will be obliged to certify opposing laws and nothing in party allegiance can compel forsaking that duty. Efforts to strike down patently constitutional legislation passed by the opposing party coalition will risk discrediting authorizing officials and imperil their reelection. Yet even if authorizing officials use their position for partisan aims indifferent to the boundary of constitutionality, the most havoc they can achieve is blocking new legislation until the end of their term. This may succeed in paralyzing self-legislation, but pending elections and legislative compromise can remove the impasse.

Although some of the appeal of parliamentary government derives from the perception that parliamentary appointment of the prime minister can forestall impasses of divided government, so long as the prime minister is chief executive and not head of state, authorizing power retains its independence from parliamentary control. Hence, parliamentary rule does not affect oppositions between the legislature and the authorizing power. If, however, parliamentary control gets extended to selection and removal of the head of state, the authorizing power loses much of its ability to forestall unconstitutional legislation. Aspects of this situation afflicted the United States during its first decades, when party congressional caucuses selected presidential nominees, whose hopes for reelection depended upon pleasing their respective party caucus.[28]

NOTES

1. United States history strongly testifies to the fallibility of the authorizing power. As the Dred Scott and early New Deal cases remind us, George Anastaplo observes, whenever Congress and the Supreme Court have differed on great matters of constitutional interpretation, Congress has been correct. See Anastaplo, *The Constitution of 1787: A Commentary* (Baltimore: Johns Hopkins University Press, 1989), p. 142.

2. Admittedly, almost all modern "parliamentary" regimes have eventually departed from the letter of social contract theory by introducing some form of authorizing power to judge the constitutionality of parliamentary bills. Whether this be done by a ceremonial head of state or a centralized constitutional tribunal, it reintroduces a separation of powers that still remains compromised by the linkage of legislature and executive in parliamentary systems.

3. Although Article 5 of the US Constitution removes from amendment the allocation of two Senate seats to each state, this obstacle to the equal political opportunity of citizens can still be circumvented without a revolution by passing amendments to reduce the functions of the Senate to those of a ceremonial counterpart of the British House of Lords. Andrew Arato points to this possibility in his essay, "The New Democracies and American Constitutional Design," *Constellations* 7, no. 3 (2000): 332.

4. James L. Sundquist describes how the American president serves as both chief executive and chief legislator, at least so long as the same party controls the presidency and Congress, averting divided rule. See Sundquist, *Constitutional Reform and Effective Government*, rev. ed. (Washington, DC: Brookings Institution, 1992), pp. 91–92.

5. As Arend Lijphart observes, although parliamentary regimes usually have a head of state separate from the prime minister, the conflation of head of state and head of government has become the normal rule for presidential systems. Lijphart himself obfuscates the distinction between authorizing and executive positions by describing parliamentary systems as having "dual executives." See Lijphart, *Patterns of Democracy: Government Forms and Performance in Thirty-six Countries* (New Haven, CT: Yale University Press, 1999), p. 126.

6. Hannah Arendt accordingly celebrates the United States Supreme Court as a great political innovation separating authority from both the legislative and executive branches while leaving the seat of authority without political power. She claims that this lack of power, combined with lifetime

appointment, signals that the Supreme Court is the ultimate seat of authority in the United States government. As we shall see, lifetime appointment is not constitutive of the authorizing power, nor does the Supreme Court have sufficient finality or scope of review to fulfill satisfactorily the role to which Arendt assigns it. See Arendt, *On Revolution* (New York: Viking, 1965), p. 201.

7. As Anastaplo points out, the moment judicial review is used for constitutional certification, the thorny question arises as to whether striking down a law is retroactive to when the law was enacted. See Anastaplo, *The Constitution of 1787*, p. 48. Right would seem to require retroactive application, but the practicalities of retroactive enforcement become progressively more challenging with the passage of time.

8. Jürgen Habermas points out that judicial review of legislation has the effect of nullifying regulations, ordinances, agency guidelines, and other administrative acts that contradict the authorized meaning of a legal statute. He refers to this effect as a relation of the legislative branch to an executive subject to the law, instead of as something mediated by the authorizing power. He thereby also ignores any direct judicial review of executive action, which will be required when the constitutionality of the enforced law is not in question. See Habermas, *Between Facts and Norms: Contributions to a Discourse Theory of Law and Democracy*, trans. William Rehg (Cambridge, MA: MIT Press, 1996), p. 173.

9. Hans Kelsen, *The General Theory of the State and Law* (Cambridge, MA: Harvard University Press, 1945), 124ff., 157, 258–59, 268–69.

10. Domestic authorization has had its finality expressly undercut by the European Convention on Human Rights, which empowers the European Court of Human Rights to invalidate any legislation or government action that it judges to violate that convention. As Arend Lijphart observes, this transnational initiative nevertheless allows judicial review to gain a foothold in the United Kingdom, whose unwritten constitution otherwise leaves constitutional certification in limbo. See Lijpahrt, *Patterns of Democracy*, pp. 19–20.

11. In this regard, Arend Lijphart points out how the unwritten constitution of the United Kingdom (1) renders the constitution devoid of a fixed character, since Parliament can change it through positive legislation, and (2) precludes judicial review, since courts have no higher law against which to test constitutionality. See Lijpart, *Patterns of Democracy*, p. 19.

12. These extreme situations underpin Anastaplo's claim that adherence to the constitution depends upon much more than judicial or any

other official supervision. See Anastaplo, *The Amendments to the Constitution: A Commentary* (Baltimore: Johns Hopkins University Press, 1995), p. 90.

13. Ronald Dworkin falls into the communitarian pitfall of relativizing the integrity of constitutional interpretation to the historical givenness of political community. His judicial Hercules then can have no ultimate reason for not subverting that political order and instituting another. After all, if the existence of every state is historically contingent, and contingent foundations are the only basis of integrity, allegiance to a specific political order becomes a groundless accident of history that any further historical transformation can destroy. Once this is recognized, the internal legitimacy of any political system becomes arbitrary and untenable on its own terms. For the most complete statement of Dworkin's historicized notion of political integrity, see Dworkin, *Law's Empire* (Cambridge, MA: Harvard University Press, 1986).

14. Indeed, as David P. Currie points out, Article 5 of the United States Constitution, which outlines the right to amend the constitution, can be looked at as the prime remedy for judicial usurpation. See Currie, *The Constitution of the United States: A Primer for the People* (Chicago: University of Chicago Press, 1988), p. 24. Or, as Anastaplo suggests, final judicial review can foster the view that the constitution is whatever the supreme court says it is. See Anastaplo, *The Constitution of 1787*, p. 145.

15. The most glaring recent example is provided by the modern-day veto record of Gerald Ford, who stymied a Democratic Congress by persistently vetoing its passed bills. See Sundquist, *Constitutional Reform*, p. 95.

16. As Anastaplo points out, congressional regulation of United States federal courts is offset by lifetime tenure and the provision that compensation may be increased but not diminished while in office. See Anastaplo, *The Amendments to the Constitution*, p. 125.

17. As Roberto Mangabeira Unger observes, this threatens the spirit of a republican constitution, although direct appeal to the electorate is too cumbersome a substitute. See Unger, *False Necessity: Anti-necessitarian Social Theory in the Service of Radical Democracy* (New York: Cambridge University Press, 1987), p. 454.

18. Lijphart describes this argument. See Lijphart, *Patterns of Democracy*, p. 224.

19. This option of an elected authorizing power defeats Robert A. Dahl's assumption that constitutional review involves a quasi-guardian who can never succeed in constraining the representatives of national electoral majorities without relinquishing democratic legitimacy. See Dahl,

Democracy and Its Critics (New Haven, CT: Yale University Press, 1989), pp. 190–91.

20. See Max Weber, *Political Writings*, ed. Peter Lassman and Ronald Speirs (Cambridge: Cambridge University Press, 1994), pp. 305–308.

21. As Currie points out, constitutional amendment procedures can be seen as an intended remedy for usurpation by the authorizing power (Currie, *The Constitution of the United States*, p. 24). They are, however, an imperfect remedy, since the authorizing power still retains ultimate authority to interpret any new amendments.

22. See G. W. F. Hegel, *Elements of the Philosophy of Right*, ed. Allen W. Wood, trans. H. B. Nisbet (Cambridge: Cambridge University Press, 1991), par. 279–80, pp. 316–21.

23. Max Weber makes this point in regard to the unity of administration. See Weber, *Political Writings*, p. 305.

24. Weber objects that judges nominated by a president, as in the United States, have far more integrity and ability than those popularly elected because presidential selection makes the president responsible for their quality (Weber, *Political Writings*, p. 174). Why their quality should be better judged by the president than by the electorate is far from self-evident, especially if the president is himself popularly elected.

25. Although the United States Constitution does not require any special qualifications for appointment as Supreme Court justice, it does, as Anastaplo notes, backhandedly emphasize concern for their competency by allowing that judges, unlike presidents and members of Congress, need not be citizens. See Anastaplo, *The Amendments to the Constitution*, p. 90.

26. John Stuart Mill claims that judicial posts are those least amenable to direct election, since judges should be most insulated from political pressures. See Mill, *Three Essays: On Liberty, Representative Government, The Subjection of Women* (Oxford: Oxford University Press, 1975), pp. 353–54. It is very dubitable, needless to say, that appointment by other elected officials, such as a president or congress, achieves the desired insulation.

27. See chap. 3, § 3.7.

28. Sundquist describes this predicament and how its threat to the separation of powers was progressively ameliorated through the rise of national party conventions and then the emergence of primary elections. See Sundquist, *Constitutional Reform*, pp. 248–51.

CHAPTER 6

THE EXECUTIVE BRANCH OF SELF-GOVERNMENT

The mandate of the executive power follows directly from the operation of its legislative and authorizing counterparts: laws passed by the legislature and certified as constitutional by the head of state now must be executed in concluding fulfillment of political freedom. Since the adoption of authorized law provides the executive power with predetermined statutes to administer, the business of execution seems to be a technical affair of supplying the appropriate means for realizing the ends given by legislation and validated by the authorizing power. Unlike legislators, who deliberate and argue about what laws are desirable, executive officials deliberate and argue among themselves over how to apply statutes in respect to contingent circumstances, issuing authoritative, rather than persuasive directions.[1]

Because the legislature must first decide what policies will be made law, legislation itself requires no competencies predicated on effecting particular goals. The goals are themselves up for grabs in legislative deliberation, albeit within the confines of right as specified in the constitution. Legislators may appeal to expert advice in comprehending particular circumstances, crafting appropriate regulations, and foreseeing the likely consequences of specific legal proposals. Nonetheless, the legislature is always in the position of drafting and choosing among different legislative initiatives. Each involves different technical considerations conditioned upon their specific goal, but for that very reason, no such consideration can supply sufficient grounds for favoring one goal over the other. The choice of which laws to adopt is never itself a technical matter, since it involves determining lawful ends and not just means. Consequently, legislators have a universal occupation, whose specification of lawful goals calls for correspondingly specific competencies of administration as the *result* of their lawmaking.

Similarly, authorization requires nothing but the same knowledge of constitutional principle that guides legislation and citizenship in general. Although authorizers may depend upon legal expertise to comprehend the vast reaches of statutory code and judicial precedent, constitutional certification itself involves an act of judgment predicated upon an understanding of the constitution and the law up for validation. That understanding cannot be beyond the capabilities of a self-governing citizenry, when citizenship involves acting in conformity with constitutional law that citizens have imposed upon themselves, albeit through representation.

By contrast, execution calls for further special expertise dictated by the particular focus of adopted legislation. Statutes addressing healthcare need to be administered by officials possessing appropriate medical and epidemiological expertise, just as statutes concerning environmental problems are best executed by officials trained in environmentally relevant fields.

6.1 THE PLACE OF BUREAUCRACY IN THE EXECUTIVE POWER

Because enforcement of authorized legislation requires special knowledge and skills dictated by the settled aims of the adopted law, execution seems to call for nothing more than bureaucracy: a professional body of technically qualified officials chosen by impartial testing of the relevant expertise. Government officials need to be professionals, that is, full-time paid employees, for the sake of both civil and political freedom. By making nonelective executive service a career, citizens need not be conscripted to fulfill executive functions, which would interfere with their economic as well as household freedom. Instead, professionalization allows citizens to enter government service through the same self-selection exercised in any earning activity in civil society. Further, failure to make administrative office an economically viable career would leave government service a privilege of the idle rich.[2] Then, the executive branch would become a field for oligarchy, where plutocrats govern the working drones who are subject to an administration to which they can never afford to belong. Alternately, administration must be taken out of private hands, overcoming the injustice of feudal times where power was a private privilege. Instead, administration must be made a public office employing professional bureaucrats, chosen from among whichever applicants best meet the requisite qualifications. To provide such professional employment for government functionaries in conformity with political and nonpolitical freedom, government must rely upon equitable taxation, levying money, not particular goods or services, from citizens at rates promoting equal economic opportunity. They thereby retain their economic freedom to decide what to buy and sell and what occupation to pursue while financing bureaucracy, as well as the salaries of elected officials.[3] On this basis, increasing bureaucratization reflects the demise of oligarchy and feudalism and increasing democratization,[4] provided those who are subject to administration also elect representative legislators and the chief officials of the authorizing power.

Bureaucracy can, of course, be detached from the legislative and authorizing organs of self-government and be an instrument of political oppression. Such has been the case when colonial bureaucracies have governed subaltern subjects who play no role in determining and validating the law that is administered upon them or when dynastic regimes have their decrees administered by bureaucracies such as Kafka experienced under the Austro-Hungarian Empire and fictionalized in *The Trial* and *The Castle*.[5] When, however, a professional officialdom enforces the law imposed by citizens upon themselves through a representative legislature and an elected authorizing power, the obstacles can be overcome that a nonprofessional or private administration poses for self-government.

Professionalism, however, is only one side of the legitimate mandate for bureaucratic administration. Because government officials administer antecedently determined ends, they must further have appropriate expertise, certified by impartial testing.[6] The requirement for specific technical qualifications here precludes filling executive positions by election or as a spoil of partisan patronage.[7] Although popular or indirect election of executive officials might seem best to integrate the executive as an instrument of self-government, general application of electoral selection would stymie the will of the state as manifest in validated legislation. Since an elected administration would lack any guaranteed competency to fulfill the specific policies mandated by the legislature and certified by the authorizing power, general election of executive officials would undercut self-rule by representative legislators. Laws might be enacted and authorized, but their execution would be captive to an unqualified, likely inept administration. The same consequence would follow from doling out executive positions as spoils of party patronage. The obligation to enforce self-rule by law would again be compromised by an extraneous concern—in this case, party loyalty. Moreover, election of all executive officials would undercut the discipline of the administrative hierarchy of executive ministries and the accountability that this hierarchy can enforce.[8] Appointment on the basis of publicly administered examinations instead promises the best-qualified staff at no worse price than offering government careers on the meritocratic principle of tested abilities.[9]

Of course, when a multitude of job candidates tie for top test results, selection must be made on some other basis that does not unduly discriminate among individuals. Appointment on a first-serve basis, through a lottery, or by means of job rotation among top contenders could all be employed without ignoring technical competency or committing any injustice.[10]

Distributing bureaucratic positions by quotas privileging members of historically disadvantaged groups presupposes that such groups still endure deficits in equal opportunity and that reserving executive positions for their members will facilitate the removal of those deficits. If such deficits do exist, reserving positions will hardly eliminate the problem, since such appointments will not alter the situation of all other group members who toil in other occupations, nor remedy the disadvantage of any other sectors of society. Besides making suspect the technical qualifications of quota appointees and fostering resentment among other groups, such measures avoid the more comprehensive remedies that a genuine civil society must undertake to remove social disadvantage and its household and political consequences.[11] Since the equal political opportunity constitutive of genuine self-government requires the achievement of equal social opportunity, the just state cannot allow any reservations by group in executive appointments. Such reservations fall within the prehistory of political justice, where their employment testifies to continued neglect of the universal measures required to eliminate social inequality.[12]

Since appointment is for the sake of efficiently achieving the administrative goals set by legislation, retention of office cannot be automatic. Tenure in the bureaucracy must instead depend upon continued performance, which must be regularly monitored by supervisory administrators qualified to make a proper assessment.

Selecting executive functionaries on the basis of tested expertise as professional bureaucrats does not necessitate restricting their political activities outside of their official activities. Admittedly, if functionaries were to use their official position to advance partisan activities instead of confining their public duties to administering the law, they would be corrupting their office. Such corruption, however, by no means requires that functionaries be prohibited from engaging in political campaigns when they are not acting in an official capacity.[13] Prohibitions of this sort would politically disadvantage executive officials without contributing at all to the workings of self-government.

Conversely, the executive branch would be compromised if professional bureaucrats could be removed and replaced for purely partisan reasons, such as occurs when large numbers of executive appointments are left to be made by a newly elected head of government. To resist the arbitrariness of patronage appointment, executive bureaucrats require a protected tenure that should only be suspended when officials no longer measure up to technical requirements, when the course of legislation no longer requires their expert administrations, or when they engage in official misconduct.

Given these provisos, appointment of government officials as professional bureaucrats with tested expertise would apply to the two constitutive fields of execution: the general administration of authorized legislation upon all political subjects and the judicial application of laws to individual cases brought to court. In both areas, the public bodies of civil society provide an officialdom ready to implement at least a portion of authorized statutes. On the one hand, the public administration of welfare already serves the ends of household and social freedom that now get regulated by political legislation. On the other hand, the civil courts and penal authorities already apply law in civil society, law which now gets promulgated in statutory, constitutionally valid codification. These civil administrations are not optional institutions over which the just state may or may not preside. Unless they are at hand, enforcing family and social rights, the equal political opportunity constitutive of self-government cannot be actual.

Given the global character of civil society and the extension of civil rights to citizens and noncitizens alike, the civil administrations of welfare and civil law may involve officials of international as well as domestic organizations. Any integration of civil institutions into the executive functions of the individual state must contend with the potential discrepancy between national legislation and transnational enforcement agencies. Although transnational administrations should be following treaty agreements in accord with right and duly enforce these international regulations, treaties may violate right and/or international enforcement may infringe upon domestic freedoms. A just government is obliged to oppose such violations to the degree that viable countermeasures are possible to uphold domestic right and reform international initiatives in the pursuit of equal opportunity in families, society, and politics the world over.

As extensive as the due activities of international and domestic civil bureaucracies may be, the administrative functions of the executive go beyond their workings. Because statutes should regulate civil society so that household and social freedom can be exercised without undermining equal political opportunity, the civil organs of public welfare and legality must be supplemented by executive agencies carrying out these tasks. New administrations are also required to execute the laws applying to the conduct of politics, both with respect to electoral campaigns, nonelectoral agitations, and the workings of political parties. These administrations are obliged to guarantee equal political opportunity in all these arenas of politics, as well as to insure that political life operate without compromising the family and social responsibilities of citizens. Finally, all these functions must be effected not only with regard to domestic affairs, but in the face of foreign relations. These external entanglements require executive efforts to conduct foreign affairs, both through diplomacy, military action, and state regulation of international commerce.

Given the multiplicity of political ends and corresponding administrative functions, the executive must itself be functionally differentiated into various agencies with their own administrative hierarchies. At the same time, the overarching imperatives of self-government require the unification of all these functions on behalf of upholding the body politic and its constitutive political and non-political rights. Not only must each executive function be subject to its own chief administrator, presiding over an appropriately subdivided administration, but all the separate ministries of executive government must be subordinate to a chief executive, charged with the general enforcement of authorized legislation in the face of both domestic and foreign conjunctures.

Due to the encompassing responsibility of the chief executive, this highest executive office transcends the particular qualifications that apply even to the apex of the separate ministries of state. Whereas ministers of foreign affairs, of defense, of transportation, of education, of housing, of health, of justice, and so forth, each preside over a functionally individuated agency calling for special expertise, the chief executive under whom they operate must achieve their unity with the general constitutional aims of the state. Such an overarching task explodes the limits of technical expertise and its specialized knowledge. Hence, the selection, prerogatives, term of office, and accountability of the chief executive have political implications that extend beyond the nonpartisan efficiencies of bureaucracy.[14] Although from a temporal point of view, the selection of the chief executive precedes the undertaking of the actual role, the specification of this highest executive office must be made first if what is being chosen is to have its proper identity. After all, if the office of chief executive remains undefined, little can be said of how it should be filled.

6.2 BASIC PARAMETERS OF THE CHIEF EXECUTIVE

The office of chief executive derives its due determination from the multiple political relationships imposed by the imperatives of political freedom. These relationships severely limit the prerogatives of the chief executive to the degree that formulating legislation falls exclusively to the legislature, just as constitutional certification falls exclusively to the authorizing power.[15] Never should the chief executive be in a position to masquerade as chief legislator or head of state. Nonetheless, execution sets the workings of the state in direct relation to individual citizens and other nations, and in this respect, the command of the chief executive has preeminent visibility.

Within the executive branch, the chief executive stands as prime minister, relating to the heads of the different executive agencies as their governing leader. This executive leadership must act with unity and ultimate administrative authority to weld government into an integral instrument of constitutional enforcement. A single individual can certainly suffice to embody this exclusive power, but it is not impossible for a plural leadership to occupy the apex of administration, provided recognized procedures could be put in place to insure that the plurality of highest command does not succumb to division and paralysis. Whether any such procedures could be reliable is open to question,[16] and, as becomes more sharply defined in connection with the form of executive elections, this difficulty undercuts the admissibility of plural leadership for the chief executive, as well as for the head of state.

In any case, even if plural leadership were admissible, it could not legitimately involve corporate or regional representations, subordinating the execution of law to a struggle of competing particular interests.[17] In order for the office of prime minister to fulfill the reflexivity and universality of self-rule, the chief executive must always act on behalf of the rights of all citizens. Only on this basis can the prime minister, be it one individual or a plural leadership, realize political freedom in commanding the various branches of administration through the mediation of their particular heads.

Historical compromises may nevertheless be required when the body politic is so divided among social groups that citizens prove unwilling to act on behalf of political justice instead of group interest. In such cases, any modicum of self-government may require mandatory power sharing on corporate lines in the executive as well as the other branches of government. Otherwise, whatever faction rules in parliament, in the authorizing branch, and/or in the executive will utilize its power to promote its interests at the expense of other groups, whose subjection may undermine their allegiance to the state and usher in civil war. For these reasons, a culturally divided nation like Belgium constitutionally requires that executive positions be apportioned among members of each of its major linguistic groups.[18] Like any such arrangement, this compromise can legitimately serve only as a temporary waystation to genuine self-government.

What is generic to political freedom is that the heads or ministers of the different executive agencies together comprise a cabinet, a council of ministers, over which the prime minister presides as ultimate executive arbiter. As subject to the leadership of the prime minister, the members of the cabinet serve as advisory subordinates, whose appointment and dismissal hinges upon the will of the prime minister, at least so long as nothing but executive prerogatives apply. Whether or not other powers of government need concur in the appointment and dismissal of cabinet officials ultimately concerns the accountability of the chief executive and whether that accountability can be sufficiently insured through due selection and dismissal of the prime minister. So long as the chief executive and cabinet ministers act within the borders of constitutionality and are not otherwise derelict in their duties, the particular policy interests of legislative majorities or authorizing officials do not warrant any intrusions upon cabinet officeholding.

Although technical expertise still plays a role in successfully administering each separate ministry, the subordination of each executive agency under the unifying governance of the prime minister involves more than performing its function in technical isolation. For this reason, lower echelons of administration may be appointed and dismissed through expert evaluations independent of any higher intervention, but the heads of each executive agency are beholden to the will of the prime minister, whose general leadership they should serve.

As chief executive, the prime minister is ultimately responsible for government action that falls within the broad guidelines of lawful implementation of the constitution. This responsibility has domestic and foreign dimensions insofar as the state must act both with regard to its internal domain and in relation to other political and nonpolitical entities outside its borders.

Although the prime minister has legitimately no authorizing role to play in certifying legislation, administering standing and new statutes involves significant initiatives. Chief among executive prerogatives is determining the allocation and level of public spending for the current administration of domestic and foreign affairs. Although budgets are commonly adopted as legislative bills, they are properly executive measures since they specify particular expenditures within a specific time frame rather than standing rules of taxation and government spending. Legislatures do have the right and duty to determine the universal principles of fair taxation, government borrowing, and government spending, but these are not themselves budget determinations. They comprise instead the lawful framework within which the executive is permitted to decide government expenditures needed to implement statutes and uphold the constitution and its system of rights.

Directing foreign policy in both peace and war also falls to the chief executive. Although ministers and their functionaries may negotiate treaties, the chief executive is ultimately responsible for deciding to what international agreements the state will adhere. Similarly, the chief executive is commander in chief of the armed forces of the state and ultimately responsible for their employment. Without the final approval of the chief executive, the state can go neither to war nor bring hostilities to an end. Civilian control over the military here has its highest expression in the power that must be wielded by the chief executive and subordinate "civilian" ministers over all military decisions, whether in peacetime or during war.[19] As history has all too often testified, the chief executive cannot rule as commander in chief unless the military has been organized and cultivated so as to be amenable to civilian control, especially when modern military technology gives civilians little defense against armed forces intent on usurping power.[20]

Of course, these executive prerogatives raise acute questions concerning the accountability of the prime minister. Some protection can be afforded by requiring public disclosure of executive deliberations and decisions.[21] Such publicity can at least enable all citizens to have an opportunity to scrutinize the official behavior of the prime minister, as well as that of any other executive official.[22] Transparency, however, only offers an occasion for remedial action. To this end, the authorizing power provides some restraint to the degree that the head of state wields the power to nullify action that is blatantly unconstitutional and to suspend the authority of the responsible executive officials, from the chief executive on down. This power can be utilized both through a continual supervision of executive action and through review of cases brought to court.[23] Of course, any checking of executive action by authorizing officials requires that they have sufficient public recognition and support to forestall resistance on the part of the administration.[24] Yet, even when this is not a problem, both of these avenues have severe limits. Unlike certification of pending legislation, which precedes legal validity, the review of executive action comes after the fact, which may be all too late when matters of war and peace hang in the balance. Further, if the chief executive presides over foreign policy, the boundaries of constitutionality allow for tremendous leeway that escape any legitimate scrutiny by the authorizing power.

Appeal to popular recall would escape the limitations of constitutional certification by leaving the boundaries of admissible executive action in the hands of popular opinion as registered in recall referenda. Nonetheless, this option suffers from two significant problems. First, popular recall would undercut executive autonomy by tending to subject the chief executive to every vicissitude of public opinion, which may be liable to manipulation by the most active and powerful social interests. Second, this procedure would require substantial time to collect recall petitions and arrange recall referenda, leaving too much opportunity for damage to be already done.

A more suitable option is to give parliament veto power in advance over any treaties, declarations of war, or budget proposals. As we have seen in considering the legislative power, this power has the advantage of being exercised *before* the executive takes final action. Further, legislative veto has only the negative effect of nullifying impending measures. Parliament cannot thereby institute treaties, wars, or budgetary spending on its own and take positive control over both legislation and execution. Accordingly, the division of powers remains intact, without jeopardy to constitutionality.

A different matter is misconduct in office by executive officials. Since here remedies must be sought after the fact, the authorizing power can rely on its capacities to scrutinize executive activity and provide judicial solutions to abuse of office. Once more, reliance on popular recall would both subject tenure in office to the unrestrained whims of public opinion and preclude an impartial investigation and adjudication of accusations of misconduct.

So restrained, but not usurped, by either legislature or authorizing power, the executive power stands under another relation of accountability. Although the chief executive may lord over the cabinet and subordinate functionaries, to be head of government equally involves serving the self-governance of the citizenry, as concretely organized into party partisans and independents, while standing in the complementary relation to the legislature and authorizing power on which constitutionality depends. These considerations bear upon the identity and selection of the prime minister, as well as the relation between prime minister and cabinet, in ways that have crucial ramifications for the controversy between "presidential" and "parliamentary" systems of government.

Simply by presiding over the execution of authorized law, the chief executive might be thought to realize the political freedom of citizens, at least insofar as legislators and the head of state are popularly elected. Yet, the mere fact that a prime minister facilitates the enforcement of self-legislation does not mean that the identity and accountability of the chief executive reflect the political self-determination of the citizenry. So long as the selection and term of the prime minister are independent of the will of citizens, who reigns as chief executive and how long that chief executive stays in office lie in other hands. To escape this domination, the choice of chief executive must be left to the will of the citizenry.

What this means concretely is, of course, far from straightforward. Citizens can codetermine who administers their government through various systems of direct election, where party candidates are chosen at party conventions or by primary elections and where final selection occurs with or without runoff elections. Alternately, the prime minister can be chosen through different sorts of indirect selection, such as those involving electoral colleges or appointment by provincial or national assemblies.

Both direct and indirect elections can keep the choice and replacement of the chief executive out of the hands of the legislature and avoid a parliamentary control of government that could enable legislators to override the limits of authorization by effectively enforcing laws as they please. What does not preclude this situation is a parliamentary system where parliamentary majorities choose the prime minister after parliamentary elections and then remain empowered to unseat a sitting chief executive through votes of no-confidence.

Although these defining powers of parliamentary systems have historically most often operated with proportional representation, nothing prevents their application to majoritarian electoral systems, as the example of British parliamentary government testifies. For this reason, the controversy between parliamentary and presidential forms of government is independent of the majoritarian-proportional representation divide.

6.3 PARLIAMENTARY GOVERNMENT AND THE SPECTER OF DIVIDED GOVERNMENT

The very liability of parliamentary systems is made their virtue by those who lament the impasse of divided government in the United States, where voting for an electoral college that elects the president permits congress to be controlled by parties opposing that of the president. That opposition can lead to legislative deadlock, however, not because the executive power is controlled by parties opposed to those ruling the legislature but because the United States president wields partial authorizing powers permitting presidential vetoes to block legislation that cannot get an overriding two-thirds supermajority. If the chief executive were strictly limited to executive functions, opposition between the prime minister's party and that of the parliamentary majority would not threaten parliamentary deadlock. The bloc controlling parliament would get its legislation through, subject to authorization by the head of state, irrespective of the party membership of the chief executive. The only results that split party loyalties could have within the legitimate limits of executive discretion would be partisan interpretations of enforcement and less alacrity in administering legislation. This would include those areas where executive action depends upon prior approval by the legislature, namely budget determination, the concluding of treaties, and the declaring of war. These are crucial fields of government activity, but each is subject to general regulation by statutes that no chief executive can legitimately evade. Moreover, even in these arenas, the head of state would monitor the constitutional fidelity of the "opposing" prime minister, providing further impediment to partisan deadlock.

By contrast, a parliamentary system that gives the parliamentary majority the power of appointing and removing the prime minister not only undercuts the division between legislative and executive powers, but threatens a dual deadlock whenever parliamentary divisions allow for no persisting majority coalition. In such all too familiar cases, the legislative process is paralyzed while the executive branch drifts without leadership so long as no prospective prime minister can muster the abiding confidence of a majority of legislators. Further, all too often the only escape is provided by compromises allowing small swing parties to extract disproportionate concessions from their coalition partners as a price for agreement on a prime minister.

These problems are somewhat mitigated by parliamentary systems allowing solely "constructive" votes of no-confidence, where parliament can dismiss the prime minister only when a parliamentary majority is united behind a successor. Then, at least, the nation does not face the prospect of waiting in limbo after dismissal of the chief executive until an otherwise divided parliament finally agrees upon a replacement. Nevertheless, the intended fix is hardly sufficient. Not only do "constructive" no-confidence procedures still subordinate executive to legislative power, but they still allow for extortion by minor parties as well as a parade of governments as short-lived and ineffectual as shifting parliamentary coalitions may be. Even if the prime minister may not be dismissed until an agreed successor has been found, that conjunction can occur and reoccur as often as a fickle parliament permits.

If "divided government" is to signify political gridlock, it will consist instead in the implacable opposition between the legislature and the head of state resulting in continual rejection of pending legislation by the authorizing power. That can be circumvented without compromising constitutionality through limiting term lengths and popular election of both legislators and the head of state.[25] Of course, no term length limits or election schedules can ever preclude paralyzing conflict between legislative and authorizing powers. Not only may citizens simultaneously choose a head of state opposing the legislature they elect, but the independence of representatives in parliament and the discretion of the head of state always allows electoral expectations of the citizenry to be disappointed.

Constitutionality is clearly imperiled by any attempt to remedy gridlock between the legislature and the authorizing power by enabling parliament to select and/or remove the head of state or, for that matter, members of a central constitutional court. Although this extension of parliamentary power does not directly determine how legislation gets certified, parliament can use it to remove authorizers until it finds a willing collaborator.

Similarly, giving a prime minister appointed by parliament the power to call for new parliamentary elections, as Mill suggests,[26] may free the prime minister from impending dismissal by a hostile parliament, but it does so at the expense of allowing executive power to encroach upon the legislature. Since the authorizing power is already at hand to counter unconstitutional usurpations by the legislature, the executive would be going beyond the bounds of enforcement to remove a legislature when nothing else indicates a violation of right.

Alleged advantages to having parliament appoint and remove prime ministers, as well as cabinet ministers, from among its own legislators are equally suspect. Nothing about the organization of either the legislative, executive, or authorizing branches prevents officials from other organs of government being called upon to give information and advice when that facilitates the functioning of each organ. Dual officeholding, however, has significant drawbacks. The more it is applied to high offices in different branches of government, the more it undercuts the division of powers. Moreover, it reduces the attention that can be paid to official duties by making the most important positions part-time occupations.

Given these problems, any version of parliamentary government loses the claim of preeminence. A presidential system in which the prime minister and head of state are directly elected may face oppositions that paralyze some legislation and certain executive functions, but it escapes weakening the division of powers and the other limitations of dual officeholding. Moreover, although presidential systems may be afflicted by fractured parliaments in which majority coalitions are continually in flux, it escapes the continual parade of changing governments that are the bane of parliamentary systems. Furthermore, direct election of prime ministers, as well as heads of states, allows the electorate to avoid another layer of distancing from its executive and authorizing chiefs.

The objection, offered by Mill, that direct election leads to prime ministers of lesser caliber than would be selected by parliament,[27] is hardly convincing, even if one abstracts from the other liabilities of parliamentary government.[28] Citizens of principle who contest popular opinion may be no more liked by parliament than by the electorate. Parliamentary leaderships may opt for lesser hacks than can command an electoral majority, just as unsung figures may come into their own on the campaign trail, despite being spurned by parliamentarians. And if legislators are themselves directly elected, why should their choice be any more worthy than that of those who gave them their office? To the extent that the added mediation of parliamentary selection and removal is both unnecessary and deleterious to the division of powers, it represents a limitation on self-rule that does not serve the cause of right.

A compromise solution following the Israeli model might seem to avoid some of these liabilities, while eliminating the deadlock of divided government.[29] On this scheme, the chief executive and the legislature are directly elected simultaneously, but parliament can dismiss the prime minister, who can equally dissolve parliament.[30] In either event, new elections are held simultaneously for prime minister and parliament. Although allowing these complementary dismissals and new elections may result in greater harmony between the executive and legislature, there is no guarantee that the opposite may not result. Admittedly, leaving selection in the hands of the electorate removes any further distancing between citizens and officials and allows each power of government to retain parity. Nevertheless, it is questionable whether empowering both the chief executive and parliament to dismiss one another serves any legitimate purpose once the division of powers is duly observed and the chief executive is unable to act as legislator in chief. Mutual power to dismiss and call new elections certainly fosters greater instability of government, without insuring that the rise and fall of governments and parliaments does not fall prey to the most petty partisan interests. Since other options can be employed for removing chief executives and legislators before the end of their term when serious misconduct is at stake, there is even less reason to allow for such potential upheaval.

6.4 THE ELECTION AND REMOVAL OF THE CHIEF EXECUTIVE

Popular election of the chief executive is subject to all the considerations that equally underpin equal political opportunity in legislative and authorizing election campaigns. To begin with, eligibility to run for chief executive should involve the same requirements that apply to general participation in self-government. Since permanent residency is sufficient to qualify an individual for political rights where they reside, any restriction of eligibility to naturally born citizens, let alone to any other class of citizens more limited than that of permanent residents, illicitly creates a divide between rulers and subjects at odds with self-government.[31] Similarly, age requirements different from those that apply to voting divide subjects into a privileged class entitled to run for office and an underprivileged class barred from officeholding.

Second, to guarantee equal opportunity to run for chief executive, individuals must be allowed to seek office as independents or as party nominees. Further, party nomination procedures must enable all citizens who wish to identify themselves as party members to have a fair chance to influence the selection of candidates. This requires that contests for party nomination be regulated to prevent party hierarchies or social interests from using their powers and resources to disproportionately dominate the outcome. The same imperatives apply to the actual campaign among party and independent candidates. Once again, campaigns must be supervised and publicly subsidized to insure that all credible candidates can make their case to the electorate without being disadvantaged through inequalities in private resources among themselves and their supporters.

Given the liabilities of parliamentary systems and the absence of any need for more than one person at the apex of executive power, proportional representation seems to have little role to play in the direct election of the chief executive. A plural chief executive could, however, be elected on the basis of proportional representation if parties offered slates of candidates for a highest council of administration. Further, since the number of officials comprising a chief executive could be small in comparison to the number of legislators, some of the most important drawbacks of proportional representation would be partly mitigated. If few enough candidates ran for nomination on each party slate, primary elections could be utilized to allow each party electorate to play some role in selecting nominees and to do so without facing too many choices to make an informed decision. The primary vote totals of each candidate could then be used to determine not only who will belong to the party slate but what ranking candidates will have in the postelectoral decision of who actually takes office. In this way, a vote for a party slate would have some, albeit limited, connection to a choice for individual candidates. If the admittance of minority viewpoints in the highest executive council were a requirement for self-government, then a plural executive leadership, elected through proportional representation, would be mandatory.

One obvious drawback of admitting proportional representation, which applies equally to extending proportional representation to the head of state, is the possibility of deadlock if the fragmentation of parties leaves no group with any abiding majority at the pinnacle of command. Such deadlocks can affect parliaments selected by majoritarian election whenever no party wins enough districts to form a stable coalition. If, however, the chief executive is a single individual, such problems are precluded. What instead remain are the perennial vicissitudes of personal decisiveness, which are inexpungible from any form of government. So long as the prime minister has been selected by the electorate under conditions of equal political opportunity, the absence of anyone from losing parties in the chief executive need not subvert the reflexivity of self-rule in the executive power. Consequently, plural leadership retains a significant disadvantage that gives cause for restricting the chief executive position to a single officeholder.

Once elected, the chief executive can be held duly accountable through the same means that apply to other elected officials as well as through specific interventions of the legislative and authorizing powers. For this reason, direct election of the chief executive does not lie on road to Caesarist acclamation, insinuating plebiscitary democracy.[32] Although the directly elected chief executive commands a popular mandate that no parliamentary prime minister can claim, the division of powers remains intact.

Like legislators and authorizing officials, the chief executive should be subject to a fixed term, long enough to allow a new administration to acclimate itself and coherently fulfill its responsibilities but short enough to enable the citizenry to be governed by an executive they have predominantly chosen and have a reasonable opportunity to replace. The limits of these extremes are contingent and cannot be precisely specified by reason.

By contrast, term limits for chief executive restrict the freedom of the electorate to be governed by candidates of its choice while providing dubious remedy to the abuse of power and misguided remedy to the electoral advantages of incumbency. So long as campaigning, both to become a party nominee and to win office in the final election, is regulated to insure equal political opportunity, incumbency need not present any barrier to electoral justice. Although term limits strictly preventing reelection can eliminate entirely any advantages to incumbency, measures to give all credible candidates equal access to campaign resources and publicity removes any legitimate rationale for restricting citizens' freedom to run for office or the electorates' freedom to choose their favorite candidate.

Once term length is properly limited, recall initiatives have little justification other than perhaps as means of remedying misconduct in office. Since self-rule does not involve any immediate identity between the decisions of government officials and current public opinion, recall has no legitimacy as a tool of making a prime minister forfeit executive autonomy and slavishly mirror the will of all. Yet, reliance on recall to counter official misconduct leaves the enforcement of executive rectitude hostage to the vagaries of public opinion, without any impartial investigation, indictment, or judicial process to establish the facts and determine punishments or compensations.

The better solution is to rely upon intervention by another power of government to judge and penalize executive officials. If the legislature were given this prerogative, it could use it to reinstate a veiled version of parliamentary rule, dismissing any chief executive who did not govern as the legislature sees fit. Although the choice of a new chief executive could still depend upon succession procedures, including early elections that are beyond legislative control, the legislature could nullify any succession by removing the new prime minister. To counter the attenuation of direct election of the chief executive and the instability to which parliamentary government is prone, legislative removal of the prime minister could require supermajorities diminishing its likelihood. Moreover, the authorizing power could step in to nullify legislative removals of prime ministers whenever executive misconduct has not been established and partisan policy agendas lie at the root of the dismissal. Then, only collusion between the legislature and the head of state could overthrow the chief executive without due cause, a collusion sufficient to endanger constitutionality in general.

Alternately, the authorizing power could be empowered to investigate, judge, and discipline the chief executive for misconduct, leaving the legislature on the sidelines. At worst, this would allow the head of state to remove the chief executive and remove any replacement not deemed satisfactory. This could leave the executive power drifting along, both with regard to domestic and foreign affairs, as functionaries perform their usual duties without new directives from the pinnacle of administration. Yet since the head of state can make no positive contribution to formulating either legislation or administrative policy, the executive power would not be usurped.

Moreover, since authorizing officials themselves have limited terms, flagrant removals of prime ministers by either the head of state or the legislature would not be endlessly repeatable without the collusion of the electorate.

6.5 THE SELECTION AND REMOVAL OF CABINET MINISTERS

If the apex of administration is held duly accountable by the above measures, selection and removal of cabinet ministers would seem to be safely left to the discretion of the prime minister. When cabinet ministers engage in official misconduct and are neither disciplined nor removed by the chief executive, the authorizing power would be in a position to hold the chief executive accountable for this lapse of administrative leadership and to take action against the miscreant ministers. This intervention by the authorizing power would allow it to suspend or remove cabinet ministers but not to appoint successors. Consequently, the divide between powers would not be breached.

Intervention by the legislature could be less benign for constitutionality. In various modern democracies, including the United States, parliament must approve cabinet appointments. Although this does not give the legislature independent initiative to put candidates forward or to remove sitting ministers, it does allow the dominant legislative coalition to prevent any cabinet appointments that do not have its approval. Under parliamentary regimes this power is redundant, since the prime minister is already a minion of the legislative majority. By leaving both the prime minister and cabinet members dependent upon the confidence of the legislature, parliamentary regimes render the cabinet collegial in the sense that the prime minister cannot independently remove ministers and must please the same parliamentary majority to which they are beholden. By contrast, a presidential system in which the chief executive unilaterally appoints and dismisses cabinet officials renders them subordinates rather than coequal colleagues.[33] Where, however, a "presidential" regime allows parliament to confirm cabinet appointees, this power engenders two disparate situations. When the chief executive makes pliant nominations, parliament can effectively determine who presides over the various ministries. When instead the chief executive is at odds with the parliamentary majority, as under "divided" government, the legislature can paralyze administration so far as rejecting cabinet nominees may keep executive functions in some degree of suspended animation. If parliament could additionally remove cabinet ministers at will and/or replace them, the division of powers would be further impaired. Even if the chief executive were immune from parliamentary appointment or dismissal, the subjection of the cabinet to the legislature would enable parliament to circumvent an independent prime minister. For all these reasons, legislative endorsement of cabinet nominees is hardly necessary, nor unequivocally conducive to self-government.

Given how chief executives may be elected as independents, as standard bearers of a majority party, or as a coalition candidate, selection of cabinet ministers by the chief executive can lead to manifold party formations within the cabinet. The variety is further enhanced by the inability of party discipline to automatically dictate what appointments will be made by a chief executive, or, for that matter, what cabinet ministers will do in overseeing their ministries under the direction of the chief executive.

By the same token, the preeminence of the chief executive with respect to cabinet ministers can be exercised in a variety of ways. Although it gives the chief executive the prerogative to act in opposition to the advice of the cabinet, the chief executive can equally choose to abide by cabinet consensus without subverting the unity of the executive power. This range applies even in a parliamentary regime where the prime minister may defy the views of some or all cabinet officials and retain the confidence of parliament.[34]

In parliamentary systems and presidential systems in which executive and legislative functions are conflated, both the prime minister and cabinet ministers often play leading roles in directing legislation, especially when they sit in parliament, enjoying dual office-holding. This gives the party composition of the cabinet added significance, especially when a cohesive parliamentary majority ensures a long tenure for cabinet members, who can exercise an enduring domination over legislation.[35] When, however, the division of powers is duly followed, neither the chief executive nor the cabinet play more than an advisory role to legislators, who retain control over the introduction, amending, and adoption of legislation.

It is worth noting that any scheme allowing parliament to determine cabinet appointments would be unlikely to replicate the diversity achieved by proportional representation in the legislature. Instead of allocating cabinet posts to party members in relation to aggregate party votes in the legislative elections, parliamentary selection of cabinet ministers would enable the sufficiently dominant party coalition to make its choice independently of the other parties. If proportionality were to be secured in the cabinet, ministerial positions would have to be allotted in respect to the relative votes of different parties in the elections for chief executive, or, in parliamentary systems, for the legislature. Proportional selection of the cabinet might allow minority party ministers to voice their partisan positions in official meetings, but this would not have any necessary impact upon executive policy if the prime minister exercises the administrative control allowing the executive to act with proper unity. The same can be said of cabinets representing multiparty coalitions.[36] Although this could indicate executive power sharing among coalition parties, that sharing remains contingent upon the will of the prime minister, unless executive supremacy is removed from the chief executive and lodged in the cabinet. In that case, of course, the prime minister is a subordinate figure head and the cabinet is actually a plural chief executive.

Similar considerations affect corporatist allotments of cabinet positions. Once more, unless cabinet ministers escape control by the chief executive, their representation of particular interests remains hostage to the discretion of their superior. In any event, since the legitimate function of the executive is to enforce law so as to uphold the rights of all citizens, subordinating the cabinet to a contest of social interests involves the same corruption of political freedom perpetrated by corporate representation in the legislature.

6.6 SHOULD EXECUTIVE OFFICIALS BE IMMUNE FROM PROSECUTION?

Upholding political right requires that official misconduct by the prime minister, cabinet ministers, or their functionaries be nullified. Although this can involve the rescinding of derelict administrative policies and suspension or removal from office, punishment and compensation can be called for when officials have maliciously violated right and/or done injury to other individuals. In addition, executive officials of any rank can also commit crimes and nonmalicious wrongs before or during their term of office that otherwise warrant timely indictment, trial, and ensuing punishment and/or compensation.

Granting immunity to a chief executive might seem particularly important given how critical the apex of administrative command can be in times of war or domestic crisis. Individual legislators and members of a constitutional court could be prosecuted without interrupting the general operations of legislation and authorization, but the individual concentration of executive control in the prime minister seems to make any suspension of immunity from prosecution a dire threat to government enforcement. Nonetheless, the pros and cons for giving the chief executive or any subsidiary executive officials immunity from prosecution for nonofficial wrongs are ultimately no different than those that apply to legislators or authorizing officials. Although granting such immunity would allow the chief executive, cabinet ministers, and their subordinates to fulfill their official duties without interruption, the right of victims to compensation and the right of civil society to punish criminals would be compromised. Those rights could be held in abeyance by suspending prosecution of executive officials until after they leave office, but that would be legitimate only if executive duties could not be fulfilled by any other means. Under certain conditions, indictments and trial could proceed without preventing executive officials from carrying out their duties, if assistance is provided by subordinates. When this is not possible, officials could be suspended and replaced for the duration of the judicial proceedings. If punishment and/or compensation is then meted out, the guilty officials could be removed from office provided the penalty cannot be served without interfering with fulfillment of official responsibilities. In the case of cabinet ministers or their subordinates, replacements could easily be made by the chief executive, subject to whatever confirmation is ordinarily required. When the chief executive is dismissed, much more is at stake, but the practicalities are hardly insurmountable. A fixed line of interim succession could already be specified constitutionally, allowing the quickest remedy. Alternately, an interim prime minister could be appointed by another power of government to serve until the next scheduled election or a special election could be promptly called to select a replacement for the remainder of the scheduled term. The head of state, rather than the legislature, could make an interim appointment with less risk of partisan manipulations effecting a reversion to parliamentary government. Whatever the procedure, triggering indictments would have to be rigorously screened to prevent bogus prosecutions from undermining the autonomy of the chief executive. On this basis, the executive power could carry on its operations without receiving immunity and derailing the wheels of justice.

6.7 THE PROBLEM OF INDEPENDENT EXECUTIVE AUTHORITIES

Although the execution of legislation requires a professional bureaucracy appointed on the basis of tested expertise, self-government becomes compromised when nonelected executive officials wield independent power to determine rather than simply implementing policies vital to the body politic and the civil society it encompasses. In recent times, such independent administrative power has been commandeered by two types of appointed officials: the heads of central national banks and the heads of self-financing public authorities. As the American examples of Federal Reserve Chairman Alan Greenspan and master builder Robert Moses have shown, a nation can be fundamentally affected by nonelected officials who control monetary supply and credit rates or initiate vast public works projects that remake the fabric of society. Moreover, given the global reach of civil society and its regulated market economy, what such officials do in one nation may have a worldwide impact.

Although officials elected directly or indirectly have generally appointed the heads of central banks and public works czars like Robert Moses, once in office, these appointees have enjoyed a power to determine policies without any further control by the electorate or their representatives. This independence has been defended as both a protection of the public interest against fickle public opinion and partisan patronage, and as an instrument for further dividing and balancing the powers of government.[37] It has also been required for participation in various transnational integrations, which use central bank independence to overcome national obstacles to global economic consolidation.[38] Whatever be the merit of these considerations, the cherished independence of these independent executive agencies comes at the expense of putting political freedom at multiple risk. To the degree that such insulated officials initiate policies of their own that are not implementations of legislation, they act by a decree that lacks the lawful character required for government to be universal in both origin and address. Further, since these officials operate independently of enforcing laws that citizens impose upon themselves through the mediation of their representatives, the activity of these autonomous agencies lacks the self-legislated character enabling rule to be self-rule. Moreover, unlike the administrative actions emanating from an elected chief executive who always retains final control, these initiatives escape higher supervision and thereby fall outside the executive realization of self-government. Finally, by retaining office without depending upon the electorate for reappointment, these lords of central banks and public works escape any regular accountability before the citizenry, who passively observe their spectacle.

To remedy such infringements on political freedom, these officials must be brought back to the fold of government administration, bound by the imperative to enforce legislation under the direction of the chief executive. This requires that the chief executive have power to appoint and dismiss the head of the central bank and of public works, as well as that authorizing authorities be prepared to curtail any unconstitutional initiatives.

Although the pivotal position of central bank director might seem worthy of direct election, this would insulate that head from control by the chief executive. Dual centers of power would result, impeding the unity of executive policy. What counts is not that such administrative positions be filled by election but that they be subordinated to the control of a chief executive, chosen by the citizenry, obliged to enforce authorized legislation, and subject to scrutiny by the head of state.

NOTES

1. Michael Oakeshott, *On Human Conduct* (Oxford: Oxford University Press, 1975), p. 166.

2. This also prevents administration from being the privilege of a premodern estate or some other status ranking antithetical to the freedoms of civil society. As Max Weber points out, the emancipation of government service from feudal private control is another achievement of modern bureaucracy, which separates the means of administration from the administrator. See Weber, *Political Writings*, ed. Peter Lassman and Ronald Speirs (Cambridge: Cambridge University Press, 1994), pp. 314–16.

3. See par. 299 of G. W. F. Hegel, *Elements of the Philosophy of Right*, ed. Allen W. Wood, trans. H. B. Nisbet (Cambridge: Cambridge University Press, 1991), pp. 337–38 for a discussion of the emancipatory character of taxation.

4. The connection between bureaucratization and democratization is pointed out by Norberto Bobbio. See Bobbio, *The Future of Democracy*, ed. Richard Bellamy, trans. Roger Griffin (Minneapolis: University of Minnesota Press, 1987), p. 38.

5. Hannah Arendt analyzes both of these deformations of bureaucratic administration, examining how rule by bureaucracy helps pave the way for totalitarian regimes. See Arendt, *The Origins of Totalitarianism*, new ed. with added prefaces (New York: Harcourt Brace Jovanovich, 1973), pp. 209, 216, 221, 243–46.

6. As Weber points out, the ancient Chinese officialdom was not a technically qualified bureaucracy insofar as the Chinese exam system tested a traditional literary-humanist formation, rather than technical expertise. See Weber, *Political Writings*, p. 156.

7. As Michael Walzer points out, if selection by election were the only consideration, it would be admissible for an elected chief executive to distribute subordinate positions as patronage, duly rewarding political loyalty. See Walzer, *Spheres of Justice* (New York: Basic Books, 1983), pp. 162–63. Although patronage appointments may well encourage local political participation and political loyalty, Walzer goes too far in claiming that complete politicization of appointments is required for a decentralized democracy (Walzer, *Spheres of Justice*, p. 163), since even here, the technical requirements of administration will still be best served by bureaucrats appointed on the basis of tested expertise.

8. Max Weber points out these shortcomings. See Weber, *Political Writings*, pp. 129, 225.

9. As Walzer points out, a universal civil service can counter the unequal effects of individual discretion, wealth, and corporate power, but filling the bureaucracy on the basis of tested merit will still result in inequalities reflecting the natural and artificial inequalities influencing such factors as educational preparation, exam-taking abilities, interview performance, and amenability to bureaucratic discipline. See Walzer, *Spheres of Justice*, p. 132.

10. See Walzer, *Spheres of Justice*, p. 136. As Walzer points out, rotation of office can coexist with technical competency, even if such schemes as Jacksonian rotation were designed to eliminate the bureaucratic monopoly of office. See Walzer, *Spheres of Justice*, pp. 133–34.

11. Walzer makes similar arguments. See Walzer, *Spheres of Justice*, pp. 148–54.

12. For a systematic analysis of what public interventions are required, see Richard Dien Winfield, *The Just Economy* (New York: Routledge, 1988), pp. 183–232.

13. Executive officials may engage in politics, but they must, as Oakeshott puts it, "notionally vacate their offices in order to participate." See Oakeshott, *On Human Conduct*, p. 167.

14. As Weber observes, the fact that the chief executive is not required to demonstrate any kind of qualification based on training is indicative of the special significance of this position (Weber, *Political Writings*, p. 160). Weber draws the contrast between administrative functionaries and the

chief executive in a telling way: whereas other executive officials are meant to follow the command of superiors, the chief executive, Weber observes, takes full personal responsibility for his or her actions, resigning whenever legislated policy contradicts his or her political convictions (Weber, *Political Writings*, pp. 161, 204). In this way, the chief executive is a politician, and not a bureaucrat, even though the division of powers limits the chief executive to enforcing laws determined by parliament. What allows the relation between legislature and chief executive to be different from that between chief executive and bureaucrat is the unifying discretion that the chief executive must wield in bringing all authorized law to a constitutional realization. Here a political, rather than technical, spirit is required.

15. Even though the United States president has partial authorizing powers and operates as a chief legislator when Congress is controlled by the same party, presidential power tends, as George Anastaplo observes, to be overestimated. Without congressional support and judicial authorization, the president can do little. Even as commander in chief, the president's hands are tied if Congress does not finance a sufficient military force. And whereas Congress can override a presidential veto, the president cannot override the Senate's refusal to approve treaties or executive appointments. See Anastaplo, *The Constitution of 1787: A Commentary* (Baltimore: Johns Hopkins University Press, 1989), pp. 110, 112, 122.

16. John Stuart Mill, for one, claims that plural leadership is flawed since responsibility becomes more difficult to assign when the decision lies in a majority of an administering board, rather than in an identifiable individual. Hence councils should be merely advisory, leaving ultimate decision in the hands of a single minister or prime minister. See Mill, *Three Essays: On Liberty, Representative Government, The Subjection of Women* (Oxford: Oxford University Press, 1975), pp. 345–47. If, however, all proceedings of executive councils are made public, responsibility becomes less mysterious.

17. The only circumstances that might require a plural chief executive, and for that matter, a plural head of state, would be situations where social groups are so divided that political unity is impossible unless these divisions find guaranteed expression at the apex of government administration. Such a situation would at best be a way station to creating the genuine bonds of citizenship, wherein individuals subordinate their particular group allegiances to the common undertaking of self-government.

18. Arend Lijphart discusses these compromise arrangements under the rubric of a consensus model of democracy, chiefly involving executive

power sharing, a multi- rather than two-party system, proportional representation, federalism and bicameralism to allow stronger representation of divided groups, and constitutional rigidity to prevent any overturning of group guarantees (Lijphart, *Patterns of Democracy: Government Forms and Performance in Thirty-six Countries* (New Haven, CT: Yale University Press, 1999), pp. 34–40). *If* all these features depend upon the risk of group domination, a duly civil society, where equal social opportunity is secured, and a just body politic that protects equal political opportunity from social power, would make them superfluous. As it turns out, however, some of these features are generic to self-government (e.g., constitutional rigidity), whereas others are tolerable, if unnecessary options (e.g., multiparty system, proportional representation, federalism, and bicameralism) that can be emancipated from corporatist limitations.

19. One can thus, following Robert A. Dahl, identify two military conditions of democratic government: (1) that the military be subject to civilian control, and (2) that the civilians in control of the military be subject to popular control. See Dahl, *Democracy and Its Critics* (New Haven, CT: Yale University Press, 1989), p. 245.

20. Dahl lists a variety of measures to secure civilian supremacy over a modern military, such as dispersal of control among local governments, universal military service and other methods for making military personnel share the civilian orientation of the citizenry, and inculcation of democratic ideals in professional soldiers and officers. See Dahl, *Democracy and Its Critics*, pp. 248–49.

21. As Mill observes, nobody can determine responsibility when officials meet behind closed doors. See Mill, *Three Essays*, p. 346.

22. Whether *all* official action should be publicized is another matter. In the second appendix to *Perpetual Peace*, Immanuel Kant argues for complete openness on the ground that "All actions affecting the rights of other human beings are wrong if their maxim is not compatible with their being made public." See Kant, *Political Writings*, trans. H. B. Nisbet (Cambridge: Cambridge University Press, 1991), p. 126. This principle suffers from the same formality as Kant's argument for the absolute prohibition against lying: it is not hard to imagine situations where government officials are obliged to maintain state secrets to protect the rights of citizens against foreign aggressors.

23. As Jürgen Habermas observes, any administrative action or inaction can be contested in court seeking nullification or mandatory injunction on the basis of infringement of rights. See Habermas, *Between Facts and*

Norms: Contributions to a Discourse Theory of Law and Democracy, trans. William Rehg (Cambridge, MA: MIT Press, 1996), p. 174.

24. Mill points this out, emphasizing how citizens' immediate contact with the executive branch tends to give it an advantage in securing the support of the citizenry in opposition to other powers. See Mill, *Three Essays*, p. 200.

25. Another possible remedy is term limits. Unlike limits on term length and popular election of legislators and authorizing officials, however, term limits restrict voter choice. This liability is reason enough for forsaking the term limit remedy since first, term length limits and popular election of both legislators and authorizers can achieve whatever benefit term limits offers, provided incumbency advantages are properly countered, and second, none of these measures can preclude recurring political divisions in the next elections.

26. See Mill, *Three Essays*, p. 352.

27. See ibid., p. 351.

28. Mill suggests that the prime minister be elected by parliament for a fixed term, without possibility of removal by votes of no-confidence, to counter the problems of parliamentary government (see Mill, *Three Essays*, p. 353). Although this gives the prime minister greater independence, it still gives parliament the power to appoint a stooge of its own.

29. Lijphart describes this hybrid as a change *in* rather than *of* the presidential system. See Lijphart, *Patterns of Democracy*, p. 123.

30. The United States Constitution comes close to this arrangement insofar as the impeachment process gives Congress the final say on who will stay president, while the president remains elected by the citizenry, albeit through the mediation of the Electoral College. See Anastaplo, *The Constitution of 1787*, p. 32.

31. Individuals who retain citizenship in a state, but have permanent residency elsewhere, cannot claim political opportunities that they cannot exercise. Although expatriate citizens may be able to cast absentee ballots, they can hardly run for or hold office in their country of origin so long as they reside abroad.

32. Weber suggests this outcome. See Weber, *Political Writings*, p. 221. Anastaplo agrees. See *The Constitution of 1787*, p. 106.

33. In drawing this contrast, Lijphart observes that presidential cabinets are effectively one-party cabinets (Lijphart, *Patterns of Democracy*, p. 105). This presumes that a multiparty cabinet is really a plural chief executive or incompatible with the subordination of ministers to the chief executive.

34. Although Lijphart acknowledges this variety of relationships between prime ministers and their cabinets, he still maintains that parliamentary systems have more collective, collegial executives than presidential systems (Lijphart, *Patterns of Democracy*, p. 118). This would hold true if the inability of the prime minister to appoint and dismiss cabinet officials were sufficient to prevent the prime minister from acting against cabinet advice.

35. Lijphart describes how this situation plays out in *Patterns of Democracy*, pp. 11–13.

36. Arend Lijphart categorizes the different possible relationships between the executive, as determined through its cabinet formation, and parties, but the differences have diminished significance if the cabinet is subordinate to the chief executive. See Lijphart, *Patterns of Democracy*, p. 3.

37. Lijphart stresses this last consideration. See Lijphart, *Patterns of Democracy*, p. 233.

38. In 1992 the Maastricht Treaty required central bank independence as a condition for joining in a common European currency. See Lijphart, *Patterns of Democracy*, p. 239.

CHAPTER 7
FEDERALISM AND POLITICAL FREEDOM

7.1 THE DUAL DIMENSIONS OF FEDERALISM

The constitutive features of the three powers of self-government operate irrespectively of whether constitutional democracy involves federalism.[1] Because these features are necessary elements of political freedom, any federalist scheme must incorporate them to have normative validity. If federalism can do so, it can be at least a legitimate option for self-government. If, however, federalism is to be not just an option, but the preeminent form of self-government, federal organization must be applicable wherever the general prerequisites of political freedom are present and contribute something to political autonomy that nonfederalist, centralist, unitary government cannot offer. Federalism would remain at best a permissible option if it instead depended upon contingencies characterizing only certain civil societies, such as deep cultural divisions or histories of group oppressions. Similarly, the just state could blamelessly do without federalism if federal government cannot enhance political self-determination.

Federalism can take various forms, but ordinarily it operates along two correlative dimensions, whose interconnection distinguishes it from corporatist arrangements that give groups political privileges in any or all the powers of government. These complementary aspects are the differentiation between national and provincial government and the incorporation of provincial representation within at least the national legislature, if not also in the national authorizing and executive powers.

The first dimension of federalism distinguishes national institutions of government from localized political bodies, subordinate to national government, but empowered within their jurisdiction to govern certain functions over which national government has no direct control. These provincial governments can have jurisdiction over geographically distinct regions. The resulting provinces may be culturally congruent with one another and thereby with the national polity as a whole. Then, whatever diversity falls within the body politic will be distributed in indifference to provincial boundaries, and provincial governance will have no particular cultural orientation. Alternately, the regions may be incongruent,[2] comprising the localities of different subcultures distinguished by language, religion, ethnicity, or any other historically given conventions that demarcate the inhabitants of one region from another.[3] In this case, the diversity of the nation as a whole gets fragmented into relatively more homogenous compartments and provincial rule derives its unifying focus from some particular subculture. The differentiation of incongruent provinces presupposes, of course, that cultural groups are geographically isolated. When this is not the case, an incongruent federalism can still operate through virtual provinces which each have jurisdiction not over a geographically defined region but over a geographically dispersed subculture, administering communal control over certain matters that are not directly governed by laws applying to all citizens, whatever be their cultural identity. Once more, the only rationale for tying citizens to their particular subfederal political body is some cultural factor that they share, in exclusion from other citizen groups.

By itself, the distinction between national and provincial rule could be assimilated into nonfederal arrangements of government hierarchy, where lower jurisdictions exercise a certain discretion in locally administering policies determined at the highest national level. This subordination operates most effortlessly when the local bodies are congruent, since then the lower level is not defined by any interest distinct from that of the nation at large. Yet even incongruent geographically isolated or dispersed communities could administer their own local affairs in line with central authority, in the manner of a corporatist municipal administration that allows particular social agendas to gain political expression. In that case, national government delegates authority to local powers, retaining central control over the political agenda that pervades all levels of government.[4]

What makes the national/local divide distinct from a hierarchy of technical specialization are two factors: (1) that local jurisdictions are empowered to pursue self-generated ends that cannot simply be derived from enforcing national legislation, and (2) that national offices be distributed to individuals as members of lower jurisdictions rather than on general principles of equal political opportunity. Although local jurisdictions here have a range of autonomy that national legislation cannot regulate, right requires that they be subject to the limits of constitutionality that insure that political and nonpolitical freedoms are not violated at either the national or "provincial" level. This subjection to constitutional stricture can only be effected by the authorizing power of the national government.[5] Appeal to any third party to mediate between alleged conflicts of "states' rights" and the federal government would introduce a sovereign that either stands outside the control of the citizenry or is nothing other than the real authorizing power of the body politic. In the former case, the institutions of political freedom would be subordinate to an external power, undermining the autonomy of self-government. In the latter case, the mediating authorizing power would be subject to the same requirements as the federal authorizing power and either merely duplicate its operations or collapse into them. Hence, it falls to the federal government to mediate conflicts between itself and local governments, just as the state must itself mediate between the demands of equal political opportunity and the interests of civil society. Nonetheless, federalism produces a certain division of power between the center and local governance that can apply whether the local level is congruent or incongruent, or defined regionally or "sociologically." Whether each of these different defining parameters of local units of government are equally compatible with self-government is another matter.

The second dimension of federalism, where certain federal offices are distributed to individuals as representatives of their local units, has commonly been associated with specific institutional modifications.[6] The implantation of provincial units into national government is often linked to a strong bicameralism, guaranteeing parliamentary representation by province in one chamber, balanced by another chamber representing individual citizens in proportion to their numbers. As we have seen, this bicameralism seeks some satisfaction for democratic principle, balancing the undemocratic inequalities of provincial representation, where members of less populous local units obtain disproportionate legislative clout. Similar balancing measures could be applied to the cabinet and constitutional courts, as unwieldy as this may be. Nonetheless, as commonplace as bicameralism has been in federal regimes, provincial representation can just as well be unicameral. After all, if seating by province has any justification that trumps equal political opportunity, that can be taken to its logical extreme in a one-chamber parliament, as well as in the authorizing and executive powers. Indeed, this is the more common pattern for the distribution of cabinet appointments and even for civil service positions, which have been doled out along communal lines in incongruent "sociological" federal systems.[7]

In addition to bicameralism, federal representation has been linked to rigid constitutional guarantees for seating by local unit, such as that of the United States Constitution, whose Article 5 forbids any amendments to alter the composition of the Senate. Such guarantees provide a bulwark against any attempts to enforce equal political opportunity by removing the inequalities of provincial representation. Of course, since a bicameral parliament might still pass legislation undercutting provincial power, the rigidity of constitutional guarantees must be supported by the same vigorous judicial review on which all constitutionality depends. These features are emblematic of how competing concerns converge upon a federalism operating on both dimensions of local autonomy and national representation by local units. This raises the question of whether federalism can serve the cause of political freedom.

7.2 LEGITIMATE AND ILLEGITIMATE USES OF FEDERALISM

Federalism can be used for various purposes—purposes that, from a normative point of view, fall into three categories. First, federalism can be advanced to privilege divisions neither consistent with nor facilitating the rise of self-government. Second, federalism can be employed as a historical compromise, securing political jurisdictions for groups and/or regions in order to best approximate and best pave the way for untrammeled self-government when entrenched divisions make political freedom otherwise unrealizable. Third, federalism can be promoted as an essential ingredient in self-government, allegedly enhancing political freedom in ways that are not dependent upon contingent cultural oppositions that may interfere with the universality, reflexivity, and supremacy of just politics. Of these three employments, only the first is devoid of any legitimacy, insofar as it offers nothing conducive to the institutions of freedom. The second use can command validity, not as an element of the just state but as a precursor that retains legitimacy so long as it serves as a temporary way station to overcoming residual impediments to full political self-determination. In this sense, such federalism falls within the prehistory of self-government, as a worthy self-eliminating stage in political emancipation. As for the third use, it commands legitimacy so far as some type of federalism best realizes self-government without further qualification.

Although only the latter two forms of federalism might be normatively justified, only the last unconditioned variety seems problematic. It is easy enough to concoct innumerable varieties of federal organization by which body politics confer special national representation and local jurisdiction to communities whose conventions are oppressive and whose political empowerment only entrenches their violations of right. It is also simple to imagine or observe federal regimes in which incongruent local units exercise autonomy and enjoy national representation in function of subcultural oppositions that otherwise imperil political unity. Less self-evident is how federal government can enhance, let alone uphold, political freedom. Depending upon the identity of provincial units, both local autonomy and national provincial representation can pose troubling challenges to self-government.

7.3 LIABILITIES OF FEDERALISM

Local autonomy challenges the reflexivity, universality, supremacy, and autonomy of self-government whenever provincial units, be they regional or "sociological," are incongruent, separating different subcultures into parallel local regimes. When incongruent provinces are regionally defined, the problem is most flagrant. If regional political unity rests on a particular cultural identity, any citizen of mixed parentage or of another subculture will be unable to fit into the scheme of provincial solidarity. Although incongruent provincial autonomy might be promoted to preserve cultural diversity, cultural diversity has no place within the homogenous ranks of each provincial homeland. The rationale of placing local government into the hands of a culturally defined group can only coincide with the self-government of its inhabitants if they all share in that identity and choose to take local political action only with those who share their culture. Any outsiders or cultural dissidents will have no right to participate on their own terms. Local self-rule will therefore depend upon a cultural cleansing, expelling heterogenous populations and preventing any such "foreign" elements from infiltrating the region.

Nonterritorial, "sociological" provinces avoid this problem by only including individuals of the same subculture. Even here, however, a culturally defined regime can conform to local self-government only if all members of the community choose to have their affairs governed on communal lines. Any diversity on this score renders cultural dissidents captive to communal solidarities that oppress rather than emancipate them. Moreover, nonterritorial communal local government has no satisfactory way of integrating individuals of mixed cultural background. They are left either "homeless," falling outside each and every community, or they get squeezed into one communal category to the exclusion of their other heritage. Even dual membership is little solace if individuals wish to join in governing their local affairs with individuals of different cultural backgrounds.

These local difficulties translate themselves into national dilemmas when offices in the federal legislature, authorizing branch, and/or executive are reserved for members of different incongruent centers of power. In such circumstances, federal representation presents a dual threat to political right. On the one hand, the distribution of positions among the different subcultural groups will damage equal political opportunity to the degree that the allotment of posts diverges from the relative populations of the different communities. Unless proportionality is maintained, citizens of some groups will have greater political power than citizens of different communities. On the other hand, communal representation reinstates the liabilities of corporatism, substituting a contest for domination among particular interests for the autonomous quest to legislate, authorize, and execute laws collectively on behalf of the rights of all.

Insofar as civil society already provides a protected arena in which different cultural groups are free to engage in distinct social activities so long as these respect the civil rights of others, the question arises as to why upholding legitimate cultural autonomy should require any further political guarantees for cultural groups. If civil society is duly regulated to ensure equal economic opportunity and equal access to the means for political participation, politically privileging cultural groups limits the opportunity to engage in the universal freedom of self-government and associate in terms of specifically political differences without necessarily enhancing the opportunity to voluntarily associate in particular cultural activities. The latter are properly civil affairs, whereas the political sphere can realize self-rule only if political activity transcends the particularities of cultural difference.

This fundamental distinction between political and cultural difference calls into question the unconditioned legitimacy of any form of incongruent federalism, which by definition binds political unity to cultural particulars. Although incongruent federalism may serve as a transitional regime when cultural divisions are too deep to allow individuals to act in terms of self-selected political programs for upholding the rights of all, the reflexivity, universality, supremacy, and autonomy of political freedom can only be realized by federalism when the units are defined independently of subcultural distinctions.

Congruent federalism escapes the particularities of its incongruent counterpart, but homogeneity among the member states of a federal union does not alone guarantee that self-government is upheld without compromise. The United States provides a telling example of the abiding problems that can afflict a federal union in which provinces are regionally defined in indifference to cultural particulars. Although the American bicameral Congress allots seats in its lower house to districts of approximately equal population, the American Senate violates equal political opportunity by giving each state two seats even though the number of citizens diverges extremely from one state to the other. This inequality intrudes not only upon legislation but upon all the other venues where votes of the Senate or state legislatures affect executive and authorizing affairs, as well as constitutional amendment ratification. The solution to such inequality is easily conceivable. Wherever political office is distributed by provincial unit, positions should be allotted in proportion to the number of citizens in each province. While such an arrangement equalizes representation for each citizen, it thereby makes bicameralism superfluous.[8] Although this equalization brings the homogeneity among member provinces of a federal union to the point where any national traces of federalism seem reduced to insignificance, congruent federalism still poses problems for self-government.

For those, like Carl Schmitt, who treat the reflexivity of ruler and ruled as an immediate identity between the will of the state and the will of all, the very presence of any provincial units threatens an opposition of the will of each and any province with the will of the people, on whose unity democratic identity depends.[9] If this threat is pinned on the differentiation of national and provincial levels of governance it is defusable, even for identity theorists. After all, if national and provincial levels have different jurisdictions, which are both subject to constitutionality, a conflict of provincial and national wills would never occur unless one or both powers transgress their proper boundaries and encroach upon the jurisdiction of another level. In that case, the national authorizing power has the right to adjudicate the dispute and reinstate the harmony among levels of jurisdiction. Moreover, since the immediate identity of the will of the state and the will of citizens is a pernicious misconstrual of self-rule, incapable of integrating political plurality with collective self-determination, disagreement among provincial representatives need not threaten the reflexivity of political autonomy. As long as representatives act independently for the sake of the rights of all citizens, their lack of unanimity need not signify the domination of one faction over the rest.

Nevertheless, provincial representation poses problems for the reflexivity of self-legislation if representatives are bound to promote regional agendas instead of the rights of all citizens. When representation by congruent province remains tied to divergent provincial interests, then legislation will either give expression to the agendas of some regions to the exclusion of others or to compromises that may leave every region without any identifiable satisfaction. These limits can be avoided if legislators make laws with autonomy for the sake of the universal aims endemic to self-government. In that case, however, their election by province has no relation to their activity as legislators, since responsible deliberation and debate requires transcending provincial partiality. Whether legislators are elected from geographical districts overlapping province boundaries would make no difference. In other words, a congruent federalism where representatives legislate, authorize, and execute laws on behalf of the rights of all citizens would no longer need to allot any national political positions by province.

The resulting federalism would reduce itself to an instrument of political decentralization, dividing power not just among branches at the same level of government but between the national and provincial levels of governance.[10] This arrangement would satisfy the requirements of political freedom, but would it add anything to self-government that would make federal organization the better body politic?

7.4 ALLEGED ADVANTAGES OF FEDERALISM

Federalism has been privileged as the preeminent form of political freedom on several grounds. First, federal organization has been praised as a fundamental political innovation that allegedly allows democratic government to retain validity by solving the conundrum of how to endow the agency founding the constitutional state with the same legitimacy that the resultant body politic should possess. If those who found a constitution cannot claim equal authority with their product, it would appear that neither they nor what they make can be valid. As Hannah Arendt argues,[11] federalism can overcome this problem by connecting the constituting will of the founders of the constitution with the constitutional willing of democratic citizens. Federalism succeeds insofar as the federation of states incorporates the same political units that participated in the constitutional convention and ratified its results. Because these political units can constitute the state without remaining outside it, they can share in its legitimacy, just as the constituted order can lay claim to their antecedent authority. These states already enjoyed democratic legitimacy as self-governing units, and the new federal regime into which they get consolidated shares in their legitimacy by both issuing from their founding act and by making room for them within the enacted order. Moreover, once established, the federal union can further enlarge, not by conquest or expansion of its units, but by incorporating new states whose retention within the enlarged republic allows constituting and constituted wills to remain in unity.[12] By contrast, any nonfederal centralized republic would automatically issue from constituting agencies who become completely superceded by their product, which places all individuals in entirely new political relations. *If* the legitimacy of the body politic rests upon the authority of its founders, then separation of constituted willing from the constituting will would signal a breach in the line of validity.

The problem with this whole argument is that it presupposes a foundational legitimation of self-government, where the authority of constitutional democracy is allegedly dependent upon the authority of its founders. Arendt may partly recognize that foundational legitimacy remains problematic so long as the foundation and what is founded are distinct, but she fails to see that a genuine identification of what founds and what gets founded eliminates the foundational difference of levels and leaves self-determination as the unique bearer of legitimacy. A self-determined body politic will therefore no longer owe its legitimacy to anything lying outside it. How it comes into being cannot be constitutive of its validity. Various prior initiatives, such as constitutional conventions, may comprise enabling conditions for sufficient recognition of and participation in the newly emergent political order, but this does not make them juridical foundations from which political legitimacy derives. The alleged conundrum of the unconstitutional character of any constituting agency is a false problem precisely because how a state is founded can have no bearing upon the legitimacy of the emergent body politic. What counts is instead the actuality of political freedom, together with that of the nonpolitical freedoms that are necessarily part and parcel of the realm of self-government. Although political autonomy is, from a normative point of view, self-grounding, it cannot contain the power to found a constitutional order. To do so would require ignoring how a self-governing citizenry is necessarily embedded within standing institutions of constitutional democracy. The ethical community of self-government may reproduce its own political practice as the continual result of its activity, but this is not equivalent to incorporating a constituting power within an established body politic. Despite Arendt's claims to the contrary, the ex-colonial governments that moved from confederation to a true federal union did not remain what they were before federation within the resultant United States. The states of the union may be connected through the history of the constitutional convention and its ratification to antecedent colonies, but this connection has no standing within the constitutional order. The states are subordinate provinces, with protected jurisdictions of their own and guaranteed representation in Congress, but none of these specifications depend upon the prior existence of any state's confederated forerunner.

If federalism is to enhance political freedom, what matters is not how a federal regime relates to its founding but how the federal division between levels of government serves self-government. Certain pragmatic considerations have often seemed decisive in supporting this division, given how federalism has been employed in maintaining political unity over relatively large territories and/or culturally diverse societies.[13] Yet when what is at issue is the actuality of self-government, rather than compromise arrangements paving the way for its emergence, the contingencies of territorial expanse and cultural division cannot suffice to make federalism an unconditionally preferential order.

The division between national and provincial levels of government can instead lay claim to a universal benefit if its dispersal of power is needed to achieve such ends as keeping national authorities in proper check, offering additional opportunities for citizen participation in self-government, and forestalling the tyranny of the majority by balancing the unduly disproportionate results of majoritarian democracy.

Is the division of powers at the national level, however, insufficient to itself uphold constitutionality, and with it, the integrity of the different spheres of right? So long as the legislature, authorizing power, and executive fulfill their constitutive functions, which include policing one another, nothing barring extensive collusion between powers or a general breakdown of rectitude among the citizenry can bring constitutionality to its knees. Although, most notably with respect to the United States, federalism has been praised as an instrument for maintaining a proper division of powers,[14] neither the distinction between national and provincial jurisdictions nor any filling of national office by province can further limit the powers of government or prevent the pervasive corruptions of constitutionality that no division of powers can forestall. Since provincial governance addresses regional affairs that are demarcated from federal jurisdiction, any usurpations at the federal level are completely untouched by provincial authority, which never legitimately intrudes upon the national arena. Further, since any conflicts between federal and provincial government must be adjudicated by the federal authorizing power to sustain the integration of provinces into a single body politic, provincial powers have no authority to counter constitutional judgments at the federal level. Moreover, federal representation of provinces in the different powers of government does not affect how the national legislature, authorizing power, and executive relate to one another. Even when provincial representation illicitly allows for disproportionate influence of less populated regions, provincial delegations are no more likely to keep law within constitutional boundaries than legislators elected independently of federal arrangements. Not only may provincial groups aim at usurping power, but legislative autonomy and the workings of national political parties diminish the significance of provincial divisions in federal government. Provincial representatives may simply follow their own drummer or act on the basis of party loyalties, already transcending provincial boundaries through national party participation in local and federal elections. Of course, within provincial government itself, the very same problems of constitutionality play themselves out, calling for the very same division of powers at the regional level, with the caveat that provincial government always remains subject to the national constitution and its federal guardian. If, on the other hand, following John C. Calhoun's states' rights interpretation, federalism were reduced to a confederation whose member states each remain empowered to judge infractions by the federal government, the body politic would be hostage to permanent minority rule, undermining any self-government by individuals in their capacity as citizens of a common state.[15] Consequently, federalism is hardly needed to uphold the constitutional division of powers.

This does not itself preclude federalism from possibly enhancing political freedom by giving citizens a regional arena in which to participate in self-rule. Yet, does the addition of provincial governance really add any dimensions to self-government not already available in the opportunities to engage as independents or party partisans in mounting electoral campaigns or lobbying elected officials at the various levels of a centralized government? Local government is hardly dependent upon federalism for its existence. Municipalities, counties, and wider districts can all be allocated their own scope of governance without either giving them representation in any central powers of government or giving them wholly separate areas of jurisdiction. Their subsidiary levels of discretion can simply be a function of extending central authority to local arenas.[16] Whatever additional venues for electoral campaigning, officeholding, and lobbying that local government provides can therefore be at hand whether or not government is federally differentiated.

As we have seen, selecting national government officials by province fully coheres with political freedom only when the provincial identity of officeholders is superceded by the universal aims and obligations of self-rule. Hence, federalism at the national level adds nothing to self-government that is not equally provided by a nonfederal differentiation of local levels of governance.

Similarly, although federalism may give regional government authority over certain affairs that national government cannot address, that empowerment does not increase the self-determination of citizens. Since these same affairs can be subject to the collective control of all citizens in a nonfederal scheme, the localization of jurisdiction does not add new fields to self-rule but only segregates control among groups of citizens. Furthermore, removing this segregation of control in no way suppresses a type of freedom such as occurs when collective control is extended to social and household affairs. Such "politicization" of family and society eliminates the space for civil and household autonomy without enhancing political freedom.

Nonetheless, the federal segregation of control has been praised as a buttress against tyranny of the majority.[17] Since federalism is required neither to uphold the constitutional division of powers, nor the demarcation between civil society and state, nor to extend the reach of self-government, those concerned about majority domination have instead laid claim to federalism's alleged restraints upon majoritarian distortions of equal political opportunity. By dividing government between central and regional power centers, federalism supposedly checks majoritarian imbalances at either level.[18] If the different centers of power could legitimately impinge upon one another, then some constraints might apply, provided electoral balances are significantly different at the local and national level. In that case, a minority political group might control a provincial government, but be shut out from national power, and then use its local prerogative to restrain the federal government. Yet this scenario presupposes two relationships that are hardly endemic to federalism: first, that political divisions at a national level and at the provincial level be incongruent, and second, that federal and local jurisdictions can restrain one another.

The first assumption of incongruent political alignments is at best a contingent happenstance. Incongruent federalism has legitimacy only when historical compromises must be made and even then, difference in subculture may not translate into political differences. Accordingly, federalism hardly insures that local governments will significantly diverge from the politics of national regimes. The second assumption, for its part, ignores that the difference of federal and local jurisdictions precludes one level restraining the other, unless local government acts unconstitutionally and must be brought to account by the national authorizing power. In every other case, the different centers of power will be operating in separate, parallel arenas such that the policies followed at the federal level will remain just as much in force no matter what provincial governments do in their legitimate arenas. Consequently, the complementary jurisdictions for national and provincial regimes leave little hope of essentially altering the outcomes of majoritarian, or, for that matter, proportional electoral systems. Under majoritarian systems, whatever imbalances prevail at the national or provincial level will play themselves out in their respective jurisdictions, just as will analogous political relations in proportional electoral systems. In either case, what happens at one level will run its parallel course without changing the balance of political forces above or below. Indeed, cases may well occur where provincial governments are prey to majoritarian imbalances more than at national or nonfederal municipal levels. Conversely, political fragmentation may be less pronounced at the provincial than at the national level under proportional or majoritarian election systems. The mere fact of federal "divided government," where national and provincial regimes are controlled by different party coalitions, neither insures political minorities enhanced autonomy nor threatens any impasse. At each level, the prevailing coalition will enjoy the same political rights as under an "undivided" political landscape and be free to exercise the prerogatives that each separate jurisdiction affords. Since jurisdictions do not intersect, different party loyalties among the ruling regimes will not produce any stalemate.

If this leaves federalism no special preeminence as a bulwark against government tyranny, it does not remove one possible advantage—that federalism allows a wider space for institutional experimentation.[19] After all, if provincial units are empowered to rule over separate jurisdictions, they each may do so with a different structure of governance. One unit may choose a majoritarian system, while others opt for any of the possible varieties of proportional representation. Or one province may institute a "presidential" governorship while others follow a parliamentary regime.[20] Yet if the choice of institutional arrangement is duly limited by a constitution guaranteeing political and nonpolitical rights and the legitimate options are equally valid, why should more numerous venues for experimentation have any inherent value? If the options have equal merit, it is a matter of indifference how many operate simultaneously. If the alternatives instead have different values, leaving greater openings for the worse choices has little to recommend it. Because political autonomy is an ethical freedom, it is tied to specific institutional forms, which cannot be left to choice. The mere fact that choices have a certain degree of variation has of itself no determinate relation to the extant of self-determination. The latter depends upon the existence of the practices and institutions constitutive of each form of right. Experimentation in and of itself is not equivalent to self-determination. For all these reasons, federalism commands no privilege as a form of self-government.

7.5 FEDERALISM REDEEMED

Although federalism may not be required for self-government, it can fully accord with right provided several basic provisos are satisfied. First, if federalism involves any distribution of national offices by province, equal political opportunity must be observed. Provincial representation must be in proportion to the relative population of each province and representatives must be free to act on behalf of the rights of all citizens, rather than being captive to regional or subcultural agendas. When these requirements are met, of course, the significance of provincial representation diminishes to the point where officials operate as agents of self-determination of the entire citizenry. In the national legislature, members chosen by provincial electorates will then function no differently than legislators drawn from any geographically drawn district or, for that matter, belonging to any party list of candidates in a proportional representation scheme. For this reason, a legitimate federalism can just as well dispense with any representation by provincial units and restrict itself to a differentiation between national and provincial levels of governance.

Second, any provincial government must rule in conformity with political and nonpolitical right as duly specified in the national constitution. This entails that provincial government meet the same general standards of the division of powers and equal political opportunity that apply to the federal government, since otherwise provincial politics will impede self-government at the local level.

Consequently, the general form of provincial politics must be mandated in the national constitution, even if provincial constitutions spell out the details.[21] Similarly, whatever matters are reserved for provincial jurisdiction must be handled in accord with the general rights that pertain. Although the political and civil rights of individuals entail general entitlements to education, health care, housing, and equal economic opportunity, as well as the enforcement of household rights, these affairs could be allotted to provincial authority provided it satisfies these universal rights while giving them a local realization.

Accordingly, provincial government must insure that every subculture enjoys and respects full civil and household freedoms, even if traditional mores violate social and family rights. Similarly, provincial government must refrain from politically privileging any cultural group. Only under conditions of historical compromise, where divisions are so pernicious that equal family, social, and political opportunity cannot be otherwise approximated, can group dispensations be tolerated. In any case, the rectitude of provincial government cannot be upheld unless province politics is subject to review by the federal authorizing power. That pinnacle of federal government not only retains final judgment on the constitutionality of provincial governance but reserves the right to adjudicate any conflicts between federal and provincial powers.

7.6 TRANSNATIONAL FEDERALISM?

The global reach of civil society and its global diaspora of cultural groups might seem to foster the expansive and multicultural body politics historically favorable to federal regimes. Yet civil society's generation of multinational economic, legal, and welfare organization has equally countered the local control of federalism with a subsumption of entire regimes under transnational institutions. These developments accentuate what already occurs on a national scale when provincial governance becomes circumscribed by the public regulation of the market and the growth of public-welfare administrations with which civil society enforces equal economic opportunity, remolding capitalism with a human face. Whereas the emergence of the welfare state and expanding national control of the economy led some commentators to pronounce federalism obsolete, the rise of transnational organization has led others to herald the emergence of a new federalism—a transnational federalism mirroring on an international scale federalism within a single country.[22]

The readiness to consider transnational developments under the banner of federalism reflects an underlying temptation to equate international and domestic politics, a temptation which has been the bane of political philosophy whenever it has turned to conceive the rights of nations.[23] Although members of transnational organizations like the United Nations and the European Community submit themselves to international controls that place certain limits upon their own domestic agendas, fundamental disanalogies cast in doubt whether the relation between these organizations and their member nations mirrors that between national and provincial government under "domestic" federalism. Although transnational bodies like the United Nations and the European Community have incorporated legislatures, executive administrations, and judicial branches, any identification between their transnational "federalism" and federalism in one country would require that these bodies be tantamount to a sovereign state and that member nations relinquish their own sovereignty in full submission to provincial status. Then, of course, the transnational organization would no longer be distinguishable from a single body politic and "transnational federalism" would be a misnomer for the federalism of an expansive state encompassing whole continents, if not all inhabited territories of the globe. If instead "transnational federalism" is to retain any discrete significance, member states will still retain political sovereignty and the transnational union will be more of a confederation than a federation. The independence of member nations will remain the underlying presupposition of the union and any common governance will remain limited by that presupposition in ways that are incongruent with the political unity of a federal state.

Certainly, individual nations can enter into a multiplicity of different relationships, just as they can lose their independence and be absorbed by larger states. Given the exclusive normativity of self-determination, all of these arrangements must be judged in respect to how they promote political freedom and the nonpolitical freedoms with which self-government is inextricably connected. Although it is not inconceivable for a free body politic to have no interaction with any other communities, the possibility of international relations has ramifications for both the internal organization and external ties of the just state. Consequently, the determination of political freedom is not complete without an account of the rights of nations in international relations.

NOTES

1. For this reason, Robert A. Dahl is wrong to suggest that the controversy between federalist and centralized government should be addressed prior to the account of the branches of government. Although federalism may well involve further alterations of these branches, this does not mean that they lack an endemic character that must be present whether or not self-government be federal or centralized. See Dahl, *Democracy and Its Critics* (New Haven, CT: Yale University Press, 1989), p. 194.

2. Charles Tarlton has suggested this distinction between congruent and incongruent federalism, cited by Arend Lijphart in *Patterns of Democracy: Government Forms and Performance in Thirty-six Countries* (New Haven, CT: Yale University Press, 1999), p. 195.

3. As Lijphart observes (Lijphart, *Patterns of Democracy*, pp. 196–97), India provides successive examples of both forms of federalism. Gaining independence with provinces originally drawn by the British colonial masters without regard for the boundaries of cultural groups, India redrew provincial boundaries during the 1950s to follow linguistic divisions, injecting the conflations of ethnic and political unity that would fuel subsequent separatist movements.

4. As Dahl points out, here national government does not alienate its authority but exercises full control over local governments, which are creations of the national legislature, mandated by its law and subject to its legal regulation. See Dahl, *Democracy and Its Critics*, pp. 197–98.

5. In this vein, John Stuart Mill argues for a Supreme Court as the

ultimate arbiter in disputes between federal and state governments. He describes such a Supreme Court as a necessarily neutral arbiter between both governments. This view could be sustained, provided one distinguishes the federal government from the federal authorizing power. Since, however, the ultimate arbiter cannot legitimately stand apart from the federal state, to which the federal authorizing power belongs, the neutrality of the Supreme Court would not have to depend upon its separation from the federal state, anymore than the division of powers between the legislature, executive, and authorizing power depend upon transcending the body politic of which they are all constitutive organs. See Mill, *Three Essays: On Liberty, Representative Government, The Subjection of Women* (Oxford: Oxford University Press, 1975), pp. 393–95.

6. Lijphart lists these as strong bicameralism, a rigid constitution, and strong judicial review. See Lijphart, *Patterns of Democracy*, p. 4.

7. Dahl discusses these arrangements under the rubric of "consociational democracy." See Dahl, *Democracy and Its Critics*, pp. 256–57.

8. Bicameralism is also superfluous when a federal union exclusively privileges states' rights at the expense of popular representation. This alternate superfluity is exemplified by the Articles of Confederation, which mandated a single-chamber legislature for its loose confederation of states, before being supplanted by the bicameralism of the United States Constitution. See George Anastaplo, *The Amendments to the Constitution: A Commentary* (Baltimore: Johns Hopkins University Press, 1995), p. 7.

9. Hence, Carl Schmitt claims to find a contradiction between democracy and federalism. See Schmitt, *Verfassunglehre—Achte Auflage* (Berlin: Duncker & Humblot, 1989), pp. 389–91.

10. Schmitt regards this as the only residue that remains when the democratic concept of the constituting power of the entire people overcomes the federal plurality of political units. See Schmitt, *Verfassunglehre*, p. 388–89.

11. Hannah Arendt, *On Revolution* (New York: Viking, 1965), pp. 165–67.

12. Ibid., p. 167.

13. Lijphart points to these bases for federalism. See Lijphart, *Patterns of Democracy*, p. 195.

14. See, for example, David P. Currie, *The Constitution of the United States: A Primer for the People* (Chicago: University of Chicago Press, 1988), p. 2.

15. Anastaplo makes this point. See Anastaplo, *The Constitution of*

1787: A Commentary (Baltimore: Johns Hopkins University Press, 1989), p. 230.

16. Mill maintains that the only rationale for local government is the presence of a common local interest not shared with the nation at large that needs to be administered and done so by those whose interest it is (see Mill, *Three Essays*, p. 368). This claim is doubly suspect. First, it presumes that government is for the sake of realizing particular interests, rather than administering a framework in which all legitimate interests are justly promoted. Second, it ignores how local government can serve to extend opportunities for participation in self-rule as well as meet administrative requirements of employing local initiative to implement collectively determined national policy in local circumstances. Mill later himself admits that there are matters of national interest, such as the administration of poor laws and sanitary regulation, that nevertheless require local management. See Mill, *Three Essays*, p. 375.

17. See Lani Guinier, *The Tyranny of the Majority: Fundamental Fairness in Representative Democracy* (New York: Free Press, 1994), p. 80.

18. Lijphart makes this argument. See Lijphart, *Patterns of Democracy*, pp. 185–86.

19. Lijphart presents this argument, without calling into question the value of such experimentation. See Lijphart, *Patterns of Democracy*, p. 197.

20. Lijphart points out how just such variety of electoral forms has played itself out in the state governments of the United States federal system. See Lijphart, *Patterns of Democracy*, p. 198.

21. Section 4, Art. 4 of the United States Constitution thus seeks to "guarantee to every state in this Union a republican form of government." As Anastaplo points out, this mandate reflects how the republican character of the federal government is duly understood to depend upon the form of government in "every State in this Union." See Anastaplo, *The Constitution of 1787*, p. 168.

22. Laski announced the obsolescence of federalism in 1939 (cited by Dahl, *Democracy and Its Critics*, p. 198), whereas Dahl diagnosed such developments as the European Community as a transnational federal system in which member states lose final control over their own political agendas. See Dahl, *Democracy and Its Critics*, p. 198.

23. For an analysis of this mistaken conflation see "Political Freedom and Territorial Rights," chap. 16 of Richard Dien Winfield, *Freedom and Modernity* (Albany: SUNY Press, 1991), pp. 287–94.

CHAPTER 8
FOREIGN RELATIONS AND SELF-GOVERNMENT

Although individuals cannot exercise self-determination without interacting with others in relationships of right, a state can practice self-government without relating to any other body politic. The self-contained character of political justice is already evident in how the institutions of political freedom are determinable without reference to foreign relations. Individuals may not be able to participate as self-governing citizens unless they also enjoy property rights, moral autonomy, and the equal family and social opportunities provided by membership in an emancipated household and a civil society. Nonetheless, the existence of these nonpolitical institutions of freedom is not something external to the democratic state, nor do they depend upon a plurality of body politics. In order for political freedom to operate, the state must incorporate these institutions within its own dominion and integrate them so that household and social activities do not undercut equal political opportunity and so that self-government does not unduly restrict nonpolitical rights. The characteristic universality, reflexivity, supremacy, and autonomy of political freedom can all be sustained through this internal relation between democracy and its civil preconditions.

This solitary independence is not refuted by the fact that the just state cannot fail to have a determinate physical reach, giving its dominion a geographic border beyond which it ceases to extend. The practices of political and nonpolitical freedom necessarily occur in time and space, and the integration of households and civil society under political sovereignty necessarily imposes a recognizable territorial limit to the jurisdiction of self-government. Family ties and social interaction may extend beyond the borders of political sovereignty. Parents, children, and spouses may live or travel outside national territory, just as members of civil society may own property, engage in commercial transactions, participate in social-interest groups, and have civil legal proceedings abroad. By the same token, foreigners may own property, do business, belong to trade unions and other professional organizations, and go to court within the territory of the state. In every case, any household and civil activities falling within the geographic domain of the just state are therein subject to the self-government which presides over that territory.

The border of the self-governing state may shift in time and space independently of any other body politics. A sedentary political community may grow or shrink in response to natural alterations and its own waxing and waning, whereas the whole body politic may follow a nomadic life, traveling across planetary or interplanetary domains to maintain itself. Whether it be relatively fixed or transient, the place for self-government must be sufficient to sustain the practices of right that serve as preconditions and as constituents of political freedom but not too great to undermine the cohesion of political solidarity.[1]

Although the domain of the just state has some limit, be it fixed or wandering, the state may have no international relations proper because of various physical, biological, or cultural reasons. The body politic may be surrounded by physical regions completely uninhabited by intelligent life or the nearest outpost of rational agents may be so remote or so barred by natural obstacles as to preclude any contact. Alternately, a self-governing citizenry may face intelligent life of such vastly different physical scale, chemical composition, metabolism, or sensory reception that any interaction is impossible. Finally, a free state may be bordered by populations who have failed to organize themselves into political communities. Although the latter predicament may not involve any relations between one state and another, it does place the one self-governing polity in a situation where a relation to politically unorganized populations outside its borders entails normative considerations.

8.1 THE NORMS GOVERNING THE RELATIONS BETWEEN A SELF-GOVERNING CITIZENRY AND POLITICALLY UNORGANIZED FOREIGN POPULATIONS

The relationship between a self-governing citizenry and bordering populations lacking political organization involves matters of right on both sides of the frontier. On the one hand, the solitary state is obliged to uphold the political and nonpolitical rights of its own citizens in face of peoples beyond its borders. Because self-rule and social and household autonomy cannot be sustained without a protected space with exclusive jurisdiction, the body politic should defend its territory, be it fixed or nomadic, against any external intrusions that interfere with its citizens' exercise of rights. This requires both military and intelligence resources to contend with hostile attacks from without. It also requires some control of peaceful entry by foreigners into the country to the extent that uncontrolled access can imperil domestic welfare by overstraining institutions and introducing communal practices violating right. Similarly, the state must supervise commercial exchanges, be it of labor, capital, or other commodities, with external populations since these can impact upon the economic preconditions of family and political freedom, as well as upon the equal economic and political opportunity of the citizenry.[2] In every case, domestic justice requires that military defense, immigration control, and regulation of external commerce be undertaken to uphold the rights of citizens, as well as the nonpolitical rights of any alien inhabitants. Only on this basis, can the national territory be one within whose frontiers all can travel freely.[3]

On the other hand, in acting vis-à-vis external communities lacking political organization, the state is obliged to respect the rights of these peoples. Since rights are determined by the concept of self-determination, which commands exclusive normativity, no individual can legitimately be deprived of the full complement of freedom, which consists in the rights to property, moral accountability, equal household opportunity, civil freedom, and political autonomy. What respecting these rights here involves depends upon the character of the nonpolitical relationships under which bordering populations live. Although politically unorganized peoples lack the institutions necessary for engaging in self-government, they may or may not participate in practices recognizing nonpolitical rights.

The possibilities are endless since what conventions happen to be followed are contingent upon the coordinated choices of individuals, which give these conventions a positive character that cannot be mandated by reason. Although what conventions exist may fall beyond rational necessity, what conventions should exist is mandated by reason, thanks to the concept of the reality of self-determination. Accordingly, the varieties of communities lacking political organization can be categorized in respect to their conformity to the conceptually specifiable institutions of nonpolitical right, namely, property rights, moral accountability, family freedom, and civil society.

At one extreme, a population may observe no property entitlements, entirely ignore moral autonomy, follow kinship relations in which self-determination is absent, and engage in social activities fixed by traditions excluding any civil autonomy. From a normative point of view, this condition can be considered the lowest depths of savagery. Its inhabitants may feel at one with nature, content and secure, but their failure to erect any institutions of freedom places them at the greatest remove from justice. At the other extreme, a population may comprise a fully functioning civil society, in which slavery is prohibited and all competent adults are recognized property owners, the right of conscience is respected, family members enjoy equal household rights, equal economic opportunity is enforced, and civil law is duly upheld. Prior upheavals may have led to political collapse, but otherwise all nonpolitical freedoms may remain in place to the extent that that is possible without political supervision. Such a community contains no institutional barriers to self-government.

Generally speaking, to respect the rights of bordering peoples who lack political community, a state should honor the nonpolitical institutions that are already functioning in accord with justice and facilitate the rise of institutions of freedom where they are lacking. Practices that violate right, such as slavery, patriarchy, caste, and any other traditions that privilege natural differences at the expense of equal opportunity, do not deserve toleration. Since the nonpolitical rights of civil society have universal application, a just state cannot permit its own citizens to engage in practices violating these rights when abroad. Holding foreigners accountable for their own oppressive behavior in their own territory is more problematic, since a state's own jurisdiction stops at its own borders. Nonetheless, sitting by when peoples subject themselves to oppression is hardly equivalent to respecting the right of a people to determine itself. Since self-determination, be it as an owner, a moral subject, a family member, a social agent, or a citizen each require specific practices and institutions, communities that lack these can hardly be called autonomous. They may be independent, in the formal sense of not being subject to an external authority, but this independence leaves the door open for the most abject servitude.

The question, however, is what should a just state do in regard to bordering peoples who are politically unorganized and whose institutions are unjust? External force can overturn oppressive practices, but instituting relations of right cannot be engineered exclusively from without. Unless individuals choose to exercise their rights in recognition of those of their counterparts, the removal of external barriers will not suffice to establish participation in households or societies, not to mention political associations, in which self-determination reigns supreme.

What complicates matters is the interdependence between the different structures of right. Although any competent rational agent is entitled to political emancipation, this is impossible so long as the preconditions of self-government are absent. The right to political freedom obliges a state to help bordering populations become self-governing, so long as doing so does not undermine that state's own constitutive freedoms. Since the identity of a citizenry is determined by adherence to a common constitution rather than by any culturally given differences, peoples without political organization can legitimately achieve political freedom by either erecting a body politic of their own or being integrated into an existing state. Either option, however, will fail to provide for self-government so long as these populations continue to follow practices that violate property rights, moral autonomy, and equal opportunity in the household and society. In particular, if a people cannot privatize its religions and allow secular institutions to operate independently of sacred control, civil and political freedom will be stifled by religious orthodoxy.[4] The scaffold of democratic institutions may be imposed, but intolerant sacred and profane traditions in family and society will prevent the prospective citizens from being able to govern themselves freely. Even when religions undergo reform and oppressive traditions have given way to institutions of civil freedom, political emancipation will not occur unless the participants are ready to pursue the universal ends of political justice instead of particular communal concerns.

For these reasons, any attempt to promote household, social, and political liberation must ultimately depend upon enlisting potential revolutionaries among unemancipated peoples. Imperialist and colonial conquests of territories lacking political organization will always face the normative problem of overcoming their own unilateral political subjugation of the colonized, of refraining from exploiting the colonial land for the exclusive welfare of the colonizer, and of giving the colonized the quickest opportunity to emancipate themselves in the household, in society, and in political life.[5]

Similar concerns apply to a free state's relation to its own citizens who enter stateless foreign territories to set up new communities of their own. Needless to say, if the indigenous inhabitants engage in practices by which they determine themselves as owners, family members, and civilians, respect for these conventions limits what the new intruders are entitled to do. If, however, the indigenous population has not instituted property relations or fixed communities, the field for entry is more open. Once more, the activities of settlers should either honor the established freedoms of the indigenous inhabitants or promote their participation in relations of right. To the extent that a state can control its citizens abroad, it should do what is possible to monitor their activities and keep them within the bounds of justice.[6]

Since the general aim of an emancipated body politic in its dealings with politically unorganized populations should be to facilitate their attainment of self-government and the household and social emancipations that make this possible, this relationship sets the stage for international relations proper, at least to the degree that the extension of political freedom may involve the establishment of additional states.

8.2 THE NORMATIVE RANKING OF NATIONS AND THE BASIC VARIETIES OF INTERNATIONAL RELATIONS

Relations between states cannot be modeled after relations between persons, moral subjects, family members, participants in civil society, or citizens for two complementary reasons.[7] First, whereas the various relations of right between individuals all involve modes of self-determination that can only be exercised within those interactions, states have a sovereignty already established by the relation between politics and prepolitical institutions, a sovereignty that does not emerge in and through intercourse between nations. Although one state's sovereignty may be curtailed by other states, acting either individually or in league with one another, it is not constituted by interaction with other states.[8] Political independence instead depends upon the self-organization of at least some citizens and the supremacy of their rule over other domestic authorities.

Even when one state grants independence to a subject nation, the withdrawal of foreign control leaves a sovereign state only insofar as domestic institutions of political association are in place to wield state power.

Second, whereas domestic rights do not allow any restriction of equal opportunities in respect to differences of merit, the normative equality of individual states is relative to the justice of their domestic institutions. Because the only ends that have intrinsic validity are those by which individuals determine themselves as free, the rights of individuals are never relative to the ends they pursue as autonomous agents. Individuals may be held liable or punished for violating the rights of others, but these remedies never involve depriving them of their rights. Rather, paying compensation or submitting to punishment is part and parcel of observing the duty to respect the rights of others, a duty that is nothing but the expression of the inherent lawfulness of rightful willing. By contrast, the independence of states does not carry with it any automatic claim to equal treatment. No matter how a state behaves to others, it possesses an identifiable internal degree of justice determined by the conformity of its domestic institutions to the standards of rights. Since promoting the institutions of freedom is the ultimate normative consideration, respect for the sovereignty of a nation hinges upon its realization of the different spheres of self-determination. Accordingly, the respective domestic justice of states is of key importance in determining how they should be treated in international relations.[9] Although states of equal legitimacy may deserve equal treatment, the same cannot be said of states of unequal justice.

As with any convention, political association has a contingent existence, whose innumerable forms have neither necessity nor conceptual transparency. Nevertheless, the structure of self-government and its enabling nonpolitical freedoms provide a yardstick by which the relative justice of different possible states can be classified. This ranking can be done in two parallel manners: first, in respect to the different structures of right, and second, in respect to the general relation to foundations embodied in the different historical projects of civilization.

To begin with, states can be normatively ranked according to how many of the spheres of self-determination they embody, as well as to how completely they realize each. In this respect, the just state proper will embody all the institutions of freedom, whereas states will have a descending legitimacy depending upon how many of the structures of right are lacking and how completely those that are present are observed. Next in rank will come states without institutions of self-government but containing a civil society in which the social, household, moral, and property rights of individuals are respected. Of lesser legitimacy will follow those regimes lacking both democratic government and civil societies but still embodying some modicum of family rights, moral autonomy, and property rights. At the bottom will lie those tyrannies in which political, social, and family freedom are absent, the right of conscience is ignored, and personhood is violated by slavery.

A complementary ordering is provided by considering states in regard to how they relate to foundations, taking into account the historical ordering these relations can take. A regime that calls into question the authority of all given foundations and demands that theory and practice be self-justifying and autonomous embraces the project that distinguishes modernity from all other types of civilization. Although modern times have been a slaughterhouse of competing worldviews, unprecedented developments, most notably the Reformation, the American and French revolutions, the rise of capitalism, the emergence of social welfare institutions, anticolonial struggles, and feminist and gay rights movements, have together contributed toward reconstructing all spheres of life as domains in which individuals can be at home with their rational autonomy. Instead of allowing given tradition to hold sway, modernity has raised the banner of autonomous reason and self-determination.

In so doing, modernity has overturned premodern regimes, characterized by an adherence to given tradition, rooted in practices that are privileged irrespectively of whether they conform to institutions of freedom. Since premodern regimes invest legitimacy in traditional mores, they are marked by a given particularity, limiting them to the locality of a specific heritage. By contrast, modernity's embrace of the foundation-free institutions of freedom and autonomous reason gives it an inherent universality, allowing modern life to be global, and indeed, interplanetary, in potential scope.

Nonetheless, the institutions of modernity will first arise in some local setting, as the result of the overthrow of prevailing premodern institutions of some particular tradition. Accordingly, modernity will first appear in a regional guise, clothed with some contingent features that are not endemic to the universal structures of freedom but reflect residual elements of its birth. In this way, modernity has made its terrestrial debut as a seeming culmination of Western civilization, and the spread of modern relations beyond its birthplace has taken the form of Westernization. To the degree, however, that self-government, civil society, the emancipated household, moral autonomy, and personhood all command universal validity in virtue of sharing the self-grounded character of freedom, distinctively modern regimes do not remain the special preserve of any particular tradition. Rather, the modern project lays claim to an authority that transcends all given heritages.[10]

By contrast, postmodernism calls into question the very possibility of reason and conduct freeing themselves from foundations. Although postmodernism diverges from premodernity by recognizing the arbitrary character of privileged foundations, it regards justification to always depend upon an appeal to givens, whose authority can never be unconditionally established. Accordingly, postmodernism regards reason and conduct to always be heteronomous, always dependent upon given foundations, whose historical contingency can never be transcended. On this view, whenever norms are advanced in theory or practice, what is actually occurring is a power play, an exercise of a will to power, where some group is attempting to impose particular values, which it has arbitrarily affirmed, as universal norms to which all others should submit. In making this diagnosis, postmodernism robs itself of the ability to account for the authority of its own hegemonic claim that reason and action are always foundation-ridden. To justify itself, postmodernism would either have to surreptitiously command a standpoint that escapes relativism, or else admit that its own diagnosis is itself relative to contingent foundations, leaving it no more authoritative than any competing analysis. For this reason, postmodernism is powerless to discredit the project of modernity.

Postmodernism can still be the ideological basis for a regime of its own, however, one that claims unique consistency by openly admitting the perspectival, relative character of its own values and how advancing them amounts to a will to power. Such a regime enlists some arbitrarily given particularity by which it identifies itself and then hegemonically advances this particularity with no excuses, avoiding the inconsistencies of those regimes that present their values as if they had genuine universality, rooted in nature and/or reason. In this way, the postmodern regime rules in consistent expression of a will to power, openly subjecting different groups to its perspectival domination. Instead of adhering to any notions of universal rights, a postmodern state follows the route of fascist regimes, asserting the supremacy of some given cultural identity, privileged by the will of an otherwise unconstrained leader, and granting no rights to nor assimilating those who are different. Although the postmodern state thereby breaks with the tradition of premodern regimes, it equally rejects the freedoms of self-government, civil society, an emancipated household, conscience, and personhood. Further, since the consistent expression of the will to power has no local limits, the postmodern state is poised to seek a global or interplanetary domination that would take premodern regimes beyond their own constitutive roots.

Although the normative differentiation of states has a conceptual basis, categorizing actual states depends upon empirical scrutiny of their domestic institutions and an act of judgment determining to what degree the empirically ascertained reality conforms to the institutions of freedom that give the project of modernity its ethical preeminence. On both counts, the identification of the respective legitimacy of an existing regime is always debatable. Moreover, the independence of nations precludes any other party from having uncontested authority to determine the normative rank of different states. For these reasons, each state must judge for itself the character of its counterparts and contend with the possibility that it will not be recognized by other nations as the type of regime it takes itself to be. This predicament, wherein states must struggle for recognition as valid regimes worthy of respect, is basic to international relations and must be kept in view in determining how nations should interact.[11]

8.3 RELATIONS BETWEEN JUST STATES

Although the application of right to individual nations may always be contestable and perilous, the principles governing the relationships between the different sorts of states are determinable by reason and provide the guide by which nations should orient their international behavior. These principles comprise a normative law of nations whose implementation is an *imperative* for all states, always depending upon their independent initiative for its realization and therefore always representing a law yet to be universally embodied. This abiding *ought* reflects the distinctive conditions of international relations, where the independence of nations precludes any ethical community among them. Because political sovereignty is a function of the internal organization of the body politic and not constituted in relations among nations, the independence of nations does not automatically sustain an international order in which the sovereignty of one state is inherently in accord with that of every other. Citizens, by contrast, enjoy rights whose exercise reproduces the institutional context constitutive of citizenship, a context in which the political self-determination of one citizen cannot occur without the political codetermination of every other. Unlike the political freedom of citizens, the sovereignty of states is not in preestablished harmony with that of one another, as if each manned a complementary station in a preexisting international community. Instead, international relations always proceed in a situation where no higher institution can command the unqualified authority that a just state exercises over its citizens. Whereas citizens enjoy their political autonomy only by acting in recognition of the constitutional order through which they govern themselves, any international body depends upon the agreement of its member states, whose individual sovereignties precede its formation and who thus always remain at liberty to withdraw their support. The enforcement of the principles of international right is always ultimately contingent upon the choice of each individual nation, whose recognition by others as an independent, legitimate regime is never secure. Although this predicament complicates the relations among nations, it does not preclude the ranking of regimes from playing a decisive role in the imperatives of international justice.

Of the different possible types of regimes, only a just state realizing the project of modernity has an unqualified right to exist and to be recognized as fully legitimate by other states. The territorial integrity of a state upholding political, social, household, moral, and property freedoms can have only one normative limit—that it not be such as to undermine the autonomy of other just states or the emancipation of unjust regimes when due adjustments could preserve its own sovereignty. Accordingly, when just states interact, they are obliged to treat one another as free and equal nations and refrain from any activities that would harm the institutions of freedom of one another. This general proviso has manifold implications, given the concrete character of the different spheres of right.

To begin with, no just state is entitled to maliciously attack another, since any intrusion by force on the territory of another violates the political freedom of its citizenry. Aggression may leave the nonpolitical institutions of freedom unperturbed, but it automatically strikes at the right of the citizenry to rule over its own territory. The same violation is committed when one just state uses the threat of aggression to extract concessions from another. The victim of aggression is entitled to resist provided the resistance is directed at the aggressor's armed forces, responsible leadership, and supporting institutions, rather than at the civilian population and the resources that are needed to sustain civil life. The latter deserve immunity insofar as the aim of resistance is not to violate the rights of the aggressor state's citizenry but to repel the intrusion on sovereignty. Hence, whatever defense is taken must be such as to lead to a just peace where the contending states retain their respective institutions of freedom and the territorial preconditions for maintaining them. The aggressor state is still liable for reparations for any damages suffered by its victim's public institutions and inhabitants, provided the reparations demanded are not such as to destroy the viability of the aggressor's own self-government and civil society. Moreover, aggressors deserve punishment. Since public officials are immediately responsible for the conduct of the state, those who initiate aggression are subject to prosecution, and the aggressor state is subject to punitive fines levied from public treasuries that once more should not be so severe as to undermine the freedoms of its inhabitants.

Enforcing any of these remedies, however, is inherently problematic. The difficulty is that the very independence of states precludes the existence of any higher power with binding authority to determine when aggression has occurred, who is responsible, and what damages and punishments are warranted, let alone to enforce these judgments. Just states may enter into league with one another to establish transnational bodies whose authority they agree to respect, but these arrangements are always contingent upon the continued adherence to such agreements by the states involved. In the end, one or more states must take the initiative to exact justice on their own, taking measures that other states may always regard as new aggressions and resist.

Analogous difficulties afflict the resolution of nonmalicious conflicts between just states. Insofar as just states recognize the same principles of right, they need not pose any irreconcilable threat to one another, at least so long as they refrain from malicious aggression. Nonetheless, they may still suffer nonmalicious wrongs at the hands of one another that call for some remedy.[12] These nonmalicious wrongs can occur either through inadvertent actions that do damage to a body politic or through disputes where one state violates the rights of another in good faith. Inadvertent wrongs can involve, for example, environmental damage one state suffers as the result of certain commercial undertakings or public works projects in another. Good faith conflicts, by contrast, can involve territorial disputes or disagreements over the terms of treaties. In these cases, each side believes it is acting in accord with the true rights of both nations, but differences in interpretations of where those rights begin and end lead one side to take action that the other regards as a violation of its sovereignty. Because the very independence of the conflicting states precludes any third party having binding authority to resolve the dispute, assignment of liability, assessment of damages, and determinations of compensation are all contingent upon the particular decisions of the governments involved. Nonmalicious disputes may be resolved by the parties agreeing upon a specific remedy or by one party simply withdrawing its conflicting claims. Alternately, the states may agree to binding arbitration by a third party, be it another state or some international organization. When, however, no such resolutions are possible, each state is left with little alternative but to use force to assert its rights or accept its injury. The justice of any ensuing war remains problematic, even if the combatants abide by their common duty to leave civilians out of the hostilities. Since no authoritative judgment is available to certify who is in the right, only capitulation by the loser resolves the underlying dispute.

Further complications in the intercourse of just states arise out of the impact of inequalities in national wealth upon social welfare and the political and cultural autonomy of nations. Although just states may enjoy equal social and political opportunity within their own borders, discrepancies in aggregate national as well as average personal wealth may place citizens of the less economically powerful nation at a disadvantage that unrestrained "free" trade may only deepen. The unrestricted operation of international market activity may overturn premodern traditional social formations that obstruct household, social, and political autonomy. Nonetheless, economic "globalization" can equally extend the monopoly advantages of established national or multinational corporations in ways that intensify international inequalities and diminish poorer nations' control of their own economic and political destiny.

To the extent that the economic preeminence of one or more nations translates itself into a predominant cultural, political, and military influence, the workings of civil society's global, if not interplanetary, market will imperil domestic equal opportunity unless countermeasures be taken. Each nation can employ its sovereign prerogatives to regulate foreign commerce and investment, but even these options may be unable to compensate for persisting imbalances in national economic power that affect the relative opportunities of citizens of different states and threaten domination at the hands of foreign interests. Transnational organizations can act on the basis of international agreements to duplicate on a broader scale the sort of public interventions that domestic civil society is obliged to undertake to defend equal household, economic, and political opportunity against the contingencies of the market.[13]

These international initiatives face two complementary obstacles with which domestic justice need not contend. First, the sovereignty of nations makes participation in such international welfare administrations contingent upon the agreement of each state. At any time, participants may balk at further engagement, and no binding enforcement is available to compel submission. Sanctions may be voluntarily imposed by other nations, but these may be ineffective and their imposers may waver whenever a participating nation finds it advantageous to rescind cooperation. Second, any redistributions of wealth among nations will be hostage to the internal decisions of the recipient regime, which may choose to use the newfound resources in ways counter to the intended benefit. Although just states of unequal wealth may all have civil welfare institutions of their own that responsibly enforce domestic equal opportunity, they may still use foreign assistance in ways that squander opportunities to diminish intrastate inequalities. Donor states may withdraw their aid, but no external pressures can be counted upon to guarantee proper employment short of aggression that violates sovereignty.

Nonetheless, if just states are to interact in terms of upholding each other's respective autonomy, the more affluent are under an obligation to insure that their commercial relations do not handicap the social and political independence of their fellow nations. Since the rights of civil society are just as universal in scope as the reach of market relations, international economic regulation in behalf of equal household, social, and political opportunity is the fitting remedy, despite the limitations of any international enforcement. Although such regulation imposes upon the domestic prerogatives of governments, it still promotes national autonomy so long as it remedies international imbalances imperiling political equality within each state, as well as independence from foreign economic domination. Given the contingencies of the international market and of extramarket circumstances that impact upon social welfare, international economic regulation is as much a perennial challenge as its domestic counterpart.

8.4 RELATIONS BETWEEN UNJUST STATES OF COMPARABLE ILLEGITIMACY

All of these imperatives that regulate the relationships of just states apply between unjust states of relatively equal legitimacy. Nations that have autocratic governments but preside over civil societies cannot claim any normative preeminence over one another. To that extent, they face one another as independent and normatively equal states, whose relationships should accordingly be governed by mutual respect. None have any special right to intervene in the affairs of their peers, so long as they maintain the same modicum of civil freedoms, nor are any exempt from the obligation to participate in international regulations to compensate for economic inequalities that threaten domestic civil societies. The resolution of disputes is regulated by the same principles that apply to those between just states and the rules of war remain the same. Although authoritarian regimes all face the obligation to reform their political practices and institute self-government, none can legitimately intervene to reform their peers without reforming themselves.

Indeed, so long as states confront others with institutions of equivalent legitimacy, principles of reciprocity apply. When premodern regimes interact, each governed by traditions excluding political freedom, as well as social and household freedom, none can claim any warrant to assert its interest at the expense of others, nor to interfere in the affairs of its neighbors, so long as they do not threaten its own welfare. Nor can any justifiably wage war against noncombatants of enemy peer nations. Even when postmodern tyrannies set one will to power against another, none can claim any justifiable ground for renouncing equal treatment, even if their self-assertion requires dominating all others. Each has as much and as little validity as its counterparts, and for this very reason, the aggression of one is duly resisted by any other.

Generally speaking, how similarly oppressive nations fare against one another is a matter of indifference for right so long as all that hangs in the balance is the rise or fall of different regimes of equivalent illegitimacy. Even a popular despot does not deserve to hold on to power, for popularity is not equal to participation in self-rule or in the freedoms of the other spheres of right. Nonetheless, relations between equally unjust regimes can impact upon the preconditions of emancipation in differential ways. Although a nation's institutions may all be oppressive, their fate may well diminish or enhance the circumstances that facilitate their transformation into first approximations of property, moral, household, social, and/or political right. Events that affect the satisfaction of survival needs, the availability of any economic surplus, the reach of education and other cultural achievements, and military development can influence what obstacles must be overcome for progress toward any sort of emancipation. In this respect, the international affairs of unjust regimes take on a normative significance above and beyond the formal equality of peers in injustice.

8.5 RELATIONS BETWEEN STATES OF DIFFERENT LEVELS OF JUSTICE

When states of different levels of justice interact, the reciprocities of formal equality become obstacles to the realization of right. If states treat one another solely in recognition of their independence, observing principles of nonintervention and strict mutuality, unjust regimes are universally tolerated and victims of domestic oppression are left at the mercy of their oppressors. Given the exclusive normativity of self-determination, the sole legitimate ends of relations among nations are sustaining and fostering the institutions of freedom. Consequently, the obligations of states toward one another must vary in function of their respective degrees of domestic emancipation.

Further complicating these obligations are the great differences in power that may exist between states, whatever be their relative justice. Such differences in economic and military might dictate very different possibilities for taking due action, as well as very different imperatives for restraint in respect of the sovereignty of legitimate states.[14] Although cooperation among less powerful nations may circumvent some of the disparities, the great powers always retain a wider field of feasible intervention that carries with it greater international responsibility.[15]

When just states interact with oppressive nations, the universal claims of freedom impose obligations upon the just states to intervene in the affairs of the less legitimate regimes, without giving these inferiors reciprocal rights of intervention. So long as a just state does not act to further domination in oppressive states, these illegitimate regimes have no right to violate the sovereignty of the just state and impinge upon its internal life. To do so would automatically impede the practices of freedom without advancing any cause of emancipation. Although oppressive states may well resist efforts undertaken by more just states to diminish their oppression, they cannot claim a right to self-defense if their rule is unworthy of preserving. A tyranny may defend itself against opponents, both domestic and foreign, but if these are acting in support of emancipation, the ruling oppressors are only upholding wrong at the expense of self-determination. By contrast, a just state cannot be indifferent to oppression in foreign nations. If just states were to honor the formal independence of other countries and observe all treaty obligations irrespective of the domestic situation in other states, the inherently universal cause of property, moral, household, social, and political right would be ignored beyond one's own frontier. Admittedly, just states have no right to appropriate the territory or harm the resources and institutions of oppressive regimes when such actions are neither required for self-defense or promotion of emancipation abroad. When, however, a nation has the opportunity to undermine oppressive rule in another state and facilitate the formation there of lacking institutions of right, the formal principle of nonintervention forfeits its applicability.

The very character of the institutions of freedom set limits to what legitimate intervention can involve, in ways analogous to those that apply to "savage" foreign peoples who have no political organization. Generally speaking, emancipation cannot be imposed entirely from without. Although oppressive institutions can be weakened or destroyed by various external initiatives, they cannot be replaced by institutions of right unless formerly oppressed populations predominantly participate in new practices in which previously absent rights are at play. This participation can be achieved both with or without the cooperation of the regime in power and with or without armed conflict. A just state can employ various nonmilitary measures to pressure another unjust regime to make due reforms. Among other options, economic and immigration sanctions can be imposed, diplomatic relations can be suspended, and opposition groups can be given support. So long as such measures lead to voluntary changes on the part of the regime under pressure and such changes are embraced by the populace, a wider exercise of freedom can be achieved. On the other hand, when rulers are intransigent oppressors, they may have to be either forced to comply with due reforms or overthrown. Other nations can achieve either outcome without direct military involvement by lending noncombat support to revolutionary movements, who, true to the name, can not only remove oppressive rulers, but win sufficient participation from the populace in establishing new institutions more in accord with right. When these indirect options are unavailable, military intervention becomes legitimate, provided it restricts itself to preventing the continuance of gross violations of right and can reasonably succeed in enlisting sufficient support from the affected populace to replace oppression with emancipated practices.[16]

Because of the interconnection of the relations of right, the possibilities of intervention, both indirect and direct, as well as peaceful and coercive, are themselves limited by both the depth of oppression and the possibilities of indigenous support for emancipation. Instituting self-government can hardly be a realistic goal if the household and social preconditions of equal political opportunity are absent. Rulers can be toppled and external control can be imposed, but unless oppression in the family and society is curtailed, individuals cannot take their place, even if they so desire, as political equals. Traditional household relations that may well entangle social roles in kinship ties pose an even more daunting challenge than political reform, given the dispersion and relative seclusion of family bonds. Social formations that assign positions independently of self-determination may well privilege traditional mores that operate outside the realm of promulgated law and are conjoined with household relations. Accordingly, they too are no easy targets for any intervention that secures the heights of political power and then uses legislation and legal enforcement to reform society. Moreover, if a firmly implanted religious culture has failed to privatize itself so as to conform to moral, household, and civil freedom, political emancipation will be hobbled unless religious reform can be sparked among the faithful.

The penetration of the global market can uproot traditional forms of production and the communal ties to which they are bound, supplanting them with commodity relations through which individuals can begin to exercise economic activity with the lawful freedom of rights. Although these economic transformations can proceed independently of state intervention, market relations can penetrate premodern regions only when their traditional practices have already been partially opened to commodity exchange. Such openings can already exist in the interstices of communal relations where trade is tolerable or be provided by voluntary reforms. Further expansion of market relations beyond the limits of traditions blocking the free development of commodity exchange will, however, require noneconomic pressures. As the history of imperialism shows, it is no easy thing to apply such pressure without succumbing to economic self-interest, dislocating and pauperizing broad sectors of the coerced nation, and creating new divides of haves and have-nots that present their own obstacles to social and political emancipation.

Moreover, inequity within unemancipated nations becomes accentuated and overlain by divisions between them and states enjoying the freedoms of civil society. To the degree that a fully developed civil society creates a regulated market economy in which continual revolutions in productivity and continual expansion of wealth become imperatives for market survival,[17] modernized regimes tend to preside over an ever-increasing share of global, if not interplanetary, economic power. This condemns members of premodern and postmodern regimes to relatively disadvantaged straits so long as obstacles to universal economic rights set limits to the accumulation of wealth and the economic mobilization of technology. So long as these inequalities in wealth and economic power undercut the current social and political opportunities and future emancipation of the inhabitants of oppressive regimes, more affluent states have an obligation to remedy the situation without undercutting the rights of their own citizens. This imperative is similar to that which applies between just states of differing economic affluence and power. Here, however, any direct redistributions of wealth or preferential trading relationships must contend with the oppressive regimes in the recipient states, who may well frustrate any attempt to get economic resources to those most in need. This may present affluent just states with the predicament of either withholding aid programs likely to be diverted or coercing the recipient regime to administer aid properly.[18]

Compounding all these difficulties is the inherent voluntarism of any foreign intervention. Although the legitimacy of every nation is objectively determined by its degree of realization of the institutions of freedom, each nation must judge for itself its own relative legitimacy and that of its counterparts.[19] In the absence of any higher authority empowered to certify the respective justice of nations, every regime must weigh the relative merit of other states and decide what, if any, interventions are called for by right. Hence, any intervention done in good faith may be regarded as an unwarranted act of aggression by others, just as intended aggressions may be clothed in the mask of wars of liberation.

8.6 THE MANDATE OF INTERNATIONAL CONFEDERATIONS AND INTERNATIONAL LAW

These problems can be addressed, if not overcome, by international confederations and other transnational organizations. Any such bodies are conditioned by two factors: first, the independence of member states, and second, the exclusive normative requirement that the different institutions of freedom be upheld and fostered internationally.

The first condition sets limits to the authority and efficacy of international organizations. Although they may take the form of a world or interplanetary government, with a legislature, an executive, and authorizing judiciary branches, such leagues of nations depend upon the agreement of member states to participate in joint operations and to accept any obligations. Unless the world or interplanetary body eliminates the political sovereignty of its members and becomes a single state, relinquishing its own international character, their independence leaves every joint action contingent upon their individual assent.

On the other hand, the legitimacy of any international body depends upon to what extent its activities promote self-government and the civil, household, moral, and property rights on which political freedom rests. This poses organizational difficulties, since states are unlikely to join a league of nations unless their independence is respected and they are protected from interventions threatening the regime in power. Consequently, a league of nations has limited options for transcending the pitfalls of equal treatment of states of unequal justice. A league can address the problem by restricting membership to states with a certain level of justice, excluding "outlaw," "barbarian" regimes whose legitimacy cannot be recognized. Then, members can treat one another with reciprocity and still retain the option of jointly combating the infamies of pariah states. Under these conditions, the league can retain the cooperation of its members by defending their institutions of freedom against these pariahs and by taking commonly acceptable initiatives to reduce the inequalities between member states that undercut equal household, social, and political opportunities.

If, however, the league extends membership to all independent nations, irrespective of their domestic justice, it faces the problem of intervening in the affairs of those whose domestic oppression is intolerable.[20] The possibility of league action depends, of course, upon the relative numbers of legitimate and illegitimate regimes and their relative economic and military strength. If outlaw states are sufficiently outnumbered and not overpoweringly mighty, the league can take measures to counter their oppressions. These can involve peaceful sanctions, such as trade and travel restrictions, which the outlaw states may only evade by relying upon one another or pressuring other vulnerable states to ignore their league commitments. Alternately, the league can take joint military action, which the pariah states can, of course, resist whether or not they resign their membership.

All of these interventions can concord with international law provided that law is properly formulated in accord with the normativity of self-government. Instead of addressing nations as persons, with no differential merit bearing upon legal right, international law should specify standards of domestic justice to which it holds all nations accountable.[21] Then, all nations can be subject to the same rule and still be treated differentially in function of their degree of justice.

The frequent appeal to "human rights" has impelled prevailing uses of international law toward this concrete approach. Admittedly, the usual application of "human rights" to international affairs restricts those rights to prepolitical civil freedoms, in recognition of the universal scope of civil society and the difficulty of challenging political oppression without openly questioning the legitimacy of prevailing regimes. Nonetheless, the right to self-government deserves recognition in international law. Then, domestic oppression, be it in the household, society, or political arena, will not be immune from the jurisdiction of international law. This lack of immunity does not subvert the sovereignty of self-government since any genuinely democratic regime will not be legitimately subject to foreign intervention for the sake of its domestic justice.

In any event, enforcement of a duly concrete international law remains beholden to the independence of nations, which international organization can never overcome without overcoming international relations themselves. The general principles of international law may be unambiguously determined by the rational content of the institutions of freedom, but international legislatures and courts still depend upon the recognition and compliance of states, who can always challenge and ignore their authority. Nevertheless, appeal to international law and international organizations can be useful instruments with which to counter the injustices of premodern and postmodern regimes and to defend and foster the triumph of every sphere of right.

NOTES

1. As Hannah Arendt observes, unlike markets, the body politic cannot be indefinitely expanded. She ascribes this limit to the inelasticity of the genuine consent at the base of the nation-state, which is difficult to win from conquered people. See Arendt, *The Origins of Totalitarianism*, new ed. with added prefaces (New York: Harcourt Brace Jovanovich, 1973), p. 126. Although this suggests a social contract construction of political authority, the same limitation applies to sustaining sufficient adherence to a common political identity and sufficient participation in common institutions of self-government across too large and too culturally fractured a territory.

2. For these reasons, any unqualified acceptance of unregulated "free trade" puts self-government in jeopardy.

3. These are the considerations that support Michael Walzer's claim that localities can be open only if nations are at least potentially closed. See Walzer, *Spheres of Justice* (New York: Basic Books, 1983), p. 38.

4. Such is the predicament of Islamist "democracy," where parliamentary elections do not prevent religious law from reigning supreme thanks to the allowance of religious political parties and the ultimate validation of legislation by a clerical authorizing power. As a result, political freedom is just as subverted as civil, household, and moral freedoms.

5. For a more detailed examination of these issues, see "Post-Colonialism and Right," chap. 14 in Richard Dien Winfield, *Autonomy and Normativity: Investigations of Truth, Right and Beauty* (Aldershott, UK: Ashgate, 2001), pp. 161–75.

6. These considerations could conceivably involve restrictions on emigration, contrary to Walzer's claim that the state is like a club that can control entry but not withdrawals (Walzer, *Spheres of Justice*, pp. 39–41).

That analogy rests on liberal assumptions that the state is a voluntary, rather than compulsory association.

7. Classical liberal theorists are divided in drawing an analogy between states and persons. Although John Locke and Thomas Hobbes regard the relation between nations as analogous to the state of nature in which individuals find themselves before entering a social contract, they argue that inequalities in power, possibilities for self-sufficiency, and the abiding independence of political sovereignty prevent states from joining together into the type of covenant from which a civil order allegedly arises. See Locke, *The Second Treatise of Government*, ed. Thomas P. Peardon (Indianapolis: Bobbs-Merrill, 1952), pp. 105, 109, 110; and Hobbes, *Leviathan*, ed. C. B. Macpherson (Harmondsworth, UK: Penguin Books, 1968), pp. 187, 188, 394. Immanuel Kant, by contrast, regards the differences in power to be normatively irrelevant and argues that states are obliged to enter into an international agreement to establish a league of nations for reasons analogous to those that oblige individuals to enter a social contract establishing a civil government. He does, however, acknowledge differences between a league of nations and civil government entailed by the abiding sovereignty of nations See Kant, *Political Writings*, trans. H. B. Nisbet (Cambridge: Cambridge University Press, 1991), pp. 102–105. Significantly, none of these figures take serious account of the normative inequality of nations.

8. For this reason, H. L. A. Hart is wrong in regarding sovereignty as nothing but the room for maneuver that a state is allowed by its relations to its counterparts. See H. L. A. Hart, *The Concept of Law* (Oxford: Oxford University Press, 1982), p. 218.

9. Although John Rawls largely follows a social contract, procedural approach to international right, which presumes equal treatment of participating nations, he identifies these as "decent liberal peoples," characterized by just constitutional democratic government, common sympathies, and a moral nature (see Rawls, *The Law of Peoples* [Cambridge, MA: Harvard University Press, 1999], pp. 23–25). Rawls distinguishes from such decent liberal peoples two broad types of regimes: decent hierarchical nondemocratic peoples who honor "human rights," are nonaggressive, and therefore can respect the territorial integrity of other states (Rawls, *The Law of Peoples*, pp. 83, 92), and expansionist, aggressive, outlaw states, who are incapable of respecting the independence of other nations (Rawls, *The Law of Peoples*, p. 125). The former can be part of the international society of peoples ordered by mutual respect insofar as they would find such an order accept-

able. He alleges that *any* society that is nonaggressive and that honors human rights has the right of self-defense" (Rawls, *The Law of Peoples*, p. 92). Even diplomatic and economic sanctions are excluded so long as the hierarchical regime fulfills nonpolitical "human rights" (Rawls, *The Law of Peoples*, p. 80). Why political oppression in such "decent" hierarchical regimes should be tolerated by just states is not satisfactorily answered by claiming that only such toleration allows for the extension of international reciprocity beyond "decent liberal" regimes. Since Rawls acknowledges that the internal justice of a state cannot be ignored in determining how it should be treated, and that decent peoples have a right to intervene in the internal affairs of indecent, outlaw regimes (Rawls, *The Law of Peoples*, p. 81), his toleration of political injustice in "decent hierarchical peoples" can no longer be justified by a procedural argument that presupposes the equal standing of each participant.

10. For a systematic exploration of the different routes to modernity that this entails, see Winfield, *Autonomy and Normativity*, pp. 163–72.

11. G. W. F. Hegel is therefore correct in characterizing international relations in terms of a struggle for recognition. See Hegel, *Elements of the Philosophy of Right*, ed. Allen W. Wood, trans. H. B. Nisbet (Cambridge: Cambridge University Press, 1991), par. 331, pp. 366–67.

12. This is why a "democratic peace" among "reasonably just constitutional democracies," who recognize each other as such, is still always subject to breakdown, even if, as Rawls observes, no such regimes have gone to war since 1800. See Rawls, *The Law of Peoples*, pp. 49–51.

13. Rawls formulates the duty of assistance as aiming not at indefinitely maximizing the average level of wealth, but realizing and preserving just institutions, which does not require equal levels of wealth in all nations (Rawls, *The Law of Peoples*, p. 107). He claims, however, that assistance is needed only by "burdened societies," societies that "lack the political and cultural traditions, the human capital and know-how, and often, the material and technological resources needed to be well-ordered" (Rawls, *The Law of Peoples*, p. 106). Yet even well-ordered societies with the full complement of the institutions of freedom can find their present and future welfare jeopardized by the presence of other just states of far greater wealth and economic leverage unless international adjustments be made. Assistance to blunt this peril may not be as desperately needed as the assistance due "burdened" regimes, but it is a matter of international right.

14. Arendt goes so far as to claim that modern power conditions make national sovereignty a mockery except for giant states (see Arendt, *The Ori-*

gins of Totalitarianism, p. 269). Although giant states can dominate other nations in violation of political and nonpolitical rights, whether they do so depends upon the statesmanship of their leaders, as well as the political decisions of their smaller counterparts. As history can testify, no empire is invulnerable to internal dissolution or external opposition.

15. As Max Weber observes, any state comprising a world power has a responsibility before history that small states lack, a responsibility involving different obligations and different cultural possibilities. See Weber, *Political Writings*, ed. Peter Lassman and Ronald Speirs (Cambridge: Cambridge University Press, 1994), p. 75.

16. This principle provides the standard for judging Vietnam's overthrow of the Khmer Rouge's more murderous communist regime in Cambodia just as much as the United States' overthrow of Saddam Hussein's Baath party dictatorship in Iraq.

17. For a systematic investigation of the dynamics of competition and their impact upon the accumulation of wealth and technological progress, see David P. Levine, *Economic Theory—Volume II: The System of Economic Relations as a Whole* (Boston: Routledge & Kegan Paul, 1981).

18. Nations, such as North Korea, who allegedly selectively withhold internationally provided famine relief from their own starving citizens, present especially cruel examples of this quandary.

19. Further, in determining what interventions are called for in a nondemocratic regime, a just state must make judgments about not just the current situation in that regime, but the dynamics of change, so that its direction and rate can be properly appraised (Robert A. Dahl, *Democracy and Its Critics* [New Haven, CT: Yale University Press, 1989], p. 316).

20. The United Nations, like the League of Nations before it, is plagued by this predicament, where commitment to the principle of nonintervention collides with lip service to the International Declaration of Human Rights.

21. Because the principles of right derive from the concept of self-determination, and the normative relations between states are predicated upon the structure of self-government, the imperatives of international law are susceptible to a single determination, overcoming the historicity to which Rawls relegates ideas of justice, resigning us to *a* rather than *the* theory of justice and *a* rather than *the* Law of Peoples. See Rawls's misleadingly titled *The Law of Peoples*, footnote 4, p. 4.

WORKS CITED

Anastaplo, George. *The Amendments to the Constitution: A Commentary*. Baltimore: Johns Hopkins University Press, 1995.

———. *The Constitution of 1787: A Commentary*. Baltimore: Johns Hopkins University Press, 1989.

Arato, Andrew. "The New Democracies and American Constitutional Design." *Constellations* 7, no. 3 (2000): 316–40.

Arendt, Hannah. *On Revolution*. New York: Viking Press, 1965.

———. *The Origins of Totalitarianism*. New ed. with added prefaces. New York: Harcourt Brace Jovanovich, 1973.

Aristotle. *The Complete Works of Aristotle*. Vol. 2. Edited by Jonathan Barnes. Princeton, NJ: Princeton University Press, 1995.

Benhabib, Seyla, ed. *Democracy and Difference: Contesting the Boundaries of the Political*. Princeton, NJ: Princeton University Press, 1996.

Bobbio, Norberto. *The Future of Democracy*. Edited by Richard Bellamy. Translated by Roger Griffin. Minneapolis: University of Minnesota Press, 1987.

———. *Which Socialism?* Edited by Richard Bellamy. Translated by Roger Griffin. Cambridge, UK: Polity, 1988.

Currie, David P. *The Constitution of the United States: A Primer for the People*. Chicago: University of Chicago Press, 1988.

Dahl, Robert A. *Democracy and Its Critics*. New Haven, CT: Yale University Press, 1989.

Dworkin, Ronald. *Law's Empire*. Cambridge, MA: Harvard University Press, 1986.

———. *Taking Rights Seriously*. Cambridge, MA: Harvard University Press, 1978.

Fishkin, James S. *Justice, Equal Opportunity, and the Family*. New Haven, CT: Yale University Press, 1983.

Foster, Michael B. *The Political Philosophies of Plato and Hegel*. Oxford: Oxford University Press, 1968.

Guinier, Lani. *The Tyranny of the Majority: Fundamental Fairness in Representative Democracy*. New York: Free Press, 1994.

Habermas, Jürgen. *Between Facts and Norms: Contributions to a Discourse Theory of Law and Democracy*. Translated by William Rehg. Cambridge, MA: MIT Press, 1996.

———. *Die postnationale Konstellation: Politische Essays*. Frankfurt am Main: Suhrkamp, 1998.

Hart, H. L. A. *The Concept of Law*. Oxford: Oxford University Press, 1982.

Hegel, G. W. F. *Elements of the Philosophy of Right*. Edited by Allen W. Wood. Translated by H. B. Nisbet. Cambridge: Cambridge University Press, 1991.

———. *Logic*. Translated by William Wallace. Oxford: Oxford University Press, 1975.

———. *Philosophy of Mind*. Translated by William Wallace and A. V. Miller. Oxford: Oxford University Press, 1971.

Hobbes, Thomas. *Leviathan*. Edited by C. B. Macpherson. Harmondsworth, UK: Penguin Books, 1968.

Kant, Immanuel. *Political Writings*. Translated by H. B. Nisbet. Cambridge: Cambridge University Press, 1991.

———. *The Metaphysics of Morals*. Translated by Mary Gregor. New York: Cambridge University Press, 1991.

Kelsen, Hans. *The General Theory of the State and Law*. Cambridge, MA: Harvard University Press, 1945.

Lenin, V. I. *State and Revolution*. Moscow: Progress Publishers, 1965.

Levine, David P. *Economic Theory—Volume II: The System of Economic Relations as a Whole*. Boston: Routledge & Kegan Paul, 1981.

Lijphart, Arend. *Patterns of Democray: Government Forms and Performance in Thirty-six Countries*. New Haven, CT: Yale University Press, 1999.

Lindblom, Charles E. *Politics and Markets: The World's Political-Economic Systems*. New York: Basic Books, 1977.

Locke, John. *The Second Treatise of Government*. Edited by Thomas P. Peardon. Indianapolis: Bobbs-Merrill, 1952.

Marx, Karl. *Early Writings*. Translated by T. B. Bottomore. New York: McGraw Hill, 1964.

Mill, John Stuart. *Three Essays: On Liberty, Representative Government, The Subjection of Women*. Oxford: Oxford University Press, 1975.

Nietzsche, Friedrich. *Twilight of the Idols/The Anti-Christ*. Translated by R. J. Hollingdale. Harmondsworth, UK: Penguin Books, 1990.

Nozick, Robert. *Anarchy, State, and Utopia*. New York: Basic Books, 1974.

Oakeshott, Michael. *On Human Conduct*. Oxford: Oxford University Press, 1975.

Plato. *The Collected Dialogues*. Edited by Edith Hamilton and Huntington Cairns. Princeton, NJ: Princeton University Press, 1961.

Putnam, Hilary. *Renewing Philosophy*. Cambridge, MA: Harvard University Press, 1992.

Rawls, John. *A Theory of Justice*. Cambridge, MA: Harvard University Press, 1971.

———. *Political Liberalism*. New York: Columbia University Press, 1993.

———. *The Law of Peoples*. Cambridge, MA: Harvard University Press, 1999.

Rorty, Richard. *Contingency, Irony, and Solidarity*. New York: Cambridge University Press, 1989.

Rousseau, Jean-Jacques. *The Social Contract and Discourse on the Origin of Inequality*. Edited with an introduction by Lester G. Crocker. New York: Washington Square Press, 1967.

Schmitt, Carl. *The Concept of the Political*. Translated by George Schwab. New Brunswick, NJ: Rutgers University Press, 1976.

———. *The Crisis of Parliamentary Democracy*. Translated by Ellen Kennedy. Cambridge, MA: The MIT Press, 1985.

———. *Verfassungslehre—Achte Auflage*. Berlin: Duncker & Humblot, 1989.

Somerville, J. and R. E. Santini, eds. *Social and Political Philosophy*. New York: Doubleday, 1963.

Sundquist, James L. *Constitutional Reform and Effective Government*. Rev. Ed. Washington, DC: The Brookings Institution, 1992.

Unger, Roberto Mangabeira. *False Necessity: Anti-necessitarian Social Theory in the Service of Radical Democracy*. New York: Cambridge University Press, 1987.

Walzer, Michael. *Spheres of Justice*. New York: Basic Books, 1983.

Weber, Max. *Political Writings*. Edited by Peter Lassman and Ronald Speirs. Cambridge: Cambridge University Press, 1994.

Winfield, Richard Dien. *Autonomy and Normativity: Investigations of Truth, Right and Beauty*. Aldershott, UK: Ashgate, 2001.

———. *Freedom and Modernity*. Albany: SUNY Press, 1991.

———. *Law in Civil Society*. Lawrence: University Press of Kansas, 1995.

———. "Modernity, Religion and the War on Terrorism." *International Readings in Theory, History and Philosophy of Culture* 18 (2004): 329–47.

———. *Overcoming Foundations: Studies in Systematic Philosophy*. New York: Columbia University Press, 1989.

———. *Reason and Justice*. Albany: SUNY Press, 1988.

———. *Stylistics: Rethinking the Artforms After Hegel*. Albany: SUNY Press, 1996.

———. *Systematic Aesthetics*. Gainesville: University Press of Florida, 1995.

———. *The Just Economy*. New York: Routledge, 1988.

———. *The Just Family*. Albany: SUNY Press, 1998.

INDEX